Sydney

Meg Mundell

LONELY PLANET PUBLICATIONS
Melbourne • Oakland • London • Paris

MAP 1 – MAP INDEX

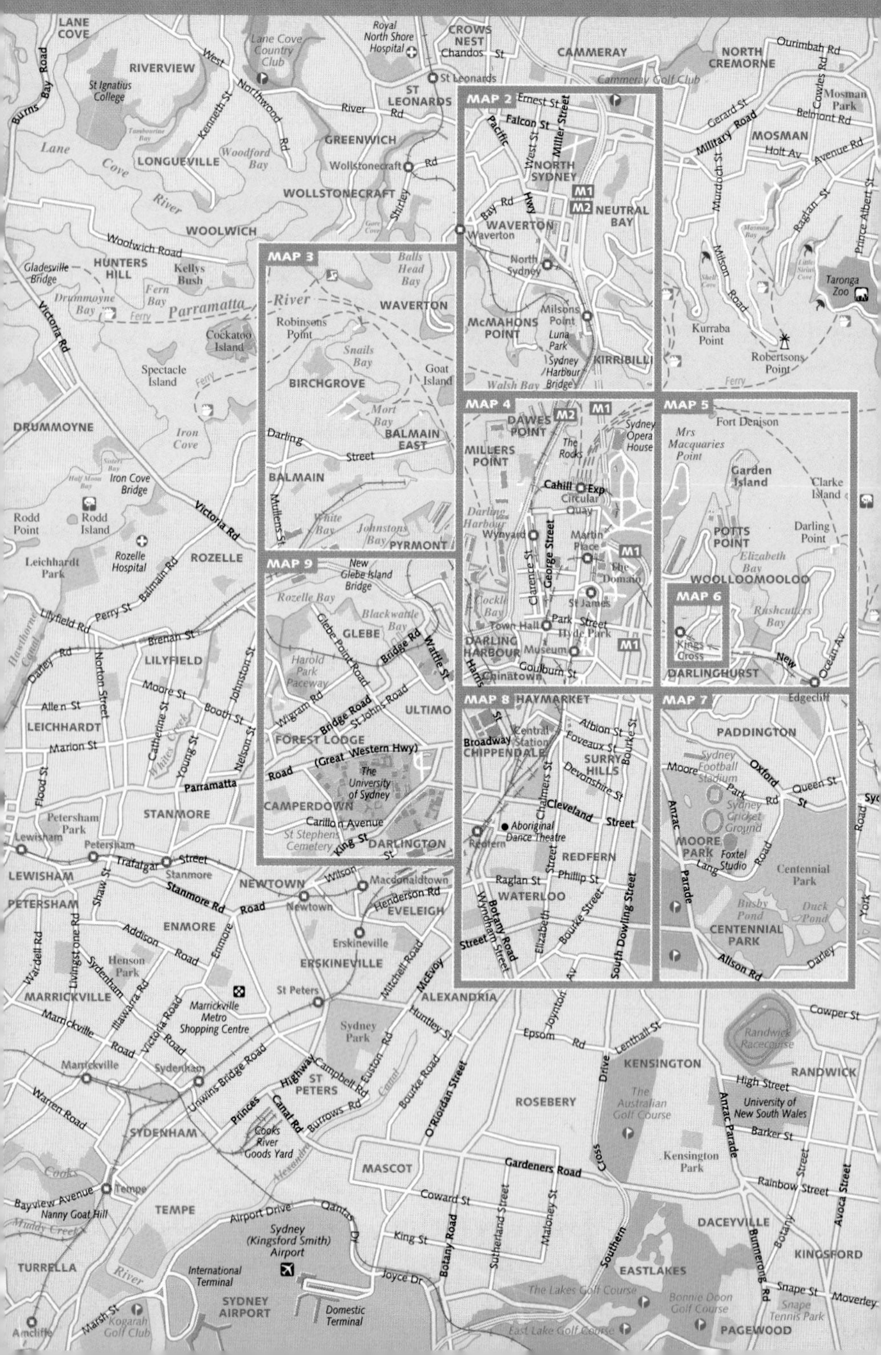

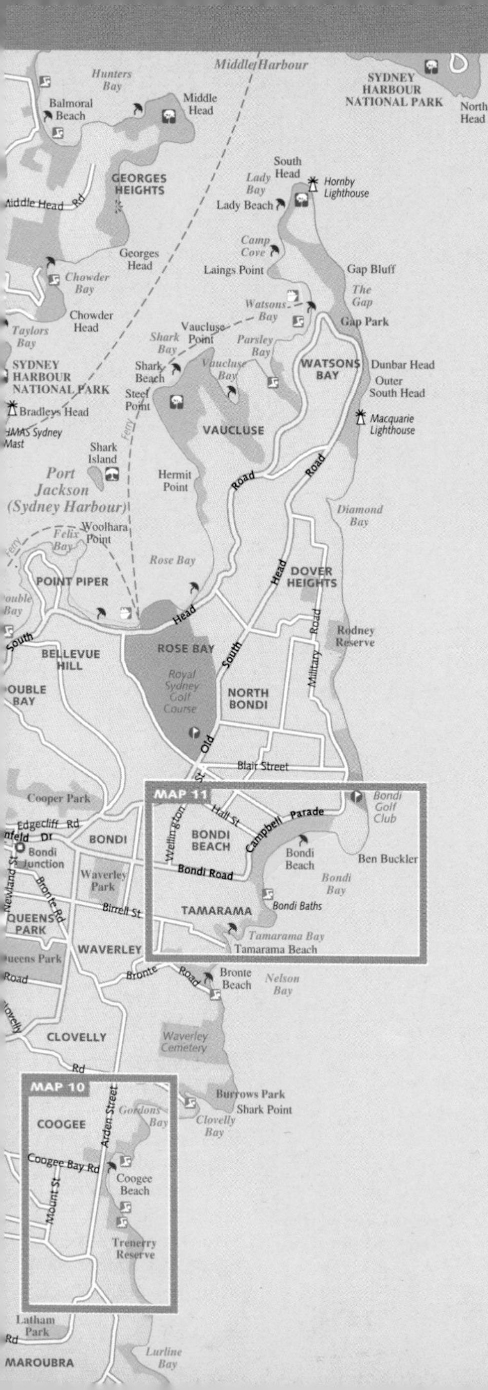
Middle Harbour
Hunters Bay
Balmoral Beach
Middle Head
SYDNEY HARBOUR NATIONAL PARK
North Head
South Head
GEORGES HEIGHTS
Middle Head Rd
Lady Bay
Hornby Lighthouse
Lady Beach
Camp Cove
Georges Head
Laings Point
Gap Bluff
Chowder Bay
The Gap
Watsons Bay
Chowder Head
Gap Park
Taylors Bay
Vaucluse Point
Shark Bay
Parsley Bay
SYDNEY HARBOUR NATIONAL PARK
Shark Beach
Vaucluse Bay
WATSONS BAY
Dunbar Head
Outer South Head
Steel Point
Bradleys Head
HMAS Sydney Mast
Macquarie Lighthouse
VAUCLUSE
Ferry
Shark Island
Port Jackson (Sydney Harbour)
Hermit Point
Old South Head Road
Diamond Bay
Woolhara Point
Felix Bay
Rose Bay
TASMAN SEA
POINT PIPER
DOVER HEIGHTS
Double Bay
Rodney Reserve
BELLEVUE HILL
ROSE BAY
Military Road
DOUBLE BAY
Royal Sydney Golf Course
NORTH BONDI
Blair Street
MAP 11
Bondi Golf Club
Cooper Park
Hall St
Campbell Parade
Edgecliff Rd
Wellington St
BONDI BEACH
BONDI
Bondi Beach
Ben Buckler
Bondi Junction
Bondi Road
Bondi Bay
Waverley Park
Newland St
Bronte Rd
Bondi Baths
Birrell St
TAMARAMA
QUEENS PARK
Tamarama Bay
WAVERLEY
Tamarama Beach
Queens Park Road
Bronte Road
Bronte Beach
Nelson Bay
CLOVELLY
Waverley Cemetery
Rd
MAP 10
Burrows Park
Shark Point
Gordons Bay
COOGEE
Arden Street
Clovelly Bay
Coogee Bay Rd
Coogee Beach
Mount St
Trenerry Reserve
Latham Park
Rd
MAROUBRA
Lurline Bay

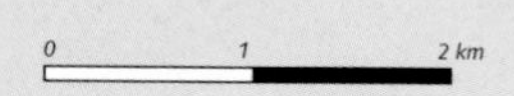
0
1
2 km

Sydney
4th edition – January 2000
First published – September 1991

Published by
Lonely Planet Publications Pty Ltd A.C.N. 005 607 983
192 Burwood Rd, Hawthorn, Victoria 3122, Australia

Lonely Planet Offices
Australia PO Box 617, Hawthorn, Victoria 3122
USA 150 Linden St, Oakland, CA 94607
UK 10a Spring Place, London NW5 3BH
France 1 rue du Dahomey, 75011 Paris

Photographs
Many of the images in this guide are available for licensing from Lonely Planet Images.
email: lpi@lonelyplanet.com.au

Front cover photograph
Sydney Harbour Bridge at night (Ross Barnett)

ISBN 0 86442 724 7

Printed by The Bookmaker Pty Ltd
Printed in China

Contents – Text

Contents – Maps

The Author

Meg Mundell

Meg is a loyal Kiwi now living in Melbourne. After studying hard for several years she realised she was too soft to be a vet, and too mad to be a psychologist. After much travel (including a nauseating but fun trans-Tasman yacht-crewing debacle) and brief stints in various odd occupations (zucchini sizer, ventriloquist's assistant, DJ), she now writes for and is deputy editor of *The Big Issue*, Australia.

From the Author

My thanks to Professor Elizabeth Webby and Trevor Howell at the University of Sydney; Mary Mihelakos from *Beat* magazine in Melbourne; Sandra at Dymocks Books in Melbourne; Susie at the Rocks visitors centre in Sydney; Carla at Bangarra Dance Theatre; and Angela and Murray in Potts Point for their info and hospitality. Thanks also to Jade, John, Rita (spellcheck queen), Hannah, Harriet, Khalil and Niamh for keeping me relatively sane while on the road; to my family for their encouragement, support and reverse-charge calls; and to Ollie for feline companionship at the keyboard.

This Book

The 1st edition of *Sydney* was written by Barbara Whiter, drawing on the Sydney section of Lonely Planet's *Australia*. The 2nd edition was thoroughly revised by Jon Murray. The 3rd edition was updated by Tom Smallman in the course of his research for the 2nd edition of *New South Wales*. This edition was updated by Meg Mundell and Liz Filleul wrote 'The Olympic Games' special section.

From the Publisher

This edition of *Sydney* was produced in the Melbourne office. The book was edited by Martine Lleonart with assistance from Jane Thompson. Pablo Gastar was the designer and Jenny Jones, Jane Hart and Helen Rowley assisted. Matt King assisted with illustrations and Maria Vallianos designed the cover. Fiona Croyden from LPI assisted by sourcing many of the images. Jane Hart and Mary Neighbour gave advice and support throughout. Thank you to Greg Alford and Jeff Trounce, in the Melbourne office, and Joanna Clifton and Charlotte Hindle, in the UK office, for their help with 'The Olympic Games' special section.

Thanks

Many thanks to Nigel Dobinson, Anthony Hutchings, Adam Kendall and Keith Stead who used the last edition and wrote to us with useful advice.

Foreword

ABOUT LONELY PLANET GUIDEBOOKS

The story begins with a classic travel adventure: Tony and Maureen Wheeler's 1972 journey across Europe and Asia to Australia. Useful information about the overland trail did not exist at that time, so Tony and Maureen published the first Lonely Planet guidebook to meet a growing need.

From a kitchen table, then from a tiny office in Melbourne (Australia), Lonely Planet has become the largest independent travel publisher in the world, an international company with offices in Melbourne, Oakland (USA), London (UK) and Paris (France).

Today Lonely Planet guidebooks cover the globe. There is an ever-growing list of books and there's information in a variety of forms and media. Some things haven't changed. The main aim is still to help make it possible for adventurous travellers to get out there – to explore and better understand the world.

At Lonely Planet we believe travellers can make a positive contribution to the countries they visit – if they respect their host communities and spend their money wisely. Since 1986 a percentage of the income from each book has been donated to aid projects and human rights campaigns.

Updates Lonely Planet thoroughly updates each guidebook as often as possible. This usually means there are around two years between editions, although for more unusual or more stable destinations the gap can be longer. Check the imprint page (following the colour map at the beginning of the book) for publication dates.

Between editions up-to-date information is available in two free newsletters – the paper *Planet Talk* and email *Comet* (to subscribe, contact any Lonely Planet office) – and on our Web site at www.lonelyplanet.com. The *Upgrades* section of the Web site covers a number of important and volatile destinations and is regularly updated by Lonely Planet authors. *Scoop* covers news and current affairs relevant to travellers. And, lastly, the *Thorn Tree* bulletin board and *Postcards* section of the site carry unverified, but fascinating, reports from travellers.

Correspondence The process of creating new editions begins with the letters, postcards and emails received from travellers. This correspondence often includes suggestions, criticisms and comments about the current editions. Interesting excerpts are immediately passed on via newsletters and the Web site, and everything goes to our authors to be verified when they're researching on the road. We're keen to get more feedback from organisations or individuals who represent communities visited by travellers.

Lonely Planet gathers information for everyone who's curious about the planet – and especially for those who explore it first-hand. Through guidebooks, phrasebooks, activity guides, maps, literature, newsletters, image library, TV series and Web site we act as an information exchange for a worldwide community of travellers.

Research Authors aim to gather sufficient practical information to enable travellers to make informed choices and to make the mechanics of a journey run smoothly. They also research historical and cultural background to help enrich the travel experience and allow travellers to understand and respond appropriately to cultural and environmental issues.

Authors don't stay in every hotel because that would mean spending a couple of months in each medium-sized city and, no, they don't eat at every restaurant because that would mean stretching belts beyond capacity. They do visit hotels and restaurants to check standards and prices, but feedback based on readers' direct experiences can be very helpful.

Many of our authors work undercover, others aren't so secretive. None of them accept freebies in exchange for positive write-ups. And none of our guidebooks contain any advertising.

Production Authors submit their raw manuscripts and maps to offices in Australia, USA, UK or France. Editors and cartographers – all experienced travellers themselves – then begin the process of assembling the pieces. When the book finally hits the shops, some things are already out of date, we start getting feedback from readers and the process begins again ...

WARNING & REQUEST

Things change – prices go up, schedules change, good places go bad and bad places go bankrupt – nothing stays the same. So, if you find things better or worse, recently opened or long since closed, please tell us and help make the next edition even more accurate and useful. We genuinely value all the feedback we receive. Julie Young coordinates a well travelled team that reads and acknowledges every letter, postcard and email and ensures that every morsel of information finds its way to the appropriate authors, editors and cartographers for verification.

Everyone who writes to us will find their name in the next edition of the appropriate guidebook. They will also receive the latest issue of *Planet Talk*, our quarterly printed newsletter, or *Comet*, our monthly email newsletter. Subscriptions to both newsletters are free. The very best contributions will be rewarded with a free guidebook.

Excerpts from your correspondence may appear in new editions of Lonely Planet guidebooks, the Lonely Planet Web site, *Planet Talk* or *Comet*, so please let us know if you *don't* want your letter published or your name acknowledged.

Send all correspondence to the Lonely Planet office closest to you:

Australia: PO Box 617, Hawthorn, Victoria 3122
USA: 150 Linden St, Oakland, CA 94607
UK: 10A Spring Place, London NW5 3BH
France: 1 rue du Dahomey, 75011 Paris

Or email us at: talk2us@lonelyplanet.com.au

For news, views and updates see our Web site: www.lonelyplanet.com

HOW TO USE A LONELY PLANET GUIDEBOOK

The best way to use a Lonely Planet guidebook is any way you choose. At Lonely Planet we believe the most memorable travel experiences are often those that are unexpected, and the finest discoveries are those you make yourself. Guidebooks are not intended to be used as if they provide a detailed set of infallible instructions!

Contents All Lonely Planet guidebooks follow roughly the same format. The Facts about the Destination chapters or sections give background information ranging from history to weather. Facts for the Visitor gives practical information on issues like visas and health. Getting There & Away gives a brief starting point for researching travel to and from the destination. Getting Around gives an overview of the transport options when you arrive.

The peculiar demands of each destination determine how subsequent chapters are broken up, but some things remain constant. We always start with background, then proceed to sights, places to stay, places to eat, entertainment, getting there and away, and getting around information – in that order.

Heading Hierarchy Lonely Planet headings are used in a strict hierarchical structure that can be visualised as a set of Russian dolls. Each heading (and its following text) is encompassed by any preceding heading that is higher on the hierarchical ladder.

Entry Points We do not assume guidebooks will be read from beginning to end, but that people will dip into them. The traditional entry points are the list of contents and the index. In addition, however, some books have a complete list of maps and an index map illustrating map coverage.

There may also be a colour map that shows highlights. These highlights are dealt with in greater detail in the Facts for the Visitor chapter, along with planning questions and suggested itineraries. Each chapter covering a geographical region usually begins with a locator map and another list of highlights. Once you find something of interest in a list of highlights, turn to the index.

Maps Maps play a crucial role in Lonely Planet guidebooks and include a huge amount of information. A legend is printed on the back page. We seek to have complete consistency between maps and text, and to have every important place in the text captured on a map. Map key numbers usually start in the top left corner.

Although inclusion in a guidebook usually implies a recommendation we cannot list every good place. Exclusion does not necessarily imply criticism. In fact there are a number of reasons why we might exclude a place – sometimes it is simply inappropriate to encourage an influx of travellers.

Introduction

Sydney, Australia's oldest and largest settlement, on one of the most spectacular harbours in the world, is a vibrant, alluring city of many natural attractions, bold colours, skyscrapers and yachts.

Sydneysiders tend to be casual, forthright, irreverent and sybaritic. According to outsiders, they're also faddish, mobile phone-addicted and obsessed with real estate. Despite the city's unhealthy fixation on waterfront properties, its corporate culture has always been balanced by the knowledge that the best things in Sydney – the beaches, the mountains, the surf and the much-loved harbour – are free.

Sydney attracts the majority of Australia's immigrants, and the city's mixture of pragmatic egalitarianism and natural indifference has made it a beacon of pluralism. It is ironic that a settlement which began life as a British Gulag has been transformed in just 200 years into one of the world's most tolerant and diverse societies. A potpourri of ethnic groups contribute to the city's cultural life. Chinese newspapers, Lebanese restaurants and Greek Orthodox churches are as much a part of the city as its Anglo-Irish traditions. Evidence of the region's original inhabitants survives in the Aboriginal stencils to be found in coastal caves, and in the indigenous names of many streets and suburbs.

Sydney has come a long way from its convict beginnings, but it still has a rough and ready energy that makes it an exciting place to visit. It offers an invigorating blend of the old and the new, the raw and the refined. You can explore the historic Rocks area in the morning, then ride the monorail to ultramodern Darling Harbour in the afternoon. While high culture attracts some to the Opera House, gaudy nightlife attracts others to Kings Cross.

Sydney is, above all, an outdoor city rich with natural assets. There are numerous options involving action and fresh air, whether it's yacht racing on the harbour, bushwalking in Sydney Harbour National Park or the Blue Mountains, or bodysurfing at Manly or Bondi Beach.

The city's beauty, its multicultural population and its environmental awareness were a major part of its successful bid to host the 2000 Olympic Games. In the lead-up to the Games, Sydney has undergone a period of extensive rejuvenation, aimed at bringing its cityscape up to a level with its natural charms.

Facts about Sydney

HISTORY

Australia was the last great landmass to be 'discovered' by Europeans. However, the continent of Australia had been inhabited for tens of thousands of years before the First Fleet arrived.

Aboriginal Settlement

Australian Aboriginal (which literally means 'indigenous') society has the longest continuous cultural history in the world, its origins dating to at least the last ice age. Although mystery shrouds many aspects of Australian prehistory, it is thought that the first humans probably came here across the sea from South-East Asia, more than 50,000 years ago.

Archaeological evidence suggests that descendants of these first settlers colonised the continent within a few thousand years. They were the first people in the world to make polished, edge-ground, stone tools; cremate their dead; and engrave and paint representations of themselves and the animals they hunted.

Aborigines were traditionally tribal people, living in extended family groups. Knowledge and skills obtained over millennia enabled them to use their environment extensively, but sustainably. An intimate knowledge of animal behaviour and plant harvesting ensured that food shortages were rare.

The simplicity of the Aborigines' technology contrasted with their sophisticated cultural life. Religion, history, law and art were integrated in complex ceremonies, which not only depicted ancestral beings who created the land and its people, but also prescribed codes of behaviour. Aborigines continue to perform traditional ceremonies in many parts of Australia.

When the British arrived at Sydney Cove, over 200 years ago, there were somewhere between 500,000 and one million Aborigines in Australia, and more than 250 regional languages – many as distinct from each other as English is from Chinese.

Around what is now Sydney, there were approximately 3000 Aborigines using three main languages to communicate, encompassing several dialects and subgroups. Although there was considerable overlap, Ku-ring-gai was generally spoken on the northern shore, Dharawal along the coast south of Botany Bay; Dharug and its dialects were spoken on the plains at the foot of the Blue Mountains.

Because Aboriginal society was based on family groups with an egalitarian political structure, a coordinated response to the European colonisers wasn't possible. Without any legal right to the lands they once lived on, Aborigines became dispossessed. Some were driven away by force, some were killed, many were shifted onto government reserves and missions, and thousands succumbed to diseases brought by Europeans. Others voluntarily left tribal lands and travelled to the fringes of settled areas to obtain new commodities such as steel and cloth, and, once there, experienced hitherto unknown drugs such as alcohol, tea, tobacco and opium.

European Settlement

Britain's prisons became badly overcrowded when the American War of Independence disrupted the transportation of convicts to North America. So when Joseph Banks suggested in 1779 that New South Wales (NSW) would be a fine site for criminals, he was taken seriously. Banks had been the scientific leader of Captain Cook's expedition, which sighted Botany Bay in April 1770.

The First Fleet landed at Botany Bay in January 1788. It comprised 11 ships carrying 759 male and female convicts, 400 sailors, four companies of marines, and enough livestock and supplies for two years. It was under the command of Captain

BEN-NIL-LONG, JAMES NEAGLE, 1798

Bennelong was one of many Aborigines captured by Arthur Phillip and taken to live in the Botany Bay settlement. He is shown here in his European clothes. (By permission of National Library of Australia, Rex Nan Kivell Collection NK 3374/5.)

Arthur Phillip, who was to be the colony's first governor. Disappointed with the land and the water supply at Botany Bay, the fleet weighed anchor after only a few days and sailed 25km north to the harbour Cook had named Port Jackson.

The settlers established themselves at Sydney Cove, named after the British home secretary at the time, Thomas Townshend, the first viscount of Sydney. From this settlement, the town of Sydney grew, clustered around what is the centre of harbour shipping to this day.

The Second Fleet arrived in 1790 with more convicts and supplies, and a year later, following the landing of the Third Fleet, Sydney's population had swelled to around 4000. The early days of the colony were tough and the threat of starvation hung over the settlement for at least 16 years.

Convicts were put to work on farms, road construction and government building projects, but Governor Phillip was convinced that the colony wouldn't progress if it relied solely on convict labour. He believed prosperity depended on attracting free settlers, to whom convicts would be assigned as labourers, and on the granting of land to officers, soldiers and worthy emancipists (convicts who had served their time).

This began to happen when Governor Phillip returned to England and his second in command, Grose, took over. In a classic case of 'jobs for the boys', Grose tipped the balance of power further in favour of the military by granting land to officers of the New South Wales Corps.

With money, land and cheap labour at their disposal, the so-called Rum Corps made huge profits at the expense of small farmers. They began paying for labour and local products in rum, and were soon able to buy shiploads of goods and resell them at up to three times their original value. Meeting little resistance, they managed to upset, defy, outmanoeuvre and outlast three governors, including William Bligh of the *Bounty* mutiny fame.

Bligh faced a second mutiny when the Rum Corps officers rebelled and ordered his arrest. The 'Rum Rebellion' was the final straw for the British Government, which in 1809 dispatched Lieutenant Colonel Lachlan Macquarie with his own regiment and ordered the New South Wales Corps to return to London. Having broken the stranglehold of the Rum Corps, Governor Macquarie began laying the groundwork for social reforms.

Colonial Expansion

In 1800, there were still only two small settlements in the Australian colony – Sydney Cove, and Norfolk Island in the Pacific Ocean. The vast interior of the continent was explored in the ensuing 40 years.

The Blue Mountains, west of Sydney, had proven an impenetrable barrier, fencing the new settlement in to the sea. But in 1813, the explorers Blaxland, Wentworth and Lawson found a route across the mountains, and a road was constructed that opened the western plains of NSW to settlers.

The discovery of gold in the 1850s resulted in significant changes to the colony's social and economic structure. Earlier gold discoveries had been all but ignored, partly because they were small and mining skills were undeveloped, but mostly because by law all gold discovered in the colony belonged to the government.

However, the 1851 discovery of large deposits near Bathurst, 200km west of Sydney, caused an exodus of hopeful miners from the city, and forced the government to abandon the law of ownership. Instead, it introduced a compulsory digger's-licence fee of 30 shillings a month. The fee was payable whether the miner found gold or not, to ensure the country earned revenue from the incredible wealth being unearthed.

In 1851, one of the largest gold discoveries in history was made at Ballarat in the newly separated southern colony of Victoria, and this was followed by further finds at the Victorian towns of Bendigo and Mt Alexander. These discoveries prompted a gold rush of unprecedented magnitude. Despite the fact that Sydney's population had almost doubled in the 1850s, the gold rush made the Victorian capital, Melbourne, the continent's largest city. Sydney, the capital of NSW, remained of secondary size and importance until the economic depression of the 1890s.

The 20th Century

During the 1890s, calls for the separate colonies to federate became increasingly strident. Supporters argued that federation would protect workers from foreign labour and improve the economy through the abolition of intercolonial tariffs.

Federation took place on 1 January 1901, and NSW became a state of the new Australian nation. However, Australia's legal ties and its loyalty to Britain remained strong. When WWI broke out in Europe, Australian troops were sent to fight in the trenches of France, at Gallipoli and in the Middle East.

Australia continued to grow in the 1920s until the Great Depression hit the country hard. In 1931, almost a third of breadwinners were unemployed and poverty was widespread. By 1932, however, Australia's economy was starting to recover as a result of rises in wool prices and a revival of manufacturing. With the opening of the Harbour Bridge in the same year, Sydney's building industry revived.

Discontent continued to escalate in Aboriginal communities and in 1938 there was a national day of protest. The 'Day of Mourning' protest was attended by Aborigines from NSW, Victoria and Queensland. In all, over 100 people attended the conference. However, it wasn't until 1967 that Aboriginal people were given the right to vote. A whopping 90.2% of voters supported changing the constitution in a national referendum on the issue.

In the years before WWII, Australia became increasingly fearful of the threat to national security posed by expansionist Japan. When war broke out, Australian troops again fought beside the British in Europe. Only after the Japanese bombed Pearl Harbor did Australia's own national security begin to take priority. A boom and net-barrage were stretched across the entrance channels of Sydney Harbour and

The 26 January 1938 'Day of Mourning' protest in Sydney brought Aboriginal communities together, pushing the agenda for Aboriginal civil rights.

gun emplacements were set up on the rocky headlands.

Sydney escaped WWII comparatively unscathed, although on 31 May 1942, several Japanese midget submarines were destroyed after becoming trapped in the harbour boom. A week later, another Japanese submarine entered the harbour, sank a small supply vessel and lobbed a few shells into the suburbs of Bondi and Rose Bay.

Ultimately, US victory in the Battle of the Coral Sea helped protect Australia from a Japanese invasion and marked the beginning of Australia's shift of allegiance from Britain towards the USA.

Post-war immigration programs brought new growth and prosperity to Australia, and Sydney spread west rapidly. Migrants at this time came predominantly from Britain, Ireland and Mediterranean countries.

Despite the influx of European immigrants and a strong trade union movement, Australia came to accept the US view that communism threatened the increasingly Americanised Australian way of life. It was therefore no surprise that in 1965 the conservative government committed troops to serve in the Vietnam War.

During the Vietnam War years, the face of Sydney changed as American GIs flooded the city for R&R (rest and recreation). Kings Cross flaunted its sleaziness, providing entertainment for the US troops. Hamburgers, Coca-Cola and 60s American rock increased in popularity. The hippie and peace movements also became established in Australia.

Support for involvement in the Vietnam War was far from absolute and the introduction of conscription troubled many Australians. Civil unrest over the situation eventually contributed to the election of the Australian Labor Party (ALP) in 1972. This was the first time in 23 years that they had been in power. The government, under the leadership of Gough Whitlam, withdrew

Australian troops from Vietnam and abolished national service.

A hostile Senate and rumours of mismanagement prompted Governor General John Kerr, the British monarch's representative in Australia, to dismiss the Whitlam government in November 1975. The position of governor general had until then been little more than ceremonial and Kerr's act was unprecedented in the history of the Commonwealth of Australia. Kerr installed a caretaker government led by the leader of the opposition, Malcolm Fraser, and despite the controversy surrounding the dismissal, a Liberal-National coalition led by Fraser won the ensuing election.

NSW reacted against the national trend at the time by electing a reformist state Labor government led by Neville Wran in 1976. Wran held office for a decade, overseeing much of the change that transformed Sydney. The booming economy of the 1980s saw Sydney flush with new skyscrapers, although the subsequent bust left a number of holes in the city centre.

The Bicentennial celebrations in 1988 and the massive Darling Harbour redevelopment project boosted the city's morale, and today the economy is doing reasonably well, though unemployment remains fairly high. After winning the bid to host the 2000 Olympic Games, Sydney began gearing up to be at the centre of the world stage at the turn of the millennium.

Australia could become a republic if voters support a republican model of government put to them in a referendum in November 1999.

Contemporary Aboriginal Issues

In 1992 the High Court ruled that Aborigines once owned Australia, and that where there was continuous association with the land they had the right to claim it back. This became known as the Mabo decision, after the indigenous activist Eddie Mabo. The decision was incorporated into subsequent federal government native title legislation.

Then, in 1996, the High Court handed down the Wik decision, which established that pastoral leases don't necessarily extinguish native title. This resulted in some fairly hysterical responses, which threatened to undermine the reconciliation process between Aboriginal and non-Aboriginal Australians.

This reconciliation was further undermined by the emergence of the right-wing conservative former independent federal MP, Pauline Hanson. She wanted to roll back gains made by Aborigines by abolishing, among other things, the Aboriginal & Torres Strait Islander Commission (ATSIC) and what she calls 'hand-outs' to Aborigines. While Hanson's star has now faded, the divisive repercussions are still being felt.

Another issue that remains unresolved is that of the 'stolen generations'. Aboriginal communities are still suffering the psychological, emotional and social consequences of children being taken from their families and put into foster homes or missions in order to assimilate them into mainstream society. At the time of writing, the federal government was being taken to court by two members of the stolen generation, and the outcome of this important test case is expected to set a precedent for the future.

There has been ongoing pressure to get the prime minister to make an official public apology for the actions of previous governments and other authorities. In mid-1999 the prime minister 'expressed regret', however many consider this to be inadequate.

GEOGRAPHY

Sydney is on Australia's populous east coast, about 870km north of Melbourne by road, and almost 1000km south of Brisbane.

The city is centred on the harbour of Port Jackson, but Greater Sydney sprawls over 1800 sq km and has grown to encompass Botany Bay in the south, the foothills of the Blue Mountains in the west and the fringes of the national parks to the north.

Sydney is hilly, and its layout is complicated by the harbour's numerous bays and headlands. It's built on a vast sandstone shelf, the rocky outcrops of which provide a dramatic backdrop to the harbour.

The inner city has an interesting mix of bohemian, gentrified, gay and working-class suburbs. There are three distinct sociogeographic areas outside the inner suburbs: the wealthy eastern suburbs stretching from the edge of Kings Cross to South Head; the middle-class North Shore, stretching from the Harbour Bridge to the edge of Pittwater; and the less wealthy western suburbs, stretching 50km from the inner-urban areas out to the foothills of the Blue Mountains.

CLIMATE

Australian seasons are opposite to those in Europe and North America. It's hot in December, while July and August are the coldest months. Summer begins in December, autumn in March, winter in June and spring in September.

Sydney is blessed with a temperate climate. It rarely falls below 10°C, except overnight in the middle of winter. The average summer maximum is a pleasant 25°C, although temperatures can soar to 40°C during hot spells. If it's hot and the humidity skyrockets, the climate can become quite oppressive.

The average monthly rainfall ranges from 75 to 130mm, and torrential-style downpours are quite common between October and March.

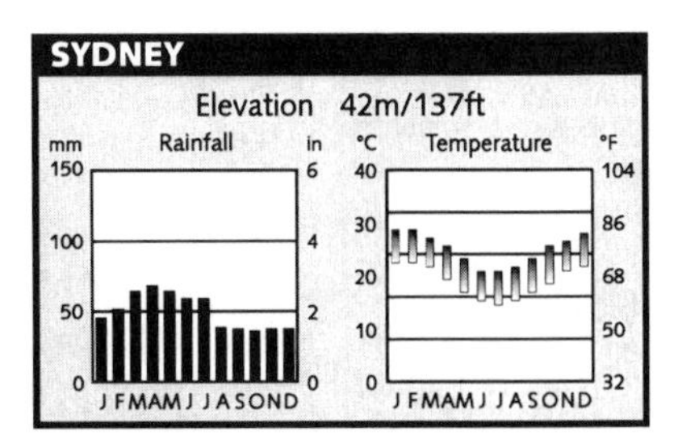

The Great Hailstorm

On 14 April 1999, a freak hailstorm struck Sydney. Giant hailstones, ranging in size from walnut to orange, thundered down from the heavens, smashing roof tiles and ravaging the eastern suburbs. Cars were heavily dented, as if they'd been attacked by baseball-bat-wielding psychopaths.

As the drama began, the weather bureau was flooded with calls from distressed people who'd had no warning of the storm. In fact, the bureau was taken by surprise, mistakenly deducing that the approaching thunderstorm would blow out to sea and would cause little harm. In the aftermath it was concluded that the storm was of a highly unusual and unpredictable variety known as a 'supercell'. It lasted for over four hours, and was the first giant hailstorm Sydney had seen for almost 200 years.

The storm has been the subject of more than 100,000 separate insurance claims, and the total damage bill is estimated at over a billion dollars – and counting.

Miraculously there was only one human casualty, a man who drowned when his boat was sunk by the hailstones.

ECOLOGY & ENVIRONMENT

As Australians have become more environmentally aware, the conservation vote has become increasingly important to political parties. This, coupled with the recognition of the value of 'green', or 'ecotourism', has resulted in many areas receiving greater, though varying, degrees of protection and management. However, problems remain.

In Sydney there's concern over pollution of the city's harbour and ocean beaches, especially after heavy rainfall, when billions of litres of rubbish and untreated effluent spew from overflow points. Millions of dollars have been spent installing pollution traps and litter booms to clean stormwater.

Noise from aircraft at Sydney's Kingsford Smith airport is a major issue for nearby residents; the state government has tried to reduce the level in the worst-affected areas by 'spreading' the flight paths.

The building of the new Eastern Distributor, a toll road through the centre of the city from the Cahill Expressway to the airport, has met with some community objections. As only part of it flows underground beneath Darlinghurst, some feel that as well as being an eyesore and blocking access to public parkland, it's also likely to increase noise and pollution levels.

However, use of public transport is increasing, and reduced car-usage should steady the air pollution levels, which are reported daily in newspaper weather sections.

In recent years, the upper Hawkesbury River has been hit by outbreaks of toxic blue-green algae, which if left unchecked can threaten marine life by absorbing all the sunlight.

If you'd like to find out more, the following agencies have offices in Sydney:

Australian Conservation Foundation (ACF)
(☎ 9247 4285) 33 George St, the Rocks. The ACF is the largest non-government organisation in NSW currently involved in protecting the environment.

Greenpeace Australia
(☎ 9261 4666) Level 4, 39 Liverpool St. One of its goals is to ensure that Sydney meets its commitment to a 'green' Olympic Games.

National Trust of Australia
(☎ 9258 0123) Observatory Hill. It is dedicated to preserving historic buildings.

Nature Conservation Council
(☎ 9279 2466) Level 5, 362 Kent St. It is an umbrella group for NSW environmental bodies.

Wilderness Society
(☎ 9552 2355) 1st Floor, 263 Broadway, Glebe. It focuses on protection of wilderness and the designation of wilderness areas.

FLORA & FAUNA

You can see a wide range of Australian flora at Sydney's Royal Botanic Gardens and its outposts Mt Annan Botanic Garden (between Camden and Campbelltown) and Mt Tomah Botanic Garden (between Bilpin and Bell). Several national parks are close to the city. Aside from many varieties of gum trees *(Eucalyptus)*, other common natives include grevillea, hakea, banksia, waratah *(Telopea)*, bottlebrush *(Callistemon)*, paperbark *(Melaleuca)*, tea tree *(Leptospermum)*, boronia and native pine *(Casuarina)*.

The native animals you're most likely to see in the wild are wallabies, kangaroos, possums and koalas, but there's often a variety of small nocturnal animals going about their business unobserved. Parks and bushland in and around Sydney are home to several protected species of bat, notably the large flying foxes, which can often be seen heading for a comfortable tree around dusk. The sacred ibis struts its stuff around Hyde Park, while the mangrove swamps around

Green & Golden Bell Frog

The first winner in the Sydney Olympics was the green and golden bell frog, a colony of which was discovered in a disused brick pit in the early 1990s, in what is now Sydney Olympic Park. The frogs are an endangered species and only a few colonies are thought to exist in Australia. Plans to build tennis courts and a multistorey car park on the site were shelved. Instead, in order to protect the frogs, a series of tunnels and ponds were built (at a cost of $400,000) to allow them to travel safely from the brick-pit site to nearby Millennium Park.

MARTIN HARRIS

The waratah is the floral emblem of NSW.

Bicentennial Park are home to pelicans and other water birds.

Parrots, cockatoos and kookaburras can sometimes be seen in the city and national parks, and you may be lucky enough to see lyrebirds at West Head. Colourful rainbow lorikeets can be spotted at Bradley's Head, while Middle Head and Obelisk Bay are home to fairy wrens and water dragons (a type of lizard). Botany Bay is a nesting and feeding site of the endangered little tern, a small migratory shore bird that divides its time between Australia and Japan.

There are many species of snake in NSW, all protected. Many are poisonous, some deadly, but they'll usually slither out of your way. Australian animals, birds and reptiles can also be seen at Taronga Zoo (see the Things to See & Do chapter) and at wildlife parks (see the Excursions chapter).

GOVERNMENT & POLITICS

Sydney is the capital of NSW and the seat of the state government. The system of government is a combination of the Westminster and US systems.

There are two main political groupings in NSW: the ALP, and a coalition of the Liberal and National parties. At the time of writing, the Labor Party was in government and Bob Carr was premier.

The balance of power in the NSW upper house is held by independents and members of a number of minor parties or groupings – notably Fred Nile of the Christian Democratic Party. Fred is the religious fundamentalist leader of the community standards organisation Festival of Light, and he and his Christian supporters are against just about everything; the Gay and Lesbian Mardi Gras really gets their blood boiling.

At local government level, the various districts of Sydney are controlled by city councils, often operating out of Victorian-era town halls, such as Sydney Town Hall on the corner of George and Druitt Sts.

ECONOMY

Sydney is Australia's chief commercial, financial and industrial centre. It is also an important transport centre. It has two harbours – Sydney Harbour (also called Port Jackson) and, about 15km south, Botany Bay – plus Australia's busiest airport and a network of roads and rail. Most of Australia's foreign trade is conducted in Sydney and NSW.

About half the workforce is employed in manufacturing and the rest in services such as transport, finance, retailing, tourism etc. Oil refining is a major local industry.

In the year prior to the Olympic Games, tourism was already Sydney's biggest overseas money-maker, and as in the rest of Australia, it continues to gain in importance. It's estimated that the games will bring in about $7 billion.

POPULATION & PEOPLE

Sydney has a population of about 3,980,000, out of the Australian total of 18.8 million. It's a multicultural city, although before WWII most Sydneysiders were predominantly of British and Irish descent. That changed dramatically in the aftermath of the war, with particularly large migrations from Italy and Greece, and significant influxes from Yugoslavia, Lebanon and Turkey.

Asian migration to Australia began in the 1850s when Chinese migrants were attracted by gold, but there were also large influxes of Vietnamese after the Vietnam War. More recently, the majority of Sydney's immigrants have come from China and New Zealand, with others arriving from Thailand, Cambodia, the Philippines and Hong Kong. Almost a quarter of the citizens of the state of NSW were born overseas, and most of these recent arrivals live in Sydney.

Aborigines

Although white Australia is at last recognising the complexities of traditional Aboriginal cultures, many nonindigenous Australians are still ignorant of the cultures of urban Aborigines, who maintain strong links with traditional ways. This causes frequent misunderstandings, and urban Aborigines are still often labelled as troublemakers because they don't conform to the norms of white Australia.

Today, more Aboriginal people live in Sydney than in any other Australian city. The Sydney region is estimated to have around 30,800 indigenous inhabitants, most of whom are descended from migratory inland tribes. This figure includes a smaller number of Torres Strait Islanders, a people native to the group of islands just off the Australian coast, near Papua New Guinea. The suburb of Redfern has a large and vital Koori population (many Aborigines in south-eastern Australia describe themselves as Kooris).

ARTS

Aboriginal Art

Art has always been an integral part of Aboriginal life, a connection between past and present, the supernatural and the earthly, people and the land.

Earthly art is a reflection of the various peoples' ancestral Dreaming – the 'Creation', when the Earth's physical features were formed by the struggles between powerful supernatural ancestors. Ceremonies, rituals and sacred paintings are all based on the Dreaming. Aboriginal art underwent a major revival in the last two decades of the 20th century. Artists throughout the country have found both a means to express and preserve ancient Dreaming values, and a way to share this rich cultural heritage with the wider community in Australia.

While the so-called dot paintings of the central deserts are the most readily identifiable and popular form of contemporary Aboriginal art, there's a huge range of material being produced – including bark paintings from Arnhem Land, wood carving and silk-screen printing from the Tiwi Islands north of Darwin, and batik printing and wood carving from central Australia.

A number of galleries specialise in Aboriginal and Torres Strait Islander art; see the Shopping chapter for details.

Dance

The Australian Ballet, the national ballet company, is considered one of the finest in the world. It tours Australia's major cities, with a mixed program of classical and modern ballets. It usually presents four ballets a year during its season at the Opera House.

Under the guidance of the artistic director, Graeme Murphy, the Sydney Dance Company (SDC) has become Australia's leading contemporary-dance company. Like the Sydney Theatre Company (STC), it's based at Pier 4, Walsh Bay, and also performs at the Opera House.

One of the country's leading Aboriginal dance companies is the Bangarra Dance Theatre. In 1999 the company performed a collaborative show with the Australian Ballet. (See also the boxed text 'Aboriginal Performance' in the Entertainment chapter.)

Music

In Sydney you can hear everything from world-class opera to grungy pub bands and live electronic acts. The city has a vital music culture and attracts many respected international musicians.

Songs are an integral part of traditional Aboriginal culture. They function not only as musical forms but as creation myths, totems and maps, and as a system of land tenure. Hybrid Aboriginal music is popular in Australia following the success of Aboriginal group Yothu Yindi and Torres Strait Islander singer Christine Anu.

The first European settlers ignored Aboriginal music. However, their bush ballads and bush songs still comprise a uniquely Australian folklore, and mark the first attempt to adapt European cultural forms to the Australian environment. The ballads and songs evolved from convict songs, English, Scottish and Irish folk songs, and campfire yarns. Part poetry, part music-hall romp, they paint an evocative picture of life in the bush in the 19th century. You can hear bush songs at several venues in the Rocks area.

Today, you're more likely to hear rock music than bush ballads. The city, which thrived on live performances and helped launch acts such as INXS and Midnight Oil, has largely lost its juice in terms of rock. This is due, in part, to the rise of dance music, and the dearth of inner-city venues – although some musicians blame the now ubiquitous 'pokies' (gambling machines), which have invaded many pubs and squeezed out the less lucrative live acts.

Local performers of note include longtime favourites Ed Kuepper, Died Pretty, the Celibate Rifles and the Hard Ons, and newer acts like the Cruel Sea, You Am I, silverchair, Frenzal Rhomb, Custard and Grinspoon. Major international acts perform regularly; the main venues for big concerts are the Entertainment Centre in Darling Harbour, Selina's at Coogee Beach, the Metro in George St and the Hordern Pavilion at Moore Park in Paddington.

Over the past few years, Sydney's dance-music scene has blossomed. While venues aren't copious, the city offers some good local DJs, as well as frequent international guests. There are clubs and dance parties catering to every sub-genre, from hip-hop to drum and bass, funk, techno and house.

Sydney also has a healthy jazz scene, centred on city venues such as the Basement, the Harbourside Brasserie and the Strawberry Hills Hotel. Top Sydney performers include Mike Nock and hip acid-jazz group DIG.

Classical music can be heard at the Sydney Opera House, the universities, and at various city venues utilised by the Conservatorium of Music. The Sydney Symphony Orchestra is Australia's largest orchestra. It performs more than 140 concerts per year, many at the Opera House. Sydney-based Musica Viva Australia is one of the world's most active chamber music organisations. It presents an ambitious program of both Australian and overseas ensembles in Australia's capital cities and regional areas.

Opera Australia is Australia's national opera company, and the third-busiest opera company in the world. In a typical year it gives around 235 performances of some 18 operas. It's based at the Opera House for seven months of the year.

The diverse strands of Sydney's musical life are brought together each January in the Domain during the month-long Sydney Festival and Carnivale.

See the Sydney Opera House section in the Things to See & Do chapter and the Entertainment chapter for information about other venues.

Literature

While Australian painters in the 1880s were developing their own style, a number of writers were creating fiction with a distinctive Australian flavour. They were known as the Bulletin School, after the magazine that published their work, and included some of Australia's most popular authors, such as Henry Lawson (1867-1922) and AB ('Banjo') Paterson (1864-1941). Despite the *Bulletin*'s propensity for tales of masculine life in the bush, it was a woman, Miles Franklin (1879-1954), who wrote *My Brilliant Career* (1901), which *Bulletin* editor AG Stephens considered 'the very first Australian novel to be published'.

The after-effects of the Bulletin School's romantic, and often melodramatic, vernacular tradition lasted many years. The so-called Jindyworobaks and the Angry Penguins tried in the 1940s to dislodge many of its tenets. But not until the 1970s (a time of renewed interest in Australian writing) were images of the bush, Australian ideas of mateship, and the chauvinism of

Australian culture fully questioned by Australian writers.

Modern Australian authors are now some of the most highly regarded in the world. Writers of international stature include Patrick White (Nobel Prize winner 1973), Thomas Keneally (Booker Prize winner 1982 – *Schindler's Ark*) and Peter Carey (Booker Prize winner 1988 – *Oscar & Lucinda*). Other authors held in high regard include David Malouf, Frank Moorhouse, Rodney Hall, Tim Winton, Helen Garner, Elizabeth Jolley and Robert Drewe.

A Sydney-centric reading list might include the following. *Seven Poor Men of Sydney* (1934) is a poetic account of a cross-section of Sydneysiders by expatriate author Christina Stead. *The Harp in the South* (1948) and *Poor Man's Orange* (1949) are New Zealand-born writer Ruth Park's accounts of life in Surrey Hills. Patrick White's *Voss* (1957) contrasts the outback with colonial life in Sydney. David Ireland's *The Glass Canoe* explores Sydney's larrikin pub culture. Frank Moorhouse's *Days of Wine and Rage* (1980) is an evocation of Sydney in the 1970s. *They're a Weird Mob* (1955) by Nino Culotta (the pseudonym of John O'Grady, who was born in NSW) is a humorous fictional tale of an Italian migrant in Sydney. Rosa Cappiello's *Oh Lucky Country* (1984) is a harrowing account of the modern migrant experience.

Offering a peek into the seamier side of Sydney are the works of prolific crime writer Peter Corris, such as *The Empty Beach* and *The Marvellous Boy*. Other noted authors to have crime novels set in the inner city include John Baxter *(Bondi Blues)* and Marele Day *(The Case of the Chinese Boxes)*.

Kate Grenville's *Lilian's Story*, loosely based on the life of Sydney eccentric Bea Miles, was made into a film. Other books worth reading are poet Dorothy Porter's lesbian thriller *Monkey's Mask*, set in the Blue Mountains, and her latest book *What a Piece of Work*, set in the old Rozelle mental hospital; Janette Turner Hospital's *The Last Magician*, set in part around Newtown train station; and Amanda Lohrey's *Camille's Bread*, a post-modern love story set in Glebe, Leichhardt and Chinatown.

Architecture

Sydney is predominantly a Victorian city, although it also has some fine early colonial buildings. Grand Victorian structures include the Town Hall, the Queen Victoria Building (QVB) and the old post office on Martin Place. Many inner suburbs have row upon row of ornate Victorian terraces. Macquarie St in the city, Parramatta and the Windsor area are home to the most impressive early colonial architecture.

Although the Australian Dream supposedly involves a quarter-acre block and a three bedroom house in the suburbs, most inner-city residents live in terrace houses, often with elaborate lace ironwork and balconies. The best examples to be found are in Paddington, where much of the iron used so effectively in the early terraces was originally used as ballast on ships sailing to Australia from abroad.

Sydney flirted with post-Regency, Gothic and Renaissance styles in the second half of the 19th century, but at the turn of the 20th century Australia developed its own style of domestic architecture, known as Federation. Unlike Victorian houses, which are basically boxes with verandas tacked on, Federation houses have red-brick or weatherboard walls, tiled roofs, casement windows, turned-timber veranda posts and fretted woodwork. Examples of this style are in the next rank of suburbs out from the inner suburbs, such as Haberfield and Strathfield in the inner west.

California Bungalow became dominant in the 1920s, while the 1930s saw the flourishing of Art Deco; there are fine examples of Art Deco apartments in Potts Point, Elizabeth Bay and Edgecliffe.

In the 1960s, the so-called Sydney School pioneered a distinctively Australian organic architecture that used over-burnt brick and native landscaping to blend into the local environment. Examples of their work can be seen in Mosman and the northern beaches.

Since the 1960s, central Sydney has become a mini Manhattan of tall buildings vying for harbour views. Many modern buildings are striking, such as the Capita Centre on Castlereagh St, and Governors Phillip and Macquarie Towers on the corner of Young and Bent Sts, but only the Sydney Football Stadium, designed by Philip Cox, approaches the flair of the city's most famous modern building, the Opera House.

In the 1990s, Art Deco is enjoying a resurgence in popularity, as seen in the design of the Coopers & Lybrand building on George St, and in the many retro-style cafes and bars.

There's an encouraging trend in the city's development that is helping to retain some of Sydney's character. Old buildings like Daking House (near Central station), home to the new Sydney YHA Hostel, are being restored and given a new lease of life. The old Customs House at Circular Quay has had a major facelift and now houses an arts and cultural centre.

Sympathetic modern extensions are being added to existing buildings; good examples include the Capitol Theatre complex, the Furama Hotel and Paddy's Markets in Chinatown. At the Museum of Sydney, the modern office tower perched atop the sandstone foundations of Australia's first Government House has won several architectural awards.

In a move to make the most of Sydney's liquid assets, the wharves at Woolloomooloo and Walsh Bay have been earmarked for development.

The controversial 'toaster' apartment blocks built near the Opera House on Circular Quay have attracted much criticism for their clunky design and view-blocking dimensions, but that hasn't stopped them from becoming some of the most expensive real estate in Australia.

Painting

It's interesting to see what the first European landscape painters made of Australia. The colours seem wrong and the features they depict aren't what would now be regarded as typically Australian. However, some early painters, such as John Glover, made a concerted effort to approach the Australian landscape on its own terms.

Colonial artists such as Conrad Martens painted Turneresque landscapes of Sydney Harbour in the 1850s that now startle Sydneysiders, who are used to seeing the foreshore dominated by exclusive housing instead of miles of bush.

Between 1885 and 1890 a distinctively Australian school of painting emerged. The painters of the so-called Heidelberg School were the first to render Australian light and colour in a naturalistic fashion. Using impressionistic techniques and favouring plein-air painting, the school represented a major break with prevailing British and Germanic tastes.

Most major painters in the Heidelberg School were from Melbourne, although Tom Roberts and fellow Melburnian Arthur Streeton established an artists' camp at Little Sirius Cove in Mosman in 1891, which became a focal point for Sydney artists.

Roberts and Streeton increasingly depicted what are now considered typically Australian scenes of sheepshearers, pioneers and bushrangers. Their paintings were powerful stimulants to the development of an enduring national mythology.

At the beginning of the 20th century, Australian painters began to flirt with Art Nouveau. Sydney Long painted bush scenes peopled with fairies in an attempt to mythologise and personify the landscape, something Aborigines had been doing successfully for thousands of years.

In the 1940s there began a flowering of predominantly expressionist art, which many considered to be the first authentically Australian art since the Heidelberg School. Again, the main practitioners were from Melbourne, but painters such as Sidney Nolan, Arthur Boyd, Albert Tucker and Russell Drysdale transcended locale to approach all Australians on the level of myth.

Mosman-based Margaret Preston's unique woodcuts and paintings combined elements of Aboriginal art, French art and simple design, and influences from her many travels in Asia, Africa and Europe.

She often utilised Australian flora and fauna as subject matter.

Drawing on popular cultural images for much of his work, Martin Sharp first rose to prominence in the 1960s as co-founder of the satirical magazine *Oz*. In the 1970s he helped restore the 'face' at Luna Park and produced many famous posters for the productions of the Nimrod theatre.

Sydney artist Brett Whiteley, who died in 1992, was an internationally celebrated *enfant terrible* who painted luscious, colourful canvases, often with distorted Bacon-like figures. His paintings of Sydney Harbour and Lavender Bay are unsurpassed; his studio, containing many of his works, has been preserved as a gallery in Surry Hills.

Probably Sydney's most commercially successful artist is Ken Done, whose simple, vivid works adorn everything from coasters to T-shirts; he has a gallery in the Rocks.

Other modern artists of note include Sandy Bruch, Ian Fairweather, Keith Looby and Judy Cassab.

Cinema

The Australian film industry began as early as 1896, a year after the Lumiere brothers opened the world's first cinema in Paris. Australia's first cinema was opened in Sydney in 1896. Maurice Sestier, one of the Lumieres' photographers, came to Australia and made the first films to be shot in the streets of Sydney and Melbourne.

One of the most successful of the early feature films was *The Sentimental Bloke* (1919), with scenes shot in Manly, the Royal Botanical Gardens and Woolloomooloo.

In the 1930s, film companies like Cinesound, which had its studio at Bondi Junction, sprang up. Cinesound made 17 feature films between 1931 and 1940, many based on Australian history or literature. *Forty Thousand Horsemen*, directed by Cinesound's great film maker Charles Chauvel, was a highlight of this era of locally made and financed films, which ended in 1959, the year of Chauvel's death. Chauvel is credited with giving Errol Flynn his first film role.

Before the introduction of government subsidies during 1969 and 1970, the Australian film industry found it difficult to compete with US and British industries. The creation of the Australian Film Commission in 1975 helped establish an ongoing renaissance of Australian cinema, and today Sydney is a major centre for film production.

Sydney has formed the backdrop to numerous movies. These include *Young Einstein* (Palm Beach), *Sweetie* (Willoughby), *Strictly Ballroom* (Pyrmont, Marrickville), *Muriel's Wedding* (Parramatta, Oxford St, Darling Point, Ryde), *Priscilla – Queen of the Desert* (Erskineville), *Lilian's Story* (Sydney Harbour), *Babe: Pig in the City*, *Romeo and Juliet*, *Dark City* (showground pavilions), *The Matrix* (inner city), and the new *Star Wars* movie. *Mission Impossible II* and the second and third episodes of *Star Wars* are to be made at the new Fox Studios complex at Moore Park.

Theatre

Sydney has something for all tastes, from imported blockbuster musicals at major venues like the State Theatre and Her Majesty's, to experimental productions in small theatres in the inner suburbs. The prestigious STC based at Pier 4, Millers Point, provides a balanced program of modern, classical, local and foreign drama. The National Institute of Dramatic Art (NIDA) in Kensington is a breeding ground for new talent and stages performances of students' work. There are also many smaller theatre companies, such as Griffin, which produce great local work.

The leading contemporary Australian playwright is Sydney-based David Williamson, whose dissections of Australian middle-class rituals began in 1971 with *The Removalists* and *Don's Party*. Recent Williamson plays include *Sanctuary*, an examination of the ethics of journalism and the dynamics of political correctness, and *Corporate Vibes*, which tackles highrise culture and the corporate ethos. Other interesting contemporary playwrights include Louis Nowra and Michael Gow.

RELIGION

A shrinking majority of people in Australia are at least nominally Christian. Most Protestant churches merged to form the Uniting Church, although the Anglican Church of Australia remains separate. The Catholic Church is popular (about 30% of Christians are Catholics), its adherents of Irish descent having been joined by large numbers of Mediterranean immigrants.

Non-Christian minorities abound, the main ones being Buddhist, Jewish and Muslim. Islam is the second-largest religion and Buddhism is one of the fastest growing. About 13% of Australians have no religion.

LANGUAGE

Visitors from abroad who think Australian (that's 'strine') is simply a weird variant of English/American will be in for a few surprises. For a start, many Australians don't even speak Australian. Italian, Turkish, Greek or Vietnamese, just to name a few, are often spoken as a first language.

English is the official and dominant language. However, about 15% of people in NSW speak a different language at home, and the proportion is probably much higher in Sydney.

For more information check out Lonely Planet's *Australian phrasebook*.

Facts for the Visitor

WHEN TO GO

Sydney is comfortable to visit at any time of the year but, unless you love sunshine, skip the Sydney summer and concentrate on autumn and spring. Autumn is delightful, with clear, warm days and mild nights. In spring there's more chance of rain, but it usually clears quickly. Sydney gets its fair share of dismal days in winter, but it's often clear and the temperatures are mild compared to European or North American winters. See the climate chart in the Facts about Sydney chapter.

If you're after sun, sea and surf, head to Sydney between November and March. If you do visit in summer, be aware that temperatures sometimes hit the high 30°Cs, and the often oppressive humidity can really sap your energy.

The other major consideration is school and public holidays – a time when everything touristy gets decidedly more crowded and accommodation rates zoom upward. Sydney students have a long summer break that includes Christmas. January is the peak of the holiday season, with most children returning to school at the end of January or by the first week in February. Other school holidays fall around March to April (Easter), late June to mid-July, and late September to early October.

ORIENTATION

Sydney wasn't a planned city. Its layout is further complicated by the convoluted harbour with its numerous inlets, and by the hilly nature of the city.

The harbour divides Sydney into northern and southern halves, which are connected by the Sydney Harbour Bridge and the Harbour Tunnel. Central Sydney and most places of interest can be found south of the harbour.

See Map 1 for an overview of central Sydney, and see Map 17 for the area surrounding Sydney.

City Centre

The central city area is relatively long and narrow, and George and Pitt Sts (the main thoroughfares) run 3km from Circular Quay south to Central station.

The historic Rocks and Circular Quay (Map 4), where you'll find the Opera House and the Harbour Bridge, mark the northern boundary of the city centre. Central station is on the southern edge, Darling Harbour forms the western boundary; and a string of pleasant parks border Elizabeth and Macquarie Sts on the east.

North of King St is the main financial and business district; south of King St is the main commercial area with lots of shops, cafes, restaurants, cinemas and a number of hotels.

Inner Suburbs

Cafes, restaurants, interesting shops and good pubs are peppered throughout the inner suburbs.

East of the city centre are Kings Cross (Maps 5 & 6), Woolloomooloo, Potts Point and Elizabeth Bay. Further east are the exclusive suburbs of Double Bay and Vaucluse. South-east of the city centre are the interesting inner suburbs (Maps 7 & 8) of Darlinghurst, Surry Hills and Paddington. At the city's eastern extreme are the oceanfront suburbs of Bondi Beach (Map 11) and Coogee (Map 10).

West of the centre is the radically changing Pyrmont and south-west of there is Glebe (Map 9), a bohemian suburb famous for its eateries. West of Pyrmont across Johnstons and White bays are Rozelle and the arty suburb of Balmain (Map 3).

Sydney airport is in Mascot, 10km south of the city centre, jutting into Botany Bay.

North Shore

Suburbs north of the bridge are known collectively as the North Shore. Mainly middle-class enclaves, they lack the vibrancy and diversity of the areas south of the harbour, but there are some excellent views, beaches and pockets of bushland.

Across the Harbour Bridge from the city centre is North Sydney, the city's second business centre. Military Rd runs east from North Sydney through the harbourside suburbs of Neutral Bay, Cremorne and Mosman. West of the bridge, Hunters Hill is one the most expensive suburbs in Sydney to live in.

To the north-east, Manly sits on a narrow peninsula near the entrance to Sydney Harbour. It fronts both the ocean and the harbour. A string of ocean beaches runs north from Manly to Palm Beach, another of Sydney's wealthy suburbs. Palm Beach fronts the Pacific Ocean and backs onto Pittwater. Ku-ring-gai Chase National Park lies on the western side of Pittwater (see the Excursions chapter).

Greater Sydney

Westward, Sydney's suburbs stretch for more than 50km, encompassing Parramatta (once a country retreat for the colony's governor), and only coming to a halt at Penrith at the foot of the Blue Mountains. South-west of the city, there's a similar sprawl of housing developments, swamping old towns such as Campbelltown and Liverpool. These red-tile-roofed, triple-fronted suburbs are where most Sydneysiders live, not beside the harbour or near a beach. Cabramatta, 30km south-west of Sydney, is a busy suburb with a large, active Vietnamese community. It has plenty of shops and restaurants.

North and south of the centre, suburbs stretch a good 20km, their extent limited by national parks.

MAPS

Lonely Planet's Sydney City Map ($7.95) is a comprehensive reference for the city centre and surrounding suburbs, as well as for important tourist sites around the city. It also features a walking tour.

For driving, or exploration beyond the city centre, a street directory is indispensable. UBD and Gregory's charge $25 to $35 for their full-sized directories, although there are smaller versions.

For maps of country areas, see the National Roads & Motorists Association (NRMA). For topographic maps, visit the Department of Land and Water Conservation (DLWC), 23-33 Bridge St; you can make credit-card telephone orders (☎ 9228 6111). If you're planning to go bush, pick up a copy of Tourism NSW's Best Bush Map ($4.95). It covers more than 1200 parks and State forests, and lists over 100 camping sites.

Several bookshops specialise in maps and travel guides, including the Travel Bookshop (☎ 9261 8200), 175 Liverpool St, and Map World (☎ 9261 3601), 371 Pitt St.

TOURIST INFORMATION

Local Tourist Offices

There's a NSW Travel Centre (☎ 9667 6050) on the international arrivals level at Sydney airport; it's open from 6 am to midnight daily. As well as being a travel agency, it sells hotel accommodation at discounted rates.

The travel centre often has the best deals, but if there's a queue you could try the nearby electronic bookings board for hotel accommodation. The useful Backpacker Board also lists 75 hostels in Sydney, and allows you to phone them for free.

Helpful City Host tourist information kiosks are located at Circular Quay, Town Hall, and Martin place. Opening hours are from 9 am to 5 pm in winter, 10 am to 6 pm in summer.

There's a Tourist Information Service (☎ 9669 5111) answering phone inquiries from 8 am to 6 pm daily. In the Sydney Coach Terminal on Eddy Ave (outside Central station), the Travellers' Information Service (☎ 9281 9366) makes bus and accommodation bookings (not hostels, but there's a hostel noticeboard) from 6 am to 10.30 pm. On Central station's main concourse is the Travellers Aid Society (☎ 9211 2469). It provides general information and assistance with travel problems, and is open weekdays from 6.45 am to 5 pm, weekends 7 am to noon; hot showers cost $3.

The Countrylink Travel Centre at Wynyard station on York St (Map 4, ☎ 13 2077) can book travel as well as hotel accommodation; it's open weekdays from 8.30 am to 5 pm.

The excellent Sydney Visitors Centre (Map 4, ☎ 9255 1788, toll-free 1800 067 676) at 106 George St, the Rocks, is open from 9 am to 6 pm daily; it can book hotel accommodation, and there's a hostel noticeboard too. There's another visitor centre (☎ 9286 0111) at Darling Harbour, next to the IMAX Cinema.

Interstate Tourist Offices

The NSW Travel Centre national toll-free number is ☎ 13 2077. It has one interstate office, in Adelaide (South Australia) at 45 King William St (☎ 08-8231 3167).

Tourist Offices Abroad

Australian Tourist Commission (ATC)

The ATC is the federal government body that informs potential visitors about the country. In the past year, the ATC has done away with telephone helplines and now conducts all of its customer relations via the Internet. There's a large and efficient Web site full of maps and information at www.australia.com, and queries can be relayed to ATC staff through the site.

Tourism NSW This body operates along the same lines as the ATC, but at a state level. It has offices in the following locations:

Japan
(☎ 03-5214 0777, fax 5214 0780)
28th Floor, New Otani Garden Court Building, 4-1 Kioi-cho, Chiyoda-Ku Tokyo 102

New Zealand
(☎ 09-379 9118, fax 366 6173)
Level 13, 48 Emily Place (PO Box 1921), Auckland 1

Singapore
(☎ 253 3888, fax 352 4888)
Unit 13-04, United Square, 101 Thomson Rd, Singapore 1130

UK
(☎ 020-7887 5003, fax 7836 5266)
Level 2, Australia Centre, The Strand, London WC2B 4LC

USA
(☎ 310-301 1903, fax 301 0913)
13737 Fiji Way, Suite C-10, Marina Del Rey, California 90292

Travel Agencies

Thomas Cook (Map 4, ☎ 9231 2877), 175 Pitt St, has a travel agency as well as a foreign exchange desk; it's open weekdays from 8.45 am to 5.15 pm, Saturday 10 am to 2 pm. American Express (Map 4, ☎ 9239 0666), 92 Pitt St, opens weekdays from 8.30 am to 5.30 pm, Saturday 9 am to 12 pm.

Quite a few travel agents cater to budget travellers/backpackers.

STA Travel (not to be confused with the State Transit Authority) has a number of branches around the city. These include its head office (Map 8, ☎ 9212 1255) at 855 George St, Ultimo; at 9 Oxford St, Paddington (☎ 9360 1822); and 127-139 Macleay St in Kings Cross, near the fountain (☎ 9368 1111).

Let's Travel Australia (Map 6, ☎ 9358 2295), 175 Victoria St near Kings Cross, is a backpacker-oriented travel agency, which means that it has dealt with every permutation and combination of the travel jigsaw. It can also help with tricky details such as car insurance. Eden Travel (Map 4, ☎ 9368 1174) at level 2, 65 York St in the city; and Backpackers World (☎ 9380 2700, fax 9380 2900), 212 Victoria St, Kings Cross are other travel agents used to dealing with backpackers.

Travellers Contact Point (Map 4, ☎ 9221 8744), 7th floor 428 George St, between King and Market Sts, is above Dymocks bookshop. You can have mail sent here, and there's information on finding work and accommodation, and a noticeboard for messages. It organises charter flights to the UK, but you need to book well in advance.

Free Publications

Several free magazines/booklets provide current listings. At the airport pick up a copy of the *Arrivals Guide* or *Sydney – The Harbour Connection* (one of the better ones, but aimed at visitors with a bit of money to spend). For budget travellers, *TNT Magazine* has heaps of info on accommodation, what to do, transport etc. Also useful are smaller publications *Aussie Backpacker* and *Sydney in your Backpack*.

A blue leaflet, the *Guide and Map to Art Galleries*, covers the inner city and eastern suburbs and is available from antique shops, galleries, cafes and the airport.

Sydney City Hub is an interesting weekly news, arts and entertainment paper available from cafes. Music-lovers can check out news and gig guides in the weekly street papers *Drum Media*, *3D World* and *Revolver*, while parents looking to keep the kids occupied can pick up a copy of *Sydney's Child*, a junior-oriented monthly. Lively gay papers include *Capital Q Weekly* and *Lesbians on the Loose*.

You'll find useful tourist tips, phone numbers and public transport information in the front of the A-K volume of the *Yellow Pages*.

Other Sources

Other excellent places to look for help and cheap travel tips are the hostel areas where most budget travellers stay – particularly Victoria St in Kings Cross and Potts Point, where there are countless posters and noticeboards offering everything from flat shares and backpacks to tours and unused air tickets. Several travel agents in Kings Cross cater to backpackers, which means they have all sorts of useful travel information.

DOCUMENTS

Visas

Visitors to Australia need a visa. Only New Zealand nationals are exempt, and even they receive a 'special category' visa on arrival. The type of visa you require depends on the reason for your visit.

Visa application forms are available from either Australian diplomatic missions overseas or travel agents; you can apply by mail or in person. Alternatively, many travel agents and airlines can now grant on-the-spot Australian visas, valid for three months, via the new ETA (Electronic Travel Authority).

Tourist Visas Issued by Australian consular offices abroad, tourist visas are the most common visa. They are generally valid for a stay of three or six months, and can be used to enter and leave Australia several times within that period. The short stay visa is valid for 12 months, with a maximum stay of three months for each entry; the long stay visa is valid for four years with a maximum of six months for each entry.

When you apply for a visa, you need to present your passport and a passport photo, as well as sign a statement that you have an onward or return ticket and 'sufficient funds' for your visit.

There is a $50 fee for visas applied for outside Australia, and a $145 fee for visas applied for within Australia.

Working Visas Young visitors (without dependent children) from the UK, the Republic of Ireland, Canada, Korea, the Netherlands, Malta and Japan may be eligible for a Working Holiday Visa. 'Young' is fairly loosely interpreted as between 18 and 26, although exceptions are made.

A Working Holiday Visa allows for a stay of up to 12 months, but the emphasis is on casual employment rather than a full-time job, so working full time for longer than three months with any one employer is not allowed.

Conditions attached to a Working Holiday Visa include having an onward ticket, and sufficient funds. You cannot enrol in formal studies while in Australia. There is a fee of $145.

See the Work section later in this chapter for more information.

Visa Extensions The maximum stay is one year, including extensions.

Visa extensions are made through Department of Immigration & Ethnic Affairs (DIMA) offices in Australia and, as the process takes some time, it's best to apply about a month before your visa expires. There's an application fee of $145 – and even if they turn down your application they can still keep your money! To qualify for an extension you must have sufficient funds and an onward ticket.

There's a DIMA office (☎ 9258 4665 or 13 1881) at 88 Cumberland St, the Rocks.

Electronic Travel Authority (ETA)

Doing away with long waits and paperwork, the ETA system allows participating airlines and travel agents to grant instant visas. This system is currently operational in around 30 countries, including Japan, the UK, the USA, Malaysia, Singapore, Germany and France. See travel agents, airlines, or the DIMA Web site at www.immi.gov.au for further details. ETAs can be granted for both business and holiday trips, and allow a stay of three months.

Travel Insurance

This not only covers you for medical expenses and luggage theft or loss, but also for cancellations or delays in your travel arrangements under certain circumstances – and everyone should be covered for the worst possible case, such as an accident requiring hospital treatment and a flight home. Cover depends on your insurance and type of ticket, so ask your insurer and your ticket-issuing agency to explain where you stand. Ticket loss is usually covered by travel insurance. Buy travel insurance as early as possible.

Check the fine print: some policies exclude 'dangerous activities' like scuba diving or motorcycling. If such activities are on your agenda, you don't want that policy. Finally, make sure the policy includes health care and medication in the countries you may visit on the way to/from Australia.

EMBASSIES & CONSULATES

Australian Embassies

Australian diplomatic missions in other countries include the following:

Canada
(☎ 613-236 0841)
Suite 710, 50 O'Connor St, Ottawa, Ontario K1P 6L2; also in Toronto and Vancouver

France
(☎ 01 40 59 33 00)
4 Rue Jean Rey, 75724 Paris, Cedex 15

Germany
(☎ 0228-810 30)
Godesberger Allee 105-107, 53175 Bonn; also in Frankfurt and Berlin

Hong Kong
(☎ 2827 8881)
23/F Harbour Centre, 25 Harbour Rd, Wanchai, Hong Kong Island

Ireland
(☎ 01-676 1517)
Fitzwilton House, Wilton Terrace, Dublin 2

Japan
(☎ 03-5232 4111)
2-1-14 Mita, Minato-ku, Tokyo 108-8361

Malaysia
(☎ 03-242 3122)
6 Jalan Yap Kwan Seng, Kuala Lumpur 50450; also in Kuching and Penang

New Zealand
(☎ 04-473 6411)
72-78 Hobson St, Thorndon, Wellington
(☎ 09-303 2429)
Floor 7 & 8, Union House, 132-138 Quay St, Auckland

Singapore
(☎ 737 9311)
25 Napier Rd, Singapore 1025

Sweden
See Germany

Switzerland
(☎ 22 799 91 00)
2 Chemin des Fins
Case postale 172, 1211 Geneva 19

Thailand
(☎ 02-287 2680)
37 South Sathorn Rd, Bangkok 10120

UK
(☎ 020-7379 4334)
Australia House, The Strand, London WC2B 4LA; also in Edinburgh and Manchester

USA
(☎ 202-797 3000)
1601 Massachusetts Ave NW, Washington DC 20036-2273; also in Atlanta, Boston, Chicago, Denver, Honolulu, Houston, Los Angeles, New York and San Francisco

Consulates in Sydney

Most foreign embassies are based in Canberra, but many countries also maintain a consulate in Sydney.

France
(☎ 9261 5779)
Level 26, St Martins Tower, 31 Market St, city

Germany
(☎ 9328 7733)
13 Trelawney St, Woollahra
Indonesia
(☎ 9344 9933)
236 Maroubra Rd, Maroubra
Japan
(☎ 9231 3455)
52 Martin Place, city
Malaysia
(☎ 9327 7565)
67 Victoria Rd, Bellevue Hill
Netherlands
(☎ 9387 6644)
500 Oxford St, Bondi Junction
New Zealand
(☎ 9247 1344)
1 Alfred St, Circular Quay
UK
(☎ 9247 7521)
1 Macquarie Place, city
USA
(☎ 9373 9200)
19-29 Martin Place, city

For others see the *Yellow Pages* under Consulates & Legations.

CUSTOMS

When entering Australia, you can bring most articles in free of duty provided that customs is satisfied they're for personal use and that you'll be taking them with you when you leave. There's the usual duty-free quota per person of one litre of alcohol, 250 cigarettes and dutiable goods up to the value of A$400.

Two issues need particular attention. Number one is illegal drugs – don't bring any in with you. If you're arriving from South-East Asia or the Indian Subcontinent you will be under even closer scrutiny from customs.

Number two is animal and plant quarantine – declare all goods of animal or vegetable origin and show them to an official. Authorities are naturally keen to prevent weeds, pests or diseases getting into the country. Fresh food and flowers are also unpopular, and if you've recently visited farmland or rural areas prior to entering Australia, it might pay to scrub your shoes before you get to the airport.

Weapons and firearms are either prohibited or require a permit and safety testing. Other restricted goods include products (such as ivory) made from protected wildlife species, non-approved telecommunications devices and live animals.

When you leave, don't take any protected flora or fauna with you. Customs comes down hard on smugglers.

MONEY

Carry some Australian currency in cash – for small transactions and for places that don't accept credit cards (some of the cheaper hotels and places to eat).

Currency

The unit of currency is the Australian dollar, which is divided into 100 cents. There are $100, $50, $20, $10 and $5 notes and $2, $1, 50c, 20c, 10c and 5c coins. The 2c and 1c coins have been taken out of circulation, although prices can still be set in odd cents. Shops round prices up (or down) to the nearest 5c on your total bill.

There are few restrictions on importing or exporting currency or travellers cheques, but if you absolutely *must* enter or leave carrying more than A$10,000 in cold hard cash, you're obliged to declare it.

Exchange Rates

The Australian dollar fluctuates quite markedly against the US dollar. Until early 1997, it stayed pretty much in the 70c to 80c range, but has since declined significantly and now hovers between 60c and 70c – a disaster for Australians travelling overseas but a real bonus for visitors. Approximate exchange values are:

country	unit		rate
Canada	C$1	=	A$1.02
euro	€1	=	A$1.53
France	10FF	=	A$2.33
Germany	DM1	=	A$0.78
Japan	¥100	=	A$1.22
Korea (South)	W100	=	A$0.13
New Zealand	NZ$1	=	A$0.79
UK	UK£1	=	A$2.35
USA	US$1	=	A$1.49

Exchanging Money

Changing foreign currency or travellers cheques is no problem at almost any bank or licensed moneychanger. The Commonwealth Bank, ANZ and Westpac banks have branches near Martin Place, and the National Australia Bank (NAB) is nearby on George St.

Thomas Cook has foreign exchange branches at 175 Pitt St (☎ 9231 2877), in the Queen Victoria Building (QVB; ☎ 9264 1267) and in the Kingsgate shopping centre (☎ 9356 2211), beneath the Coca-Cola sign in Kings Cross. The QVB branch is open daily, the others Monday to Saturday. American Express (☎ 9239 0666), 92 Pitt St, opens weekdays and Saturday morning.

Travellers Cheques Travellers cheques generally enjoy a better exchange rate than foreign cash. American Express, Thomas Cook and other well-known brands are widely used. A passport is usually adequate identification, but a driver's licence, credit card or plane ticket can also be useful in case of problems.

Buying Australian-dollar travellers cheques is worth considering. These can be exchanged immediately at the cashier's window without being converted from a foreign currency and subject to commissions, fees or exchange-rate fluctuations.

Fees for changing foreign-currency travellers cheques vary widely from bank to bank. Westpac charges $7 for amounts below $500, but no fee thereafter. At the National Australia and Commonwealth banks it's $5, and at ANZ the fee depends on the amount being changed.

ATMs There are 24-hour automatic teller machines (ATMs) at the branches of most banks in Sydney. Most of the major banks have reciprocal arrangements: Westpac, Commonwealth Bank, National Bank and ANZ Bank ATMs generally accept each other's cards – but charge you a small fee for the privilege.

Most banks place a $1000 limit on the amount you can withdraw daily.

Credit Cards Visa, MasterCard, Diners Club and American Express are widely accepted. Cash advances from credit cards are available over the counter and from many ATMs.

A credit card makes renting a car much simpler; many agencies simply refuse to rent you a vehicle if you don't have one.

Costs

Compared to other major world cities, Sydney is cheaper in some ways and more expensive in others. Manufactured goods like clothes tend to be more expensive, but food and wine are both high in quality and low in cost.

Many places to stay have high and low-season prices, and special deals lower than the standard room-rate. Prices in this book are generally standard high-season ones, unless otherwise stated.

At the budget end, a dormitory bed in a hostel costs from $15 to $22 a night, a cheap hotel room starts at $35/50 a single/double. A modest B&B costs around $50/70, and a mid-range hotel room with *en suite* starts at around $65/95. You can eat for as little as $4 or $5 at one of the food courts; dinner with a beer or wine in a reasonable restaurant or cafe costs about $15 to $30.

Tipping

While tipping is becoming more common, and might be expected in more upmarket restaurants and cafes, it isn't yet an entrenched practice. A tip of around 10% is average, but feel free to vary the amount depending on your satisfaction with the service. Taxi drivers don't expect to be tipped, but 'rounding up' the fare to the nearest dollar is common.

Taxes

As of July 2000, the Australian government will introduce a 10% goods and services tax (GST). This tax will be automatically added to virtually everything you buy, from taxi fares and accommodation, to clothing – even a humble cup of coffee.

If you purchase new or second-hand goods with a total minimum value of $300 from any one supplier within 28 days of departure from Australia, you will be entitled to a refund of any GST paid. Contact the Australian Taxation Office (ATO) on ☎ 13 6320 for details.

POST & COMMUNICATIONS

Post

Australia Post (☎ 13 1318) runs the country's mail system. Most post offices are open weekdays from 9 am to 5 pm, but you can often get stamps from post offices operating out of newsagencies, or from some Australia Post retail outlets on Saturday from 9 am to noon.

Sydney's original general post office (GPO), in the grand Victorian building on Martin Place, has been refurbished and should have reopened by the time you read this. It will open from 10 am to 2 pm weekdays and on Saturday.

Another post office (with counter service) operates from 130 Pitt St. Post Restante (☎ 9744 3732) and PO boxes are located at 310 George St, in the Hunter Connection Bldg near the Wynyard station entrance; it's open from 8.15 am to 5.30 pm on weekdays.

Sending Mail It costs 45c to send a postcard or standard letter within Australia, while aerograms cost 70c.

Airmail postcards/letters cost 70/75c to New Zealand, 80/85c to Singapore and Malaysia, 90/95c to Hong Kong and India, 95c/$1.05 to the USA and Canada, and $1/1.20 to Europe and the UK.

Receiving Mail The Poste Restante at 310 George St has computer terminals that enable you to check if mail is waiting for you. Remember to bring some identification. You can also have mail redirected to any suburban post office for a small fee.

American Express and Thomas Cook (see Money, earlier) provide mail services for their clients. Alternatively, there's Travellers Contact Point (☎ 9221 8744), Suite 11-15, 7th floor, 428 George St or Internet Bakpak Travel (☎ 9360 3888), a backpackers' resource provider at 3 Orwell St, Kings Cross.

Telephone

There's a wide range of local and international phonecards. Lonely Planet's eKno Communication Card is aimed specifically at travellers and provides cheap international calls, a range of messaging services and free email – for local calls, you're usually better off with a local card. You can join on-line at www.ekno.lonelyplanet.com, or by phone from Australia by dialling toll-free ☎ 1800 674 100. Once you have joined, to use eKno from Australia, dial toll-free ☎ 1800 11 44 78.

Telstra Phone Centre, at 231 Elizabeth St, has booths of coin, phonecard and credit card telephones. It's open daily. The 24-hour Translating & Interpreting Service (☎ 13 1450) can help with language difficulties. For help in finding a number within Australia, call directory assistance (☎ toll-free 1223) or Yellow Pages Direct (☎ 13 1319, business numbers only).

Local Calls Local calls from public phones cost 40c for unlimited time; most phones take coins and/or phonecards. You can also make local calls from gold or blue phones (often found in hotels, shops, bars etc) and from payphone booths.

STD Calls The 02 code covers NSW, 03 is for Victoria and Tasmania, 07 covers Queensland and 08 is for South Australia, Western Australia and the Northern Territory. There is no need to dial the area code when making local calls.

You can make long-distance (STD – Subscriber Trunk Dialling) calls from virtually any public phone. Many public phones accept Telstra phonecards, which come in $5, $10, $20 and $50 denominations, and are available from retail outlets that display the phonecard logo. Otherwise, use coins. STD calls are cheaper in off-peak hours – see the front of a local telephone book for the different rates.

Some public phones take only bank cash cards or credit cards. The minimum charge for a call on one of these phones is $1.20.

International Calls You can make ISD (International Subscriber Dialling) calls from most STD phones.

To call Australia from abroad dial ☎ 61. When dialling Australia from abroad drop the zero from the area code.

Dial ☎ 0011 for overseas, the country code (44 for Britain, 1 for North America, 64 for New Zealand etc), the city code (0207 or 0208 for London, 212 for New York etc) then the telephone number. (For free international directory assistance, call ☎ 1225.) Off-peak rates apply on weekends – between midnight Friday and midnight Sunday is the cheapest time to ring.

It's possible to make ISD calls through either of Australia's two main telecommunications companies, Optus or Telstra, from private phones in most areas. Phone Optus (☎ toll-free 1800 500 002) for details on how to access their services.

Telstra rates for calls from public phones are roughly double those for calls from private phones. Calls to the USA and UK cost $1.60 a minute (80c off-peak); calls to NZ cost $1.20 a minute (80c off-peak). Call ☎ toll-free 12 552 for international rates.

Country Direct gives travellers in Australia direct access to operators in nearly 50 countries, to make collect or credit-card calls. For a full list of the countries hooked into this system, check the local *White Pages* telephone book. They include: Canada (☎ toll-free 1800 881 150), Ireland (☎ toll-free 1800 881 353), New Zealand (☎ toll-free 1800 881 640), the UK (☎ toll-free 1800 881 441) and the USA (☎ toll-free 1800 881 011).

There are several companies offering discounted international calls, especially around Kings Cross. One company selling overseas phonecards is One.tel (☎ toll-free 1800 501 110). A travellers' communications specialist with telephones and Internet access, the Global Gossip chain (☎ 9326 9777) has outlets in several locations around Sydney, including one at 111 Darlinghurst Rd, Kings Cross.

Other Calls Many businesses and some government departments operate a toll-free service from around the country with the prefix 1800. Other companies have six-digit numbers beginning with 13. Calls to these numbers are charged at the rate of a local call.

Phone numbers with the prefixes 014, 015, 017, 018, 041 or 0409 are mobile or car phones. Calls to mobile numbers can be quite expensive.

Numbers starting with 1900 are usually recorded information services provided by private companies. Watch out – your call can cost as little as 35c to as much as $45 per minute! Numbers starting with 1300 are also information lines, but dialling them costs the same as a local call.

Fax

You can send a fax from post offices and some agencies. To send one to another fax machine or to a postal address within Australia, post offices charge $4 for the first page and $1 for subsequent pages. If the fax is sent to a postal address, it goes first to the local post office and is either delivered by normal mail, or is collected by the recipient. Overseas faxes, either to a private fax machine or the local mail service, cost $10 for the first page, $4 for following pages.

If you're sending a fax to a fax machine, it's worth finding a business that offers a fax service because it's usually a lot cheaper than the post office. Kinko's (☎ 9267 4255) at 175 Liverpool St, opposite Hyde Park, charges $1 a page for local faxes, and is open 24 hours. You can receive faxes for free at Backpackers World (☎ 9380 2700, fax 9380 2900), 212 Victoria St, Kings Cross. The international code for sending faxes is 0015.

Email & Internet Access

Internet 'cafes' have been popping up all over Sydney, and while few of them offer anything resembling food, the resulting price war is good news for travellers.

FACTS FOR THE VISITOR

RICHARD I'ANSON

View of the city at night from Harbourside

ROSS BARNETT

The Monorail crossing the old Pyrmont Bridge, Darling Harbour

C GROENHOUT

The view of the Opera House at dusk

Kings Cross has the highest concentration of Internet cafes, several of which are open 24 hours. Besides allowing you to access email and surf the Web, many offer word-processing, fax, scanning, and printing services too.

Global Gossip (☎ 9326 9777) is open from 8 am until at least midnight, and has locations at 770 George St in the city; 108 Oxford St, Darlinghurst; and 111 Darlinghurst Rd, Kings Cross. Backpackers World (see the Fax section earlier) also has Internet access. For good specials, check out the late-night Kings Internet Cafe (☎ 9356 2311), 41 Darlinghurst Rd, Kings Cross.

Serving both food and coffee, Well Connected (☎ 9566 2655), at 35 Glebe Point Rd, Glebe, is Sydney's longest-running and most comfortable Internet cafe. If you fancy logging on with a beer, there's the pricier Hotel Sweeney (☎ 9267 1116), at 236 Clarence St in the city.

Other places include Newtown Internet Salon (☎ 9519 0010) at 423 King St, and Idle Tank (☎ 9365 5266) at 84 Campbell St, Bondi Beach. Coin-operated computer stations that look like video game machines are also popping up, but they're relatively expensive. Most libraries offer free Internet access, but you need to book ahead. Many hostels are also getting wired up.

An excellent option for travellers are the free email accounts offered by companies such as Hotmail (www.hotmail.com), Yahoo (www.yahoo.com) and Excite (www.excite.com).

INTERNET RESOURCES

The Internet is a rich resource for travellers. You can research your trip, hunt down bargain air fares, book hotels, check on weather conditions or chat with locals and other travellers about the best places to visit (or avoid!).

There's no better place to start your Web explorations than the Lonely Planet Web site (www.lonelyplanet.com). Here you'll find succinct summaries on travelling to most places on earth, postcards from other travellers and the Thorn Tree bulletin board, where you can ask questions before you go or dispense advice when you get back. You can also find travel news and updates to many of our most popular guidebooks, and the subWWWay section links you to the most useful travel resources elsewhere on the Web.

Other useful Web sites are:

Active Sydney
 www.active.org.au
 (news, views and links for activist events around Sydney)
Australian Tourist Commission (ATC)
 www.australia.com
 (huge official site: maps, information, queries answered)
Izon's Backpacker Journal
 www.izon.com
 (full of backpacker-friendly information and useful links)
State Transit Authority (STA)
 www.sydneytransport.net.au
 (information on bus, train, and ferry services)
Sydney Morning Herald's city guide
 www.citysearch.com
 (entertainment, the arts, dining, accommodation and shopping options)
Youth Hostel Association
 www.yha.org.au
 (heaps of info on hostelling around Australia)

BOOKS

For information on Sydney's bookshops see the Shopping chapter.

Lonely Planet

Lonely Planet's *New South Wales* guide includes extensive coverage of the whole state, so if you plan to visit more of the state, check it out. Lonely Planet's *Bushwalking in Australia* details the walk in the Blue Gum Forest in the Blue Mountains. For extensive information on Sydney's eateries, get a copy of Lonely Planet's *Out to Eat – Sydney*.

If you are travelling elsewhere in Australia, Lonely Planet publishes *Australia*, individual state and city guides *(Melbourne, Islands of Australia's Great Barrier Reef, Outback Australia)* and the *Australian phrasebook*.

Can't Find a Book?

Most books are published in different editions by different publishers in different countries. As a result, a book might be a hardcover rarity in one country and readily available in paperback in another. Fortunately, bookshops and libraries search by title or author, so your local bookshop or library is best placed to advise you on availability.

Guidebooks

There's a good range of guidebooks concentrating on particular aspects of the city, including a number on exploring the city on foot. Joan Lawrence has written several books describing short walks in many Sydney suburbs, including *Balmain, Glebe and Annandale Walks*, *Eastern Suburbs Walks* and *North Shore Walks*. *Sydney by Ferry & Foot*, by John Gunter, describes 16 walks mainly near the harbour.

If you want to find out more about the history and character of various areas of the city, look for the *Book of Sydney Suburbs*.

A gem of a book to take with you when exploring Sydney's bushland is *Burnum Burnum's Wildthings Around Sydney* by Geoff Sainty et al. It's full of colour photographs and brief descriptions.

See the Cycling section of the Things to See & Do chapter for books on cycling and the boxed text 'A Guide for the Serious Foodie' in the Places to Eat chapter.

Travel

A great book is *Sydney*, by Jan Morris, one of the best travel writers around. In Lonely Planet's *Sean & David's Long Drive*, an offbeat road book by Sean Condon, the protagonists visit Sydney.

History & Politics

A good introduction to Australian history is Manning Clark's *A Short History of Australia*. Clark also wrote the controversial, six-volume *History of Australia*, which was condensed into a palatable single volume.

Robert Hughes' best-selling account of the convict era, *The Fatal Shore*, is a very good read. Russel Ward's *Concise History of Australia* provides a quick introduction.

Sydney 1842-1992 by Shirley Fitzgerald details 150 years of the city's history. *Old Sydney Buildings* by Margaret Simpson gives a history of the city through its architecture.

Aboriginal History & Culture

In *The Other Side of the Frontier*, Henry Reynolds uses historical records to give a vivid Aboriginal view of the arrival of Europeans in Australia. Geoffrey Blainey's award-winning *Triumph of the Nomads* provides another historical perspective. Sally Morgan's prize-winning autobiography, *My Place*, traces the author's discovery of her Aboriginal heritage. Roberta Sykes' autobiographical trilogy gives an insight into the life of this eminent Australian. *My People* by Oodgeroo Noonuccal (formerly Kath Walker) is recommended reading for anyone interested in Aboriginal culture. *The Stolen Children*, edited by Carmel Bird, features harrowing and tragic accounts from victims of this one-time government policy.

Day of the Dog, by Aboriginal writer Archie Weller, has been made into a film called *Blackfellas*.

Children's Books

Norman Lindsay's *The Magic Pudding* and May Gibbs' *Snugglepot & Cuddlepie* are classics for younger children. Lindsay's home near Springwood in the Blue Mountains is now a museum, as is Nutcote, May Gibbs' house in North Sydney.

General

There are some good coffee-table books about Sydney that make excellent souvenirs, such as *Sydney Harbour* by Rodney Hall & David Moore. *Sydney from Below* (1995), edited by Finbar McCarthy, takes a warm, hopeful look at the plight of Sydney's homeless.

NEWSPAPERS & MAGAZINES

The *Sydney Morning Herald* is one of the best newspapers in the country. It's a serious broadsheet, but also captures some of Sydney's larrikinism. The other Sydney paper is the relatively tame Murdoch tabloid, the *Daily Telegraph*.

Two national newspapers are available in Sydney: the *Australian*, a conservative daily that has an interesting weekend edition; and the business-oriented *Australian Financial Review*. There are also a healthy number of weekly newspapers for Australia's ethnic communities – some are published in English.

The *Bulletin* is a venerable, conservative weekly news magazine, which carries a condensed version of *Newsweek*. It was first published in 1880.

Widely available international papers include the *International Herald Tribune*, the *European* and the *Guardian Weekly*. *Time* produces an Australian edition, as does *Rolling Stone*.

Australians are avid consumers of magazines, and Sydney is home to most of the country's glossies. Published bi-monthly, *HQ* is one of the better reads.

RADIO & TV

Sydney's radio dial is crowded with over 20 stations, plus another dozen short-range community FM stations. The Australian Broadcasting Commission (ABC) has Radio National (576 AM), 2BL (702 AM) and Fine Music (92.9 FM). Triple J FM (105.7) is the ABC's excellent 'youth' station. There's also the SBS multilingual station, 2EA (1386 AM). Koori Radio broadcasts on 88.9 FM.

Sydney has five TV channels: two – the government-funded ABC station; seven, nine and 10 – standard commercial fare; and SBS – a UHF channel devoted to multicultural programs. SBS invariably has the best news, the best movies, and some good arts and music programs.

PHOTOGRAPHY & VIDEO

Australian film prices are similar to those in the rest of the western world, but if you arrive via Hong Kong or Singapore, it's probably worth buying film there. A 36-exposure Kodachrome 64 or Fujichrome 100 slide film costs around $25 to $28, including developing.

Developing standards are high, with many places offering one-hour service for colour print film. Film is susceptible to heat, so protect your film by keeping it cool and having it processed as soon as possible. Dust and humidity also affect film.

The best photographs are taken early in the morning or late in the afternoon, especially in summer when the sun's glare tends to wash out colours. Ask before taking pictures of people.

Many camera shops also do repairs. One is Paxton's (☎ 9299 2999) downstairs at 285 George St, a large camera and video store specialising in duty-free gear.

At airports, X-ray machines don't jeopardise lower-speed film, but it's best to carry your film and camera with you and ask the X-ray inspector to check them visually.

Overseas visitors thinking of purchasing videos should remember that Australia uses the Phase Alternative Line (PAL) system, which isn't compatible with other standards unless converted.

TIME

NSW uses Eastern Standard Time (as do Queensland, Victoria and Tasmania), which is 10 hours ahead of GMT/UTC (Greenwich Mean Time).

Other time zones in Australia are Central Time (half an hour behind Eastern Standard, and used in South Australia and the Northern Territory) and Western Time (two hours behind Eastern Standard, and used in Western Australia). Broken Hill, in western NSW, uses Central Time.

At noon in Sydney it's 2 am in London, 3 am in Rome, 9 am in Bangkok, 2 pm in Auckland, 6 pm the previous day in Los Angeles and 9 pm the previous day in New York.

From the last Sunday in October to the last Sunday in March, NSW is on Eastern Summer Time, which is one hour ahead of standard time.

ELECTRICITY

Voltage is 220-240V and plugs are flat three-pin, but not like British three-pin plugs. Except in fancy hotels, it's difficult to find converters to take either US flat two-pin plugs or European round two-pin plugs used for electric shavers or hair driers. Adaptors for British plugs are found in good hardware shops, chemists and travel agents.

WEIGHTS & MEASURES

Australia uses the metric system, though in country areas you may hear people talking in imperial units. When you're getting directions, make sure people are talking about kilometres, not miles.

LAUNDRY

Most hostels and cheaper hotels have self-service laundry facilities, while the more expensive hotels will return your clothes washed, dried and neatly folded. Otherwise there are self-service laundrettes, or dry-cleaning places, many of which open daily. Washing costs around $1.50 to $2 per load, and drying another $2 for 30 minutes. Some laundrettes have attendants who wash, dry and fold your clothes for an additional fee. To find a laundrette, look in the *Yellow Pages* under 'Laundries – Self-Service'.

While your clothes are washing at My Favourite Laundrette (☎ 9332 1843), 249 Darlinghurst Rd south of Kings Cross, you can pop over the road to Fishface for a meal. You can do the same at Fitzroy Laundry (no phone), 61 Fitzroy St, next to Johnnie's Seafood Cafe, Surry Hills. Wash on the Rocks (☎ 9247 4917) is at 9a Argyle Place, the Rocks; it's closed Sunday.

LEFT LUGGAGE

There is a cloakroom at Central station (☎ 9379 4395) where you can leave luggage for 24 hours at $1.50 per item, but unless you pay this levy in person on a daily basis, you'll be charged $4.50 a day. The cloakroom opens daily from 6.30 am to 10.30 pm.

There are luggage lockers in the Greyhound Pioneer office on Eddy Ave outside Central station. They cost $4 to $8 for 24 hours, depending on the size of your bag. Some of the backpacker service specialists in Kings Cross also store luggage.

HEALTH

Vaccinations aren't required for entry to Australia unless you've visited an infected country in the preceding 14 days (aircraft refuelling stops don't count).

Medical care in Australia is first class and only moderately expensive. A typical visit to the doctor costs around $35 to $40. Health insurance is available, but there's usually a waiting period after you sign up before you can make a claim.

There's universal health care in Australia (for Australians and citizens of nations with reciprocal rights) and you can choose your own doctor. Visitors from Finland, Italy, Malta, the Netherlands, New Zealand, Sweden, Ireland and the UK have reciprocal health rights and can register at any Medicare office. Seeing a doctor is simply a matter of finding one nearby – check the *Yellow Pages* under 'Medical Practitioners'.

If you have an immediate health problem, attend the casualty section at the nearest public hospital; in an emergency, call an ambulance (☎ 000).

It's a good idea to travel with a basic medical kit (including aspirin or paracetamol, antiseptic, elastic plasters etc), even when your destination is a country like Australia where first-aid supplies are readily available. Don't forget any medication you're already taking.

Health Precautions

The sun can be very intense in Australia and ultraviolet rays can burn you badly even on an overcast day. Australia has the world's highest incidence of skin cancer, so cover up and slather on the sunscreen. The sun is at its fiercest between 11 am and 3 pm, so be especially careful during this period.

Too much sunlight whether direct or reflected (glare) can damage your eyes. Good-quality sunglasses that filter out UV radiation are important.

Dehydration or salt deficiency can cause heat exhaustion. Take time to acclimatise to high temperatures and make sure you drink sufficient liquids. Wear loose clothing and a broad-brimmed hat. Heat stroke occurs when the body's heat-regulating mechanism breaks down and body temperature rises to dangerous levels. If you arrive during a hot period avoid excessive alcohol and strenuous activity.

For advice on HIV/AIDS call the 24-hour HIV/AIDS Information Line (☎ 9332 4000) or contact the AIDS Council of NSW (☎ 9206 2000, toll-free 1800 063 060), PO Box 350, Darlinghurst, NSW 2010.

The contraceptive pill is available by prescription only, so a visit to a doctor is necessary first.

Salbutamol inhalers (Ventolin) are available without prescription, but you must give your name and address to the chemist.

Condoms are available from supermarkets, chemists, convenience stores, and vending machines in hotel toilets.

Vaccinations

Several places give vaccinations and advice, but you need to book an appointment.

The Traveller's Medical & Vaccination Centre (☎ 9221 7133), Room 12, 7th Floor, 428 George St above Dymocks bookshop, opens weekdays from 9 am to 5 pm and Saturday to noon.

Kings Cross Travellers' Clinic (☎ 9358 3376), Suite 1, 13 Springfield Ave, opens weekdays from 9 am to 1 pm and 2 to 6 pm, Saturday from 10 am to noon.

Hospitals & Pharmacies

The city's public hospitals, many of which have casualty and out-patient departments, include:

New Children's Hospital
(☎ 9845 0000) Hawkesbury Rd, Westmead
Prince Henry Hospital
(☎ 9382 5555) Anzac Parade, Lavender Bay
Royal North Shore Hospital
(☎ 9926 7111) Pacific Hwy, St Leonards
Royal Prince Alfred Hospital
(☎ 9515 6111) Missenden Rd, Camperdown
St Vincent's Hospital
(☎ 9339 1111) on the corner of Victoria and Burton Sts, Darlinghurst
Sydney Children's Hospital
(☎ 9382 1111) High St, Randwick
Sydney Hospital & Sydney Eye Hospital
(☎ 9382 7111) Macquarie St, city

For pharmacies, check the *Yellow Pages* under 'Chemists – Pharmaceutical'. Some chemists with longer opening hours are:

Blake's Pharmacy
(☎ 9358 6712) 28 Darlinghurst Rd, Kings Cross. Open daily from 8 am to midnight.
Darlinghurst Prescription Pharmacy
(☎ 9361 5882) 261 Oxford St, Darlinghurst. Open daily from 8 am to 10 pm.
Park Chemist
(☎ 9552 3372) 321 Glebe Point Rd, Glebe. Open daily from 8 am to 8 pm.
Wu's Pharmacy
(☎ 9211 1805) 629 George St, city. Open Monday to Saturday from 9 am to 9 pm, Sunday to 7 pm.

WOMEN TRAVELLERS

Sydney is generally safe for women travellers, although you should avoid walking alone late at night. Sexual harassment and discrimination, while uncommon, can occur and shouldn't be tolerated. If you do encounter infantile sexism from drunken louts in pubs or bars, the best option is to leave and choose a better place – there are plenty.

Some of the major women's organisations (which can direct you to local services) are:

Royal Hospital for Women
(☎ 9382 6111) Barker St, Randwick
Women & Girls Emergency Centre
(☎ 9360 5388) 177 Albion St, Surry Hills
Women's Legal Resources Centre
(☎ 9637 4597, toll-free 1800 801 501)
Women's Liberation House
(☎ 9569 3819) Level 1, 26 Hutchinson St, Surry Hills

GAY & LESBIAN TRAVELLERS

Gay and lesbian culture is so strong in Sydney that it's almost mainstream. Oxford St, especially around Taylor Square, is the centre of what's probably the second-largest gay community in the world, and the suburb of Newtown is home to Sydney's lesbian scene. Sydney is one of the top three holiday destinations for North American gays and lesbians. The Gay & Lesbian Mardi Gras in February/March is the biggest annual tourist event in Australia. It culminates in a spectacular parade along Oxford St, watched by approximately 650,000 people.

Despite this, there's still a strong homophobic streak among 'dinkum' Aussies, even in Sydney, and violence against homosexuals isn't unknown.

For the record, it's legal in NSW for a man to have sex with a man over the age of 18, and for a woman to have sex with a woman over the age of 16. Laws in other states differ.

Free gay papers, *Capital Q Weekly* and *Sydney Star Observer* and publications such as *Lesbians on the Loose (LOTL)* have extensive listings.

For information on tickets to the Gay & Lesbian Mardi Gras, contact the Mardi Gras office (☎ 9557 4332, 1900 957 800), 21-23 Erskineville Rd, Erskineville. There is a Web site at www.mardigras.com.au See Special Events later in this chapter for more information about the Mardi Gras.

For counselling and referral call the Gay & Lesbian Line (☎ 9207 2800, toll-free 1800 805 379), daily from 4 pm to midnight.

DISABLED TRAVELLERS

Useful Organisations

The following organisations offer useful information and services for people with disabilities:

ACROD (Australian Council for the Rehabilitation of the Disabled)
(☎ 02-9743 2699)
24 Cabarita Rd, Cabarita 2137
(industry association for disability service providers)

Deaf Society of NSW
(☎ 02-9893 8555, TTY 9893 8858, fax 9893 8333)
Level 4, 169 Macquarie St, Parramatta 2150

Independent Living Centre
(☎ 02-9808 2233, TTY 9808 2477, fax 9809 7132)
600 Victoria Rd, Ryde 2112
(equipment and information service for disabled and older people)

NICAN (National Information & Communication Awareness Network)
(☎ 06-285 3713, toll-free 1800 806 769, fax 6285 3714)
Box 407 Curtin 2605 ACT
(information on recreation, tourism, sport and the arts for disabled people; Web site: www.nican.com.au)

Paraplegic & Quadriplegic Association of NSW
(☎ 02-9764 4166)
33-35 Burlington Rd, Homebush

Royal Blind Society of NSW
(☎ 02-9334 3333, toll-free 1800 424 359, TTY 9334 3260, Braille TTY 9334 3466)
4 Mitchell St, Enfield 2136

Useful Publications

The following publications contain useful information on access for travellers:

Access Illawarra – A Guide to Wollongong, Shell Harbour & Kiama for People with Disabilities & the Elderly, Illawarra Disabled Persons' Trust. Available from Australian Quadriplegic Association (☎ 02-4272 9356, Illawarra)

Accessing Sydney. Available from ACROD NSW ($19.95)

Blue Mountains Access Guide. Available from PO Box 189, Katoomba 2780

Easy Access Australia – A Travel Guide to Australia. Available from PO Box 218, Kew VIC 3101 ($24.85, including postage)

Visitors Guide – National Parks in NSW and ***Outdoor Access for Everybody***, National Parks & Wildlife Service. Call ☎ 02-9585 6444 for a copy.

SENIOR TRAVELLERS

Travellers with an Australian Pensioners Card are entitled to many discounts including public transport and admission fees. Few discounts apply to senior citizens from abroad, though some places may agree to give you a discount if you show your seniors card from home.

In your home country you may be entitled to interesting travel packages and discounts (on car hire, for instance) through organisations and travel agents that cater to senior travellers. Start hunting at your local senior citizens' advice bureau.

For information on recreational and other activities contact the Seniors Information Service (☎ 131244), 6th Floor, 93 York St, Sydney 2000. Each March, there's a Seniors Week with exhibitions, concerts, seminars etc.

SYDNEY FOR CHILDREN

Successful travel with young children requires effort, but a bit of forethought can make all the difference. Try not to overdo things and consider using some sort of self-catering accommodation as a base. Include children in the planning process; if they've helped to work out where you're going, they'll be more interested when they get there. Include a range of activities – balance a visit to the Art Gallery of NSW with one to the Powerhouse Museum. During school holidays many places put on extra activities for children; the Opera House has an interesting range of entertainment tailored to juniors.

Look for copies of *Sydney's Child*, a free monthly paper listing businesses and activities for ankle-biters. The Visitors Centre at the Rocks, the Powerhouse Museum and Captain Cook Cruises at Circular Quay are some of the many places that stock it.

For more general information see Lonely Planet's *Travel with Children*.

CULTURAL CENTRES

Among the many foreign cultural centres in Sydney are:

Alliance Française
(☎ 9267 1755) 257 Clarence St, city
British Council
(☎ 9326 2022) 203 New South Head Rd, Edgecliff
Goethe-Institut
(☎ 9328 7411) 90 Ocean St, Woollahra
Italian Institute of Culture
(☎ 9392 7939) 1 Macquarie Place, city
Japan Cultural Centre
(☎ 9954 0111) Level 14, 201 Miller St, North Sydney

DANGERS & ANNOYANCES

Sydney isn't a dangerous city but the usual big-city rules apply: never leave cars or rooms unlocked, never leave luggage unattended, never show big wads of money and never get drunk in the company of strangers. Use extra caution in Kings Cross, which attracts drifters from all over Australia and gutter-crawlers from all over Sydney.

Places where you may be hassled for small change are Kings Cross, George St near the cinema complex, Oxford St between Taylor Square and Hyde Park, and along Eddy Ave outside Central station.

If you're unlucky enough to have something stolen, immediately report it to the nearest police station. If your credit cards, cash card or travellers cheques have been taken, notify your bank or the relevant company immediately (most have 24-hour 'lost or stolen' numbers listed under 'Banks' or 'Credit Card Organisations' in the *Yellow Pages*).

Swimming

It seems superfluous to mention it, but don't go swimming if you've been drinking alcohol. Swimming after a heavy meal is also unwise.

The surf lifesaving clubs aren't there for show – many people are rescued from the surf each year. To signal that you're in trouble in the water, raise your arm and keep it raised while treading water or floating. If you're at a patrolled beach (indicated by flags) help will come quickly.

Shark attacks are extremely rare. Some major beaches, especially around Sydney, have shark-netting to deter sharks from cruising along the beaches and checking out the menu. The more popular beaches have shark-spotting planes at peak times. If a siren sounds while you're swimming leave the water quickly but calmly.

There are a few poisonous marine animals (such as the blue-ringed octopus, which can be fatal) – basically, if you don't know what it is, don't touch it.

Some beaches are unsuitable for swimming because of pollution caused by stormwater runoff; some local radio stations give updates on the latest conditions.

Snakes & Spiders

Snakes are protected. Although there are many venomous snakes in Australia, few are aggressive, and unless you have the bad fortune to tread on one you're unlikely to be bitten. Taipans and tiger snakes, however, will attack if alarmed.

To minimise your chances of being bitten, always wear boots, socks and long trousers when walking through undergrowth where snakes may lurk. Don't poke your fingers into holes and crevices, and be careful when collecting firewood.

Snake bites don't cause instantaneous death and antivenenes are usually available. Keep the victim calm and still, wrap the bitten limb tightly, as you would for a sprained ankle, then attach a splint to immobilise it. Then seek medical help, if possible with the dead snake for identification. Don't attempt to catch the snake if there's even a remote possibility of being bitten again.

There are a few nasty spiders too, including the funnel-web, the redback and the white-tail. The funnel-web bite is treated in the same way as snake bite. For redback bites, apply ice and seek medical attention.

Ticks & Leeches

The common bush tick can be dangerous if left lodged in the skin because the toxin it excretes can cause paralysis and sometimes death. Check your body for lumps every night if you've been bushwalking. Remove a tick by dousing it with methylated spirits or kerosene and levering it out intact.

If you're out walking in muddy fields north of Sydney check yourself for leeches.

Bushfires

In dry, hot weather, bushfires can raze thousands of hectares of eucalypt forest. Be *extremely* careful of fire when camping in summer. Many catastrophic bushfires are started by people, accidentally or deliberately.

Apart from the real risk of dying in the fire, you can be hit with huge fines, and even jail sentences if you light a fire during a total fire ban. This includes stoves fuelled by gas or liquid. *Never* throw a cigarette butt out of a car.

Bushwalkers should take local advice before setting out. If there's a total fire ban in operation, delay your trip until the weather changes. A recorded message service (☎ 9898 1356) gives current fire restrictions. If you're out in the bush and you see smoke, even at a great distance, take it seriously. Go to the nearest open space, downhill if possible – a forested ridge is the most dangerous place.

EMERGENCY

In a life-threatening emergency, dial ☎ 000. This call is free from any phone and the operator will connect you with the police, ambulance or fire brigade.

There are several police stations in the city, including one at 192 Day St (☎ 9265 6499) near Darling Harbour, another in the Rocks on the corner of George and Argyle Sts (☎ 9265 6366), and one in Kings Cross behind the El Alamein fountain at 1-15a Elizabeth Bay Rd (☎ 8356 0099).

Sydney Hospital (Map 4, ☎ 9382 7111) on Macquarie St, and St Vincent's (Map 5, ☎ 9339 1111) on the corner of Victoria and Burton Sts, Darlinghurst, are two of the many public hospitals with casualty departments (see the Health section earlier).

Foreigners (except those from countries that have reciprocal health agreements with Australia – see the Health section earlier) are charged at least $75 for a visit to casualty. They bill your home address, so you'll be treated before they see your money.

The Wayside Chapel (☎ 9358 6577, 24 hours), 29 Hughes St, Kings Cross, is a crisis centre that provides useful local information and can help solve problems.

Some other useful emergency numbers include:

Chemist	☎ 9235 0333
Dentist	☎ 9369 7050
Interpreter Service	☎ 131450
Life Crisis	☎ 131114

FACTS FOR THE VISITOR

Poisons	☎ 13 1126
Rape Crisis Centre	☎ 9819 6565/7842
Salvo Care Line	☎ 9331 6000
Youth Line	☎ 9951 5522

LEGAL MATTERS

The legal drinking age is 18 and you may need photo ID to prove your age. Stiff fines, jail and other penalties could be incurred if you're caught driving under the influence of alcohol. During festive holidays and special events, random breath-testing stations (booze buses) are often set up to deter drink-driving. The legal blood-alcohol limit is 0.05%.

Traffic offences (illegal parking, speeding etc) usually incur a fine payable within 30 days.

The importation and use of illegal drugs is prohibited and punishable by imprisonment.

If you need legal assistance contact the Legal Aid Commission of NSW (☎ 9219 5000), 323 Castlereagh St; it has several suburban branches.

BUSINESS HOURS

Most offices and businesses are open weekdays from 9 am to 5 pm, some until 5.30 pm. Banking hours are Monday to Thursday from 9.30 am to 4 pm, Friday to 5 pm. Some large city branches open from 8 am to 6 pm weekdays. Some stay open Friday until 9 pm.

Most shops are open weekdays from 8.30 or 9 am to 5 or 5.30 pm, with hours extended Thursday to 9 or 9.30 pm. Many shops open all day Saturday, but some close at noon. On Sunday, many shops close, but there are exceptions, especially in Kings Cross and Oxford St where delicatessens, milk bars and bookshops stay open late every day.

PUBLIC HOLIDAYS

On public holidays, government departments, banks, offices, large stores and post offices are closed. On Good Friday and Christmas Day, newspapers aren't published and about the only stores you'll find open are 7-Eleven-style convenience stores. Note that some consulates close for 10 days over the Christmas to New Year period.

Public holidays include:

New Year's Day
  1 January
Australia Day
  26 January
Easter (Good Friday/Easter Monday)
  March/April
Anzac Day
  25 April
Queen's Birthday
  2nd Monday in June
August Bank Holiday
  1st Monday in August
Labour Day
  1st Monday in October
Christmas Day
  25 December
Boxing Day
  26 December

Most public holidays become long weekends (three days), and if a fixed-date holiday such as New Year's Day falls on a weekend, the following Monday is usually a holiday.

SPECIAL EVENTS

Major celebrations on the Sydney calendar are:

Spring

September

Royal Botanic Gardens Spring Festival
Mid-September; includes concerts, brass bands and a plant market; display of spring flowers in David Jones' city store.

Festival of the Winds
Second Sunday; kite-flying festival with a multicultural theme at Bondi Beach; includes competitions for best home-made kites.

Taylor Square Arts Festival
Mid-September; week-long; wide range of events, many involving local Oxford St businesses.

Rugby League Grand Final
Held at Sydney Football Stadium.

October

Manly Jazz Festival
Labour Day long weekend; styles range from traditional and big band to fusion, bop and contemporary.

November

Kings Cross Carnival
First weekend; busking competition, food and wine tastings.

Summer

December

Christmas Party
25 December; impromptu party on Bondi Beach, a favourite with travellers, improved by being made alcohol-free.

Sydney to Hobart Yacht Race
26 December; Sydney Harbour is crowded with boats farewelling yachts competing in the race.

New Years Eve
31 December; Circular Quay and Darling Harbour are popular; huge fireworks display.

January

Sydney Festival & Carnivale
Most of January; wide range of events from in-line skating and street theatre to huge, free concerts in the Domain.

Great Ferry Boat Race
Australia Day (26 January); contested by the city's ferries, decorated with balloons and streamers for the race from the Harbour Bridge to Manly and back.

Survival Festival
26 January; Aboriginal Australia Day, marked by Koori music, dance, arts and crafts.

Flickerfest
Ten-day international short film festival, held at Bondi Pavilion. Call ☎ 9211 7133 for details.

January/February

Chinese New Year
January or February; celebrated (literally with a bang!) in Chinatown.

Hunter Vintage Festival
January to March; Hunter Valley; attracts hordes of wine enthusiasts for tastings, and grape-picking and treading contests.

February/March

Gay & Lesbian Mardi Gras
February and early March; attracts more visitors and generates more tourist dollars than any other event in Australia; month-long festival includes a sports carnival, the Blessing of the Mardi Gras, theatre, arts festival and *lots* of parties; culminates in amazing parade (first Saturday in March) and Mardi Gras Party. Tickets normally sell out by mid-January, and are usually only available to Mardi Gras members, though interstate and overseas visitors can get temporary membership. See the Gay & Lesbian Travellers section earlier for details.

Autumn

March/April

Golden Slipper
March; Sydney's major horse race, which is held at Rosehill.

Royal Easter Show
Sydney Showground at Homebush Bay; 12-day event traditionally beginning with a massive parade of farm animals; has a distinctly agricultural flavour, but has plenty of events to entertain city slickers.

Sydney Cup
April; the second-most major horse race, held at Randwick.

Winter

June

Sydney Film Festival
At the magnificent State Theatre; subscribe to the whole season or buy tickets to special screenings. Call ☎ 9660 3844 for details.

Sydney Biennale
In even years; international arts festival at the Art Gallery of NSW and other city venues.

July

Yulefest
In the Blue Mountains; guesthouses and restaurants celebrate Christmas. If you're lucky there might be snow.

August

City to Surf Run
Second Sunday; more than 40,000 runners pound the 14km from Park St in the city to Bondi Beach; some are deadly serious, some are in it for fun, and everyone gets their name and finishing position published in the *Sydney Morning Herald*; entry forms appear in the *Herald* months before the race, but you can enter on the day (about $20).

DOING BUSINESS

Sydney is Australia's chief commercial, financial and industrial centre. Many major international companies have their Australian and Asia-Pacific headquarters here. With its harbour, road and rail network and Australia's busiest airport, Sydney is also an important transport centre. Its location means that it has similar business hours to Tokyo and Hong

Kong. The Sydney stock exchange (☎ 9227 0000), 20 Bond St, is the largest in the country. The NSW Chamber of Commerce (☎ 9350 8100) is at Level 12, 83 Clarence St. A number of countries have set up trade promotion offices in Sydney; a list of these can be found in the *Yellow Pages* under 'Trade Centres' and 'Trade Commissioners'.

The *Australian Financial Review* and the *Business Review Weekly* are Australia's foremost publications on business and finance.

Many top-end and higher mid-range hotels provide business facilities (eg conference rooms, private office space, secretarial services, fax/photocopying services, use of computers and Internet access). Some also provide specialist translation services.

At Kingsford-Smith airport, the Qantas business lounge offers business travellers a range of services, including individual workstations equipped with telephone, fax, modem point and photocopier. A number of telecommunications services catering to travellers offer good business-oriented facilities – see Post & Communications earlier in this chapter.

WORK

Many backpacker hostels find work for guests, but much of it involves collecting for charities or door-to-door sales. A few hostels have telephones in the rooms, which makes job-hunting easier, and some backpacker specialists provide a voicemail service.

Alternatively, you could do as Sydneysiders do and get a mobile phone (pre-paid services, rather than contracts, are the best option for travellers). Some train stations have vending machines that let you whip up a presentable business card in a jiffy.

TNT Magazine lists private employment agencies that specialise in finding work for travellers, or look in the *Yellow Pages* under 'employment agencies'. There are also job noticeboards around Kings Cross.

The government-run Centrelink offices (☎ 13 2850) have touch-screen computers listing jobs, but most of what's available for travellers is seasonal work like harvesting and fruit-picking. The main office is at 477 Pitt St. Overseas visitors must present their work permits.

The nationwide employment scheme, Job Network, is similarly geared towards Australian citizens, but it too may offer seasonal work. Employment National's Harvestline (☎ 1300 720 126) is another option. Be sure to re-confirm all the details with your prospective employer before you head off to the back of beyond for a picking spree.

There are strict regulations governing overseas visitors working in Australia. Call DIMA (☎ 6264 1111) or visit the Web site at www.immi.gov.au if you're in any doubt.

Getting There & Away

AIR

Departure Tax

There's a departure tax of $27 payable by everyone leaving Australia, which is incorporated into your air fare. Sydney has a 'noise' tax of $3.40 (see Ecology & Environment in the Facts about Sydney chapter); again, this is included in your air fare.

Other Parts of Australia

The major domestic carriers are Ansett (☎ 13 1300) and Qantas (☎ 13 1313). Both fly between Sydney and the other state capitals, and both have subsidiaries that fly smaller planes on shorter interstate and intrastate routes: Eastern Australia is part of Qantas; Ansett Express is part of Ansett. Smaller airlines include Hazelton (☎ 13 1713) and Impulse (☎ 13 1381).

You don't have to reconfirm domestic flights on Ansett and Qantas, but to check flight details, the numbers to call are ☎ 13 1515 (Ansett) and ☎ 13 1223 (Qantas). Ansett has a Web site at www.ansett.com.au and Qantas' is at www.qantas.com.au.

All airports and domestic flights are non-smoking areas.

Fares Few people pay full fare on domestic travel because the airlines offer a wide range of discounts. These come and go, and there are regular 'spot specials', so keep your eyes open. If you book and pay one, two or three weeks in advance, you'll get a corresponding discount (up to 50%) off the standard return fare – the further ahead you book, the bigger the discount.

International travellers (Australians and foreigners) can get a 25% to 40% discount on Qantas or Ansett domestic flights simply by presenting their passport and international ticket (any airline, one way or return) when booking. The discount applies only to the full economy fare, so in many cases it'll be cheaper to take advantage of other discounts. Both Ansett and Qantas offer good discounts for YHA, VIP and ITC cardholders.

Interstate Distances

Travelling interstate from Sydney is a major journey unless you fly. The nearest state capital is Melbourne, 870km away by the shortest road route. To Brisbane it's almost 1000km; to Adelaide at least 1400km; Darwin is 4000km; and Perth is 4100km. Sydney to Darwin via Adelaide is 4450km, and it's nearly 5000km via Townsville.

Air Passes If you book in advance you'll find that some discounted fares are cheaper than air passes and have fewer restrictions. However, air passes are worth checking out.

Qantas and Ansett both offer two types of pass. The Qantas Australia Explorer Pass can only be purchased overseas and involves buying a coupon for each sector: a Sydney-Melbourne one-way flight costs $280; Sydney-Perth $365. Prices vary depending on when you travel and for how long.

The Qantas Backpackers Pass can only be bought in Australia with identification such as a YHA, VIP Backpackers or Independent Backpackers membership card. You must purchase a minimum of three sectors, which must be used over a minimum period of seven days. The discount is quite substantial; a sample fare with this pass is Sydney-Uluru for $310 one way, as against the full economy fare of $576.

Ansett's Kangaroo Airpass gives you two options – 6000km with a minimum/maximum of two/three stopovers for $949 ($729 for children) or 10,000km with a minimum/maximum of three/seven stopovers for $1499 ($1149). These tickets can be good value if you want to see a lot of the country in a short time. Although restrictions apply, you don't need to start and finish at the same place.

Other Countries

Most visitors to Australia arrive by air at Sydney's Kingsford Smith airport.

Air fares to Australia are expensive – it's a long way from anywhere and flights are often heavily booked. If you're flying to Australia at a busy time of year (the middle of summer, ie Christmas time, is notoriously difficult) or on a particularly popular route (eg Hong Kong-Sydney or Singapore-Sydney), plan well ahead.

Sydney travel agents are predicting that air fares from Australia to Europe may rise by as much as 50% in 2000 as Australians head overseas to participate in pre-planned millennial events.

Advance-purchase fares and other special deals can reduce ticket prices considerably. When choosing a ticket consider its validity (you don't want to buy a return ticket that's only valid for two weeks) and the number of stopovers. As a rule, the cheaper the ticket, the fewer stopovers allowed. Also, think about how much hassle it'll be if you have to change planes on the way to Australia. Sometimes paying more for a ticket is worth it to avoid languishing in a foreign departure lounge for hours on end.

Qantas and Ansett offer air passes that give reasonable discounts on flights within Australia, although they have complex rules and restrictions. See Air Passes under Other Parts of Australia earlier.

The approximate fares quoted in this chapter are for the high season.

Arriving & Departing The large number of visitors to Sydney causes frequent bottlenecks at Sydney airport. Delays of arrival or departure are common. Even when you're on the ground it can take ages to get through immigration and customs.

Travellers with Special Needs If you have broken a leg, are vegetarian or require a special diet, are travelling in a wheelchair, taking a baby, petrified of flying, or whatever, let the airline staff know so that they can make the necessary arrangements. Remind them when you reconfirm your booking (at least 72 hours before departure) and again when you check in at the airport. Before deciding who to fly with, it's worth asking various airlines how they will handle your particular needs.

Airports and airlines can be helpful, but they need advance warning. Most international airports provide escorts from the check-in desk to the aeroplane where needed, and there should be ramps, lifts, and accessible toilets and phones. Aircraft toilets, however, are likely to present a problem; travellers should discuss this with the airline early on and, if necessary, with their doctor.

Guide dogs for the blind often travel in a specially pressurised baggage compartment with other animals, away from their owners;

Air Travel Warning

The information in this chapter is particularly vulnerable to change: prices for international travel are volatile, routes are introduced and cancelled, schedules change, special deals come and go, and rules and visa requirements are amended. Airlines and governments seem to take a perverse pleasure in making price structures and regulations as complicated as possible. You should check directly with the airline or a travel agent to make sure you understand how a fare (and ticket you may buy) works. In addition, the travel industry is highly competitive and there are many lurks and perks.

The upshot of this is that you should get opinions, quotes and advice from as many airlines and travel agents as possible before you part with your hard-earned cash. The details given in this chapter should be regarded as pointers and are not a substitute for your own careful, up-to-date research.

smaller guide dogs, however, may be admitted to the cabin. Australia is free of rabies and guide dogs and other animals are subject to tough quarantine laws when entering.

Deaf travellers can ask for airport and inflight announcements to be written down.

Children under two travel for 10% of the standard fare (or free on some airlines) as long as they don't occupy a seat. They don't get a baggage allowance either. 'Skycots' should be provided by airlines if requested in advance; these take a child weighing up to about 10kg. Children aged two to 12 years can usually occupy a seat for half to two-thirds of the full fare, and get a baggage allowance. Pushchairs can often be taken as hand luggage.

Round-the-World Tickets Round-the-World (RTW) tickets are often real bargains and many take you through Australia. Since Australia is on the other side of the world from Europe and North America, it can sometimes be cheaper to continue in the same direction rather than return the way you came.

Official airline RTW tickets are usually put together by two airlines and permit you to fly anywhere on their route systems as long as you don't backtrack. Other restrictions (usually) include booking the first sector in advance; cancellation penalties then apply. There may be restrictions on how many stops you're permitted and normally the tickets are valid from 90 days up to a year. Typical prices for RTW tickets with South Pacific stopovers are around £760 or US$1170.

An alternative RTW ticket is one put together by a travel agent using a combination of discounted airline tickets. A UK agent like Trailfinders can put together interesting London-to-London RTW combinations via Australia for around £800 to £1100.

Circle-Pacific Tickets Circle-Pacific fares are similar to RTW tickets, using a combination of airlines to circle the Pacific – combining Australia, New Zealand, North America and Asia. Some examples are Qantas-Northwest Orient, and Canadian Airlines International-Cathay Pacific.

As with RTW tickets, there are advance-purchase restrictions and limits on how many stopovers you can make. Typically, fares range between US$1760 and US$2240. A possible Circle-Pacific route is Los Angeles-Hawaii-Auckland-Sydney-Singapore-Bangkok-Hong Kong-Tokyo-Los Angeles.

The UK The cheapest tickets in London are provided by 'bucket shops' (discount-ticket agencies), which advertise in magazines and papers like *Time Out*, *Southern Cross* and *TNT*. The magazine *Business Traveller* also has good advice on air fare bargains. Most bucket shops are trustworthy and reliable, but the occasional sharp operator appears – *Time Out* and *Business Traveller* give useful advice on precautions.

Trailfinders (☎ 020-7938 3366), 46 Earls Court Rd, London W8, and STA Travel (☎ 020-7581 4132), 74 Old Brompton Rd, London SW7 and 117 Euston Rd, London NW1 (☎ 020-7465 0484), are good, reliable agents for cheap tickets.

The cheapest London to Sydney bucket-shop tickets are about £335/499 one way/return. They are usually only available if you leave London in the low season (March to June). In September and mid-December, fares go up about 30%; the rest of the year they're somewhere in between.

From Australia, you'll pay from around A$1000/1500 one way/return to London and other European capitals, with stops in Asia on the way.

North America There are a variety of connections across the Pacific from Los Angeles, San Francisco and Vancouver. These include direct flights, flights via New Zealand, island-hopping routes and more-circuitous Pacific-rim routes via Asia. Qantas, Air New Zealand and United fly USA-Australia; Qantas, Air New Zealand and Canadian Airlines International fly Canada-Australia. An interesting option from the east coast is Northwest

Airlines' flight via Japan. Air Pacific flies via Fiji.

One advantage of flying Qantas or Air New Zealand is that if your flight goes via Hawaii, the west coast to Hawaii sector is not treated as a domestic flight (as it is on US airlines). This means you don't pay for drinks and headsets, which are free on international sectors.

For an idea of fare prices, check the travel ads in the Sunday travel sections of papers like the *Los Angeles Times*, *San Francisco Chronicle-Examiner*, *New York Times* or Canada's *Globe & Mail*. You can typically get a return ticket from the west coast for around US$1150, from the east coast for US$1550. Council Travel and STA Travel are good sources for discount tickets in the USA and have lots of offices around the country; in Canada, Travel CUTS offers a similar service. Fares from Vancouver are similar to the US west-coast prices. From Toronto, fares go from around C$1880 return.

If Pacific island-hopping is your aim, check out the airlines of Pacific island nations; some have good deals on indirect routes. Qantas can give you Fiji or Tahiti along the way, while Air New Zealand offers both and the Cook Islands. See Circle-Pacific Tickets earlier for more details.

Typical one-way/return fares from Australia include: San Francisco A$1010/1620, New York A$1180/1800 and Vancouver A$1010/1200.

New Zealand Air New Zealand and Qantas operate a network of trans-Tasman flights linking Auckland, Wellington and Christchurch in New Zealand with most major Australian cities. You can also fly directly between many other places in New Zealand and Australia.

From New Zealand to Sydney costs around NZ$600 one way or return. From Sydney to New Zealand expect to pay from A$370 one way, and A$415 or more return, depending on the time of year. The competition on this route means you'll find good discounts.

Asia Ticket discounting is widespread in Asia, particularly in Singapore, Hong Kong, Bangkok and Penang. There are numerous fly-by-nights in the Asian ticketing scene, so care is required. Also, Asian routes have been caught up in the capacity shortages on flights to Australia. Hong Kong-Australia flights are notoriously heavily booked; those to/from Bangkok and Singapore are often part of the longer Europe-Australia route, so are also sometimes full. Plan ahead.

Typical one-way fares to Sydney are S$690 from Singapore, HK$4350 from Hong Kong. From Australia's east coast, some typical one-way fares to Singapore, Kuala Lumpur and Bangkok start from A$470 to A$770, and to Hong Kong from A$900 to A$1600.

You can pick up interesting tickets in Asia to include Australia on the way across the Pacific Ocean. Qantas and Air New Zealand offer discounted trans-pacific tickets.

Africa The number of flights between Africa and Australia has increased markedly in the last few years, and there are several direct flights each week, but only between Perth and Harare (Zimbabwe) or Johannesburg (South Africa). Qantas, South African Airways and Air Zimbabwe fly this route.

Other airlines that connect southern Africa and Australia include Malaysia Airlines (via Kuala Lumpur) and Air Mauritius (via Mauritius), both of which have special deals from time to time.

From East Africa the options are to fly via Mauritius, or via the Indian subcontinent and on to South-East Asia, then connect from there to Australia.

Sydney to Harare or Johannesburg costs about A$1810 return.

South America Two routes operate between South America and Australia. The long-running Chile connection involves Lan Chile's Santiago-Easter Island-Tahiti twice-weekly flight, from where you fly Qantas or another airline to Australia. The other route, operated twice-weekly by

Aerolıneas Argentinas, skirts the Antarctic Circle, flying from Buenos Aires to Auckland and Sydney. Sydney to Santiago or Buenos Aires costs about A$1485 return.

BUS

Sydney coach terminal (Map 8, ☎ 9281 9366), on Eddy Ave outside Central station, is open daily from 6 am to 10.30 pm. Greyhound Pioneer (☎ 13 2030) and McCafferty's (☎ 9361 5125) have offices on Eddy Ave, while Premier (☎ 1300 368 100) and Firefly Express (☎ 9211 1644) have offices around the corner on Pitt St. Many bus lines stop in suburbs on the way in/out of the city, and some have feeder services from the suburbs.

Greyhound Pioneer is the only national bus network. See its Web site at www.greyhound.com.au. McCafferty's is the next-largest, although it doesn't go Australia wide. Its Web site is at www.mccaffertys.com.au. For destinations along the Princes Highway (Hwy) within NSW, Pioneer Motor Service (☎ 13 3410, 24 hours) often has the best fares. There are a few other companies running less-extensive routes.

It pays to shop around for fares. Students, YHA members and, sometimes, backpackers, in general get discounts of at least 10% with many long-distance companies. On straight point-to-point tickets, there are varying stopover deals. Some companies give one free stopover on express routes, while others charge a fee, maybe $5 per stopover. This fee might be waived if you book through certain agents, such as hostels.

Major routes from Sydney are:

Canberra
: Murrays (☎ 13 2251) has three daily express buses that take under four hours to reach Canberra and cost $28 one way. The fare with both McCafferty's and Greyhound Pioneer is also $28; McCafferty's has the most frequent Canberra service.

Melbourne
: It's a 12 to 13 hour run to Melbourne via the Hume Hwy, the most direct route – longer still if you go via Canberra. McCafferty's and Firefly Express charge $50, other companies charge around $60. Greyhound Pioneer also offers a Princes Hwy coastal route, which is much prettier but takes about 18 hours, for $60.

Brisbane
: It takes about 16 hours via the Pacific Hwy and the standard fare is around $70. You often need to book in advance. Some buses don't stop in all the main towns en route. Companies running the Pacific Hwy route to Brisbane include Greyhound Pioneer, Premier and McCafferty's.

Northern NSW
: Fares between Sydney and destinations in northern NSW include: Port Macquarie $50 (seven hours), Coffs Harbour $57 (9½ hours) and Byron Bay $69 (13 hours). Greyhound Pioneer and McCafferty's also have services to northern NSW via the inland New England Hwy, which take an hour or two longer but cost about the same. Book at their offices or at Sydney coach terminal.

Adelaide
: Sydney to Adelaide takes 18 to 25 hours and costs around $96. Services run via Canberra or Broken Hill. Travelling Sydney-Melbourne-Adelaide with Firefly is cheaper ($85) than travelling Sydney-Adelaide with other companies. Countrylink's daily Speedlink service consists of a train to Albury, then a bus to Adelaide; the standard fare is $130, but discounts may be available.

Elsewhere in Australia
: The 52 to 56 hour trip to Perth costs $295. To Alice Springs it's about 42 hours (plus some waiting in Adelaide) and $231, all the way to Darwin it's 67 hours and $376, via Mt Isa.

Bus Passes

If you're planning to travel extensively in Australia, check Greyhound Pioneer's excellent bus pass deals. If a bus pass is what you want, make sure you get enough time and stopovers.

Bus Tours

A good way of travelling between Sydney and Byron Bay is with Ando's Opal Outback Tours (☎ 9559 2901, toll-free 1800 228 828), which takes five days and travels inland via Lightning Ridge. Tours depart Sydney every Sunday and include opal and gold mining, camel riding, optional horse riding, and accommodation in miners' cabins, outback pubs and cotton plantations. Now run by Ando's nephew, this tour has received good feedback. It costs $425 ($399 for YHA, ISIC, Nomads and VIP cardholders).

The popular Wayward Bus (☎ toll-free 1800 882 823) offers a range of tours covering Australia's central and south-eastern regions, including five-day trips between Sydney and Melbourne via Victoria's High Country for $190 (plus accommodation). Its Web site is at www.waywardbus.com.

Pioneering Spirit (☎ toll-free 1800 672 422) runs a three day bus trip from Sydney to Byron Bay via the coast for $195 (another $20 takes you on to Brisbane), including accommodation, breakfast and dinner. It describes itself as a mobile hostel, and leaves Sydney every Friday; you need to book in advance.

Oz Experience (☎ 9368 1766) is a backpackers' bus line offering frequent services along the east coast, with off-the-beaten track detours to cattle stations and national parks. There are 18 different tours ranging in price from $55 to $1275 depending on distance, and tickets are valid for six to 12 months.

TRAIN

Interstate and principal regional services operate to and from Central station (Map 8). Most people just call it Central, but it's also known as Sydney Terminal station.

Within New South Wales

Countrylink's rail network within NSW is the most comprehensive in Australia. Trains and connecting buses take you quickly (if not frequently) to most sizeable towns. Most Countrylink services have to be booked (☎ 13 2232 daily from 6.30 am to 10 pm).

Intrastate economy fares from Sydney include: Albury, 643km, $75; Armidale, 530km, $69; Bathurst, 240km, $32; Bourke, 841km, $85; Broken Hill, 1125km, $100; Byron Bay, 883km, $85; Coffs Harbour, 608km, $69; Cooma, 446km, $57; Dubbo, 431km, $57; Orange, 323km, $39; Tamworth, 455km, $62.

CityRail (Sydney metropolitan service) runs frequent trains south through Wollongong ($7.20 one way) to Bomaderry ($12.80); west through the Blue Mountains to Katoomba ($10.80) and Lithgow ($14.60); north to Newcastle ($14.60); and south-west through the Southern Highlands to Goulburn ($22). Some duplicate Countrylink services, but are a little slower and much cheaper, especially if you buy a day-return ticket. You can't book seats on CityRail trains. Off-peak return fares are available after 9 am weekdays, all day on weekends.

Other Parts of Australia

For interstate service information and bookings call the Central Reservation Centre (☎ 132232 daily from 6.30 am to 10 pm) or a Countrylink Travel Centre (same central number). There are Countrylink Travel Centres on the main concourse at Central station; at Circular Quay on Alfred St under the expressway behind Wharf 5; at 11-31 York St in the city (☎ 9224 4744); and in the Queen Victoria Building (QVB) arcade near Town Hall. These are fully fledged travel agencies and keep to business hours, but you can buy a train ticket at the Central station office on the concourse daily from 6 am to 9.35 pm. You can also make phone bookings and collect your tickets from a Countrylink Travel Centre or a train station.

Call ☎ 13 2232 for recorded information on arrival/departure times.

Interstate trains can be faster than buses, and there are often special fares that make the prices competitive. On interstate journeys, you can arrange free stopovers if you finish the trip within two months (six months on a return ticket).

As well as high-speed XPT trains (some with sleepers) there are the zippy Explorer trains. Trains run to capital cities Melbourne, Canberra, Adelaide, Perth and Brisbane. There are discounts of up to 40% on all standard rail fares if you book two weeks in advance, but this is sometimes waived.

Interstate routes and standard fares from Sydney are:

Canberra
  Three trains daily; about 4 hours: $42/58 in economy/1st class.

Melbourne
: A nightly XPT; 10½ hours: $96/134/229 in economy/1st class/1st-class sleeper.

Brisbane
: A nightly XPT; about 13½ hours: $96/134/229. This train connects with a bus at Casino for passengers travelling to the far north coast of NSW, and Queensland's Gold Coast. You can also take the train between Sydney and Murwillumbah, just south of the Queensland border ($91/125). There's a bus from Murwillumbah to the Gold Coast.

Adelaide & Perth
: The twice-weekly *Indian Pacific* goes to Perth via Adelaide; the 25 hour trip to Adelaide costs $162/480 in economy/1st class sleeper. The 65 hour trip to Perth costs $400/1261, or $823 for an economy sleeper. The 1st-class fares include meals. There's also a daily bus/train connection to Adelaide called Speedlink, which is cheaper at $130/255, and five or six hours faster.

CAR & MOTORCYCLE

There are four main road routes out of Sydney: the Sydney-Newcastle freeway/Pacific Hwy, which runs north to Newcastle and eventually to Brisbane (cross the Harbour Bridge and follow the Pacific Hwy to the start of the freeway in Hornsby); the Western Motorway, which runs west to Penrith and the Blue Mountains, and becomes the Great Western Hwy (follow Parramatta Rd west to Strathfield); the Hume Hwy, which runs south-west to Mittagong and Goulburn and on to Melbourne (follow Parramatta Rd west to Ashfield); and the Princes Hwy, running south to Wollongong and the south coast (follow South Dowling St south from Surry Hills).

See the Getting Around chapter for information on car rental.

HITCHING

Hitching is never entirely safe in any country and we don't recommend it. Travellers who do hitch should understand that they're taking a small but potentially serious risk. History shows that Australia certainly isn't exempt from danger. Even people hitching in pairs aren't necessarily safe. Before hitching, talk to local people about the danger. If you decide to hitch, let someone know where you're trying to hitch to before setting off. An alternative to hitching is to check university and hostel noticeboards for fellow travellers with cars heading in your direction. They may advertise rides in exchange for sharing petrol expenses. Noticeboards are also a good place to look for hitching partners.

BOAT

Cruise liners and yachts regularly call at Sydney. The liners aren't a feasible way of travelling from point A to B unless you have money to burn, but yachts looking for crew might be, especially if point B is a Pacific island. Ask at yacht clubs and check hostel noticeboards. *Sydney Afloat* is a free monthly paper that occasionally has ads for crew. You'll find a copy at most yacht clubs. If you're determined to try yacht crewing and have some spare time and money, it might help to do one of the courses offered in Sydney. See Sailing & Boating in the Things to See & Do chapter.

It might also be possible to travel on a cargo ship. This will certainly be more expensive than flying (although a lot cheaper than a cruise ship), but could be interesting. Ask travel agents for details of shipping companies with berths available.

Getting Around

The fairly short distances involved make walking a good way to explore the city and inner suburbs. There are several steep hills, but the climb is invariably short. See the Things to See & Do chapter for some suggestions on walking routes.

The State Transit Authority (STA) of NSW controls most public transport in Sydney. Call ☎ 13 1500 between 6 am and 10 pm daily for information about Sydney buses and ferries and CityRail, or visit its separate information booths at Circular Quay. Also check the front of the A-K *Yellow Pages* telephone directory. Children (under 16) pay half-price on STA services.

THE AIRPORT

Sydney's Kingsford Smith airport is about 10km south of the city centre. The international and domestic terminals are a 4km bus trip apart ($2.50 with STA). Ansett and Qantas have separate domestic terminals. In the arrivals hall at the international terminal there's an airport information desk and a branch of the NSW Travel Centre. All terminals have foreign-exchange facilities.

TO/FROM THE AIRPORT

Airport Express (☎ 13 1500) is a special STA service that travels to/from the airport via Central station, with bus No 300 continuing to Circular Quay and bus No 350 going to Kings Cross. The green-and-yellow Airport Express buses have their own stops. The one-way fare is $6; a return ticket, valid for two months, is $10. The trip from the airport to Central station takes about 15 minutes, to Circular Quay or Kings Cross about 30 minutes.

These buses leave the airport for the city every 10 minutes. Buses leave Circular Quay and Kings Cross for the airport every 20 minutes, but both stop on Eddy Ave at Central station along the way, so a bus leaves there every 10 minutes. The service runs from 5 am to 11 pm.

Some ordinary STA buses also service the airport, but don't run as frequently. These are bus No 100 to North Sydney, bus No 305 to Railway Square (via Redfern) and bus No 400 to Bondi Junction.

Kingsford Smith Transport/Airporter (☎ 9667 0663/3800, 24 hours) runs a door-to-door service between the airport and places to stay (including hostels) in the city and Kings Cross. The fare is $6/11 one way/return. Heading out to the airport, you must book at least three hours before you want to be collected.

Avis (☎ 9667 0667), Budget (☎ 9669 2121), Hertz (☎ 9669 2444) and Thrifty (☎ 9669 6677) have rental desks at the airport's international and domestic terminals.

Depending on traffic conditions, taking a taxi (via the traditional route) from the airport to Circular Quay costs $20 to $25, to Central station $15 to $20. The new Eastern Distributor toll road, to be completed in June 2000, should reduce travelling time between the airport and city (and will cost $3 for northbound traffic).

A rail link between the airport and the city is due to be completed in May 2000.

DISCOUNT PASSES

The composite SydneyPass is great value if you intend to use different forms of transport. If you just want to get to places, you're better off buying a TravelPass.

SydneyPass

The SydneyPass offers bus, rail and ferry transport, travel on the Sydney Explorer and Bondi & Bay Explorer buses, harbour ferry cruises and the Airport Express. Passes are valid for a week; a three day SydneyPass costs $85 ($75 children), five days $115/100 and seven days $135/120. Family tickets are also available. The trip back to the airport is valid for two months, but it must be your last trip because you then have to surrender the ticket.

TravelPass

The TravelPass offers cheap weekly, quarterly or yearly travel on buses, trains and ferries. It's designed for commuters, but is useful for visitors. There are various colour-coded tickets offering different combinations of distances and services. The Green TravelPass is valid for extensive bus and train travel, and all ferries except the RiverCat and the Manly JetCat (before 7 pm). At $33 for a week, it's a bargain. If you buy a TravelPass after 3 pm, your week begins the following day. TravelPasses are sold at newsagents, train stations and STA offices.

TravelTen & FerryTen

The colour-coded TravelTen ticket gives a sizeable discount on 10 bus trips. The blue ticket is valid for two zones and costs $9.50. The FerryTen also allows 10 trips, starting at $23 for travel on the inner harbour.

Day Passes

The BusTripper allows unlimited travel on Sydney bus routes for $8.30. The Bus/Ferry DayPass costs $12.

The CityHopper costs $6.60/5.40 peak/off-peak and gives you unlimited train travel within the city centre and on all normal buses. On the trains you can go north to North Sydney, south to Central station and east to Kings Cross. The DayRover ($20) adds unlimited travel on ferries.

Combination Passes

Several transport-plus-entry tickets are available for STA services, and work out cheaper than paying separately. The ZooPass pays for your ferry to/from Taronga Zoo, the short bus ride from the wharf to the zoo entrance, zoo entry and the 'Aerial Safari' cable car ride. It costs $21 ($10.50 children; family tickets available). There are similar passes for the National Aquarium in Darling Harbour and Oceanworld in Manly.

The Rocks and Darling Harbour also have composite tickets offering sightseeing, travel and admission to several attractions. See the Things to See & Do chapter.

BUS

The bus information kiosk on the corner of Alfred and Pitt Sts (behind Circular Quay) is open daily. There are other offices on Carrington St (by Wynyard Park) and outside the Queen Victoria Building (QVB) on York St. For further information, call the bus, train and ferry Infoline (☎ 13 1500).

Buses run almost everywhere, but they're slow compared to trains. However, some places – including Bondi Beach, Coogee, and the North Shore east of the Harbour Bridge – aren't serviced by trains. On the eastern suburbs line you can get a combination bus/rail ticket from some stations, which enables you to change from a train to a bus for a destination such as Bondi Beach. This works out cheaper than buying separate tickets.

Sydney is divided into seven zones, the city centre being zone 1. The main bus stops in the city centre are Circular Quay, Wynyard Park on York St and Railway Square.

Nightrider buses provide an hourly service after regular buses and trains stop running. They operate from Town Hall station and service suburban train stations. Return and weekly train-tickets are accepted; otherwise most trips cost $3.60.

Some useful bus routes from Circular Quay are:

destination	bus Nos
Balmain	441, 442, 445, 446
Bondi Beach	380, 382, 389
Coogee	314, 315, 316, 372, 373, 374, 377, X13, X74
Darling Harbour	443, 456, 500, 501, 506, 888
Glebe	431-4
Kings Cross	200, 323, 324, 325-7, 333 (free bus)
La Perouse	393, 394, 398
Leichhardt	370, 413, 436-440, 445, 446, 468, 470
Newtown	355, 370, 422, 423, 426, 428
Paddington	378, 380, 382
Surry Hills	301, 302, 303, 304, 375, 390, 391
Watsons Bay	324, 325

For Manly, take bus No 151 or 169 from Wynyard Park.

Special Bus Services

Sydney Explorer The red Sydney Explorer is an STA bus that runs a two hour circular route from Circular Quay to Kings Cross, Chinatown, Darling Harbour and the Rocks, linking many inner-city attractions. It runs approximately every 20 minutes, departing Circular Quay from 8.40 am to 5.25 pm daily. There's an on-board commentary, you can get on and off as often as you like, and your ticket includes discounted entry to many attractions. This is a good way to orient yourself, as well as see a lot of sights.

The 22 Explorer stops are marked by green and red signs. It's cheaper to get to places on its route by ordinary bus (in fact, it's possible to walk around the circuit), but the Explorer is less hassle because you don't have to work out routes. You can use the Explorer ticket on ordinary buses between Central station and Circular Quay or the Rocks until midnight, and the ticket entitles you to big discounts on some tours (conditions apply). You can buy a ticket ($28; $20 children) on the bus, from STA offices and elsewhere. A detailed map of the route comes with the ticket.

Bondi & Bay Explorer This operates along similar lines to the Sydney Explorer, but has a much larger route, which includes Circular Quay, Kings Cross, Paddington, Double Bay, Vaucluse, Watsons Bay, the Gap, Bondi Beach and Oxford St. The circular route takes two hours, and if you want to get off at many of the 19 places of interest along the way, you'll need to start early. The bus departs Circular Quay half-hourly from 9.15 am to 4.15 pm daily. The ticket entitles you to use ordinary buses south of the harbour until midnight. Ticket prices are the same as the Sydney Explorer, or you can buy a two day pass for $50 ($40 children, $140 family), which gives you use of the Sydney Explorer as well. Five and seven-day passes are also available. A map comes with the ticket.

TRAIN

CityRail (☎ 13 1500), Sydney's suburban rail network (Map 15) services a substantial portion of the city. It has frequent trains and is generally much quicker than the bus. Getting around the city centre by train is feasible (if disorienting). At Circular Quay, under the Cahill Expressway behind Wharf 5, is a CityRail booth open daily from 9 am to 5 pm.

The rail system consists of a central City Circle and a number of lines radiating out to the suburbs. Clockwise, stations on the City Circle starting at the southern end are Central, Town Hall (on George St between Bathurst and Park/Druitt Sts), Wynyard (York St at Wynyard Park), Circular Quay, St James (northern end of Hyde Park) and Museum (southern end of Hyde Park). A single trip anywhere on the City Circle or to a nearby suburb such as Kings Cross costs $1.60; an off-peak return trip costs $2. Most suburban trains stop at Central station and at least one of the other City Circle stations. A combined ticket for light rail and trains, called TramLink, is available at all stations.

Trains run from around 4 am to about midnight, give or take an hour. After the trains stop, Nightrider buses provide a skeleton service.

There are automatic ticket machines at most train stations. The machines accept $5 and $10 notes, and all coins except 5c coins. You can buy an off-peak return ticket for not much more than a standard one-way fare after 9 am on weekdays and at any time on weekends.

MONORAIL

The monorail (☎ 9552 2288) circles Darling Harbour and links it to the city centre. There's a train every four minutes, and the full circuit takes 14 minutes. A single trip costs $3 (free for children five and under), but with the $6 day pass you can ride as often as you like between 7 am (8 am Sunday) and 10 pm (midnight Thursday to Saturday). A family day pass costs $19. See Map 8 for the monorail route.

SYDNEY LIGHT RAIL

In the 1930s Sydney had more than 250km of tramway, but by the early 1960s the last tram had lowered its pantograph and that fine metaphor for a hasty departure, 'pulled out like a Bondi tram', became meaningless. However, in 1997 the tram made a return albeit with its name changed to Sydney Light Rail (SLR; ☎ 9660 5288). It's only another monorail in terms of usefulness to commuters, and operates 24 hours between Central station and Pyrmont via Darling Harbour and Chinatown. The service runs as far as Wentworth Park, although there is a planned extension to Lilyfield. If you travel the full distance the fare is $4 return.

CAR & MOTORCYCLE

Australians drive on the left side of the road. The minimum driving age is 18 years old. Overseas visitors can drive in Australia with their domestic driving licences, but have to take a driving test to obtain a NSW driving licence if they take up temporary or permanent residency. Speed limits in Sydney are generally 60km/h, rising to 100 or 110km/h on freeways. Seat belts must be worn.

You'll need a street directory to drive around the city, but with such good public transport why bother? The city centre has an extensive and maddening one-way-street system; parking is hell in most of the inner city and tow-away zones lurk in wait. Car parks in the inner city area include: the Goulburn St Parking station (☎ 9212 1522) on the corner of Goulburn and Elizabeth Sts; KC Park Safe (Map 4, ☎ 9211 4877), 581 George St near Chinatown; Grimes Parking (Map 4, ☎ 9247 3715) on Gateway Plaza at Circular Quay; the Rocks Space station (Map 4, ☎ 9247 6222), 121 Harrington St, the Rocks; and Kings Cross car park (Map 6, ☎ 9358 5000) on the corner of Ward Ave and Elizabeth Bay Rd. Many maps indicate with a 'P' where you can park your car. See also the *Yellow Pages* under 'Parking Stations'.

If you have a car, make sure that your hotel has parking (many cheaper places don't) or you'll have to pay for commercial parking, which is fairly expensive.

The blood-alcohol limit of 0.05% is enforced with random breath-checks and severe punishments. If you're in an accident (even if you didn't cause it) and you're over the alcohol limit, your insurance will be invalidated.

The new Eastern Distributor toll road, to be completed in June 2000, should reduce travelling time between the airport and city (and will cost $3 for northbound traffic).

Rental

The larger companies' metropolitan rates are typically about $55 a day for a small car (eg Ford Laser), about $65 a day for a medium-sized car (eg Holden Apollo) and about $85 a day for a big car (eg Holden Commodore or Ford Falcon). These rates sometimes also include insurance and unlimited kilometres.

There are usually discounts for rentals of three or four days or longer. Check the small print on your rental agreement to see exactly where you can take the car (some firms don't allow driving on dirt roads) and what your insurance covers.

The major companies – Avis (☎ 9353 9000), Budget (☎ 13 2727) and Hertz (☎ 13 3039) – have offices at the airport and around the city. Thrifty is a smaller, national company with desks at the airport (☎ 9669 6677) and an office (Map 8, ☎ 9380 5399) in the city at 75 William St. It offers small manual/automatic cars for $47/53 – both with insurance and unlimited kilometres.

The *Yellow Pages* is crammed with other outfits. Many offer deals that appear better than those offered by the major companies, but advertisements may be misleading, so read the small print carefully and ring around first.

There are plenty of places renting older cars, which range from reasonable transport to frustrating old bombs, although there are no huge bargains. Check for things like bald tyres and bad brakes *before* you sign anything – some of these outfits have all the compassion of used-car saleyards (which some of them are). Also check the fine print regarding insurance excess – the amount you pay before the insurance takes over. It can be high. One small company offering competitive rates is Bayswater Rental (☎ 9360 3622), 120 Darlinghurst Rd, Kings Cross, with small manual cars for $30 a day including insurance and 100km free.

Motorcycle rentals are available from Bikescape Motorcycle Rentals and Tours, (Map 8, ☎ 9699 4722, fax 9699 4733), on the corner of Abercrombie and Cleveland Sts, Chippendale, a five minute walk from Central station. Rates start from $60 per day, including gear.

Automobile Associations

The National Roads & Motorists Association (NRMA), the NSW motoring association, provides 24-hour emergency roadside assistance, road maps, travel advice and insurance, and discounted accommodation. It has reciprocal arrangements with the other state associations and similar organisations overseas. If you belong to another motoring organisation, bring proof of membership with you. The NRMA's head office (Map 4, ☎ 13 2132) is on the corner of George and King Sts in the city.

TAXI

Taxis are easily flagged down in the city centre and the inner suburbs. You'll also often find cabs at taxi ranks at Central, Wynyard and Circular Quay train stations, and at the large rank just off George St on Goulburn St. Service standards have improved in recent years. Most drivers are required to wear a uniform of sorts, and it's planned for all cabs to be white. The four big taxi companies offer reliable telephone services: Taxis Combined (☎ 8332 8888), 357 Glenmore Rd, Paddington; RSL Taxis (☎ 13 2211), 20 O'Riordan St, Alexandria; Legion (☎ 13 1451), 7 Foveaux St, Surry Hills; and Premier Cabs (☎ 13 1017), 33 Woodville Rd, Greenvale.

Taxi fares include $1 telephone booking fee, $2 flagfall, and $1.17 per kilometre. The waiting fee is 55c a minute, and there's a luggage charge of 10c per kilogram for luggage over 25kg (often waived). These fares apply any time of the day or night. Tipping isn't mandatory but 'rounding-up' the bill is common: if the fare is $9.20 you might say 'call it $10, mate'; the driver may say the same to you if the fare is $10.20. If you take a taxi via the harbour bridge or tunnel (or any other toll road), expect to pay the driver's return toll.

Water Taxis

Water taxis are pricey, but a fun way of getting around the harbour. Companies include Water Taxis (☎ 9955 3222) and Harbour Taxis (☎ 9555 1155). Fares vary slightly between companies, but generally up to four people can travel from Circular Quay to Watsons Bay for $35 for the first person, $5 for each extra person; to Clarke Island it costs $25 for the first person, to Shark Island $30.

FERRY

Sydney's ferries (☎ 13 1500) are one of the nicest ways of getting around. The picturesque, old, green and yellow boats are supplemented by speedy JetCats to Manly, and sleek RiverCats running up the Parramatta River.

All the harbour ferries (and the Cats) depart from Circular Quay (Map 4). The STA, which runs most ferries, has a ferry information office (which also sells tickets) on the concourse under the Cahill Expressway opposite the entry to Wharf 4; it's open Monday to Saturday from 7 am to 5.45 pm, Sunday 8 am to 5.45 pm. Many ferries have connecting bus services.

In getting to Manly, you have the choice of a roomy ferry, which takes about 30 minutes and costs $4 ($3 children), or a JetCat, which does the trip in half the time and costs $5.20 (no concessions). The ferry trip is more pleasant because you can walk around, and there's a basic snack bar on board. The JetCats have only a small outdoor area, and if you're stuck inside, the windows can be a long way away. The JetCat is the only craft running to Manly after 7 pm, but you can take it for the normal ferry fare. If you're staying in Manly, consider buying a Manly FerryTen pass (10 trips for $34) or, better still, a Green TravelPass (see the Discount Passes section earlier).

Hegarty's Ferries (☎ 9206 1167) run from Wharf 6 at Circular Quay to wharves directly across the harbour: Lavender Bay, McMahons Point and two stops in Kirribilli. These services cater to peak-hour commuters and stop early in the evening. The one-way fare is $2.45 ($1.20 children). The Hunters Hill ferry stops at Balmain and Birchgrove.

You can catch a RiverCat upriver to the Olympic Park wharf at Homebush Bay ($3.40), and some even go as far as Parramatta ($5).

See Map 16 for ferry routes.

BICYCLE

See the Cycling section in the Things to See & Do chapter for cycling tips, information on buying or hiring a bike, and recommended spots for a leisurely pedal.

ORGANISED TOURS

There is a vast array of city and area coach tours. For details, check the free magazines at hotels, or ask at Australian Travel Specialists (☎ 9555 2700), at Circular Quay's Wharf 2; it's open from 7 am to 9 pm weekdays, 8 am to 9pm weekends.

Australian Pacific (☎ 9247 7222), AAT King's (☎ toll-free 1800 334 009), Newmans (☎ 9247 7222), Murrays (☎ 13 2259), Clipper Gray Line (☎ 9241 3983) and Great Sights Tours (☎ 9241 2294) carry most tourists around town. You can join a half-day city or koala-cuddling tour (from around $40 to $50), or a full-day city tour (from around $60 to $70). Many companies also offer tours outside Sydney, to the Blue Mountains, Jenolan Caves, Hunter Valley, Canberra etc. See the Excursions chapter for some options.

Sydney Aboriginal Discoveries (☎ 9368 7684) offers a variety of interesting tours focused on indigenous culture and history. Outings cost from $25 (concession) to $60, and include a harbour cruise, a camping trip, a walk-about tour, a feast of native Australian foods, and an Aboriginal philosophy meeting (adults only).

The National Parks & Wildlife Service (NPWS) runs tours of Sydney's historic forts and islands. See Sydney Harbour National Park section in the Things to See & Do chapter.

Blue Thunder Bike Tours (☎ 9977 7721) and Eastcoast Motorcycle Tours (☎ 9555 2700) show you Sydney from the back of a Harley-Davidson. Blue Thunder can take you up into the Blue Mountains. With Eastcoast, a one hour tour of the harbour costs $80; it also offers day trips out of the city. Both have set tours or you can plan your own itinerary.

If a birds-eye view of the city appeals, South Pacific Seaplanes (☎ 9544 0077) runs scenic flights of the harbour, starting from $60 for a 15 minute flight.

Critical Mass

Sydney is awash with bicycles on the last Friday of the month, when hundreds of cyclists (plus joggers and inline skaters) gather to travel through the city in peak-hour traffic. The event is called Critical Mass and the aim is to raise awareness of Sydney's traffic conditions. Originating in San Francisco, it takes its name from a scene in the film *Return to the Scorcher*, in which a lone cyclist on a four-way street can't make a left turn because of the motorised traffic. He waits patiently and is eventually joined by so many other cyclists that the traffic is forced to stop as they make the turn together.

Cyclists meet from 5 pm onwards at Hyde Park and everyone heads off together at 6 pm. The route changes every month and the journey takes an hour or more. For more information call ☎ 9614 0777 (ext 26) or visit the Web site at www.criticalmass.com.au.

Tours of Sydney Olympic Park

Several companies run guided tours from the city centre to Sydney Olympic Park in Homebush Bay.

Red Terra Tours (☎ 9874 4200) offers guided tours of all the Homebush Bay landmarks including Stadium Australia, the Superdome, Aquatic Centre, showgrounds, railway, Bicentennial Park, and the Athletes' Village. Buses leave from the city twice daily, with free pickup and return to city hotels. The tour takes four hours and costs $65 ($52 children). If you want a birds-eye view, there are also helicopter options.

Australian Pacific Tours (☎ 9252 2988) runs a similar tour (minus the helicopter option) for $65 ($32.50 children).

The Sydney Olympic Explorer is a hop-on, hop-off service that makes 10 pit-stops around the Olympic Park site, including the Sydney Superdome, Stadium Australia, the State Sports Centre, and Bicentennial and Archery Parks. Buses leave from the Homebush Bay information centre every 20 minutes between 9 am and 3 pm daily ($10 adults, $5 children).

The quickest way to get to Olympic Park is to catch a train to Lidcombe station, then board the Olympic Park Sprint service, which runs every 10 minutes between 6 am and 11 pm ($3.20 one way). Alternatively, you can catch a train from Central station to Strathfield, then the No 403 bus to the park. You can also catch a RiverCat from Circular Quay up the Parramatta River to the Olympic Park wharf ($3.40 one way).

See also the special section 'The Olympic Games'.

Harbour Cruises

A wide range of cruises from Circular Quay offer relatively inexpensive excursions on the harbour. You can book most at Australian Travel Specialists (☎ 9555 2700), at Circular Quay's wharves six and two (and at offices in Manly, Darlinghurst, Darling Harbour and the Centrepoint tower). It's open from 7 am to 9 pm weekdays, 8 am to 9pm weekends. Captain Cook Cruises (☎ 9206 1111) has its own booking office at Wharf 6.

STA ferries offer some good-value cruises, such as the 2½ hour trip that goes as far as Sydney Head and the Spit Bridge (departs at 1 pm weekdays, 1.30 pm weekends). Tickets cost $19 ($12 children). For sparkling views of the city at night, there's a Harbour Lights cruise, departing 8 pm Monday to Saturday ($16.50/10.50). There's also a one hour morning cruise of the eastern bays, departing at 10 and 11.15 am ($13/8.50). STA cruises depart from Wharf 5, and tickets can be bought from the ferry information office under the Cahill Expressway opposite Wharf 4.

The Sydney Harbour Explorer, run by Captain Cook Cruises, is a hop-on, hop-off service that stops at the Opera House, Watsons Bay, Taronga Zoo, The Rocks and Darling Harbour. Boats run every two hours from 9.30 am to 3.30 pm ($20/12 children).

Sail Venture Cruises (☎ 9262 3595) sails big catamarans around the harbour five times a day. They depart from Darling Harbour's Aquarium wharf and also pick up at Circular Quay's East Pontoon (note that you get a longer cruise for the same price if you start at Darling Harbour). The trip takes about 2½ hours. The different options include the coffee cruise for $25 ($12 children), buffet lunch cruise for $48/24, or dinner cruise for $90/45.

Sailing cruises are also offered on the *Bounty* (☎ 9247 1789), a replica of the ship lost by the infamous Captain Bligh in the famous mutiny – this one was made for the film starring Mel Gibson. It sails twice daily on weekdays and three times on weekends. There is a choice of cruises available. Prices range from $45 for the 1½ hour Sunday morning brunch sail, to $80 for the 2½ hour daily evening dinner cruise. The boat leaves from Campbell's Cove at the Rocks. The *Svanen* (☎ 9698 4456) also sails from here.

Walking Tours

See Walking Tours in the Things to See & Do chapter for information on guided walking tours around Sydney.

Bicycle Tours

CTA Cycle Tours (☎ toll-free 1800 353 004) runs weekend day tours for $45 ($40 YHA), including gear and ferry transport.

THE OLYMPIC GAMES

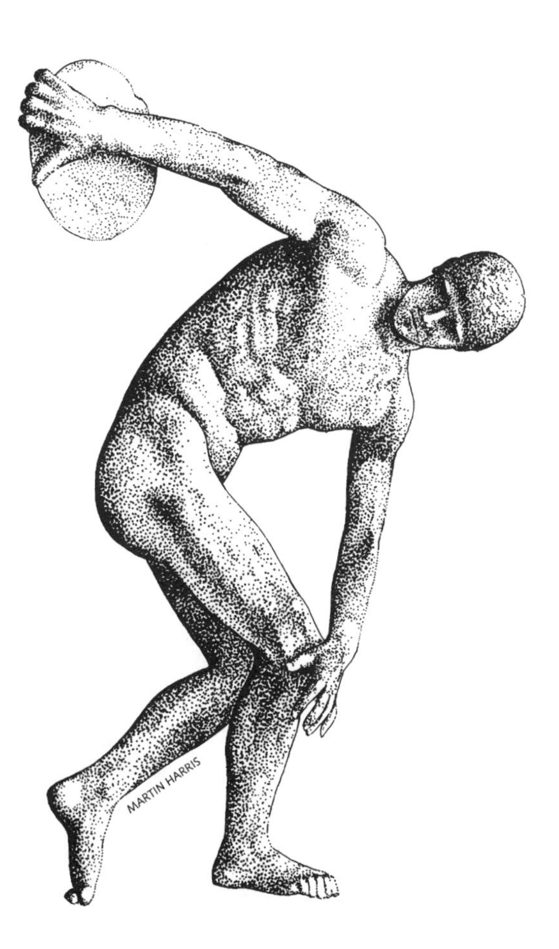

In September 2000, sportspeople from all over the globe will converge on Sydney to take part in the world's greatest sporting event – the Olympic Games. For two weeks, the eyes of the world will be on these athletes as they strive to become the first Olympic gold medallists of the new millennium.

ANCIENT OLYMPICS

The Ancient Olympics were held in Olympia, Greece every four years from at least 776 BC. Some evidence dates the Games even earlier, to around 900 BC; other historians believe a similar festival existed at least four centuries previously.

Initially the Olympics only lasted one day with a single event – a running race for one length of the stadium (about 190m). In time the event was extended to five days, and four running events (including a race in armour), combat sports, a chariot race and a pentathlon (long jump, javelin, discus, sprint, wrestling) gradually made their way into the Games. Some nonsporting activities also muscled in, including a trumpeting contest.

Competitors had to be free-born male Greeks. From 750 BC they competed in the nude; prior to that they wore a shorts-like garment. Women and slaves were forbidden, under threat of death, to even attend the Games. However, it was possible for a woman to win an Olympic event. In the chariot race the crown of wild olive leaves was awarded to the owner of the horses and not the drivers. So Bėlistike of Macedonia won the two-horse chariot race in 268 BC.

In addition to a crown of wild olive leaves, winners were often richly rewarded by their home states and sometimes became wealthy. The importance of winning at Olympia, and the reflected glory it bestowed on the winner's birthplace, led cities to hire professionals and bribe judges. The farce that the Olympics were to become was symbolised by Nero's appearance in the chariot race in 66 AD: he was drunk, there were no other competitors, and he did not even finish the course, but he was declared the winner.

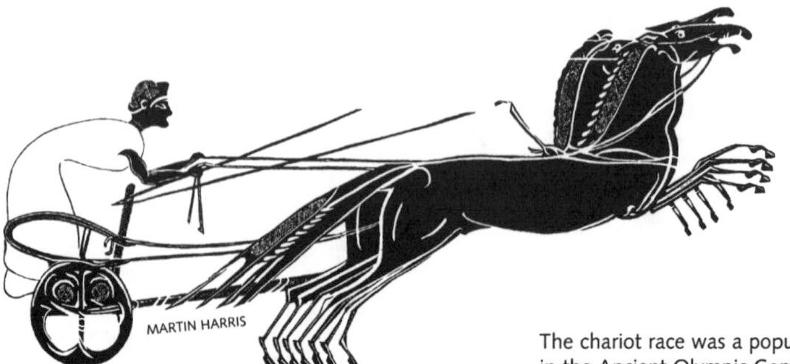

The chariot race was a popular event in the Ancient Olympic Games.

Dead Good

In the Ancient Olympics, the *pankration* event was a brutal combination of boxing and wrestling in which virtually anything was permitted. Arrachion of Phigalia was awarded the title in 564 BC because his opponent 'gave up' – though Arrachion himself was by then lying dead in the arena. He remains the only dead person to become an Olympic champion.

The Myth of the Marathon

Everyone thinks they know the story of the marathon – even if you don't, the story gets another run (so to speak) every Olympic Games. In 490 BC, the small army of the Athenians, having defeated the much larger Persian forces at the battle of Marathon, sent a famed runner, Pheidippides, to Athens, a distance of 26 miles and 385 yards (about 42km), to deliver the good news. He had just completed a 300 mile (480km) round trip to Sparta in a vain attempt to enlist their support; nevertheless, he ran to Athens, gasped out his message and, in extreme exhaustion, collapsed and died.

So, is it true? Well, partly, but not the most famous bit that everyone believes. Pheidippides certainly did exist: Herodotus, the earliest and most reliable historian of this era, mentions him in two paragraphs (Book VI, 105-6), written about 40 years later. These clearly state that Pheidippides ran to Sparta and back in about three days – and that's it. There's no mention of him at Marathon.

Subsequently, though, Pheidippides ran out of the pages of history and into the realm of mythology. The modern marathon was supposed to be the exact distance he ran from Marathon to Athens. But there is no record of this in Herodotus; later Greek and Roman historians invented the more romantic 'Marathon' story.

Pheidippides was a professional messenger; even so, his run to Sparta is one of the great feats of endurance in history, especially as much of it was through very rugged terrain. Thus, Pheidippides' actual deeds far surpass any mere marathon. So the modern marathon rightly celebrates Pheidippides' prowess – only in not quite the way most people think. So when you're lining the marathon route among the wildly cheering crowds at Sydney 2000, spare a thought for Pheidippides and the real story of his remarkable run.

Greg Alford

In 393 AD the Olympics were abolished by the Christian emperor Theodosius, and Olympia was buried under earthquakes until excavated between 1875 and 1881: it was these excavations that turned Baron Pierre de Coubertin's mind towards resurrecting the Games.

MODERN OLYMPIC HISTORY

The history of the modern Olympic Games has been a turbulent one. Almost from their inception, the Games have faced disruption courtesy of political crises – including two world wars, boycotts and terrorist attacks – and their demise has frequently been predicted. Despite this, the Games have always gone on and, 104 years after the first Olympics of the modern era took place in Athens, winning an Olympic gold medal remains the ultimate ambition of sportspeople throughout the world.

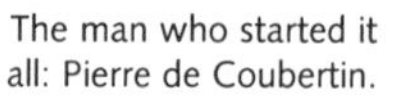
The man who started it all: Pierre de Coubertin.

The modern Olympic Games was the brainchild of the Frenchman Baron de Coubertin. In 1892, inspired by epic tales of the Ancient Olympics and by the public school games of 19th century Britain, de Coubertin proposed the idea of reviving the Olympic Games. He invited interested parties to participate in a world sports congress in Paris in 1894. This congress spawned the International Olympic Committee (IOC) and, consequently, the decision to revive the Olympics in 1896.

De Coubertin intended the Games to be for amateurs only (with the exception of professional fencing masters), that competitors should be adult males, and that the Olympics should be held every four years in different venues. At the turn of the 21st century the only stipulation that has stood the test of time is that the Games are staged in different cities.

The 1896 Games, which were jointly funded by wealthy Greek architect Georgios Averoff, a lottery, and the world's first collection of sporting postage stamps, were well attended and successful. However, the following two Games, held in Paris and St Louis, were appalling: they were staged as an appendage to the World Exhibition, and the sporting events were held over a periods of five and 4½ months respectively. Additionally, the organisation was so bad that in Paris many competitors had no idea they were taking part in the Olympics, and in St Louis many of the events were open only to Missouri residents.

The Olympic movement might have died then, had it not been for the successful 'Intercalated' Games held in Athens in 1906 to mark the ten-year anniversary of the Games. The London Games of 1908 were marked by controversy, with the USA in particular accusing the British officials of favouring British athletes. However, the well organised Games of Stockholm in 1912 attracted athletes from five continents, and the future of the Olympics at last looked promising. WWI prevented the 1916 Games from going ahead, and the fact that athletes gathered for the Games in war-torn Antwerp in 1920 was a major achievement for the IOC.

Famous Five

Only five sports have been on the program of every modern Olympic Games since 1896 – cycling, fencing, gymnastics, swimming and track and field athletics. Rowing should have been included with them, but rough seas caused its cancellation in 1896.

The post-WWI years saw increased public interest in the Games, with distance runner Paavo Nurmi and swimmer Johnny Weissmuller (who later played Tarzan in the films of the 1930s and 40s) becoming the first 'household names' of Olympic sport. The 1920s and 30s also witnessed the gradual admission of more female competitors in the Games, with track and field and gymnastics being added to the women's program in Amsterdam in 1928. The final Games before the outbreak of WWII were held in Berlin in 1936.

Nova Peris-Kneebone will be the first torchbearer in Australia.

The Journey of the Olympic Torch

The world has the Nazis to thank for the concept of the Olympic flame and torch relay. The brainchild of Carl Diem, head of the organising committee for the Berlin Olympics, the Olympic flame was ignited in Olympia, Greece for the first time in 1936, and was carried from there to Berlin by 3075 torchbearers, all running just slightly over one mile of the journey.

The Sydney 2000 Olympic torch relay will travel over 27,000km and be carried by 10,000 torchbearers in what is to be the longest torch relay in Olympic history.

Apart from being carried by torchbearers, the Olympic flame will travel on a surf boat at Bondi Beach, on the *Indian Pacific* train across the Nullarbor Plain, on a Royal Flying Doctor Service aircraft in the remote outback, and by camel on Cable Beach at Broome. Before reaching Australia, the torch will be taken by plane to Guam, where it will begin a 20 day journey visiting the 12 Pacific Island countries that make up the Oceania ring of the Olympic nations. It will then visit every state and territory in Australia over 100 days. The first person to carry the torch in Australia will be Australian Olympic hockey gold medallist-turned-sprinter Nova Peris-Kneebone.

History at a Glance

Olympic Games	Highlights	Leading Nations
1896 – Athens, Greece Male (M): c. 200, Female (F): 0	Greek peasant Spiridon Louis wins the marathon.	USA (11 gold), Greece (10), Germany (7)
1900 – Paris, France M: 1206, F: 19	Australian Frederick Lane wins swimming's obstacle race – climbing over and diving under boats.	France (29), USA (20), GB (17)
1904 – St Louis, USA M: 681, F: 6	'Winner' Fred Lotz, an American, is disqualified from the marathon for taking a lift.	USA (80), Germany (5), Cuba (5)
1908 – London, GB M: 1999, F: 36	First gold medals awarded. Briton Wyndham Halswelle wins a 'walkover' 400m courtesy of partisan judging.	GB (56), USA (23), Sweden (7)
1912 – Stockholm, Sweden M: 2490, F: 57	The photo finish and electronic timer are introduced. American Jim Thorpe wins the pentathlon and decathlon, but is later stripped of his medal due to his professional status.	Sweden (24), USA (23), GB (10)
1920 – Antwerp, Belgium M: 2591, F: 77	French Wimbledon champion Suzanne Lenglen takes tennis gold.	USA (41), Sweden (17), GB (15)
1924 – Paris, France M: 2956, F: 136	Finnish athlete Paavo Nurmi takes his total of gold medals to five.	USA (45), Finland (14), France (13)
1928 – Amsterdam, Netherlands M: 2724, F: 290	American Johnny Weissmuller takes his gold medal tally to five.	USA (22), Germany (10) Finland (8)
1932 – Los Angeles, USA M: 1281, F: 127	American Babe Didrikson wins two athletics golds.	USA (41), Italy (12), France (10)
1936 – Berlin, Germany M: 3738, F: 328	American Jesse Owens wins four athletics golds to dominate the 'Aryan Games'.	Germany (33), USA (24), Hungary (10)
1948 – London, UK M: 3714, F: 385	Fanny Blankers-Koen of the Netherlands wins four athletics golds.	USA (38), Sweden (16), France (10)
1952 – Helsinki, Finland M: 4407, F: 518	Czech Emil Zatopek wins the 5000m, 10,000m and the marathon and his wife, Dana, wins gold in the javelin.	USA (40), USSR (22), Hungary (16)
1956 – Melbourne, Australia M: 2813, F: 371	Australian Dawn Fraser wins the first of three consecutive 100m freestyle golds.	USSR (37), USA (32), Australia (13)

BERGMAN / SPORT • THE LIBRARY •

CHRIS ELFES / SPORT • THE LIBRARY •

The grand opening of Sydney Olympic Park in 1999

CHRIS ELFES / SPORT • THE LIBRARY •

Sydney Aquatic Centre will be host to a few world records in 2000.

PRESSE SPORTS / SPORT • THE LIBRARY •

Speed star Rebecca Twigg (USA) leads the charge for gold.

RUDIGER FESSEL / SPORT • THE LIBRARY •

Russian Dimitri Saoutine wins gold in Atlanta.

DAVID CALLOW / SPORT • THE LIBRARY •

Marcus Stephen (Nigeria), worth his weight in ...

SPORT • THE LIBRARY •

Australia's golden girl, Cathy Freeman

History at a Glance

Olympic Games	Highlights	Leading Nations
1960 – Rome, Italy M: 4736, F: 610	Ethiopian Abebe Bikila wins the marathon barefoot.	USSR (42), USA (34), Italy (13)
1964 – Tokyo, Japan M: 4457, F: 683	The first Games televised internationally. Soviet sisters Irina and Tamara Press take three gold medals between them.	USA (36), USSR (30), Japan (16)
1968 – Mexico City, Mexico M: 4749, F: 781	American Bob Beamon sets long jump world record. American sprinters Tommie Smith and John Carlos give 'black power' salute on victory podium and are sent home.	USA (45), USSR (29), Japan (11)
1972 – Munich, FRG M: 6065, F: 1058	American Mark Spitz wins seven golds in swimming.	USSR (50), USA (33), GDR (20)
1976 – Montreal, Canada M: 4781, F: 1247	Romanian gymnast Nadia Comaneci scores seven perfect tens.	USSR (49), GDR (40), USA (34)
1980 – Moscow, USSR M: 4043, F: 1124	British arch rivals Steve Ovett and Seb Coe win a gold each in middle distance running.	USSR (80), GDR (47), Bulgaria (8)
1984 – Los Angeles, USA M: 5230, F: 1567	American Carl Lewis wins four athletics golds.	USA (83), Romania (20), FRG (17)
1988 – Seoul, South Korea M: 6279, F: 2186	East Germany's Kristin Otto wins six gold medals. American Ben Johnson is stripped of his 100m gold after testing positive to anabolic steroids.	USSR (55), GDR (37), USA (36)
1992 – Barcelona, Spain M: 6657, F: 2707	South Africa competes in Games for the first time since 1960 and Germany competes as one nation for the first time since 1964. The USA's 'Dream Team' dominates the men's basketball.	Unified Team* (45), USA (37), Germany (33)
1996 – Atlanta, USA M: 6797, F: 3513	Ireland's Michelle Smith wins more golds individually (three) than any Irish team in the history of the Games. American Michael Johnson takes the 200m and 400m double.	USA (44), Russia (26), Germany (20)

** The Unified Team was made up of representatives of the Commonwealth of Independent States, the former USSR.*

DAVID CALLOW / SPORT • THE LIBRARY •

The Nazis turned them into a propaganda event, presenting the image of a democratic, peace-loving Third Reich. However, Hitler's hope that the Games would prove the superiority of the Aryan athletes was undermined by the performances of USA's black athletes, in particular the incredible Jesse Owens, winner of four gold medals for track and field.

PRESSE SPORTS / SPORT • THE LIBRARY •

Carl Lewis wins one of four golds in the 100m at the LA Games in 1984.

The post-war era saw the Olympics used as a battleground between the capitalist countries of the western world and the communist countries of Eastern Europe to 'prove' which ideology was best. The Eastern European practice of mass-producing athletes in elitist sports schools led to accusations of 'shamateurism' by western nations who found they could not effectively compete against the USSR and East Germany. There were boycotts of Olympic Games held between 1954 and the end of the Cold War era. Some of the world events that influenced the boycotts were: the Soviet invasions of Hungary (1956), Czechoslovakia (1968) and Afghanistan (1979); the apartheid regimes of South Africa and Rhodesia; and the British intervention in the Suez crisis (1956). The boycotts hit their peak in 1980 when the USA, Canada and Germany refused to attend the Moscow Olympics because of the Soviet invasion of Afghanistan. Four years later the Soviets and most of their East European satellites carried out a tit-for-tat boycott of the Los Angeles Olympics.

The use of the Olympics for political ends turned to tragedy in 1972 when 11 Israeli athletes were killed by Palestinian terrorists during the Munich Games. It is to the credit of the athletes that the Games continued to increase in prestige and public popularity during the 1960s and 1970s – Bob Beamon's world record long jump in Mexico, swimmer Mark Spitz's seven gold medals in Munich, and Nadia Comaneci's perfect ten scores in Montreal remained in the memories of sports fans long after boycotts and terrorism had almost been forgotten.

The LA Games marked a turning point in Olympic history. Up till that point, Olympic Games had proved far from lucrative and countries showed little interest in staging an event that had become a security nightmare as well as a financial one. Montreal was still paying off debts accrued from its Olympics way into the 1990s.

But LA turned the Games into a commercial success thanks to marketing, sponsorship and revenue from TV rights. Since then, cities have clamoured for the right to stage the Games, now regarded as a huge money-spinner. With the dismantling of the Eastern Bloc in 1989-90, the days of tit-for-tat boycotts were over, so all the top sportspeople started turning up for the Games. Additionally, professionals were allowed to take part in the Games from 1988 onwards, and 'shamateurism' became a term of the past.

Today some aspects of this commercialisation of the Olympics undermine their integrity and public image. Pressure on athletes to perform is immense. The issue of drugs also refuses to go away. Ben Johnson's positive test of 1988 led many sports bodies and fans to believe that plenty of other athletes remained uncaught. There have been allegations – most notably by Andrew Jennings, author of *The Lords of the Rings* (1992) and *The New Lords of the Rings* (1996) – that positive tests have been covered up in recent Olympics.

Jennings' books also revealed another 'dark side' to the Olympics: corruption and bribery, he claimed, was rife in the bidding process for Olympic Games, with organising committees showering IOC officials and their families with gifts to encourage them to vote for their city. In 1998-99 these allegations were taken more seriously when the IOC admitted that some of its officials had accepted bribes from the organising committee of the Salt Lake City Winter Games of 2002. In 1999 Australian Olympic Committee president John Coates admitted that inducement payments were made to Kenyan and Ugandan officials to encourage them to vote for the Sydney bid.

The anger these revelations provoked among athletes, sports fans and the organisers of failed Olympic bids resulted in IOC president Juan Antonio Samaranch ordering an inquiry into the bribery scandal. But the news that he had received gifts from Nagano and Salt Lake City prior to their cities being granted the Winter Olympics of 1998 and 2002 respectively did not instil critics with confidence in his ability to weed out corruption. (Incidentally, as IOC president, Samaranch is not entitled to a vote during the bidding process ...)

At present corruption and drugs seem to pose the greatest threat to the future of the Greatest Show on Earth. However, the Games have survived plenty of turmoil over the past 104 years and it has always been the marvellous performances of the athletes that has helped to sustain them. Whatever else happens in Sydney, it will be the performances of the next Carl Lewis or Nadia Comaneci that will be remembered after external politics have been forgotten.

Identity Crisis

In the early Olympic years, competitors were regarded as individuals and so could represent any country. For example, Stanley Rowley (Australia) won bronze medals in the 60m, 100m and 200m in 1900 representing Australasia. He was then drafted into the British team for the 5000m team race and won a gold medal, although he didn't finish the race.

Women at the Olympics

Like the ancient Greeks before him, de Coubertin believed that 'Women have but one task, that of crowning the winner with garlands'. So the first Olympics was for men only. Ironically, women made their Olympic debut in de Coubertin's home city – but they were permitted to compete only in 'genteel' sports like tennis and golf. The first female Olympic champion was Charlotte Cooper of Great Britain, who won the tennis singles and went on to win the mixed doubles.

After 1900, women's participation in Olympic sport evolved torturously slowly. Women's swimming (the 100m freestyle and a relay) and highboard diving were added to the program in 1912. It was not until 1928 that women were allowed to compete in track and field events. Unfortunately, so many competitors collapsed after the 800m that the distance was declared unsafe for women, and women weren't permitted to run farther than 200m in Olympic Games until 1960. Since the late 1970s, the IOC has made a concerted effort to increase women's Olympic participation and in Sydney women will compete in some 24 sports including, for the first time, weightlifting.

Paralympic Games

The Paralympics began when the British government set up a spinal injuries centre for ex-servicemen at Stoke Mandeville hospital in 1944. As part of their therapy, patients were introduced to a number of sports and in 1948 a sports competition involving patients from various rehabilitation centres took place. Three years later, competitors from Holland took part in these games and the international Paralympic movement was born. Now, the Paralympics – the name is derived from 'parallel to the Olympics' – take place every four years, in the wake of the Olympics. Since 1976 the Winter Paralympics have followed the Winter Games.

No Handicap

Perhaps the most amazing Olympic competitor of all time was American gymnast George Eyser. In 1904 he won three gymnastics events, despite the fact that he was well over 30 and had a wooden leg! Incredibly, he also competed in the all-around track and field contest (forerunner of the decathlon).

THE SYDNEY GAMES

The 2000 Olympic Games will take place in Sydney from 15 September to 1 October, bringing together more than 10,000 competitors from 198 countries.

Sydney 2000 will feature 28 sports (seven of which include multiple disciplines – eg swimming, diving, synchronised swimming and water polo are disciplines in the sport of aquatics) including, for the first time, the triathlon and taekwondo.

Shortly after the Olympic Games have finished, disabled sportspeople from some 198 countries will converge on Sydney for the 2000 Paralympic Games, held from 18 to 29 October.

Harbour of Life Arts Festival

If you're in Sydney during the 2000 Games you'll find a variety of things to do. In addition to the Games, there'll be the Harbour of Life Arts Festival, which will begin in August 2000 and continue until the conclusion of the Paralympic Games on 24 October. There'll be plenty of street entertainment including outdoor concerts, performing arts, visual arts, film, literature and music activities. Tickets for the festival went on sale in October 1999.

For up-to-the-minute information on all the events taking place, check the daily papers and the official Web site for the Games (www.Sydney.Olympic.org) or call the info service on ☎ 13 63 63.

Venues

Most of the Olympic events will take place at Sydney Olympic Park in Homebush Bay, with some sports being held in western Sydney, eastern Sydney and Darling Harbour.

The centrepiece of Sydney Olympic Park is the 110,000-capacity Stadium Australia. The stadium will stage the opening and closing ceremonies as well as the athletics events and the soccer (football) final.

Also in the Olympic Park is the Sydney International Aquatic Centre, which holds 17,500 people. The gymnastics events and the basketball finals will be held in the 18,000-seat Sydney Superdome. The Baseball Stadium, Hockey Centre, Tennis Centre and Bicentennial Park (where the modern pentathlon will take place) are also in Olympic Park.

Western Sydney will stage the water polo at Ryde Water Polo Pool, rowing and canoeing at the Regatta Centre in Penrith, the cycling at Dunc Gray Velodrome, Bankstown and the three day eventing at the appropriately named Horsley Park.

In eastern Sydney, spectators can watch sailing at Rushcutters Bay, beach volleyball at Bondi Beach, and football at Sydney Football Stadium.

Boxing, weightlifting, judo and fencing will take place at the Sydney Exhibition Centre and Convention Centre in Darling Harbour. Finally, preliminary soccer matches will take place at various venues in Australia: Brisbane's Gabba, Adelaide's Hindmarsh Stadium, Canberra's Bruce Stadium and Melbourne's MCG.

Tickets

Olympic tickets range from A$105 to A$1382 for the opening and closing ceremonies, through A$65 to $455 for athletics events, down to A$30 to $80 for rowing. For Australians, ticket applications closed in July 1999. However, tickets for less popular sports will possibly remain on sale right up to and during the Games themselves. Keep an

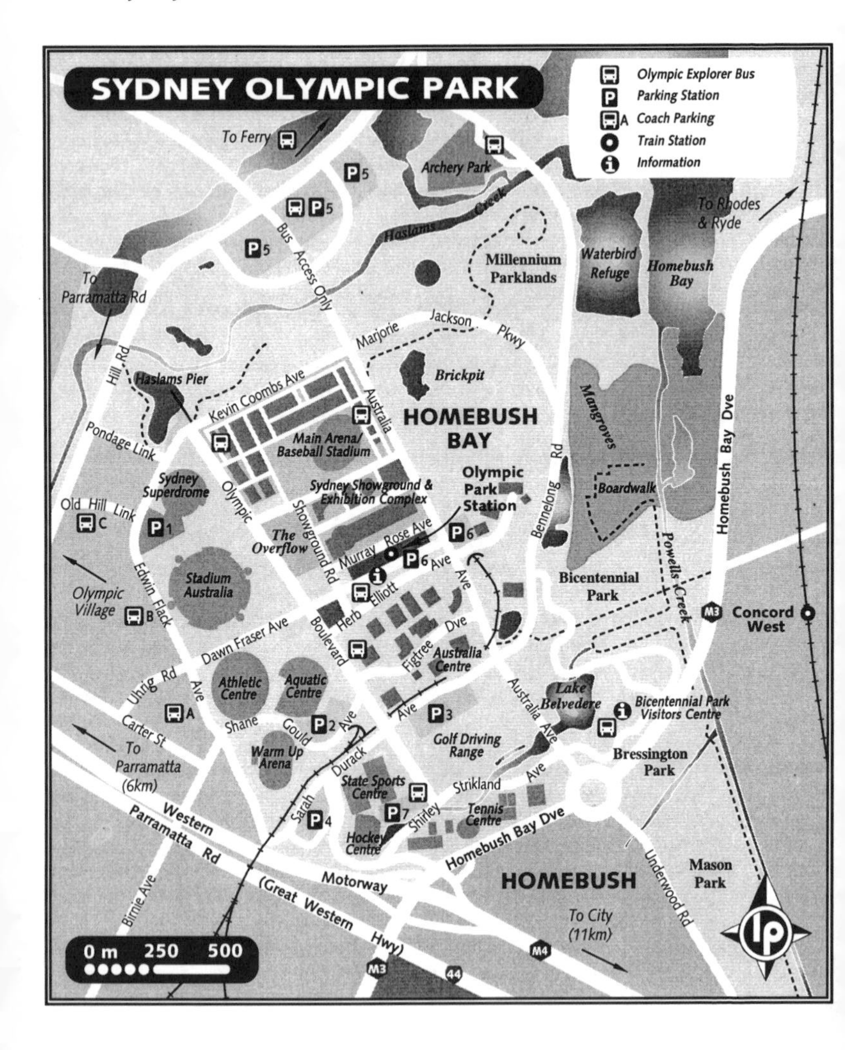

eye on the official Olympic Web site or call ☎ 13 63 63 to see which events can still be attended. Paralympics tickets went on sale in October 1999.

Overseas visitors can purchase tickets for the Olympics through agents appointed by their National Olympic Committee. See the Web site www.olympic.org/ioc/e/org/noc/noc_list_e.html for a list of all the

Marvellous Melbourne

This will be the second time the Olympics have been staged in Australia – Melbourne hosted the Games in 1956. The Melbourne Games were memorable for the gold-medal-winning performances of the host nation, especially in the pool, and for Soviet runner Vladimir Kuts' victories in the 5000m and 10,000m. Melbourne also marked the first and only time that the complete Olympic program could not take place within the host country – Australia's quarantine laws meant that the equestrian events had to be staged in Sweden.

committees around the world. Some National Olympic Committees are listed below.

Australia
(☎ 02-9245 2000, fax 9245 2098)
Level 13, The Maritime Centre, 207 Kent St, Sydney NSW 2000
Canada
(☎ 514-861 3371, fax 861 2896)
Olympic House, Ave Pierre Dupuy 2380, Montreal, Quebec H3C 3R4
France
(☎ 01-40 78 28 00, fax 40 78 29 51)
Maison du Sport Français, 1 Ave Pierre de Coubertin, 75640 Paris, Cedex 13
Great Britain
(☎ 020-8871 2677, fax 8871 9104)
1 Wandsworth Plain, London SW18 1EH
Germany
(☎ 69-670 02 02, fax 677 12 29)
Postfach 71 02 63, 60492 Frankfurt-am-Main
Ireland
(☎ 01-668 04 44, fax 668 06 50)
27 Mespil Rd, Dublin 4
Japan
(☎ 03-3481 2286, fax 3481 0977)
1-1-1 Jinnan, Tokyo 150-8050
Netherlands
(☎ 26-483 44 00, fax 483 44 44)
PO Box 302, Papendallaan 60, 6800 AH Arnhem
New Zealand
(☎ 04-385 0070, fax 385 0090)
Olympic House, 3rd Floor, 97-99 Courtenay Place, Wellington
USA
(☎ 719-632 5551, fax 632 4180)
Olympic House, 1750 East Boulder St,
Colorado Springs, CO 80909-5764

Freebies

You won't have to be wealthy to watch Olympic sport live. In fact, some of the Sydney events can be seen free of charge. These are:

Marathons The women's marathon will take place from 9 am on 24 September, and the men's will be on 1 October from 4 pm (followed by the closing ceremony). The 42km course runs from North Sydney Oval through the city centre and out to Stadium Australia in Homebush, and thousands are expected to watch from the roadside.

Racewalking The men's 20km and 50km walks and the women's 20km walk will also take place in Sydney's streets, on 22, 28 and 29 September.

Cycling The road race route will go through Sydney's eastern suburbs, starting and finishing at Moore Park. Road racing can be seen on 25 (training only), 26 and 27 September.

Triathlon Spectators will be able to watch the swimming stage of this event free from the harbourside. The event will take place from 10 am to 1 pm on 16 and 17 September.

Sailing Sydney's famous harbour will play host to the sailing events. Yachts will carry special symbols, probably their national flag, to help spectators identify them. The sailing events will take place every day from 16 to 30 September, from noon.

In addition to the sporting events, free concerts and street entertainment will be provided for the duration of the Games. These events will be centred on the Olympic Boulevard and Millennium Park at Homebush Bay, and around the waterfront at Circular Quay and Darling Harbour.

Transport

Games ticket holders can travel free on the Sydney Olympic transport system on the day of the event until 4 am the following day. Transport will run 24 hours a day. The system covers all CityRail trains and the bus network covering the venues. Olympic Park train station will run up to 30 trains an hour and there will be frequent buses to Olympic Park and the other venues. The free transport zone includes central Sydney and extends to Newcastle, Dungog and Scone in the north of NSW, to Port Kembla and Nowra in the south, Goulburn in the south-west and Bathurst in the west.

Further Reading

Chronicle of the Olympics, pub. Dorling Kindersley
The Complete Book of the Olympics, David Wallechinsky
The History of the Olympics, ed. Martin Tyler & Phil Soar
The Lords of the Rings, Andrew Jennings
The New Lords of the Rings, Andrew Jennings
The Olympics at 100, Associated Press

Liz Filleul

Things to See & Do

Most interesting things to see in Sydney are in the city centre or nearby inner suburbs. They're all easy to get to on foot or by public transport. (See also the Free Entertainment section in the Entertainment chapter.)

WALKING TOURS

Setting out on foot is a good way to explore Australia's largest city.

A City Stroll

One way to orient yourself is to start in **Hyde Park** (Map 4) at Museum station's Liverpool St exit. Walk north through the park past the **Anzac Memorial**. On the right, on College St, is the **Australian Museum**. From here William St (the eastward extension of Park St) heads east to **Kings Cross**. Across Park St, at the end of the avenue of trees, is the wonderful **Archibald Fountain** (Map 4). To the north on College St is **St Mary's Cathedral**.

Keep going north to reach **Macquarie St** with its collection of early colonial buildings and, after a few blocks, **Circular Quay** and the **Opera House**. On the west side of Circular Quay, behind the **Museum of Contemporary Art**, George St meanders through **the Rocks**.

Walk north on George St, which curves around under the **Harbour Bridge** into Lower Fort St. Turn right (north) for the waterfront or left to climb **Observatory Hill**. From here Argyle St heads east, through the skinny **Argyle Cut** and back to the Rocks.

Nearby on Cumberland St you can climb stairs to the Harbour Bridge and walk across to **Milsons Point** on the North Shore, where you can catch a train back to the city.

This walk covers about 7km and takes about 2½ to three hours.

It's also worth wandering along Oxford St from Hyde Park's south-eastern corner to **Paddington** (Map 7). You can catch a bus back to the city from Paddington, or, if you keep going to **Bondi Junction**, catch a train.

Highlights

- Taking a cruise or ferry trip on Sydney Harbour – one of the best ways to view the city
- Enjoying the view from an alfresco cafe table at Campbells Cove in the Rocks, or Circular Quay
- Bushwalking in Sydney Harbour National Park – spectacularly scenic and right in the city!
- Joining in the parade (or just watching) at the vibrant Gay & Lesbian Mardi Gras
- Catching a performance at the Sydney Opera House
- Seeing displays at the Powerhouse Museum and Art Gallery of NSW
- Visiting the beaches – from crowded Bondi and lively Manly to beautiful, remote Whale Beach
- Eating a pie at Harry's Cafe de Wheels in Woolloomooloo
- Soaking up the sleaze (and fun) in Kings Cross
- Coming face-to-face with a shark at Sydney Aquarium
- Catching an outdoor movie at the summer Moonlight Cinema in Centennial Park

Harbourside Walks

At the entrance to the harbour, near Watsons Bay, there's a rather fine short walk around **South Head**. It begins at Camp Cove and passes by Lady Bay, Inner South Head and **the Gap** (a popular place for watching sunrises and sunsets), ending at Outer South Head. From Circular Quay, catch Bus No 325 (or an infrequent ferry) to Watsons Bay.

There's a good 5km coastal walk running from Bondi Beach along the clifftops to Tamarama, Bronte, Clovelly and Coogee.

On the North Shore, the Sydney Harbour National Park includes the 4km **Ashton Park track** that begins below Taronga Zoo and rounds Bradleys Head, skirting Taylor's Bay to reach Clifton Gardens. Take the Taronga Zoo ferry from Circular Quay to get to Ashton Park. From Taronga, you can also wander west to **Cremorne Point** via a combination of parks, stairways, streets and pockets of bush.

One of the best walks in the park is the 8km **Manly Scenic Walkway**, which takes about four hours and follows the shore from Manly to Spit Bridge, where there are buses back to the city centre. Points of interest, from the Manly end, include Fairlight, Forty Baskets and Reef beaches (the latter, a nude beach, involves a swerve off the main track), and ancient Aboriginal rock carvings on a sandstone platform between the Cutler Rd Lookout and Grotto Point. The route can be tricky to discern at times, so grab a leaflet from Manly's Visitor's Information Bureau. For more information call the National Parks & Wildlife Service (NPWS, ☎ 9977 6229) or Manly Municipal Council (☎ 9976 1500).

For a more urban waterside wander, head west of Hyde Park along Market St, which leads to Pyrmont Bridge (for pedestrians and the monorail only) and **Darling Harbour** (Map 4). On the other side of Darling Harbour, Pyrmont Bridge Rd leads to **Glebe Island Bridge** and **Pyrmont Fish Markets** (Map 9). If you continue along Pyrmont Bridge Rd you'll eventually end up in **Glebe** (Map 9).

Sydney Harbour Ferries publishes a useful pamphlet detailing some picturesque harbourside strolls.

Guided Walks

Several people offer guided walks in Sydney. Maureen Fry (☎ 9660 7157), 15 Arcadia Rd, Glebe, caters mainly for groups of about eight people, but she can take individuals or perhaps fit you in with a group. A two hour guided walk costs $15.

The Rocks Walking Tours (☎ 9247 6678) offers guided 75-minute walks ($12 adults, 8.50 children; children under 10 free) from the visitors centre at 10.30 am, 12.30 and 2.30 pm on weekdays, 11.30 am and 2 pm on weekends. If you'd rather soak it up at your own pace, hire a Rocks Walking Adventure cassette (☎ 018 111 011) for $8.

Sydney Aboriginal Discoveries (☎ 9368 7684) offers a variety of outings with an indigenous focus, including walkabout tours of city landmarks and sacred places.

SYDNEY HARBOUR (MAP 1)

The harbour has melded and shaped the Sydney psyche since the first days of settlement, and today it's both a major port and the city's playground. Its waters, beaches, islands and waterside parks offer all the swimming, sailing, picnicking and walking you could want.

Officially called **Port Jackson**, Sydney's extravagantly colourful harbour stretches some 20km inland to join the mouth of the Parramatta River (Map 17). The headlands at the entrance are known as North Head and South Head. The city centre is about 8km inland and the most scenic area is on the ocean side. The harbour has multiple sandstone headlands, beautiful bays and beaches, numerous inlets and several islands. **Middle Harbour** is a large inlet that heads north-west a couple of kilometres inside the Heads.

At weekends, the harbour is carpeted with the sails of hundreds of yachts, and following the 18-footer yacht races on Sunday (from mid-September to late March) is a favourite activity. (See the Spectator Sports section in the Entertainment chapter.)

The best way to view the harbour is to persuade someone to take you sailing, take a harbour cruise (see the Getting Around chapter) or catch any one of the numerous ferries that ply its waters. The Manly ferry offers vistas of the harbour east of the bridge, while the Parramatta RiverCats cover the west. You can also visit some of the small islands, which are part of Sydney Harbour National Park (see later).

For details of Sydney Harbour's beaches see Beaches later.

Sydney Harbour National Park

This park protects the scattered pockets of bushland around the harbour and includes several small islands. It offers some great walking tracks, scenic lookouts, Aboriginal carvings, beaches and a handful of historic sites. The park headquarters (☎ 9337 5511) is at Greycliffe House in Nielsen Park, Vaucluse; the information centre for the park is at Cadman's Cottage, in the Rocks. On the south shore, the park incorporates South Head and Nielsen Park; on the North Shore it includes North Head, Dobroyd Head, Middle Head and Ashton Park. George's Head, Obelisk Bay and Middle Head, north-east of Taylor's Bay, are also part of the park, as are the islands.

Islands Previously known as Pinchgut, **Fort Denison** is a small fortified island off Mrs Macquarie's Point. It was originally used as a punishment 'cell' to isolate troublesome convicts, until it was fortified in the mid-19th century during the Crimean War, amid fears of a Russian invasion.

The largest island in the bay, **Goat Island**, west of the Harbour Bridge, has been a shipyard, quarantine station and gunpowder depot in its previous lives, and is now a filming location for the popular 'Water Rats' TV show. Fort Denison and Goat Island are heritage sites, so you'll need to join a tour if you want to visit them – contact NPWS (☎ 9247 5033) at Cadman's Cottage, 110 George Street, the Rocks. At the time of writing, Fort Denison was temporarily closed for conservation work. Goat Island tours depart from Cadman's Cottage Monday, Friday and Saturday at 1 pm, and cost $12 adults, $8 children. There's also a 'Water Rats' tour ($13/9), and a Gruesome Tales tour ($18) – this is not suitable for children!

Clarke Island, off Darling Point, **Rodd Island**, at Iron Cove near Birkenhead Point, and **Shark Island**, off Rose Bay, make great picnic getaways, but you'll need to hire a water taxi or have access to a boat to reach them. To visit these islands you need a permit ($3 per person) from Cadman's Cottage.

THE ROCKS (MAP 4)

Sydney's first non-Aboriginal settlement was made on the rocky spur of land on the western side of Sydney Cove, from which the Harbour Bridge now crosses to the North Shore. It became known as the Rocks because of the prominent outcrops of sandstone on the hillside. Today, the site is unrecognisable from the squalid and overcrowded place it was when the sewers were open and the residents were raucous.

Soon after settlement, the Rocks became the centre of the colony's maritime and commercial enterprises. Warehouses and bond stores were built, and the area thronged with convicts, officers, ticket-of-leavers, whalers, sailors and street gangs. Brothels and inns soon followed (this is the spot to look for several of Australia's oldest pubs).

In the 1820s and 30s, the nouveaux riches built three-storey houses on what is now Lower Fort St (which overlooked the slums), but the area remained notorious right into the 20th century. In the 1870s and 80s, the infamous Rocks 'pushes' used to haunt the area, snatching purses, holding up pedestrians, feuding and generally creating havoc. The area fell into decline when modern shipping and storage facilities moved away from Circular Quay, and slumped further following an outbreak of bubonic plague in 1900, which led to whole streets being razed. The construction of the Harbour Bridge two decades later resulted in further demolition.

The Rocks as we know it today was created by visionaries in the building industry and the union movement. Redevelopment, which began in the 1970s under the auspices of the Sydney Cove Redevelopment Authority, has turned the Rocks into a sanitised, historical tourist precinct, full of narrow cobbled streets, fine colonial buildings, converted warehouses, tearooms and stuffed koalas. If you ignore the kitsch, it's a delightful place to stroll around, especially in the narrow backstreets and in the less-developed, tightly knit, contiguous community of Millers Point.

Orientation & Information

The main street leading into the Rocks is George St, which runs north through the city centre from Railway Square. George St curves under the Harbour Bridge and meets Lower Fort St, which leads south to Observatory Park and north to the waterfront near Pier 1. Cumberland St is parallel to George St, and almost all of the area's attractions are jammed into the narrow paths and alleyways between the two streets. The Argyle Cut on Argyle St is the short cut between the eastern and western sides of the peninsula.

The Sydney Visitors Centre (☎ 9255 1788 or toll-free 1800 067 676), in the old Sailors Home at 106 George St in the Rocks, opens from 9 am to 6 pm daily. It has an exhibition on the colourful and shameful history of the Rocks and shows the video *Story of the Rocks* in its upstairs theatre (free). The centre sells the Rocks Ticket ($46, $28 children), which gives entry to a couple of attractions, and includes a meal, a walking tour and a harbour cruise.

The visitors centre has a good range of publications and souvenirs, and maps of self-guided walking tours for $1. The Rocks isn't large, but there are many small streets and hidden corners, so a map is handy. Make sure you see Millers Point on the western side of the Bradfield Highway (Hwy) – the elevated Harbour Bridge approach road – where there are some charming old terrace houses and the Sydney Observatory.

Things to See & Do

The oldest house in Sydney is **Cadman's Cottage** (1816), 110 George St, close to the visitors centre. It was once the home of the last government coxswain, John Cadman. When the cottage was built, it was actually on the waterfront, and the arches to the south of it housed longboats. The cottage is now an NWPS office (☎ 9247 5033), open from 9 am to 5 pm daily, which helps organise tours of the harbour islands.

Susannah Place, 58-64 Gloucester St, is a terrace of tiny houses dating from 1844. It's one of the few remaining examples of the modest housing that was once standard in the area.

The Rocks has several interesting shopping centres. They include the **Argyle Centre** on Argyle St, which was originally built as a bond store between 1826 and 1881, but today houses shops, studios, and eateries; the **Rocks Centre**, also on Argyle St; and the **Metcalfe Arcade** on George St.

The work of Sydney artist Ken Done is on show at the **Ken Done Gallery** (☎ 9247 2740), 1 Hickson Rd, in a converted warehouse. It's open from 10 am to 5.30 pm daily.

A short walk west along Argyle St through the **Argyle Cut** – an old tunnel excavated by convicts through the hill – takes you to the other side of the peninsula and **Millers Point**, a delightful district of early colonial homes.

At the far end of the cut is **Garrison Church** (1848), the first church in Australia. Soldiers of the 50th Queen's Own Regiment once said their prayers in the church and the first prime minister of Australia, Edmund Barton, received his primary education in the parish hall that once stood here. Nearby are **Argyle Place** (an English-style village green), and the secular delights of the Lord Nelson Brewery and Hero of Waterloo hotels, which vie for the title of Sydney's oldest pub.

Further north at 53 Lower Fort St is the **Colonial House Museum** (☎ 9247 6008), a private house jam-packed with colonial-era furniture and knick-knacks. It's open from 10 am to 4.30 pm daily; admission is $1 (50c children).

Built in the 1850s, the historically and architecturally interesting **Sydney Observatory** (☎ 9217 0485) has a commanding position atop Observatory Hill overlooking Millers Point and the harbour. This was the second observatory to be built on the hill – the first was constructed in 1821. Before that, the hill's exposed position made it an ideal site for a windmill to grind wheat. The colony's first windmill was built here in

1796, but its canvas sails were stolen and the structure eventually collapsed.

The observatory has an interesting little museum with interactive displays and videos. Daytime admission is free; the observatory opens from 10 am to 5 pm daily. A small planetarium has shows weekends at 11.30 am and 3.30 pm ($2). The observatory also opens nightly at 6.15 and 8.15 pm for a tour of the building, video screenings and telescope viewing. These must be booked and cost $8/3 children.

Close by, the **National Trust Centre** (☎ 9258 0123) in the old military hospital houses the SH Ervin Gallery, which has changing exhibitions; it's open from 11 am to 5 pm Tuesday to Friday, from noon on weekends; admission is $6 ($3 concession).

The waterfront from Dawes Point to Darling Harbour was Sydney's busiest before container shipping and the construction of new port facilities at Botany Bay. Although Darling Harbour has been redeveloped, many wharves and warehouses around Dawes Point are in a state of decay. **Pier 1**, at the tip of Dawes Point, has been renovated, but is an under-used shopping and leisure complex. **Pier 4** (also known as Wharf Theatre) is home to the renowned Sydney Theatre and Sydney Dance companies. Tours of the theatre company are held at 10 am Thursday (or by appointment) and cost $5 – bookings are advisable (☎ 9250 1700 or inquire at the box office).

You can find the site of the **public gallows**, in use until 1804, and Sydney's first jail on Essex St. The Essex St gallows were given a second lease of life (so to speak) from 1820 to 1840 while the Darlinghurst Gaol was built.

See the Walking Tours section in this chapter for guided walks around the Rocks.

SYDNEY HARBOUR BRIDGE (MAPS 2 & 4)

From the northern end of the Rocks, the imposing 'old coat hanger' crosses the harbour at one of its narrowest points, linking the southern and northern shores and joining central Sydney with the satellite business district North Sydney. Although some people consider the bridge ugly, it has always been a popular icon, partly because of its sheer size, simplicity and symmetry; partly because of its function in uniting the city; and partly because it kept a lot of people in work during the Depression.

The two halves of the mighty arch were built out from each shore, supported by cranes. After nine years of work, when the ends of the arches were only centimetres apart and ready to be bolted together, a gale blew up and winds of over 100km/h set them swaying. But the bridge survived and the arch was soon completed.

The bridge cost $20 million, a bargain in modern terms, but took until 1988 to pay off! Normally giving it a new coat of paint takes 10 years, but the painting cycle was stepped up prior to the 2000 Olympics.

You can climb inside the south-eastern stone pylon, which houses the small **Harbour Bridge Museum** (☎ 9247 3408). It's open from 10 am to 5 pm daily ($2). The pylons supported the cranes used to build the bridge, but today they're purely decorative.

Cars, trains, cyclists, joggers and pedestrians use the bridge. At night there are also huge cockroaches and rats. The cycleway is on the western side, the pedestrian walkway

Opening the Bridge

The Harbour Bridge was opened in 1932 – twice. Before the NSW premier, Jack Lang, could cut the ribbon, a Captain de Groot charged up on horseback and cut it with his sword, declaring the bridge open on behalf of 'decent and loyal citizens'. The captain was a member of the New Guard, right-wing revolutionaries outraged that Lang was shepherding NSW through the Depression with socialist ideas, such as feeding the poor. After de Groot was led away, Lang opened the bridge on behalf of 'the people of New South Wales', 750,000 of whom were present.

on the eastern; stair access is from Cumberland St in the Rocks and near Milsons Point station on the North Shore.

The best way to experience the bridge is undoubtedly on foot; don't expect much of a view crossing by car or train. Driving south (only) there's a $2 toll; there's no toll in the other direction.

If you don't suffer from vertigo (and you can afford the steep fee), you can climb to the peak of the bridge itself with a guided tour group – see the boxed text 'City Views' in this chapter.

The bridge shares Sydney's voluminous trans-harbour traffic with the **Harbour Tunnel**. The tunnel begins about half a kilometre south of the Opera House, crosses under the harbour to the east of the bridge and meets the Warringah Freeway (the road leading north from the bridge) on the northern side. There's also a $2 southbound-only toll. Heading from the North Shore to the eastern suburbs, it's easier to use the tunnel; for Glebe, Pyrmont and Darling Harbour use the bridge.

SYDNEY OPERA HOUSE (MAP 4)

Australia's most recognisable icon sits dramatically on Bennelong Point on the eastern headland of Circular Quay. The Opera House's soaring shell-like roofs were actually inspired by palm fronds, but look a little like white turtles engaging in congress. Started in 1959, the Opera House was officially opened in 1973 after a tumultuous series of personality clashes, technical difficulties and delays.

It's truly memorable to see a performance here, visit the Sunday market or sit at an outdoor cafe and watch harbour life go by. The Opera House itself looks fine from any angle, but the view from a ferry coming into Circular Quay is one of the best.

The Opera House (☎ 9250 7777) has four main auditoriums and stages dance, theatre, concerts and films, as well as opera. There's also a new venue called The Studio, which stages contemporary arts events.

There are tours (☎ 9250 7250) of the building, and although the inside isn't as spectacular as the outside, they're worth taking. Tours are held daily every half hour (approximately, depending on what's happening) between 9 am and 4 pm for $12.90 ($8.90 children and students). Not all tours can visit all theatres at any given time because of the various activities taking place. You're more likely to see everything if you take a tour early in the day or go on a Sunday. There are also intermittent backstage tours ($20.90).

On Sunday there's a market near the front entrance selling Australian-made arts and crafts.

The bi-monthly *Opera House Diary* details forthcoming performances and is available free at the Opera House.

Buying a Ticket

The box office (☎ 9250 7777) opens from 9 am to 8.30 pm Monday to Saturday, 2½ hours before a Sunday performance. You can also book by fax (☎ 9251 3943) if you quote your credit card details (includes a $6 service fee); by writing to the Box Office Manager, Sydney Opera House, PO Box R239, Royal Exchange, 1225; or on-line at bookings@soh.nsw.gov.au. Children under five aren't admitted to most performances so check before you book.

Despite the price, popular operas sell out quickly, but there are often 'restricted view' tickets available for about $30. Some seats may have no view, which you might consider as an option for an opera performance. Decent seats to see a play or hear the Sydney Symphony Orchestra are more affordable from around $28. People under 27 qualify for 'Big Rush' rates – otherwise-empty seats to some performances cost $25 in advance, or $15 on the day.

The 'Sundays 'round the House' program offers some of the best deals, with a wide variety of events, and most tickets priced at $20.

CIRCULAR QUAY (MAP 4)

Circular Quay, built around Sydney Cove, is one of the city's focal points. Sydney Cove was the landing place of the First Fleet, and the first European settlement

The Soap Opera House

The hullabaloo surrounding construction of the Sydney Opera House was an operatic blend of personal vision, long delays, bitter feuding, cost blowouts and narrow-minded politicking.

The NSW government held an international design competition in 1956, which was won by Danish designer Jorn Utzon, with plans for a $7 million building. Construction of Utzon's unique design began in 1959, but the project soon became a nightmare of cost overruns and construction difficulties. After political interference and disagreements with his consultants about construction methods, Utzon quit in disgust in 1966, leaving a consortium of three Australian architects to design a compromised interior. The parsimonious state government financed the eventual $102 million cost in true-blue Aussie fashion through a series of lotteries. The building was completed in 1973.

After all the brawling and political bickering, the first public performance staged was, appropriately, Prokofiev's *War & Peace*. The preparations were a debacle and a possum appeared on stage during one of the dress rehearsals.

In 1995, the resident Opera Australia staged *The Eighth Wonder*, dramatising the events surrounding the building of the Opera House.

grew around the Tank Stream, which now runs underground into the harbour near Wharf 6.

The quay was created by a huge landfill built using convict labour between 1837 and 1844 and was originally called Semi Circular Quay. In the 1850s it was extended further, covering the Tank Stream, and was given its present name. Circular Quay was for many years the shipping centre of Sydney; early photographs and paintings show a forest of masts crowding the skyline. Today it's both a commuting hub and a recreational space.

There's no finer way of getting around Sydney than by ferry, and waiting for one on Circular Quay among the crowds and the buskers is an experience in itself.

Circular Quay is the departure point for all harbour ferries, the starting point of many city bus routes, and is a train station on the City Circle. It has ferry and bus information booths, and a Countrylink Travel Centre (☎ 13 2232). The elevated Cahill Expressway, running above Alfred St behind the ferry wharves, rather isolates the quay from the rest of the city.

Circular Quay East runs out beside the Royal Botanical Gardens to Bennelong Point with the Opera House perched on the end. Along Circular Quay West is the small **First Fleet Park**, a good place to pause after pounding the pavements; the **Overseas Passenger Terminal**, where liners moor; and the little bay of **Campbells Cove**, backed by the low-rise Park Hyatt Sydney.

The **Museum of Contemporary Art** (MCA, ☎ 9241 5892, 9252 4033), 140 George St fronting Circular Quay West, is set in a stately Art Deco building. It has a fine collection of modern art, and temporary exhibitions of the sublime and the ridiculous. It's open from 10 am to 6 pm Wednesday to Monday (closes 4 pm in winter); admission is $6 ($4 children). There are discounts for YHA, VIP and ISIC cardholders. The MCA bookshop has good postcards, and the cafe serves classy food.

Customs House

Built in 1885, the grand old Customs House (☎ 9247 2285) on Alfred St has been totally re-vamped, and now houses an impressive arts and cultural centre. The Djamu gallery (☎ 9320 6429) features works by contemporary Aboriginal, Torres Strait Islander and Pacific artists; the Object gallery showcases modern art, craft and design. Upstairs is the City Exhibition Space, with a huge scale model of Sydney, and other exhibits documenting the changing face of the city.

The Writers' Walk

Every day at Circular Quay, thousands of feet pass over an odd but interesting collection of musings. Set into the promenade alongside the wharves is a series of round metal plaques – a selection of ruminations from a handful of Australian writers (and the odd literary visitor), reflecting on the place they call home.

Contributors include internationally acclaimed art critic and historian Robert Hughes; feminist, academic and author Germaine Greer; and writers Thea Astley, Peter Carey, Dorothy Hewitt and James A Michener.

Subjects range from indigenous rights and identity, to the paradoxical nature of glass; offerings range from eloquent poems addressing the human condition, to an irreverent ditty about a meat pie by Barry Humphries (associate of the famous Dame Edna Everage).

Several of the writers are Australians now living overseas. A wistful entry from the expatriate (and apparently homesick) author and entertainer Clive James reads:

> In Sydney Harbour the yachts will be racing on the crushed diamond water under a sky the texture of powdered sapphires. It would be churlish not to concede that the same abundance of natural blessings which gave us the energy to leave has every right to call us back.

SIMON BRACKEN

There are also gallery shops and eateries. It's open from 7 am to 5 pm daily. Entry is free, except for entry to the Djamu gallery, which costs $8 ($5 YHA, $2 children).

MACQUARIE PLACE & AROUND (MAP 4)

Narrow lanes lead south from Circular Quay towards the city centre. At the corner of Loftus and Bridge Sts, under the shady Moreton Bay figs in Macquarie Place, are a cannon and anchor from the First Fleet flagship, HMS *Sirius*. Other pieces of **colonial memorabilia** in this interesting square include gas lamps, an ornate drinking fountain dating from 1857, a National Trust-classified gentlemen's convenience (not open) and an obelisk, erected in 1818, indicating road distances in miles to various points in the nascent colony.

The square has some pleasant outdoor cafes and is overlooked by the rear façade of the imposing 19th century **Lands Department building**, on Bridge St, with its statues of surveyors, explorers and politicians.

Museum of Sydney

The excellent Museum of Sydney (☎ 9251 5988), 37 Phillip St, is east of Martin Place, on the site of the colony's first and infamously fetid Government House (built in 1788). The museum uses installation and multiple-perspective art to explore Sydney's early history – including the early natural environment, the culture of the indigenous Eora people and convict life. It's open from 9.30 am to 5 pm daily; admission is $6 ($3 children).

Justice & Police Museum

Designed by colonial architect James Barnet, and completed in 1886, the museum (☎ 9252 1144) is in the old Water Police Station at 8 Phillip St. It was in use until 1979 and is now set up as a late-19th century police station and court. It has various exhibits on criminal activity, once a major industry in the nearby Rocks. You can even take part in mock trials. The museum only opens from 10 am to 5 pm weekends; admission is $6 ($3 children, ISIC and YHA members).

CITY CENTRE (MAPS 4 & 8)

Central Sydney stretches from Circular Quay in the north to Central station in the south. The business hub is towards the northern end near Circular Quay, but most redevelopment is occurring at the southern end and this is gradually shifting the focus of the city.

Sydney lacks a true civic centre, but **Martin Place** lays claim to the honour, if only by default. This grand pedestrian mall extends from Macquarie St to George St and is lined by the monumental buildings of financial institutions and the colonnaded, Victorian, former general post office (GPO). The Commonwealth Bank on the corner of Martin Place and Elizabeth St, and the Westpac on George St opposite the western end of Martin Place, have impressive old banking chambers.

The street has a couple of fountains, plenty of public seating and an amphitheatre – a popular lunchtime entertainment spot, especially during January's Festival of Sydney, when there's free entertainment daily.

Near the George St end of Martin Place is the **Cenotaph** commemorating Australia's war dead. This is where Sydney's Christmas tree is placed, in December's summer heat.

Barrack St, west of Martin Place, another pedestrian area, has fruit barrows and good views of Martin Place and the GPO. East of Martin Place are the delightful historic buildings of **Macquarie St** and the parks and gardens of the city centre's eastern edge (these are detailed later).

The huge, sumptuous **Queen Victoria Building** (QVB), next to Town Hall, takes up the entire block bordered by George, Market, York and Druitt Sts. It houses about 200 shops, cafes and restaurants. It was built in 1898, in the style of a Byzantine palace, to house the city's fruit and vegetable market. They don't build markets like this any more! There are guided tours (☎ 9265 6864) twice daily. Outside the QVB is an imposing statue of Queen Victoria herself, and nearby is a wishing well featuring a small bronze statue of her beloved pooch, Islay (which, quite disconcertingly, speaks aloud in a deep baritone).

A few blocks south, the old civic locus used to be the plaza containing Town Hall and St Andrew's Cathedral, but traffic and insensitive development have diminished the area's authority. The ornate exterior of Town Hall (1874), on the corner of George and Druitt Sts, is matched by the elaborate chamber room and concert hall inside. The concert hall houses an impressive organ and is a venue for free, monthly lunchtime concerts (☎ 9265 9007). Across the open space to the south, **St Andrew's Cathedral** (☎ 9265 1661), dating from the same period, is the oldest cathedral in Australia. At the time of writing it was being restored, but free organ recitals will recommence upon completion.

Opposite the QVB, underneath the Hilton Hotel and the Royal Arcade, is the **Marble Bar**, an extravagant piece of Victoriana. The bar was built by George Adams, the founder of Tattersalls lotteries. When the old Adams Hotel was torn down to build the Hilton, the bar was carefully dismantled and reassembled. The city's other ostentatious building is the splendidly gothic **State Theatre**, to the north at 49 Market St. It was originally built as a movie palace during Hollywood's heyday and is now a National Trust-classified building. Except during the Sydney Film Festival in June, it stages only live shows. Tours of the opulent interior (☎ 9373 6660) run Tuesday to Sunday, and cost $12/$8.

On Pitt St, a block south of Martin Place, is the busy **Pitt St Mall**, with shopping arcades and department stores nearby. The lovingly restored **Strand Arcade**, which houses speciality shops and designers, runs west off the mall to George St. On the eastern side of the mall is the modern **Skygarden** arcade; take the long 'express' escalator straight to the top. **Centrepoint**, at the bottom of the Sydney Tower (see the 'City Views' boxed text in this chapter), is another large complex. Two large department stores, Grace Brothers and the more upmarket David Jones, are nearby on Market St. Gowings, on the corner of Market and George Sts, is an old-fashioned-style department store for men and boys.

To the south-west are the lively **Chinatown** and the much smaller **Spanish Town**. Chinatown, west of George St between Liverpool and Quay Sts, is a colourful and bustling area, encompassing Dixon St and **Haymarket**, and the restored Paddy's Markets. Spanish Town is along Liverpool St between George and Sussex Sts. A block east, **World Square**, once a big hole in the ground, is slowly taking shape. See Map 4 for World Square monorail station.

The dynamism of this part of the city is spreading south to breathe life back into the zone around **Central station** (1906) and **Railway Square** at the intersection of Broadway, George and Regent Sts on the city centre's southern periphery. At the turn of the 20th century, this was Sydney's business district. Running beneath Central from Railway Square is a long pedestrian subway, emerging at Devonshire St in Surry Hills. It's usually crowded with commuters (and buskers), but late at night it can be spooky.

DARLING HARBOUR & PYRMONT (MAP 4)

This huge, waterfront leisure park on the city centre's western edge was once a thriving dockland area with factories, warehouses and shipyards lining Cockle Bay. In a state of decline for many years, it was reinvented and opened in 1988. It hasn't been the success that was hoped for, though further developments like Darling Walk and the snazzy new wining-and-dining precinct of Cockle Bay Wharf will no doubt attract more visitors. Facing Harbourside across the water, it comprises a concentrated cluster of mostly upmarket eateries and bars, with a shop or two in between.

The Harbourside shopping centre has recently undergone a $50 million face-lift, and although this is the supposed centrepiece, the real attractions are the aquarium, the state-of-the-art Powerhouse Museum, the IMAX Theatre, and the lovely Chinese Garden.

Darling Harbour Visitors Centre (☎ 9286 0111), under the elevated freeway near the IMAX Theatre, opens daily during business hours. You can also call the Infoline (☎ 1902 260 568) for recorded information about activities and events.

Although the complex covers a large area it's possible to see it all on foot. If you're bent on seeing everything, consider the Darling Harbour Superticket ($29.95, $19.50 children), which gives you a harbour cruise, entry to the aquarium and Chinese Garden, a restaurant meal, a monorail ride and a discount on a tour of Sydney Olympic Park. You can buy the Superticket at the aquarium, monorail stations, the Chinese Garden or through Matilda Cruises (☎ 9264 7377); it's valid for one month.

Harbourside

This large, graceful structure, faintly reminiscent of public buildings from the reign of Queen Victoria, is basically a shopping mall. Most shops are open from 10 am to 9 pm daily. One of the main attractions is **Gavala** (☎ 9212 7232), which, as well as exhibiting Aboriginal arts and crafts, puts on cultural performances including traditional dancing and didgeridoo playing.

Harbourside (☎ 9281 3999) is close to Pyrmont Bridge (the old bridge that crosses Cockle Bay), a short walk west from the city centre via Market St, and it is also a stop on the monorail.

Sydney Aquarium

This aquarium (☎ 9262 2300), displaying the richness of Australian marine life, consists of three 'oceanariums' moored in the harbour, with sharks, rays and big fish in one, Sydney Harbour marine life and seals in the others. There are also transparent underwater tunnels and informative, well-presented exhibits of freshwater fish and coral gardens.

The aquarium is near the eastern end of Pyrmont Bridge and opens from 9.30 am to 9 pm daily; admission is $15.90 ($8 children, $36.90 family).

Australian National Maritime Museum

It's not hard to spot the maritime museum (☎ 9552 7777) at the western end of Pyrmont Bridge, with its billowing, sail-like roofs echoing the roof shapes of the Opera House. The museum tells the story of Australia's relationship with the sea, from Aboriginal canoes and the First Fleet to surf culture and the America's Cup.

Vessels moored at the wharves and awaiting exploration include a racing yacht, a Vietnamese refugee boat and the naval destroyer HMAS *Vampire*. There's an audiovisual display of sailing life, maritime craft demonstrations and entertainment.

The admission price varies depending on how much you want to see. To see the lot – the museum, HMAS *Vampire* and the moored vessels – costs $9 ($4.50 concession, $19.50 family, children under 15 free). Prices include guided tours, which take place on the hour 10 am to 3 pm daily. The complex opens from 9.30 am to 5 pm daily.

Powerhouse Museum

Sydney's most spectacular museum (☎ 9217 0111), 500 Harris St, is housed in a vast building that was once the power station for Sydney's now-defunct trams.

The museum covers the decorative arts, social history, science and technology with exhibits on anything from costume jewellery to space capsules. The superbly displayed collections emphasise interaction and education through enjoyment, with video and computer activities, experiments, performances, demonstrations and films. There are a variety of free tours, including a tour of the museum's highlights at 1.30 pm weekdays. Guided tours in a community language can be booked by phoning ☎ 9217 0495.

The museum opens from 10 am to 5 pm daily. Admission is $8 ($2 children, $18 family); entry is free the first Saturday of every month.

IMAX Theatre

The IMAX Theatre (☎ 9281 3300) with its yellow-and-black chequered façade rises up between two elevated freeways. It shows eye-popping, 45-minute feature films on its giant six storey screen daily on the hour 9 am to 10 pm, but it's not cheap – admission costs $13.95 ($9.95 children). The films are so realistic that there's a sign warning patrons that they may experience physical discomfort.

Chinese Garden

The exquisite 10-hectare Chinese Garden (☎ 9281 6863/0111), the biggest outside China, is an oasis of tranquillity. It was designed by landscape architects from NSW's Chinese sister province, Guangdong, to commemorate Australia's bicentenary in 1988.

After entering through the Courtyard of Welcoming Fragrance you'll see distinct geographical features including mini mountains, wilderness, forest and a lake, interspersed with pavilions, waterfalls and lush plants. Round off the experience with tea and Chinese cakes in the teahouse (open 10 am to 5 pm) overlooking the lotus pond.

The garden opens from 9.30 am to sunset daily; admission is $4 ($2 children).

Australia's Northern Territory & Outback Centre

This centre is both a tourist agency for the Northern Territory region, and a retail outlet for Aboriginal artefacts and Australiana-type goods. Objects of interest include woomeras (spears), *kalis* (jumbo-sized boomerangs), musical clap sticks and bull-roarers. It's next to Segaworld and is open daily (☎ 9283 7477).

Tumbalong Park & Around

The pleasant grassy area in the centre of the Darling Harbour complex is Tumbalong Park. The park has an amphitheatre that hosts free entertainment most lunchtimes and on weekends.

The **Sydney Convention Centre** and the **Sydney Exhibition Centre** on the western edge of the park were designed by Australian architect Philip Cox, who also designed the aquarium, the maritime museum and the Sydney Football Stadium. The centres' roofs are suspended from steel masts, continuing Darling Harbour's maritime theme.

South of the Chinese Garden, the old pumphouse that used to supply hydraulic power to Sydney's lifts is now the **Pumphouse Tavern Brewery**, which brews its own beer. Further south again, on the edge of Chinatown, is the **Sydney Entertainment Centre**, a venue for rock concerts and sporting events.

Darling Walk, on the eastern side of the park, is a new development containing **Sega World** (☎ 9273 9273), Australia's first indoor theme park. It uses the latest in computer graphics and virtual technologies and there are live stage shows. Beneath Sega World is a complex with cafes, restaurants, shops and a performing-arts space.

Motor Vehicle Museum

The Motor Vehicle Museum (☎ 9552 1210), Level 1, 320 Harris St, is a short walk from the Powerhouse Museum. It has over 175 vehicles on display, from vintage beauties to Morris Minors. It's open from 10 am to 5 pm Wednesday to Sunday and school holidays; admission is $10 ($5 children).

Star City Casino Complex

Built near the waterfront in Pyrmont on the north-eastern headland of Darling Harbour, the new casino complex offers the usual gaudy assortment of 24-hour gambling rooms, shops and theme bars, as well as two large theatres (the Lyric and the Showroom), a nightclub and a five-star hotel. For information call ☎ 9657 8393 or toll-free ☎ 1800 700 700.

Pyrmont Fish Markets (Map 9)

Fish auctions are held on weekdays at these markets west of Darling Harbour on the corner of Pyrmont Bridge Rd and Bank St, beside the approach roads to Glebe Island Bridge. They begin at 5.30 am and last from three to six hours, depending on the size of the catch. The complex includes fabulous fish shops, fruit and vegetable stalls, delis and several eateries.

Call ☎ 9660 1611 for information about these tours.

Getting There & Around

The two main pedestrian approaches to Darling Harbour are footbridges from Market and Liverpool Sts. The one from Market St leads onto the lovely old Pyrmont Bridge, a pedestrian and monorail-only route that crosses Cockle Bay. It was famous in its day as the first electrically operated swing span bridge in the world.

Town Hall is the closest train station, from where it's a short walk down either Druitt or Market Sts.

Monorail The monorail (☎ 9552 2288) circles Darling Harbour and links it to the city centre. Some say its steel track, winding round the streets at 1st-floor level ruins some of Sydney's best vistas, but the initial fuss has died down. As a transport system, the monorail isn't great, but for sightseeing it's worth $3 ($6 for the whole day). Get off at Haymarket for the Powerhouse Museum or at Harbourside for Harbourside shopping centre, the National Maritime Museum and Pyrmont Bridge.

Bus & Train Bus No 456 connects Circular Quay with the Powerhouse Museum and the casino. The Sydney Explorer bus (see the Getting Around chapter) stops at five points around Darling Harbour every 20 minutes.

The light-rail transit (read tram) system runs from Central station to Darling Harbour and Pyrmont. A one-way fare is $2, return $3.

Ferry State Transit Authority (STA) ferries leave Circular Quay's Wharf 5 every 30 minutes from 8 am to 7.30 pm weekdays (til 10 pm weekends), and cost $3.20 ($1.60 children) per trip. They stop at Darling Harbour's Aquarium wharf, and the Pyrmont

Bay wharf near the casino. Matilda Cruises (☎ 9264 7377) operates the Darling Harbour Rocket ferry, which leaves the Harbourmaster's Steps at Circular Quay West every 20 minutes ($3.25/1.60).

People Mover The People Mover (☎ 018 290 515) is an incongruous, trackless, toy-town style mini-train that makes a 20 minute loop around Darling Harbour's sights from 10 am to 5 pm for $2.50 (children $1.50).

MACQUARIE ST (MAP 4)

Sydney's greatest concentration of early public buildings graces Macquarie St, which runs along the eastern edge of the city from Hyde Park to the Opera House. The street is named after Governor Lachlan Macquarie, who was the first governor to have a vision of the city extending beyond a convict colony. In the early 19th century he commissioned convicted forger Francis Greenway to design a series of public buildings. There are excellent views of Greenway's buildings from the 14th-floor cafeteria of the Law Courts building, on the corner of Macquarie St and Queens Square.

Hyde Park Barracks Museum & St James Church

These two Greenway gems, on Queens Square at the northern end of Hyde Park, face each other across Macquarie St. The barracks (1819) were built originally as convict quarters, then became an immigration depot and later a women's asylum. They now house a museum that concentrates on

City Views

The most elevated view in Sydney is from **Sydney Tower** (☎ 9231 1000), the 300-metre needle soaring from the Centrepoint shopping centre on the corner of Market and Pitt Sts. The views extend west to the Blue Mountains and east to the ocean, as well as to the streets of inner Sydney below. The tower is open daily from 9 am to 10.30 pm (11.30 pm on Saturday); entry costs $10 ($8 concession). To get to the tower, enter Centrepoint from Market St and take the lift to the podium level where you buy your ticket.

The **Harbour Bridge** offers excellent views. You can get onto the bridge from a stone staircase off Cumberland St in the Rocks or from near Milsons Point train station on the North Shore. A footpath runs right across. If the view from the footpath isn't enough, you can climb the 200 stairs inside the south-east pylon for panoramic views of the harbour and city. For the intrepid view-seeker, Bridgeclimb (☎ 9252 0077) offers a breath-taking 1500-metre climb to the top of the bridge for $98 during the week, $120 on the weekend. Wear rubber-soled shoes, and don't hit the bottle beforehand – you may be breath-tested!

For a sea-level view of the Opera House, harbour and bridge, walk to **Mrs Macquarie's Point**, at the headland east of the Opera House. The point has been a lookout since at least 1810, when Elizabeth Macquarie, wife of Governor Lachlan Macquarie, had a stone chair hewn into the rock so she could sit and watch ships entering the harbour and keep an eye on hubby's construction projects just across Farm Cove. The seat is still there today.

If you're in the vicinity of Kings Cross, the northern end of Victoria St in **Potts Point** is a good vantage point for views of the cityscape and its best-known icons, especially at night.

To get the best views of all, catch a **ferry** – the Manly ferries are especially good because they traverse the length of the harbour east of the Harbour Bridge. The ferries that travel west of the bridge (such as the Hunters Hill ferry) are also worth catching, both for the experience of cruising under the bridge and to see the narrow waterways humming with workday activity.

the barracks' history and provides an interesting perspective on Sydney's social history. The museum (☎ 9223 8922) opens from 9.30 am to 5 pm daily; admission is $6 ($3 children).

St James (1819-24) was restored in the 1950s. It contains traditional stained glass, but also the more modern, striking 'creation window' in the Chapel of the Holy Spirit.

Sydney Mint Museum

This lovely building (1816) housing the Sydney Mint Museum was originally the southern wing of the infamous Rum Hospital. It was commissioned by Macquarie in 1814 and became a branch of the Royal Mint in 1854, the first to be established outside London. The museum has exhibits on the gold rush, coins, stamps, minting and a collection of decorative arts. At the time of writing, it was closed for renovations, but there are plans to reopen it. For inquiries, call the Historic Houses Trust (☎ 9692 8366).

Parliament House

Parliament House (1810), used by the Legislative Council of the colony from 1829, is still used by the NSW Parliament. This elegant two storey, sandstone, verandaed building was originally the northern wing of the Rum Hospital and is the world's oldest continually operating parliament building. It's open from 9 am to 4 pm weekdays; admission is free. There are free tours (☎ 9230 2111) at 10, 11 am and 2 pm on non-sitting weekdays. The public gallery is open on sitting days; question time is at 2.15 pm, Tuesday to Thursday.

Sydney Hospital & Sydney Eye Hospital

Just south of Parliament House is the country's oldest hospital (☎ 9382 7111). Dating from the early 1880s, it was the site of the first Nightingale school, and the home of nursing in Australia. In front of the hospital is the bronze **Little Boar**, a copy of a statue in Florence, with water dripping from its mouth. Rubbing its polished snout – coupled with a donation that goes to the hospital – is said to grant you a wish. There's a pleasant cafe in the hospital courtyard.

State Library of NSW

The state library (☎ 9273 1414) is more of a cultural centre than a traditional library. It has one of the best collections of early works on Australia, including Captain Cook's and Joseph Banks' journals, and Captain Bligh's log from the *Bounty*. The library's exhibition galleries open from 9 am to 5 pm weekdays, 11 am to 5 pm weekends.

Conservatorium of Music

The conservatorium (☎ 9351 1222), at the northern end of Macquarie St, was built by Greenway as the stables and servants' quarters of Macquarie's planned new government house. However, Macquarie was replaced as governor before the rest of the new house could be finished. Greenway's life ended in poverty because he couldn't recoup the money he had invested in the building.

The building was closed for renovations at the time of writing, but should reopen in early 2001. Meanwhile, the conservatorium's students continue to fine-tune their jazz, classical music and singing at a temporary location, and host concerts at venues around the city – including the popular, free 'Lunchbreak' series (1.10 pm Tuesday during term time) at St Andrew's Cathedral next to Town Hall.

Other Things to See

History House, at 133 Macquarie Street, is a Victorian townhouse built in 1853 which now houses the Royal Australian Historical Society. The **Royal College of Physicians** building, just up the street, is one of the last surviving verandaed Georgian townhouses in the city.

ROYAL BOTANIC GARDENS (MAP 4)

The Royal Botanic Gardens encompass Farm Cove, the first bay east of Circular Quay. It has a magnificent collection of South Pacific plant life; an old-fashioned, formal rose garden; an arid garden featuring cacti and succulents; and a dark, dank bat colony complete with upside-down mammals. The visitors centre (☎ 9231 8125) opens from 9.30 am to 4.30 pm daily.

The gardens were established in 1816, and include the site of the colony's first vegetable patch. There's a fabulous tropical display housed in the interconnecting Arc and Pyramid glasshouses, which are open from 10 am to 4 pm daily. It's a great place to visit on a cool, grey day. The multistorey Arc has a collection of rampant climbers and trailers from the world's rainforests, while the Pyramid houses the Australian collection, including monsoonal, woodland and tropical rainforest plants – although at the time of writing, the Pyramid Glasshouse was closed for repairs (the $2 entry fee will rise when it reopens).

The gardens open daily from sunrise to sunset. Free guided walks leave daily at 10.30 am from the visitors centre and are extremely informative.

The Trackless Train (similar to Darling Harbour's People Mover) does a circuit of the gardens for $3 ($2 children).

THE DOMAIN (MAP 4)

The Domain is a large, grassy area south of Macquarie St, which was set aside by Governor Phillip in 1788 for public recreation. It also contained Australia's first farm. It's separated from the Royal Botanic Gardens by the Cahill Expressway, but you can cross the expressway on the Art Gallery Rd bridge.

Today, it's used by workers for lunchtime sports and as a place to escape the bustle of the city. It's the Sunday-afternoon gathering place for impassioned soapbox speakers who do their best to entertain or enrage their listeners. Free events are staged here during the Festival of Sydney in January, as is the popular Carols by Candlelight at Christmas. The Domain is also the venue for the Tropfest film festival (see Free Entertainment in the Entertainment chapter).

ART GALLERY OF NSW (MAP 4)

The Art Gallery of NSW (☎ 9225 1744) is in the north-eastern corner of the Domain, a short walk from the city centre. It has an excellent permanent display of Australian, European, Japanese and tribal art, and has some inspired temporary exhibits. It was built in 1880, but has modern extensions discreetly moulded into the hillside.

It's open from 10 am to 5 pm daily, and free guided tours are held at 1 and 2 pm; Tuesday to Friday there are also tours at 11 am and 12 pm. Tours of the Aboriginal and Torres Strait Island gallery run at 11 am Tuesday to Friday, and there's a free Aboriginal dance performance at 12 pm Tuesday to Saturday. Admission is free, but you have to pay to see some temporary exhibitions.

AUSTRALIAN MUSEUM (MAP 4)

Established only 40 years after the First Fleet dropped anchor, the Australian Museum (☎ 9320 6000), 6 College St across from Hyde Park, is a natural history museum with an excellent Australian wildlife collection. One gallery traces Aboriginal history and Dreamtime.

Guided 30-minute tours occur on the hour from 10 am to 4 pm. There are also plenty of activities to keep children amused. The museum opens from 9.30 am to 5 pm daily; admission is $5 ($2 children, $12 family).

HYDE PARK & AROUND (MAP 4)

The pleasant Hyde Park is large enough to offer a break from traffic and crowds, but retains a city feel.

At the northern end is the richly symbolic Art Deco **Archibald Memorial Fountain**. Sidney Archibald, founding editor of *Bulletin* magazine, bequeathed the fountain to the city. The statues are from Greek mythology. Near Liverpool St, at the southern end, is the dignified **Anzac Memorial** (1934), which has a small free exhibition of photographs and exhibits covering the wars Australians have fought in. There are tours at 11.30 am and 1.30 pm daily. Some pines near the memorial were grown from seeds gathered at Gallipoli.

St Mary's Cathedral (1882), across College St from the park's north-eastern corner, took 14 years to build. Despite lacking spires, and though you can hardly tell from outside, it's one of the largest cathedrals in the world. A free tour of the cathedral and crypt is held at noon Sunday, departing from the College St entrance.

The impressive 1873 **Great Synagogue** (☎ 9267 2477) is diagonally opposite St Mary's, across the park on Elizabeth St north of Park St. A free 45 minute tour takes place at noon Tuesday and Thursday from the entrance at 166 Castlereagh St.

There's an entrance to **Museum station** in the south-western corner of Hyde Park, near the park cafe. Many people dislike it, others find it a charming period piece. It depends on whether those dim tunnels of glazed tiles remind you of film noir or a public toilet. Museum station and nearby renovated St James date from the 1920s and were Sydney's first underground stations.

KINGS CROSS & AROUND (MAPS 5 & 6)

The Cross is a bizarre cocktail of strip joints, prostitution, crime and drugs, peppered with a handful of classy restaurants, designer cafes, upmarket hotels and backpacker hostels. It attracts an interesting mix of lowlife, sailors, travellers, inner-city trendies, tourists by the bus-load, and suburbanites looking for a big night out.

The Cross has always been a bit raffish, from its early days as a centre of bohemianism to the Vietnam War era, when it became the vice centre of Australia. Today, the Cross retains its risqué aura, with a hint of menace and more than a touch of sleaze. Sometimes the razzle-dazzle has a sideshow appeal; sometimes walking up Darlinghurst Rd, the main drag, can be an unappetising experience. On a Friday or Saturday night in particular, it pays to watch where you're putting your feet.

However, there's much more to this insomniac region than sleaze. It's the travellers' headquarters of Sydney, with many people beginning and ending their Australian travels here. It has Australia's greatest concentration of hostels and late-night Internet cafes; weary travellers can even pull up a milk crate along Darlinghurst road for a (therapeutic) Chinese massage. There are also many good (and increasingly trendy) places to eat, and plenty of entertainment that doesn't involve the sex industry. You don't have to walk far from the neon lights to find gracious old terraces in tree-lined streets.

Darlinghurst Rd is the trashy main drag. It dog-legs into Macleay St, which continues into the more salubrious suburb of Potts Point. Most hostels are on Victoria St, which diverges from Darlinghurst Rd north of William St, near the iconic Coca-Cola sign.

The Cross is a good place to swap information and buy or sell things. Noticeboards can be found in hostels, shops and along Victoria St. At Kings Cross Car Market (☎ 9358 5000), on the corner of Ward Ave and Elizabeth Bay Rd, travellers buy and sell vehicles.

The most notable landmark in Kings Cross is the thistle-like **El Alamein Fountain** in the brick-paved Fitzroy Gardens. The fountain is known locally as 'the elephant douche'. Bunkered down behind the fountain is a fortress-like police station (☎ 9265 6233).

Nearby, to the north, in the suburb of Elizabeth Bay is the 1839 **Elizabeth Bay House** (☎ 9358 2344), 7 Onslow Ave. Once known as 'the finest house in the colony', it was meticulously restored by the Historic Houses Trust, and has fine views of the harbour. It was designed in English neoclassical revival style for the then colonial secretary of NSW, Alexander Macleay. It has been refurbished with early 19th century furniture, and the original colour scheme has been reproduced. The house opens from 10 am to 4.30 pm Tuesday to Sunday; admission costs $6 ($3 children, $15 family).

The suburb of **Woolloomooloo**, wedged between the city and the Cross and affectionately known as 'the loo', is one of Sydney's older areas. It's crammed with narrow streets and was run-down in the early 70s, but was given a face-lift and is now a pleasant place to explore.

On Cowper Wharf Roadway is **Harry's Cafe de Wheels**, the famous Woolloomooloo pie cart, which has been open since 1945. Nearby is the Fingerpoint Wharf, jutting into Woolloomooloo Bay, which is being redeveloped into a residential, shopping, hotel and entertainment complex. Opposite is the innovative **Artspace** gallery.

Getting There & Away

The simplest way to get to the Cross is on a CityRail eastern suburbs train from Martin Place, Town Hall or Central station. It's the first stop outside the city loop on the line to Bondi Junction.

The STA's Airport Express bus No 350 runs to Kings Cross, as does the private Kingsford Smith Transport (see the Getting Around chapter). From Circular Quay, bus Nos 200, 323-327, and 333 (a free service) run to Kings Cross; from Railway Square take bus No 311.

You can walk from Hyde Park along William St in 15 minutes. A longer, more interesting route involves crossing the Domain, crossing the pedestrian bridge behind the Art Gallery of NSW, walking past Woolloomooloo's wharf and climbing McElhone Stairs to the northern end of Victoria St.

INNER EAST (MAPS 7 & 8)

The lifeblood of Darlinghurst, Surry Hills and Paddington, **Oxford St** is a strip of shops, cafes, bars and nightclubs, and is one of the more happening places for late-night action. Its flamboyance and spirit are largely attributed to its vibrant and vocal gay community, and the route of the Sydney Gay & Lesbian Mardi Gras parade passes this way.

The main drag of Oxford St runs from the south-eastern corner of Hyde Park to the north-western corner of Centennial Park, though it continues in name into Bondi Junction. Taylor Square, at the junction of Oxford, Flinders and Bourke Sts, is the hub of social life in the area. (Be warned: tricky Oxford St street numbers restart west of the junction with South Dowling and Victoria Sts, on the Darlinghurst-Paddington border.) South-east of Taylor Square, Darlinghurst Rd and Victoria St run north off Oxford St to Kings Cross, while Oxford St continues on through Paddington and Woollahra, eventually reaching Bondi Junction. Bus Nos 380 and 382 from Circular Quay, and No 378 from Railway Square, run the length of the street.

Darlinghurst

Darlinghurst is the inner-city mecca for groovy young things wanting to be close to the action and the cafe lattes. It's a vital area of trendy, self-conscious, urban cool that's fast developing a cafe monoculture. There's no better way to soak up its studied ambience than to loiter in a few alfresco cafes and do as the others do. Darlinghurst encompasses the vibrant 'Little Italy' of Stanley St in East Sydney, and is wedged between Oxford and William Sts.

Facing Taylor Square is **Darlinghurst Courthouse** (1842) and behind it is the **Old Darlinghurst Gaol**, where author Henry Lawson was incarcerated several times for debt. He called it 'Starvinghurst' jail. Today it houses East Sydney TAFE College.

The **Sydney Jewish Museum** (Map 5, ☎ 9360 7999), 148 Darlinghurst Rd at the corner of Burton St, has exhibits on the holocaust and Australian Jewish history. It's open from 10 am to 4 pm Monday to Thursday, to 2 pm Friday, 11 am to 5 pm Sunday. Admission is $6 ($3 children).

Surry Hills

South of Darlinghurst, Surry Hills, squeezed between the east side of Central station and South Dowling St, is a former working class neighbourhood that's undergoing gentrification. Originally the centre of Sydney's rag trade and print media, it's an interesting multicultural area with some good cafes and restaurants, and a handful of funky boutiques and record stores. The main attraction is the **Brett Whitely Gallery** (☎ 9225 1881/1744), 2 Raper St, in a small lane in a quiet part of the suburb. The gallery, in the former studio of this renowned modern Australian painter, houses a selection of his paintings and drawings. It's open from 10 am to 4 pm weekends; admission is $6 ($4 children).

Surry Hills is a short walk south of Oxford St. Catch bus Nos 301-304, 390 or 391 from Circular Quay.

Paddington

Paddington, 4km east of the city centre, is an attractive inner-city residential area of leafy streets and tightly packed terrace houses. It was built for aspiring artisans in the later years of the Victorian era. During the lemming-like rush to the dreary outer suburbs after WWII, the area became a slum. A renewed interest in Victorian architecture, combined with a sudden recollection of the pleasures of inner-city life, led to the area's restoration during the 1960s. Today it's a fascinating jumble of beautifully restored terraces tumbling down steeply sloping streets. Paddington is a fine example of unplanned urban restoration, and it's full of trendy shops and restaurants, art galleries, bookshops and interesting people.

You can wander through Paddington's streets and winding laneways any time, although the best time is from around 10 am Saturday, when the **Paddington Village Bazaar**, in the grounds of the Uniting Church on the corner of Newcombe and Oxford Sts, is in full swing. The crowds are as interesting as the myriad stalls.

The magnificent, restored **Juniper Hall**, on Oxford St diagonally opposite Paddington Town Hall, was built by Robert Cooper as a family home in 1824, with profits from his gin business. He named it after the juniper berries from which he distilled his gin. It's owned by the National Trust but isn't open to the public.

There are free tours of the stately **Victoria Barracks** (☎ 9339 3000), on Oxford St between Oatley and Greens Rds; tours run at 10 am Thursday, and include a performance by the military band. The **Army Museum** is open between 10 am and 3 pm on Sunday (admission is free).

The **Australian Centre for Photography** (☎ 9331 6253), 257 Oxford St, has regular exhibitions on show.

The utilitarian **Moore Park**, south of Paddington, bordering Surry Hills, has a playing field; a walking, cycling and skating track; horse trail; a golf-driving range and grass skiing. It's also home to the historic **Sydney Cricket Ground** (SCG) and the **Sydney Football Stadium**. Sportspace (☎ 9380 0383) offers behind-the-scenes guided tours of the facilities, which include historic displays featuring great players (and commentators) associated with sports played there. Tours are held at 10 am, 1 and 3 pm daily (except on match days), and cost $18 ($12 for children) for 1½ hours.

Much of the former **Royal Agricultural Society's (RAS) Showgrounds** has been taken over by the new **Fox Studios** film and entertainment complex (☎ 9383 4000). As well as a professional film studio, the completed complex will include 16 Hoyts cinemas, a shopping and dining precinct, an outdoor live entertainment venue, and an interactive display area.

Centennial Park, Sydney's biggest park, is further east again, south of Woollahra. It has running, cycling and horse tracks, barbecue sites, football pitches and more. You can hire bikes and inline skates from several places on Clovelly Rd, Randwick, near the southern edge of the park, or hire horses ($35) from one of five stables situated around the park – contact the stable manager (☎ 9332 2809).

At the southern edge of the park is **Randwick Racecourse**, and south of there is the **University of NSW**. The university is on Anzac Parade, which becomes Flinders St and runs into Taylor Square. Many buses run along Anzac Parade, including No 336 from Circular Quay.

EASTERN SUBURBS (MAPS 5 & 7)

The harbourside suburbs east of Kings Cross are some of Sydney's most expensive. The main road through this area is New South Head Rd, the continuation of William St.

Darling Point, east of Rushcutters Bay, was a popular place for the city's first merchants to build mansions. Inland is the suburb of **Edgecliff**, centred on New South

Galleries

The Art Gallery of NSW and the Museum of Contemporary Art shouldn't be missed. Other galleries abound, especially in the inner eastern suburbs, where there is the highest concentration of art galleries in Australia.

The blue *Guide and Map to Art Galleries* is a free annual pamphlet with gallery listings, available from bookshops, cafes and galleries in the eastern suburbs. The *Sydney Morning Herald*'s Friday 'Metro' section lists galleries and art exhibitions, but for more detailed information look for the monthly *Art Almanac* ($2) at galleries and newsagents. Pick up a copy of *Paddington Galleries & Environs* from one of the many galleries in that suburb, or at the New Edition bookshop (☎ 9360 6913), 328 Oxford St, Paddington.

Galleries to look out for include the following:

Artspace
(☎ 9368 1899) The Gunnery, 43-51 Cowper Wharf Rd, Woolloomooloo. Open from 11 am to 6 pm Tuesday to Saturday; changing contemporary avant garde exhibitions.

Australian Centre for Photography
(☎ 9331 6253) 257 Oxford St, Paddington. Open from 11 am to 6 pm Tuesday to Sunday.

Australian Galleries
(☎ 9360 5177) 15 Roylston St, Paddington. Open from 10 am to 6 pm Tuesday to Saturday.

Boomalli Aboriginal Artists Co-operative
(☎ 9560 2541) 27 Abercrombie St, Chippendale. Open from 10 am to 5 pm Tuesday to Friday.

Brett Whitely Gallery
(☎ 9225 1744/1881) 2 Raper St, Surry Hills. Open from 10 am to 4 pm weekends.

The Cartoon Gallery
(☎ 9267 3022) Level 2, Queen Victoria Buillding (QVB). Open daily from 10 am to 5 pm (to 5 pm Sunday, to 9 pm Thursday); animation and comic strip art.

Coo-ee Aboriginal Art Gallery
(☎ 9332 1544) 98 Oxford St, Paddington. Open from 10 am to 6 pm Monday to Saturday and 11 am to 5 pm Sunday.

Ken Done Gallery
(☎ 9247 2740) 1 Hickson Rd. Open from 10 am to 5.30 pm daily; colourful, naive art by a popular designer.

Stills Gallery
(☎ 9331 7775) 36 Gosbell St, Paddington. Open from 11 am to 6 pm Wednesday to Saturday; photography.

Tin Sheds Gallery
(☎ 9351 3115) 154 City Rd, University of Sydney. Open from 11 am to 5 pm Monday to Saturday; contemporary.

Wagner Art Gallery
(☎ 9360 6069) 9 Gurner St, Paddington. Open from 11 am to 5.30 pm Tuesday to Saturday; famous Australian art.

Watters Gallery
(☎ 9331 2556) 109 Riley St, East Sydney. Open from 10 am to 5 pm Tuesday and Saturday, until 8 pm Wednesday to Friday; contemporary.

Wentworth Galleries
(☎ 9331 8633) 31 Norfolk St, Paddington. Open from 11 am to 5 pm Wednesday to Saturday; contemporary.

Head Rd. The wealthy harbourside suburb of **Double Bay** is further east. Double Bay's main shopping street is Bay St, which runs north off New South Head Rd and eventually leads to a quiet waterfront park and the ferry wharf. Double Bay is worth a visit.

There are plenty of cafes and patisseries that don't necessarily cost a fortune, and you can at least window shop for some designer clothes.

There's a small beach near the ferry wharf and a saltwater pool to the east, near Seven Shillings Beach. The latter is actually part of **Point Piper**, the headland that separates Double Bay from **Rose Bay**. Rose Bay has a pair of longer beaches visible at low tide, though people rarely swim here. It's also served by ferries. Inland behind the wharf area is the Royal Sydney Golf Course.

Rose Bay curves north onto the peninsula that forms the southern side of the entrance to Sydney Harbour. On the harbour side of the peninsula is **Vaucluse**, the most exclusive suburb of all. Vaucluse was a desirable address even in the colony's early days, but it's ironic that **Vaucluse House** (1828), one of its finest mansions, was built by William Wentworth, whose democratic leanings saw him outcast from high society (he suggested that Australian-born colonials were the equals of the English).

Vaucluse House (☎ 9337 1957) opens from 10 am to 4.30 pm Tuesday to Sunday; admission is $6 ($3 concession). Built in fine grounds in the Gothic Tudor style, it's an imposing, turreted example of 19th century Australiana. Catch bus No 325 from Circular Quay and get off a couple of stops past **Nielsen Park**, which is part of Sydney Harbour National Park.

Watsons Bay is nestled on the harbour side of the peninsula as it narrows towards South Head. On the ocean side is **the Gap**, a dramatic clifftop lookout. On the harbour north of Watsons Bay are the small fashionable beaches of **Camp Cove** and **Lady Bay**. At the tip of the peninsula is **South Head**, with great views across the harbour to North Head and Middle Head.

Getting There & Away

The closest suburb to a rail link is Double Bay, which is north-east of the Edgecliff train station on the eastern suburbs line. Take the New South Head Rd exit from the station, turn right and follow New South Head Rd to the nearby corner of Ocean Ave. Head down to the corner of Cooper St, which leads to Bay St. Alternatively, you could stay on New South Head Rd until you meet Bay St, but it's a less pleasant walk.

Ferries run from Circular Quay to Double Bay and Rose Bay and, on weekends, to Watsons Bay. See the Places to Eat chapter for information on private boats to Watsons Bay. Bus Nos 324 and 325 run from Circular Quay to Watsons Bay.

INNER WEST (MAPS 3 & 9)

Balmain & Birchgrove

Once a tough, working-class neighbourhood, Balmain attracted artists in the 1960s and has been prime real estate for some time, rivalling Paddington in Victorian-era trendiness. There's nothing special to do or see, but there are some good places to eat and pleasant walks.

William Balmain was a high achiever who arrived on the First Fleet, and within a decade was principal surgeon, a magistrate and collector of customs. He was rewarded with several land grants, including the 220 hectares of headland which bear his name.

Most construction in Balmain occurred between 1855 and 1890, although there are Georgian colonial and early Victorian houses still standing. Most streets worth visiting are north of Darling St, towards Birchgrove. A stroll around the wharf area at the end of Darling St, and through the park and the maze of tiny streets behind, is also worthwhile.

Darling St, Balmain's spine, runs the length of the peninsula. It has bookshops, restaurants, antique stores, bakeries and boutiques. There's a market every Saturday from 8.30 am to 4 pm at St Andrew's Congregational Church on Darling St.

The suburbs between Balmain and Glebe – **Annandale** and **Leichhardt** (its lesbian population dubs it 'dyke-heart') – also attract interesting people and have good eateries.

A major attraction when visiting Balmain is the journey on the Hunters Hill ferry from Circular Quay; it stops at Thames St, Darling St and Birchgrove wharves. Bus Nos 441, 442, 445 and 446 also come here.

Glebe

Glebe is south-west of the city centre, close to the University of Sydney. It has been going up the social scale in recent years, but still has a bohemian atmosphere. The main thoroughfare, Glebe Point Rd, runs the length of the suburb from Broadway to Glebe Point and offers affordable restaurants, recycled clothing shops and second-hand bookshops. (It also has the wonderful Valhalla Cinema, but screening has ceased, at least temporarily, and its future remains undecided.) There are several good places to stay, and its proximity to the city makes it an interesting alternative to the Cross.

The area has been inhabited since the First Fleet's chaplain was granted the first church land (or glebe), covering an area of 160 hectares. Around 1826, the Church of England sold the land to wealthy settlers, who built mansions. After 1855, church land was leased for building downmarket housing, and it was subdivided. A century later, the estate had deteriorated into slums. In the mid-1970s, the federal government bought the estate and rejuvenated the area for low-income families, many of whom had lived here for generations.

Glebe's **Buddhist Temple**, on Edward St, was built by Chinese immigrants who arrived in Australia during the 1850s goldrush, and has been fully restored by Sydney's Chinese community. It welcomes visitors, but remember that it's a holy place. At the northern tip of Glebe Point Rd is **Jubilee Park** with views across the bay to Rozelle and back towards the city.

Getting There & Away From the airport you can take the Kingsford Smith Transport (☎ 9667 3221) bus; from the city and Railway Square, bus Nos 431-4 run along Glebe Point Rd.

On foot, head south on George St and Broadway, turning right into Glebe Point Rd about a kilometre south-west of Central station. A more interesting daytime walk begins at Darling Harbour's Pyrmont Bridge, which leads to Pyrmont Bridge Rd. After passing Pyrmont Fish Markets (see under Darling Harbour & Pyrmont earlier) on Blackwattle Bay, follow the road past Wentworth Park. Turn right onto Burton St, and take the steps up to Ferry Rd, which leads into Glebe Point Rd. Turn left into Glebe Point Rd for shops and cafes, right for Jubilee Park.

A Balmain & Birchgrove Stroll

Balmain (Map 3) is full of pretty Victorian houses and offers interesting views of Sydney Harbour. To get a feel for this attractive suburb, begin on **Darling St**, the suburb's main thoroughfare, and turn north into Rowntree St. Follow Rowntree St to the junction with Ballast Point Rd. Turn right into Ballast Point Rd then left into Lemm St and follow it through to **Wharf Rd**, which has an attractive stretch of waterfront homes.

Follow Wharf Rd west, turn left into Grove St then right into The Terrace, which takes you through Birchgrove Park, then right into Rose St and right again into Louisa Rd. This road winds down to the Birchgrove wharf at **Yurulbin Point** and reserve. There are good views up the harbour towards the Harbour Bridge from the point. From here you can take a ferry back to Circular Quay.

Yurulbin Point used to be called Long Nose Point but the name was changed to acknowledge the Aboriginal heritage of the area. Yurulbin means 'swift running water'. This area was occupied by the Wangal clan, of which Bennelong is thought to have been a member.

Allow 45 minutes to walk from Darling St to Yurulbin Point.

Rozelle

This suburb lies across Rozelle Bay from Glebe. The main attraction around here is the **Sydney Maritime Museum Restoration Site** (☎ 9818 5388) at James Craig Rd, beside the bay. Moored here are two fully restored vessels, the *Lady Hopetoun*, a VIP yacht built in 1902, and the tugboat *Waratah*, from the same era. Undergoing restoration are the *John Oxley*, a large Scottish pilot boat dating from 1928, and the harbour ferry *Kanangra*, built early this century. The museum runs a 'Fish & Ships' tour of the vessels that includes a 20 minute boat trip across Blackwattle Bay to Pyrmont Fish Markets.

The site opens from 9 am to 4 pm Tuesday, Thursday and Saturday (later in summer); admission is free, but there's a donation box to help with restorations. Take bus No 440 from Circular Quay.

Newtown

Bordering the south of the University of Sydney, Newtown is a melting pot of social and sexual subcultures, students and home renovators. King St, its downbeat main drag, is packed with funky clothes stores, bookshops, cafes and Thai restaurants. The backstreets are full of aerosol graffiti art, the cafes full of creative types. While it's definitely moving up the social scale, Newtown comes with a healthy dose of grunge and political activism, and harbours several live-music venues. The best way to get there is by train, but bus Nos 355, 370, 422, 423, 426 and 428 from the city run along King St.

Leichhardt

Predominantly Italian, Leichhardt, south-west of Glebe, is increasingly popular with students, lesbians and young professionals. Its Italian eateries on Norton St have a city-wide reputation. Bus Nos 436-440 run here from the city.

INNER SOUTH (MAPS 8 & 9)

South-west of Central station, the small suburb of **Chippendale** is a maze of Victorian terrace houses – an unscrubbed version of Paddington. South of Railway Square, near the corner of Lee (George) and Regent Sts, is the quaint neo-Gothic **Mortuary Station**, where coffins and mourners once boarded funeral trains bound for Rookwood Cemetery, which is now in the city's western suburbs.

Chippendale borders the east of the **University of Sydney**, Australia's oldest tertiary institution. **Nicholson Museum** (☎ 9351 2812), in building A14 on the main quadrangle at the university, displays Greek, Assyrian, Egyptian and other antiquities. It's open from 8.30 am to 4.30 pm weekdays. Admission is free.

Redfern, south of Central station, but on the eastern side of the tracks, is one of the few inner suburbs to escape gentrification and remains predominantly working class. A few sections come close to slum conditions. Redfern tends to buck the system, and relations between the police and the community (especially the large Koori community) are at times bad. The suburb is also an area of Aboriginal self-reliance and defiance, with a strong sense of community; it has become something of a sanctuary from white authorities, but now has high drug abuse and crime rates.

Some of the restored workshops at the site of the former Eveleigh Locomotive Workshops, corner of Garden and Boundary Sts, are home to the National Technology Park and National Innovation Centre. Some of the buildings contain Victorian steam-powered blacksmithing equipment, used by Wrought Artworks (☎ 9319 6190) to manufacture artefacts. The curious can wander in and watch them at work.

BONDI BEACH (MAP 11)

Although it's Australia's most famous beach, Bondi Beach isn't as glamorous as tourist brochures might suggest. It's still largely working class and successive waves of migrants have made it their home. In recent years, it has become more fashionable and has received a huge face-lift. Today, its unique flavour is a blend of old Jewish and Italian communities, dyed-in-the-wool Aussies, New Zealand, Irish and UK expats, working travellers and devoted surfers, all bonded by their love for the beach.

Orientation & Information

Campbell Parade is the main beachfront road where most shops, hotels and cafes are located. The corner of Campbell Parade and Hall St is the hub. The main road into Bondi Beach is Bondi Rd, which branches off from Oxford St east of the mall in Bondi Junction. This is the same Oxford St that begins at Hyde Park and runs through Darlinghurst and Paddington.

The post office is on the corner of Jacques Ave and Hall St. A little further up Hall St, you enter a small Jewish area, with kosher shops and the Hakoah Club.

Although Bondi Beach is usually referred to simply as Bondi, the suburb of Bondi is actually inland, between Bondi Junction and Bondi Beach.

The beach itself will be the venue for the beach volleyball competitions at the 2000 Olympics, but many residents are far from ecstatic about the idea.

Things to See & Do

The main reason for coming is the beach, where you can swim, surf or just hang out. If the water's too rough there are sea-water swimming pools at either end, including a children's pool at the eastern end. **Bondi Pavilion**, on the esplanade, has change rooms and showers, as well as a theatre and gallery hosting cultural and community events.

Accessible **Aboriginal rock engravings** are a short walk north of Bondi Beach on the golf course in North Bondi. A beautiful coastal walking path leads south to the beaches at Tamarama, Bronte and Coogee.

Getting There & Away

Bondi Junction is the terminus of the eastern suburbs CityRail line, and the nearest train station to Bondi Beach. From there, you can take bus No 380, 382 or 389 to Bondi and Bondi Beach. Alternatively, you can take these buses from Circular Quay or bus No 378 from Railway Square, which continues south to Bronte; bus Nos 378 and 380 run along Oxford St.

Buses stop along Campbell Parade terminating at Brighton Blvd in North Bondi.

TAMARAMA & BRONTE

South of Bondi, Tamarama (or 'Glamarama', as it's sometimes called) is a lovely cove with strong surf, popular with Sydney's 'beautiful people'. Get off the bus just before it reaches Bondi Beach; Tamarama is a five minute walk down the hill.

At Bronte, south of Tamarama, there's a superb family-oriented beach hemmed in by a bowl-shaped park and sandstone headlands. A toy train chugs around during the warmer months, offering children's rides. Cafes with outdoor tables, picnic areas and barbecues make it the perfect place for a day of doing very little. Catch bus No 378 from the city, or take a train to Bondi Junction and pick the bus up there. You can walk along the wonderful clifftop footpath from Bondi Beach or from Coogee via Gordon's Bay, Clovelly and the sun-bleached Waverley Cemetery.

COOGEE (MAP 10)

Coogee, about 4km south of Bondi Beach, is almost a miniature carbon copy, minus the crowds or glitzy development. While increasingly popular with visitors, it still has a relaxed atmosphere, few airs and graces and a good sweep of sand.

The main beachfront street is Arden St, and the junction of Arden St and Coogee Bay Rd is the commercial hub of the suburb. Like Bondi, Coogee's main attraction is its beach and this is a great spot for a snorkel. From Coogee, the spectacular clifftop footpath runs north along the coast to Bondi Beach passing Gordon's Bay, Clovelly, Bronte and Tamarama.

Getting There & Away

Bus Nos 373 and 374 run from Circular Quay; bus Nos 371 and 372 run from Railway Square; and bus Nos 314 and 315 run from Bondi Junction.

THE NORTH SHORE (MAP 2)

The North Shore is the unofficial but universally recognised name applied to the suburbs north of the harbour. The area's pretty bays and beaches, good shopping and eateries, make it worthwhile leaving the cosmopolitan delights of the southern side to see how wealthier Sydneysiders live.

Kirribilli & Milsons Point

The Sydney residences of the governor general and the prime minister are on Kirribilli Point, east of the Harbour Bridge. The prime minister stays in **Kirribilli House** (1854) and the governor general in **Admiralty House** (1846). Admiralty House is the one nearer the bridge.

To the north of Kirribilli Point is the **Royal Sydney Yacht Squadron** headquarters. Yachting has been popular on the harbour since the 1830s, and the Australian Yacht Club was formed in 1862.

Luna Park amusement park, at Milsons Point on the edge of Lavender Bay immediately west of the Harbour Bridge, was at its peak in the 1930s, when thousands of people flocked across the harbour on the new bridge. The park closed in the 1970s, but after a long battle was restored and proclaimed a public reserve. It has opened and closed a couple of times since then, but there are plans for it to reopen at the end of 2000.

McMahons Point is a pleasant, sleepy suburb on the next headland west. It's tipped by **Blues Point Reserve**, named after the Jamaican-born Billy Blue, who ferried people across from Dawes Point in the 1830s. Blues Point Tower was designed by the architect Harry Seidler. It was one of the first high-rise buildings on the harbour. If you follow Blues Point Rd north from the ferry wharf it'll bring you to North Sydney.

Kirribilli, Lavender Bay and Blues Point are serviced by ferries from Circular Quay. Other ways of getting here include walking across the bridge or taking a North Shore train to Milsons Point.

North Sydney & Crows Nest

North Sydney is north-west of the Harbour Bridge. The suburb's historical connections have become difficult to find since it became Sydney's second CBD.

The grand Victorian **North Sydney Post Office** (1889) is on the corner of Miller St and the Pacific Hwy, one of Sydney's busiest intersections. To the left along Mount St at No 7 is **Mary MacKillop Place** (☎ 9954 9688) with displays telling the life story of the girl from the bush who became a nun – and Australia's first saint. The museum is open from 10 am to 4 pm daily; admission is $7.50 ($3 children).

A kilometre or so north along the Pacific Hwy from North Sydney is the suburb of Crows Nest, which has a string of good eateries. The 1880s **Sexton's Cottage Museum** (☎ Stanton Library 9936 8400), in St Thomas' Rest Park at 250 West St, next to the old St Thomas' Church, has displays relating to the early European settlement of the area. It's open from 1 to 4 pm Thursday and 2 to 4 pm the first Sunday of the month. Entry is free.

Balls Head Reserve

Balls Head Reserve not only has great views of the harbour, but also old Aboriginal rock paintings and carvings, although they're not easily discernible. The park is two headlands west of the Harbour Bridge. Take a train to Waverton, turn left when you leave the station and follow Bay Rd, which becomes Balls Head Rd.

Hunters Hill & Woolwich

The elegant Victorian suburbs of Hunters Hill and Woolwich are on a spit at the junction of the Parramatta and Lane Cove rivers. In 1834, Mary Reiby built a riverside cottage here. She was followed in 1847 by the Joubert family, who operated a fleet of ferries for nearly 50 years. The Joubert brothers began to build houses, and it's said that 200 of them still stand.

The National Trust **Vienna Cottage** (☎ 9817 2510), 38 Alexandra St, Hunters Hill, is a stone cottage built in 1871 by Jacob Hellman and is typical of the era. It's open from 2 to 4 pm the second and fourth Sunday of the month; entry is $3.

Hunters Hill ferries from Circular Quay stop at Woolwich's Valentia St Wharf.

SIMON BRACKEN

ust in case ... life preservers at Darling Harbour

SIMON BRACKEN

Matilda III at Darling Harbour

SIMON BRACKEN

Model whale skeletons, Darling Harbour

ROSS BARNETT

National Maritime Museum, Darling Harbour

SIMON BRACKEN

Sega World, Darling Harbour

SIMON BRACKEN

Lyric Theatre

SIMON BRACKEN

The upmarket Chifley Plaza

ROSS BARNETT

The 'Egg Crate' crown of Governor Phillip Tower

SIMON BRACKEN

The Star City Casino complex

SIMON BRACKEN

Badde Manors cafe, Glebe

CHRIS MELLOR

Centrepoint Tower

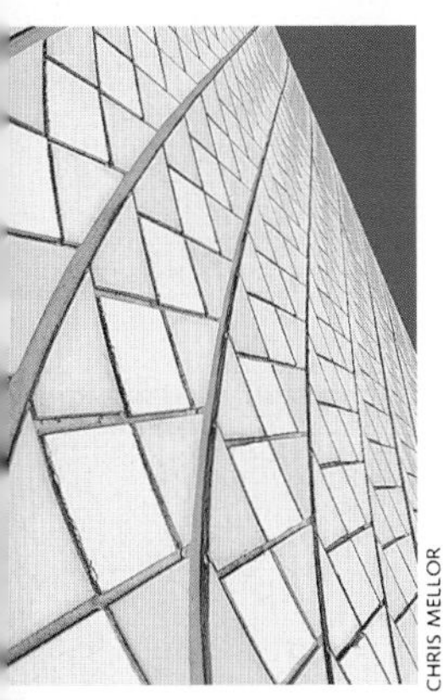

CHRIS MELLOR

The tiles on the Opera House

RICHARD I'ANSON

Catching a ferry is the most scenic way to get around the harbour.

RICHARD I'ANSON

NSW National Museum

COLIN K BARNES

Glebe Island Bridge

SIMON BRACKEN

Painted tiles on a Newtown shop

SIMON BRACKEN

A Newtown antique shop

SIMON BRACKEN

Mambo designer wear

SIMON BRACKEN

Dinosaur Designs

SIMON BRACKEN

The entrance to Macdonnas Cafe, Newtown

Mosman & Around

East of the Harbour Bridge, Mosman, **Neutral Bay** and **Cremorne**, have good shopping centres and some beautiful foreshore parks and walks. Mosman is on the large chunk of land separating Middle Harbour from the main harbour. Cremorne and Neutral Bay are further west. The beachside suburb of **Balmoral**, north of Mosman, faces Manly across Middle Harbour. It has three fine beaches (one with a shark net) and some good restaurants.

You can walk north from Kirribilli, past Careening Cove, to Neutral Bay, where pleasant Anderson Park leads down to the waterfront. East of here is **Nutcote** (☎ 9953 4453), 5 Wallaringa Ave, the former home of well-known and loved Australian children's author May Gibbs. It's now a museum containing exhibits on her life and work; volunteer guides can show you around and there are beautiful gardens. Nutcote opens from 11 am to 3 pm Wednesday to Sunday; entry is $6 ($3 children). It's a short walk from the Neutral Bay ferry wharf.

To the south is Kurraba Point. Off Bogota Ave you can pick up a footpath that runs through bushy gardens to the end of **Cremorne Point**. This is an excellent spot to picnic on the grass reserve or go for a swim, with great views of the harbour. The point is especially popular on Christmas Day and New Year's Eve as a vantage point for the annual fireworks. From here, you can continue up the other side to Mosman Bay and Taronga Zoo.

The main road through this area is Military Rd, which branches east off the Warringah Freeway (the northern side of the Harbour Bridge) near North Sydney. Military Rd crosses Middle Harbour at Spit Bridge then runs north, changing names several times. It bypasses Manly, eventually reaching **Palm Beach**, Sydney's northernmost beachside suburb.

Bus No 190 runs a limited-stop route from Wynyard in the city to Palm Beach via Military Rd; bus No 182 from Wynyard runs to Cremorne and Mosman. Buses also run to Military Rd from the North Shore suburb of St Leonards.

Taronga Zoo

The 30-hectare Taronga Zoo (☎ 9969 2777), a short ferry ride from Circular Quay, has an attractive hillside setting overlooking the harbour. It houses over 4000 critters, including a substantial number of Australian ones.

The zoo is open 9 am to 5 pm daily; admission is $16 ($8.50 children). Ferries to the zoo depart from Circular Quay's Wharf 2 half-hourly from 7.15 am on weekdays, 8.45 am Saturday and 9 am Sunday. The zoo is on a steep hillside and it makes sense to work your way down if you plan to depart by ferry. If you can't be bothered to climb to the top entrance, take the bus. (The 'Aerial Safari' cable car was closed at the time of writing.) A ZooPass ticket, sold at Circular Quay and elsewhere, costs $21/10.50 and includes return ferry rides, the bus to the entrance (and a bus to the top of the hill for those daunted by the climb) and zoo admission. A ZooLink ticket is similar to the ZooPass but includes train travel.

MANLY (MAP 12)

The jewel of the North Shore, Manly sits on a narrow peninsula that ends at the dramatic cliffs of North Head. It was one of the first places in Australia to be named by Europeans – Arthur Phillip named it after the 'manly' physique of the Aborigines he saw here in 1788. Sun-soaked Manly boasts all the trappings of a full-scale holiday resort and a sense of community identity, but isn't afraid to show a bit of tack and brashness to attract visitors. It makes a refreshing change from the prim upper-middle-class harbour enclaves nearby.

It's half an hour by ferry from Circular Quay (15 minutes by JetCat) and the trip offers fantastic views of the city.

Orientation & Information

Manly straddles the narrow isthmus leading to North Head, and has both ocean and harbour beaches. The ferry wharf is on Manly

Cove, on the harbour side, and the Corso (the main commercial strip) runs from here to the ocean, where Manly Beach is lined with Norfolk pines. Most of the Corso is a pedestrian mall.

Manly Visitors Information Bureau (☎ 9977 1088), open from 10 am to 4 pm daily, is on Manly Beach (South Steyne) near the Corso. It has useful, free pamphlets on the 8km Manly Scenic Walkway and sells Manly Heritage Walk booklets ($3.50). There are small lockers where you can leave your things while you go for a swim. There's a bus information booth at the entrance to the wharf.

Things to See

The long ocean beach north of the Corso is **North Steyne Beach**; the shorter stretch of beach running south is usually called **Manly Beach**, but it's technically South Steyne Beach. The beachfront road is called North Steyne and South Steyne. At the southern end of Manly Beach is the Manly Life Saving Club, from which a path leads around the rocky headland to tiny **Fairy Bower Beach**, which has a small saltwater swimming pool. Further around is beautiful **Shelly Beach**. The large building on the hill south-east of the town centre is **St Patrick's College** (1889). Manly Hospital is nearby.

North Steyne Beach runs up to **Queenscliff Beach**, near the steep Queenscliff headland. There's a lifesaving club here as well. Around the headland (although not easy to get to on foot) is **Freshwater Beach**.

There's another stretch of sand on the harbour side at **Manly Cove**, backed by the East and West Esplanade. In the centre is **Manly Wharf**, which has cafes, restaurants, shops and a small amusement park.

Oceanworld (☎ 9949 2644), West Esplanade, is on the headland at the western end of Manly Cove. It's a good oceanarium and its program includes turtle and shark feeding, and an eerie underwater perspex tunnel lets you eyeball the fish (and vice versa) in close-up. The sharks are handfed at 11.30 am Monday, Wednesday and Friday, and there's a 15 minute seal show at 11.45 am and 2 pm daily. It's open from 10 am to 5.30 pm weekdays; admission is $14.50 (children $7.50, family $39, concession $10).

Manly Art Gallery & Museum (☎ 9949 2435), next to Oceanworld, has exhibitions on beach themes and local history (much the same thing in Manly). It's open from 10 am to 5 pm Tuesday to Sunday; admission is $3 (children free).

See Harbourside Walks earlier in this chapter for details of the lovely **Manly Scenic Walkway**.

North Head

Spectacular North Head, at the Sydney Harbour entrance about 3km south of Manly, offers good views of the ocean, harbour and city skyline. The peninsula has dramatic cliffs, several coves and lookouts with views of the cliffs, the harbour and the city centre. Most of the headland is in the Sydney Harbour National Park; contact the NPWS office (☎ 9977 6522) near the Quarantine Station for information.

The **Quarantine Station** housed suspected and real disease carriers from 1832 to 1984 and many people died here. The station is run by the NPWS and you have to book a guided tour to visit. These 1½-hour tours are held at 10.40 am weekdays, 1.25 pm weekends; admission is $10 ($7 children and concession). The station is reputedly haunted and there are spooky three-hour ghost tours at 7.30 pm Wednesday and Friday to Sunday; admission is $17 ($20 Sundays).

The centre of the headland is an off-limits military reserve, but you can visit the **National Artillery Museum** (☎ 9976 3855) in North Fort Manly. It's open from noon to 4 pm Wednesday, Saturday and Sunday; admission is $4 ($2 children).

Getting There & Away

See the Getting Around chapter for details on ferries to Manly. Alternatively, bus No 169 runs from Wynyard Park in the city. The No 135 bus from outside Manly Wharf covers North Head; the one-way fare is $2.50.

SYDNEY OLYMPIC PARK (MAP ON PAGE 70)

Sydney Olympic Park in the suburb of Homebush Bay, 14km west of the city centre, is the main venue for the 2000 Games. It also contains the Olympic Village where all the athletes will stay. **Sydney International Athletic Centre**, **Sydney International Aquatic Centre**, the **Tennis Centre** and **Stadium Australia** are open to visitors. You can swim at the aquatic centre or walk through the **Leisure Garden**, which depicts Australia's different natural habitats. There are guided 90-minute tours for $14 ($9 children and seniors) at 10 am, noon and 2 pm on weekdays, noon and 2 pm weekends. Call ☎ 9752 3666. Also here is the **Sydney Showground**, new home of the Royal Easter Show.

For details on how to get to Olympic Park, and sites to check out once you get there, see the boxed text 'Tours of Sydney Olympic Park' in the Getting Around chapter.

BEACHES

Sydney's beaches are some of its greatest assets. They're popular on weekends but Sydneysiders also often swim before or after (or instead of) going to work. The beaches are easily accessible and usually good, although some, like Balmoral, post warnings that swimming is inadvisable after heavy rains because of stormwater runoff.

There are two types of beaches – harbour beaches (Map 1), which are sheltered, calm and generally smaller, and ocean beaches (Map 17), which often have good surf.

Although they get busy on hot summer weekends, Sydney's beaches are never really packed. Swimming is generally safe, but at the ocean beaches you're only allowed to swim within the 'flagged' areas patrolled by the famed life-savers. Efforts are made to keep surfers separate from swimmers. High points of Sydney's beach life are the surf life-saving competitions held at various beaches during summer.

Shark patrols operate during the summer, and ocean beaches are generally netted. Try to keep the *Jaws* terrors in perspective – Sydney has only had one fatal shark attack since 1937. See also Dangers & Annoyances in the Facts for the Visitor chapter.

Many of Sydney's beaches are 'topless', but some aren't: do as the locals do. There are also a couple of nude beaches.

Harbour Beaches

Sydney's harbour beaches are generally sheltered, calm coves with little of the frenetic activity of the ocean beaches.

Immediately inside the Heads, on the southern side, is tiny **Lady Bay Beach**, a nude beach, mainly gay. South of Lady Bay is **Camp Cove**, a small but pleasant sliver of sand popular with families and topless bathers. This is where Arthur Phillip first landed in Sydney. South of Camp Cove is **Watsons Bay**, which hosts two of the delightful Doyle's outdoor seafood restaurants. Another popular harbour beach is the family-oriented **Shark Beach** at Nielsen Park in Vaucluse. These beaches can be reached by bus No 324 or 325 from Circular Quay.

On the North Shore, there are harbour beaches at **Manly Cove** (suburban beach), **Reef Beach** (nudist), **Clontarf** (families), **Chinaman's Beach** (quiet hideaway) and **Balmoral** (popular day trip for North Shore residents). The Manly ferry docks at Manly Cove, and Reef Beach is a couple of kilometres walk along the Manly Scenic Walkway. To get to Balmoral, take the No 247 from Wynyard to Mosman Junction, then change to the No 257. For Clontarf, catch the No 131 or 132 from Wynyard. The other beaches are accessible, with a bit of walking, by catching bus No 175 or 178 from Wynyard Park, which travel along Military Rd and cross Spit Bridge.

Southern Beaches

South of the Heads, there is a string of ocean beaches all the way to Botany Bay. **Bondi Beach**, with its crowds and surfers, is the best-known beach in Australia and a favourite with young out-of-towners.

Tamarama, a little south of Bondi, is a pretty cove with strong surf. Take bus No 361 from Bondi Junction or catch a Bondi Beach bus and walk from the bottom of Bondi Rd. Next south is **Bronte**, a broader beach popular with families. Take bus No 378 from the Central depot (Eddy Ave), or Bondi Junction. The tiny inlet of **Clovelly** is nestled between Bronte and Coogee. It has a breakwater that makes it safe for swimming. Catch bus No 339 from George St in the city or No 329 from Bondi Junction. **Coogee** has a wide, sweeping beach and is a good spot to rest up from the rigours of the surf. Take bus No 373 or 374 from Circular Quay, or the 372 from Central. **Maroubra** is further south again; take bus No 376, 377 or 395 from Circular Quay. Botany Bay itself is more for sailing than swimming, due to its large shark population.

Northern Beaches

A string of ocean-front suburbs stretches 30km north along the coast from Manly, ending at beautiful, well-heeled Palm Beach and spectacular Barrenjoey Head at the entrance to Broken Bay. There are plenty of beaches along the way. **Freshwater**, the first north of Manly, attracts a lot of teenagers; then there's **Curl Curl** (families and surfers); **Dee Why** and **Collaroy** (families); and the long sweep of **Narrabeen** (surfers). The most spectacular are **Whale Beach** and **Bilgola**, near Palm Beach, which both have dramatic steep headlands. Fans of Aussie soap operas will want to make a pilgrimage to **Palm Beach** because many outdoor scenes in the TV show 'Home & Away' are shot here. The northern end of Palm Beach is for nude bathers.

Avalon Beach, south of Palm Beach, was earmarked in early 1999 as a proposed location for the buffed and chesty 'Baywatch' TV series, but indignant residents vetoed the plan.

Several of the northernmost beach suburbs back onto **Pittwater**, a lovely inlet off Broken Bay and a favoured sailing spot.

Bus Nos 136 and 139 run from Manly to Freshwater and Curl Curl. Bus No L90 from Wynyard Park stops at Collaroy, Narrabeen, Bilgola, Avalon and Whale beaches, and continues north to Palm Beach. From Manly, take bus No 155 or 157 to Mona Vale and pick up No 190 there.

This route is popular as the first step on the journey to NSW's northern coast and as a weekend excursion to the Central Coast.

Surf Beaches

With so many good beaches it's easy to see why surfing is a popular pastime in Sydney. For surfing see the Activities section later in this chapter.

PARKS & GARDENS

Sydney has plenty of parks, many with harbour views, making it a wonderful city for a picnic or a stroll.

The Royal Botanical Gardens, the Domain and Hyde Park (see those sections earlier in this chapter) border the eastern side of the city centre. There are also a few smaller parks in the city centre, which provide relief from the cement. **Wynyard Park** is a wedge of Victoriana on York St outside Wynyard station; the smaller **Lang Park** is a few blocks north; and **First Fleet Park** is north again, at Circular Quay. **Observatory Park**, on the western side of the Bradfield Hwy, is a pleasant place with old trees and good views.

There are two small parks at Elizabeth Bay, north-east of Kings Cross: the delightful **Arthur McElhone Reserve** opposite Elizabeth Bay House and **Beare Park**, down by the water. But the nearest swathe of green to the Cross is **Rushcutters Bay Park**, a pretty waterfront area to the east with sporting facilities and good views of the yachts.

East of Surry Hills and south of Paddington are the adjacent Moore and Centennial parks, both large recreational areas (see under Paddington earlier).

Many headlands and bays on the North Shore have small parks, including Blues Point, Kirribilli (Careening Cove), Neutral Bay (Anderson Park), Cremorne Point and Mosman (Reid Park). Finding them without a street directory can be difficult.

On the North Shore there's an 8km corridor of bushland called **Garigal National Park** stretching from Bantry Bay on Middle Harbour north to Ku-ring-gai Chase

National Park at St Ives. **Lane Cove National Park**, between the suburbs of Ryde and Chatswood, is also on the North Shore. Both parks have extensive walking tracks and Lane Cove has lots of picnic areas. You may see lyrebirds in Garigal; the males make their spectacular mating displays May to August.

See also Sydney Harbour National Park earlier in this chapter.

ACTIVITIES

The *Sydney Morning Herald*'s Friday 'Metro' guide lists activities. Noticeboards at hostels are usually crammed with suggestions, and travel agents often have good information on day trips.

Swimming

Sydney's harbour beaches offer sheltered water for swimming. Nothing beats being knocked around in the waves that pound the ocean beaches, where you're safe if you follow instructions and swim within the flags. There are some notorious but clearly signposted rips – even at Sydney's most popular beaches – so don't underestimate the surf just because it doesn't look threatening.

There are more than 100 public swimming pools in Sydney, including: the saltwater Andrew 'Boy' Charlton pool (Map 4, ☎ 9358 6686) in the Domain on the edge of Woolloomooloo Bay; the Prince Alfred Park pool (Map 4, ☎ 9319 7045), near Central station; the North Sydney Olympic Pool (Map 2, ☎ 9955 2309) in Milsons Point; the Victoria Park Pool (☎ 9660 4181) on Broadway, next to the University of Sydney; the Leichhardt Park Aquatic Centre (☎ 9555 8344) in Leichhardt Park overlooking Iron Cove; the tiny saltwater pool at Fairy Bower Beach, Manly; and the two ocean-side pools at Coogee, one of which, McIvers Baths, is for women only. Both the Boy Charlton pool and the Prince Alfred Park pool close during winter.

Surfing

South of the Heads, the best spots are Bondi, Tamarama, Coogee and Maroubra. Cronulla, south of Botany Bay, is also a serious surfing spot. On the North Shore, there are a dozen surf beaches between Manly and Palm Beach; the best are Manly, Curl Curl, Dee Why, North Narrabeen, Mona Vale, Newport Reef, North Avalon and Palm Beach itself.

In Manly, Aloha Surf (Map 12, ☎ 9977 3777), 44 Pittwater Rd, rents surfboards and boogie-boards (wetsuits included) for $20/30 for a half/full-day (until 7 pm). At Bondi Beach, you can hire surfboards and boogie-boards with wetsuit from Bondi Surf Company (Map 11, ☎ 9365 0870), 72 Campbell Parade. The cost is $20 to $30 for three hours, $40 for the day (passport or credit card identification required).

In Coogee, Surfworld (Map 10, ☎ 9664 1293) is at 250 Coogee Bay Rd.

For windsurfers, Balmoral Sailboard School (☎ 9960 5344) hires sailboards and gives tuition on Middle Harbour.

Sailing & Boating

There are plenty of sailing schools in Sydney and even if you're not serious about learning the ropes, an introductory lesson is a fun way of getting onto the harbour.

The sociable EastSail Sailing School (☎ 9327 1166) at d'Albora Marina, New Beach Rd, Rushcutters Bay, runs a range of courses from introductory to racing level.

The friendly Sunsail (☎ 9955 6400), 23A King George St on McMahon's Point in Lavender Bay, runs an introductory course over two full days for $350.

If you want to learn to sail a dinghy, contact Northside Sailing School (☎ 9969 3972), Spit Road, Spit Bridge, Mosman. Two six-hour lessons costs $290, boat hire is around $50 for two hours, and they offer a range of kids' activities.

If you'll be in Sydney for a while and you'd like to learn how to sail a yacht, contact the Australian Sailing School (☎ 9960 3999), The Spit, not far from Northside Sailing School. It has four-week courses catering for all skill levels for $360 to $390.

Pittwater and Broken Bay offer some of the world's best sailing. Scotland Island

Schooners at Church Point has a sailing school (☎ 9999 2285) specialising in ocean-going boats. It takes some months to earn the internationally recognised Certificate of Competency – but what a qualification to have!

Diving

The best shore dives in Sydney are the Gordons Bay Underwater Nature Trail, north of Coogee; Shark Point, Clovelly; and Ship Rock, Cronulla. Popular boat dive sites are Wedding Cake Island, off Coogee; around the Sydney Heads; and off the Royal National Park. In Manly, you can make beach dives from Shelly Beach.

Plenty of outfits will take you diving and many run dive courses. Pro Dive (Maps 4 & 10) has several outlets in and around Sydney, including at 428 George St (☎ 9264 6177) in the city, and 27 Alfreda St, Coogee (☎ 9665 6333). Four-day diving courses cost from $245, boat dives cost $105, and shore dives $55 (gear included). In Manly, the Dive Centre Manly (Map 12, ☎ 9977 4355), 10 Belgrave St, has one-day courses for $95. It also hires snorkelling gear ($15) and wetsuits ($12). Pacific Coast Divers (Map 12, ☎ 9977 5966), 169 Pittwater Rd, Manly, is similar. Snorkelling gear is $10.

Canoeing & Kayaking

The NSW Canoe Association (Map 9, ☎ 9660 4597), Wentworth Park Complex, Ultimo, has information on clubs that provide lessons, and also conducts kayak and canoe tours of Sydney Harbour. Call from 9 am to 5 pm weekdays.

Sydney Kayak Centre (☎ 9969 4590), at the southern end of Spit Bridge in Mosman, rents sea kayaks to paddle on Middle Harbour. Single kayaks cost $10 per hour for the first two hours, $5 for subsequent hours. Double kayaks cost twice that.

Natural Wanders (Map 3, ☎ 9899 1001), 45 Wharf Rd, Birchgrove, has weekend kayak tours of the harbour. From Lavender Bay, they head under the Sydney Harbour Bridge to Bradley's Head, stopping in secluded bays, and at Taronga Zoo for brunch. Patrick, the tour operator, who'll tailor a tour to suit you, relates the history and architecture of the area. The tour takes four hours and costs $75. No prior experience is necessary.

Cycling

The steep hills, narrow streets and busy traffic don't make Sydney a particularly bicycle-friendly city. Some roads have designated cycle lanes but these often run between parked cars and moving traffic. Bicycle NSW (☎ 9283 5200), Level 2, 209 Castlereagh St, publishes a handy book called *Cycling around Sydney* ($10), detailing routes and cycle paths in and around the city. It also publishes booklets detailing cycle routes throughout NSW.

With less-hectic traffic and long cycle paths, both Manly and Centennial Park are popular pedalling spots. The Road Transport Authority (RTA) issues maps of metropolitan Sydney's cycle path network – phone ☎ toll-free 1800 060 607 or download them at the Web site www.rta.nsw.gov.au.

Bicycles can travel on suburban trains for concession rates during peak hours, and for free outside peak times. Cycling is prohibited in Darling Harbour and Martin Place. Innes Bicycles (Map 4, ☎ 9264 9597), 222 Clarence St, the city, sells bicycles and does repairs.

For bike hire, check out Inner City Cycles (Map 9, ☎ 9660 6605), 31 Glebe Point Rd, Glebe, which rents good quality mountain bikes for $30/50/80 a day/weekend/week (including gear).

Woolys Wheels (Map 7, ☎ 9331 2671), 82 Oxford St, Paddington, across from the Victoria Barracks, rents hybrid bikes for $30 a day (24 hours). In Manly, you can hire bikes from Manly Cycle Centre (Map 12, ☎ 9977 1189), 36 Pittwater Rd, for $10/$25 an hour/day.

Most places require a hefty deposit, but accept credit cards.

See the Getting Around chapter for cycle tours of Sydney.

Inline Skating

The beach promenades at Bondi and Manly are the favoured spots for skating, but Coogee and Bronte are becoming popular too.

Manly Blades (☎ 9976 3833), in Manly Beach Plaza, 49 North Steyne, hires out skates for $10 an hour, $15 for two hours, or $20 for the day. It also offers lessons. You can also hire skates at Manly InLine Action (☎ 9976 3831), 93 North Steyne.

Bondi Boards & Blades (Map 11, ☎ 9365 6555), 148 Curlewis St, back from Campbell Parade, rents skates for $10 for the first hour, $5 for subsequent hours. Protective gear is free.

Jogging

The foreshore from Circular Quay around Farm Cove to Woolloomooloo Bay and through the Royal Botanical Gardens and the Domain is popular with joggers. Running across the Harbour Bridge is a popular, if polluted, way for North Shore residents to commute to work in the city.

Centennial Park and the promenades at Bondi Beach and Manly are the best jogging spots. The cliff trail between Bondi Beach and Bronte is also good.

Horse Riding

There are four outfits offering horse rides in Centennial Park – contact the stable manager (☎ 9332 2809) for details. They're based at the RAS Showgrounds (enter on the corner of Lang and Cook Rds). Prices start from around $30 per hour, and bookings are necessary.

Golf

The most central of Sydney's 40-odd public golf courses is Moore Park (Map 4, ☎ 9663 3960) on Centennial Ave, which charges $27 for 18 holes on weekends, $24 on weekdays. Other public courses include Bondi (☎ 9130 3170) on Military Rd in North Bondi, and Barnwell Park (☎ 9713 1162) on the corner of William St and Lyons Rd in Five Dock. Hudson Park (☎ 9746 5702) is a golf driving range at Homebush Bay.

Tennis

There are tennis courts for hire all over the city, including the following:

Coogee South Squash & Tennis
(☎ 9344 7976) 222 Malabar Rd, Coogee

Jensen's Tennis Centre
(☎ 9698 9451) next to Central station, Broadway, Surry Hills

Miller's Point Tennis Court
(☎ 9256 2222) Kent St, the Rocks

Parklands Tennis Centre
(☎ 9662 7521) on the corner of Anzac Parade and Lang Rd, Moore Park, Paddington

Places to Stay

There's a huge variety of accommodation available in Sydney with good options in every price range.

Almost every hotel and hostel lifts its rates or cancels special deals during the busy summer months, and school holidays (and February's Mardi Gras) can make accommodation both scarce and pricey. But in winter, when things are slow, it's worth seeking out bargains by ringing around.

Many larger hotels cater primarily to business people, so their rates may drop on weekends. Some bigger hotels include breakfast and parking in their rates. Mid-range and top-end hotels publish 'rack' (standard) rates, but there are often special deals and it's worth ringing to inquire about these. Prices are usually quoted per room, depending on the facilities and/or the view.

For longer-term stays, there are places in the 'flats to let' and 'share accommodation' ads in the *Sydney Morning Herald* on Wednesday and Saturday. Many people find flats to share through other travellers. Hostel noticeboards are another good source. Serviced apartments often sleep several people; lower weekly rates can be inexpensive for a group.

Disabled travellers can get information on accommodation options in Sydney from NICAN and Accessing Sydney (see Disabled Travellers in the Facts for the Visitor chapter).

In the summer holiday season (November to February) prices at beachside resorts can be as much as 40% higher than low-season rates. The rates quoted here are for the high season.

PLACES TO STAY – BUDGET

Camping

Sydney's caravan parks, most of which also have sites for tents, are a fair way out of town. The following are 26km or less from the city centre.

Bed Tax

In September 1997 the NSW government introduced a controversial 10% inner-Sydney bed tax. The tax is added to the standard room rate of hotels, serviced apartments and B&Bs in the CBD. Add 10% to rates listed in this chapter. However, as of 1 July 2000, the bed tax will be replaced by the GST (also 10%).

East's Lane Cove River Caravan Park *(☎ 9888 9133, Plassey Rd, North Ryde)*, 14km north, has van sites from $17 to $20, cabins for $65 a double.

Harts Caravan Park *(☎ 9522 7143, 215 Port Hacking Rd, Miranda)*, 24km south, has sites for $18/110 per night/week; vans cost $30/150, cabins $30/150 a double.

Lakeside Caravan Park *(☎ 9913 7845, Lake Park Rd, Narrabeen)*, 26km north, has sites/cabins for $20/70 a double, seventh night free.

Sheralee Tourist Caravan Park *(☎ 9567 7161, 88 Bryant St, Rockdale)*, 13km south, has sites for $20/120 per night/week, vans $40/160 a double.

The Grand Pines Caravan Park *(☎ 9529 7329, 289 The Grand Parade, Sans Souci)*, 17km south, has sites for $29, vans/cabins from $50/70 to $70/130 a double.

Hostels

Sydney has a huge number of hostels. The largest concentration is in Kings Cross, but there are others in Bondi, Coogee, Glebe, Surry Hills and Manly. Facilities vary from dorms with *en suite*, TV, fridge and cooking facilities to just a bare room with a couple of bunks; many also offer single and/or double accommodation. YHA hostels are often better run and cleaner than many backpacker places. Some hostels have set hours for checking in and out, though all have 24-hour access once you've paid.

The average low-season price for a dorm bed is around $16, but in summer this can rise to $21. Many hostels offer reduced weekly rates, and most are acutely aware of the competition. The prices quoted here could easily fluctuate by a few dollars depending on demand. Winter rates are often a little lower. Hostelling International (HI) and YHA members usually receive discounts, as do members of VIP Backpackers International.

If you're Australian, finding a hostel that will accept you might be tricky if you can't prove you're travelling. Some Sydney hostels ban Australians altogether to stop locals using hostels as dosshouses and because of bad experiences with lecherous drunks. Hostels may demand a passport as identification, although in the low season these standards sometimes vanish. YHA hostels take members of any nationality.

The YHA's Membership & Travel Centre (☎ 9261 1111), 422 Kent St, can book you into any YHA hostel in Australia, and many others around the world. The centre is also a domestic and international travel agency. It's open from 9 am to 5 pm weekdays (to 6 pm Thursday), 10 am to 2 pm Saturday.

As well as the backpacker-only hostels, many pubs and boarding houses fill spare rooms with bunks. Some are perfectly OK, but most lack the hostel atmosphere and the essential information grapevine. If you're staying in a pub and need a good night's sleep, check the location of the jukebox or band in the downstairs bar before choosing a room.

City Centre (Maps 4 & 8) The slick 532-bed ***Sydney Central YHA*** *(☎ 9281 9111)*, on the corner of Pitt St and Rawson Place, is near Central station in the renovated, heritage-listed Daking House. It's the largest hostel in the world (just outdoing the one in Amsterdam) and has a heated rooftop pool, sauna and licensed cafe. Dorms cost $20 per person ($23 nonmembers), doubles $33 per person, and twins from $29. All *en suite* twin rooms ($66) are set up for disabled travellers. Double and twin rooms are for YHA members only. It's advisable to book ahead.

The super-civilised ***YWCA*** *(☎ 9264 2451, 5-11 Wentworth Ave)* has an enviable position, with Hyde Park across the road and both the city centre and Oxford St a short walk away. The standard is high, with simple but spotless well-furnished rooms, and a cafeteria downstairs. Unfortunately, there's a fairly high price for this: $60/80/90 for singles/twins/triples or $95/115/125 with attached bathroom. There's a 10% discount on weekly rates if you pay in advance. Dorm accommodation is $24 a night, but the maximum stay is three nights. Both genders can stay.

Kings Cross & Around (Maps 5 & 6) There are heaps of hostels in the Cross and there's little to distinguish many of them. Eva's has one of the best reputations, followed by Backpackers Headquarters. Barncleuth House/Pink House is for those who like their hostels a little more lived in and cosy. The Jolly Swagman hostel has the best-organised social life.

Heading north along Victoria St from Kings Cross station, the first hostel you come to is ***Plane Tree Lodge*** *(☎ 9356 4551, 174 Victoria St)*. It's a fairly average Kings Cross hostel, with a variety of rooms, each with TV and fridge. Rates are $20 in a dorm, $45/50 for an acceptable twin/double.

Highfield House Private Hotel *(☎ 9358 1552, 166 Victoria St)* caters primarily to overseas travellers. It's secure, clean and has a good atmosphere. Rates stay much the same all year, with singles/doubles for $37/52 ($220/310 weekly). Dorm beds cost $19/110, and all rooms have shared bathrooms.

Many of the fine old terrace houses along Victoria St have been converted into hostels. ***Original Backpackers*** *(☎ 9356 3232, 162 Victoria St) is* the original backpacker hostel in this area and, having expanded, is going strong. The atmosphere is good, it's clean and there are decent sized common areas, with a courtyard, pool table and jukebox out the back. Dorms cost $20/120 a night/week, singles $30/270, and twins and doubles $50/300. The noticeboard is full of ads and information, and staff can assist with finding work.

The cosy ***Travellers Rest*** *(☎ 9380 2044, 156 Victoria St)* is popular for long-term stays. Its comfortable, well-equipped rooms each have a phone, sink and TV, and all but singles have a fridge. Some have balconies overlooking Victoria St. It's well run, and management has useful work contacts. Rates tend to stay the same all year: three to four-bed dorms cost $17/110 a night/week; twins $38/230; doubles cost $40/240 without bath, $45/260 with bath.

Virgin Backpackers *(☎ 9357 4733, 144 Victoria St)*, on the site of the old Jolly Swagman, is the new kid on the block. There are plans to incorporate a cafe and bar into the hostel once it's completed.

The family owned and operated ***Eva's Backpackers*** *(☎ 9358 2185, 6-8 Orwell St)* is clean, friendly and well run. There's a rooftop barbecue area and a sociable kitchen/dining room. Dorms cost $20, doubles or twins $48, triples $20 per person. It's so popular that it's often full, even in winter. The desk is staffed from 7 am to 1 pm and 5.30 to 7.30 pm.

Further up Orwell St is the clean and cheery ***Sydney Central Backpackers*** *(☎ 9358 6600, 16 Victoria St)* – not to be confused with Sydney Central YHA in the city. Dorm beds cost $18/108 per night/week, doubles $45/270. There's a rooftop garden with views of the Opera House and Harbour Bridge, and a kitchen with free tea and coffee.

Over the road is the busy ***Jolly Swagman*** hostel *(☎ 9358 6400, 14 Springfield Mall)*. It has a good atmosphere, good security and Internet access, and there's someone at the desk 24 hours. Dorms cost $19/120 per night/week, doubles $45/270. Rooms have fridges and each bed has its own reading light.

The long-established ***Rucksack Rest*** *(☎ 9358 2348, 9 McDonald St)* is tucked away down a relatively sedate cul-de-sac off Macleay St, in Potts Point. It's quiet, clean and in reasonable condition. The rooms are fairly small, but comfortable, and dorms sleep no more than three people. Dorm beds go for $17, single rooms $30, twins and doubles around $40 (depending on the size of the room). If you stay a week, you only pay for six nights.

A popular Kings Cross hostel is ***Barncleuth House Travellers Hostel*** *(☎ 9358 1689, 6 Barncleuth Square)*, east of Darlinghurst Rd. Not far from the main drag, it's also called the Pink House Travellers Hostel. It has a courtyard garden, log fires and a (loud) loudspeaker system. Dorm beds cost from $18 to $19 ($114 weekly), doubles and twins $20-21 per person ($126 weekly). The uninhibited can also take a double bed in one of the dorms, for $14/90 nightly/weekly per person.

The sherbet-coloured ***Backpackers Headquarters*** *(☎ 9331 6180, 79 Bayswater Rd)* has beds for $19/114 per night/week in 10-bed dorms, $20/120 in 6-bed dorms. There's one double room for $54/324. (Rooms on the side away from busy Kings Cross Rd are quieter.) There's good security, and the place is often full.

A touch more luxurious, just west of the Cross is ***Forbes Terrace*** *(☎ 9358 4327, 153 Forbes St, Woolloomooloo)*. It's clean, quiet and has a good courtyard area. It charges $18 to $20 for a dorm bed, $60 for twins and doubles. If you stay for six nights, the seventh night is free. Rooms have TV, fridge and tea and coffee-making facilities. Clean linen is supplied free.

Funk House *(☎ 9358 6455, 23 Darlinghurst Rd)* is a relative newcomer but rates high on the fun scale. It's a colourful, bustling place with dorm beds for $20 ($120 weekly) and doubles for $48. It's also a fully-fledged travel agency. Enter from Llankelly Place.

Surry Hills (Maps 7 & 8) Set in an old house, ***Kangaroo Bakpak*** *(☎ 9319 5915, 665 South Dowling St)* is a relaxed and friendly place that gets consistently good feedback. Dorm beds cost $18 ($100 weekly), and the rooms at the front have balconies. Doubles and twin rooms cost

$50/250 per night/week. From Central station, take bus No 372, 393 or 395. ***Nomads Backpackers*** *(☎ 9331 6487, Captain Cook Hotel, 162 Flinders St)* has beds in 10-bed dorms for $17, four-bed dorms for $20; double and twin rooms cost $44. Weekly rates are available. It's on a busy intersection near the Moore Park cricket ground and football stadium, and gets booked out when big games are on.

The ***Excelsior Hotel*** *(☎ 9211 4945, 64 Foveaux St)* is only a few blocks from Central station. Most rooms offer reasonable pub accommodation (but the bands in the downstairs bar can be a bit raucous), and most dorms have between three and six beds. Dorm beds/doubles cost $19/49 ($108/220 weekly). VIP cardholders get discounts.

Alfred Park Private Hotel *(☎ 9319 4031, 207 Cleveland St)* is also close to Central station. Occupying two adjacent houses, it has plain but clean rooms of varying sizes and ambience. (The house next door to the mauve one has better rooms.) There's a pleasant courtyard and kitchen and a balcony overlooking the park; rooms have TV and fridge. Dorms with attached bathrooms cost $18. Both singles and twins cost $60 ($80 if you want your own bathroom). There are cheaper weekly rates.

Glebe (Map 9) The hostels, restaurants and entertainment options in Glebe make it a good area to stay in.

Located in a large, brick block, the friendly ***Glebe Point YHA Hostel*** *(☎ 9692 8418, 262-64 Glebe Point Rd)* has five-bed dorms for $19, four-bed for $21 and clean but bare twin/double rooms for $50. (Non-YHA members add $3.) It offers a large range of activities as well as luggage storage.

Two doors down is ***Glebe Village Backpackers*** *(☎ 9660 8133, 256-58 Glebe Point Rd)*. Set in a sprawling old house, this is a hostel suited to travellers who place sociability above cleanliness. It's well-worn, but people like the lively atmosphere; there's a crowded noticeboard and plenty of outside seating. Dorms cost around $20 ($125 per week), doubles and twins $50 ($300 per week). The cafe downstairs does $5 breakfasts.

Wattle House *(☎ 9692 0879 or 9552 4997, 44 Hereford St)* is a small hostel in a pleasant, old house. It's clean, renovated and has nice extras, such as free linen and doonas. The owners are friendly. This is *not* a hostel for party animals. It has a minimum stay of three nights for advance bookings. Rates are a touch higher than at other hostels, but the standard of accommodation makes it worthwhile. Rooms are often full. A bunk in a four-bed dorm costs $20 ($130 to $140 weekly), twin and double rooms $55 to $60 ($350 weekly).

Dorm beds are available for $20 at the spotless ***Alishan International Guesthouse*** *(☎ 9566 4048, 100 Glebe Point Rd)*. See also Glebe under Places to Stay – Mid Range.

Newtown (Map 9) The YHA operates a summer hostel at ***St Andrews College*** *(☎ 9557 1133)* at the University of Sydney, where dorms cost $18, twins and doubles $22 per person. Take bus No 422, 423, 426 or 428 from Railway Square.

Billabong Gardens *(☎ 9550 3236, toll-free 1800 806 419, 5-11 Egan St)* is a lovely hostel, built by one of Sydney's original hostel owners. It's clean and quiet. There's a small solar-heated pool surrounded by thriving native plants, and a large professional-looking kitchen. Dorms cost $18 ($105 weekly) with shared bathroom, or $19 ($115 weekly) with *en suite*; twins/doubles cost $49 nightly (280 weekly) with bathroom. Triples ($65) and a family room ($75) are also available.

The hostel picks travellers up at the airport by arrangement. From Railway Square, catch bus No 422, 423, 426 or 428 up Newtown's King St, and get off at Missenden Rd. By train, go to Newtown station and turn right; Egan St is about four blocks along, on the left.

Bondi Beach (Map 11) There's a range of accommodation in Bondi, not all of it appealing, but with the beach on your doorstep you're unlikely to spend much time in your room. This is a popular base for long-term, working travellers, and there are plenty of inexpensive flats available.

The long-running ***Lamrock Hostel*** *(☎ 9365 0221, 7 Lamrock Ave)*, a block back from Campbell Parade, is a well-worn but bright house with dorm beds for $20 ($100 weekly), singles $140 weekly (a nightly rate of $25 is available once you've stayed a week); doubles and twins cost $40/220 nightly/weekly. Studio flats are $90 per person per week, and sleep four to five people.

Nomads Backpackers Bondi *(☎ 9130 1366, toll-free 1800 814 885, 2 Campbell Parade)* is at the southern end of the beach. It's a well-run place in a great location, with worn but clean rooms. Singles, doubles and twins with shared bathroom are all $45/315 a night/week. Some rooms sleep up to four people; an extra person costs $10. Beds in three to four-bed dorms cost $20/140, six-bed dorms $18/126; most rooms have TV and fridge, and there's a good lounge with pinball machines and a pool table.

Other places in Bondi have shared rooms; see the Hotels & Guesthouses section later.

Coogee (Map 10) It's further from the city than Bondi and other traveller centres, but Coogee's relaxed atmosphere and low-season specials make it a popular spot. It's worth ringing hostels before arriving because some have limited office hours.

Surfside Backpackers Coogee *(☎ 9315 7888, 186 Arden St)* is opposite the beach and main bus stop. The entrance is on Alfreda St. It's a fine hostel with a five-backpack rating and has balconies, some with views of the beach. Dorm rates are $19 ($130 weekly) in a four bed dorm, $18 ($115) in a 16 bed dorm.

The popular ***Coogee Beach Backpackers*** *(☎ 9315 8000, 94 Beach St)* is a short, stiff walk up the hill at the northern end of the beach. It occupies a Federation-era house and a modern block next door. There are good common areas and a deck with great views of the ocean. Dorms cost $20, doubles $48.

The smaller ***Indy's*** *(☎ 9315 7644, 302 Arden St)* is on the hill at the southern end, in a pleasant, old Victorian-era house. Beds in four-bed dorms cost $18/118 nightly/weekly; some rooms on the lower floor are a bit musty, so investigate first. There's a TV room, and rates include breakfast.

Manly (Map 12) Manly has great ocean and harbour beaches and few city hassles, and is only 30 minutes by ferry (15 minutes by JetCat) from Circular Quay.

The ***Manly Beach Resort Backpackers*** *(☎ 9977 4188, 6 Carlton St)* is part of a motel. Backpackers have their own section. The spacious, clean dorms cost $18/119 per night/week, twin and double rooms $40/250. The long-running, pleasant, and strictly run ***Manly Astra Backpackers*** *(☎ 9977 2092, 68 Pittwater Rd)* is nearby. Bunks in dorms cost $18/98 per person, doubles $20/108 per person.

Actually about a block from the beach, ***Manly Backpackers Beachside*** *(☎ 9977 3411, 28 Raglan St)* has beds in modern three-bed dorms for $19/120 and in four to six-bed dorms for $18/115. It also has twins/doubles for $50 and doubles with *en suite* for $55.

Alcohol-free ***The Wharf Backpackers*** *(☎ 9977 2800, 48 East Esplanade)* is near Manly wharf. It has three kitchens, a garden/barbecue area, and an Internet lounge in the foyer. Dorm beds cost $17 to $18, twin rooms $23 nightly per person, or $150 a week.

The ***Steyne Hotel*** *(☎ 9977 4977, 75 The Corso)* has bunks in four-bed dorms at a relatively pricey $35 a night, including breakfast. There are good shared kitchen facilities, and bistro-style meals available in the bar downstairs.

North Shore Being the affluent area that it is, there's not a lot of budget hostel accommodation on the North Shore. If you want to get out of the city, the relaxed beachside suburb of Avalon has the ***Avalon Beach Hostel*** *(☎ 9918 9709, 59 Avalon Parade)*. It's a sociable place, but it's not particularly clean or quiet. Beds in dorms cost $20 ($125 weekly) or $18 in a smaller dorm. Doubles cost $44. Phone in advance because it's often full.

Take bus No L90 from Town Hall or Wynyard Park in the city, or No L88 from Town Hall. Ask for Avalon Beach (1¼ hours, $4.60).

Hotels & Guesthouses

A wide variety of accommodation falls into this category. There are some fine budget hotels and guesthouses, which work out only fractionally more expensive than hostels if you're travelling with friends. A refundable key deposit of $10 is often required.

Some cheaper, older hotels in and near the city centre have so far survived Sydney's redevelopment.

City Centre (Map 4 & 8) The rambling ***CB Private Hotel*** *(☎ 9211 5115, 417 Pitt St)* first opened in 1908 and was once the largest residential hotel in the country, with over 200 (mostly single) rooms. It's plain, well run, and reasonably clean with fresh linen supplied, though it has seen a lot of wear, and most of the aging rooms lack power points. Nightly rates are $34/54/64 for singles/doubles/triples with shared bathroom; beds in four-bed dorms cost $18 a night.

The ***George Hotel*** *(☎ 9211 1800, 700a George St)* is one of the best innercity budget hotels. It's plain, clean and equipped with cooking and laundry facilities. Singles/doubles with common bathroom cost $36/54, and a double with TV and attached bathroom is $75. Weekly rates are available.

The basic ***Sydney Central Private Hotel*** *(☎ 9212 1005, 75 Wentworth Ave)* is a short walk from Central station and Oxford St. It has cooking and laundry facilities. Singles/doubles with shared bathroom cost $35/55 ($125/200 weekly), doubles with private bathroom cost $75. The traffic can be noisy, but staying six nights gets you a seventh night free.

Crystal Palace Hotel *(☎ 9211 0957, 789 George St)* is a pub with OK singles/doubles for $45/65 nightly ($180/240 weekly). Double rooms have attached bathrooms, and all have fridges. The bistro downstairs serves $5 pastas. The ***Criterion Hotel*** *(☎ 9264 3093)*, on the corner of Pitt and Park Sts, is a large pub with rooms from $50/60, or $80/90 with attached bathroom. An extra person costs $10.

The Rocks (Map 4) The small ***Harbour View Hotel*** *(☎ 9252 3769, 18 Lower Fort)* should have been renamed the 'Bridge View' back in 1932 because it's beside an approach pylon. There's some noise from trains, even more from the bands in the bar, but with clean singles/doubles at $50/65 (including breakfast), it's pretty good value for the location.

Palisade Hotel *(☎ 9247 2272, 35 Bettington St)* stands sentinel-like at Millers Point. Originally constructed to house the men who built the Harbour Bridge, it's a lovely old heritage building, offering bright, clean pub rooms with shared bathroom and views for $88 a double.

Pyrmont (Map 10) The ***Woolbrokers Arms*** *(☎ 9552 4773)*, on the corner of Allen and Pyrmont Sts, is close to Darling Harbour. It offers reasonable motel-style B&B for $85 a double. Rooms vary in size, and all have TV and fridge; bathrooms are separate, but they're numerous enough to ensure privacy.

Kings Cross (Maps 5 & 6) There are some reasonable hotels in the heart of the Cross. The friendly ***Bernly Private Hotel*** *(☎ 9358 3122, 15 Springfield Ave)* has uninspiring but acceptable singles/doubles with shared bathroom for $45/50. It also has 'deluxe' *en suite* rooms with telephones for around $80.

Similar in style but a little more basic is ***Orwell Lodge*** *(☎ 9358 1745, 18-20 Orwell St)*, which charges $160/180 weekly – nightly rates aren't available in the high season.

Springfield Lodge *(☎ 9358 3222, 9 Springfield Ave)* with its pink-painted exterior, is hard to miss. The rooms are average, and all have fridge, TV and tea and coffee-making facilities. Singles/doubles with shared bathroom cost $35/45 ($210/270 weekly), and with attached bathroom it's $60/70 ($360/420). You're advised to book ahead.

Palms Private Hotel *(☎ 9357 1199, 23 Hughes St)* is a quiet guesthouse with a TV lounge and communal kitchen. Reception hours are from 8 am to 8 pm. It has singles/doubles for $40/50 with fridge and shared bathroom, doubles with *en suite* for $70; it's a good idea to book.

Montpelier Private Hotel *(☎ 9358 6960, 39A Elizabeth Bay Rd)* has plain but cheap rooms for $30/40 ($150/180 weekly) with shared bathroom, tea and coffee-making facilities, TV and fridge.

Potts Point (Map 5) Not as cheap as it once was, but in a good spot nonetheless, is the low-key, well-maintained ***Challis Lodge*** *(☎ 9358 5422, 21-3 Challis Ave)*. In a pair of renovated cavernous terraces not far from the Cross, it has simple but clean *en suite* singles/doubles for $45/55 ($270/330 weekly), and rooms with a private balcony for $70/420. Singles/doubles without bathroom cost $35/45. Rooms on the upper floors are quieter and get better light.

The ***Point Inn*** *(☎ 9357 3878, 31 Challis Ave)* is a quiet, friendly guesthouse in a great location. Like many places pre-Olympics, it was being refurbished at the time of writing, but rooms should cost $35/45 or $40/60 with bathroom.

Around the corner, ***Macleay Lodge*** *(☎ 9368 0660, 71 Macleay St)* has good-value, bright single rooms from $35/210 per night/week, doubles from $40/240 (the better rooms on the upper floors cost more). Nearby, ***Holiday Lodge Hotel*** *(☎ 9356 3955, 55 Macleay St)* has basic motel-style rooms with air-con, TV, phone and fridge for $50 to $60.

Newtown Despite its worn exterior, ***Australian Sunrise Lodge*** *(☎ 9557 4400, 485 King St)* is a clean, pleasant place with parquet floors and potted plants. It has reasonable motel-style singles/doubles with TV and fridge for $45/55, or *en suite* rooms for $65. Turn left when you leave the station.

Bondi Beach (Map 11) Hotels in Bondi are prone to summer price-hikes, like in most beachside suburbs. Rates vary depending on demand; those listed are for the busy summer season. However, these summer rates may rise on weekends and the bargain weekly rates may be dropped. There are better deals when trade is slow.

The renovated ***Biltmore Private Hotel*** *(☎ 9130 4660, 110 Campbell Parade)* has a TV lounge, kitchen and laundry. It charges $20/120 for dorm beds and $35/45 ($190/280 weekly) for singles/doubles; rooms vary widely in size and quality, so check this before you check in.

Hotel Bondi *(☎ 9130 3271, 178 Campbell Parade)* is the peach-coloured layer-cake on the beachfront. It has small single rooms (men only) for $45, as well as a range of other accommodation (see Bondi under Places to Stay – Mid-Range).

Thelellen Lodge *(☎ 9130 1521, 11a Consett Ave)* is a modest but friendly operation in a renovated house two blocks back from the beach. It's clean, has a modern kitchen and singles/doubles for $45/49. All rooms have TV, fridge, toaster, and tea/coffee facilities. Occupying the three houses next door is ***Bondi Beach Guesthouse*** *(☎ 9389 8309, 11 Consett Ave)*, with dorm beds for $20 ($120 weekly) and singles/doubles for $30/50. Most rooms have TV and fridge, and there are laundry facilities and some off-street parking.

The large, pink-painted ***Bondi Lodge*** *(☎ 9365 2088, 63 Fletcher St)* is a short walk up the hill from the southern end of the beach, but close to neighbouring Tamarama Beach. It offers a deal including dinner, bed and breakfast for $30 in a dorm ($175 weekly), and from $60/80 in singles/doubles ($300/400 weekly).

Coogee (Map 10) At Coogee's southern end is the ***Grand Pacific Private Hotel*** *(☎ 9665 6301)*, at the bottom of Carr St, near the beach. Once truly grand, it's now pretty dilapidated, but in a charming kind of way. Rooms have TV, fridge and tea and coffee-making facilities, and some have sea views. Bathrooms are communal, and there's a guests' kitchen and laundry. Rates for singles/doubles are $35/45 for the first two nights, less thereafter.

Coogee Beach Private Hotel *(☎ 9665 1162, 171 Arden St)*, at the northern end of the beach, has dorm beds for $20/120, doubles for $55/330, including breakfast. The four to six-bed dorms are basic but clean; those on the upper floors get more light. There's a barbecue area up top.

Manly (Map 12) Manly is a popular holiday resort, so it's particularly susceptible to summer price-rises.

The large ***Eversham Private Hotel*** *(☎ 9977 2423, 27-29 Victoria Parade)* has been undergoing structural renovations for some time now, but rooms rates have remained constant. Unpromising singles cost $28/123 nightly/weekly; the weekly rate for doubles/twins is $133 for one person, $150 for two. There's a dining room and some deals include meals.

Ask at Manly Lodge (see Places to Stay – Mid-Range) about the secluded ***Manly Cove Guest House*** *(51 Wood St)*; singles cost $70 a night, but all weekly rates are between $190 and $220.

North Shore ***St Leonards Mansions*** *(☎ 9439 6999, 7 Park Rd, St Leonards)* occupies three old houses and has well-equipped, clean singles/doubles for $60/80 ($255/290 weekly). Triple rooms cost $400 a week. Most rooms have phone, fridge, cooking facilities and *en suite*, and some have balconies with city views. A light breakfast is free if you're paying nightly rates, and there are laundry and parking facilities. From St Leonards station, head west along the Pacific Highway (Hwy); Park Rd is the second street on your left.

North Sydney Lodge *(Map 2, ☎ 9955 1012, 310 Miller St, North Sydney)* is a pleasant guesthouse opposite St Leonards Park. All rooms have bathrooms and rates include breakfast; both singles and doubles cost $82.

The quiet suburb of Kirribilli, north-east of the bridge, has several guesthouses. ***Tremayne Private Hotel*** *(Map 2, ☎ 9955 4155, 89 Carabella St)* is a large, clean, quality guesthouse originally built as accommodation for country girls attending school in Sydney. Rates for singles/doubles are $25/35 ($150/230 weekly) with shared bathroom, $180/250 weekly with *en suite*. There's a minimum stay of two nights, and some rooms have harbour views.

Nearby is ***Kirribilli Court Private Hotel*** *(Map 2, ☎ 9955 4344, 45 Carabella St)*, with its mock-Tudor frontage and leafy surrounds. It offers fairly unremarkable singles/doubles with shared bathroom for $30/40 ($150/190 weekly). Dorm beds cost $15 ($80 weekly).

Glenferrie Private Hotel *(Map 2, ☎ 9955 1685, 12a Carabella St)* to the south, is in a large, old house. It's been refurbished in a fairly chintzy style, but the rooms are clean and each has a fridge. Singles/doubles with shared bathroom cost $68/96 ($408/576 weekly) including a buffet-style breakfast and dinner; there are sometimes discounts for students and longer stays.

Neutral Bay Motor Lodge *(Map 2, ☎ 9953 4199)*, on the corner of Kurraba Rd and Hayes St, Neutral Bay, is near the ferry wharf. It's a quiet, friendly guesthouse with clean, tasteful rooms. Rates are $60/70 ($360/420 weekly) with a private bathroom; singles with shared bathroom range from $130 to $150 a week, doubles from $180 to $200.

University Colleges

Many residential colleges accept casual guests. Those listed accept nonstudents and both men and women. Unless otherwise stated, rooms are available during holidays only, mainly the long mid-December to late January break.

Although most places quote meal-inclusive rates, it's often possible to negotiate a lower bed-only rate. Ask about weekly or fortnightly rates which, if available, might also be cheaper.

University of Sydney (Map 9) The uni is south-west of Chippendale, close to Glebe and Newtown.

International House *(☎ 9950 9800, 96 City Rd, Chippendale)* has fully serviced B&B rooms for $35, full board for $45.

St Johns College *(☎ 9394 5200, 8a Missenden Rd, Camperdown)* has rooms available all year-round. B&B *en suite* rooms cost $55-$67 nightly, $220 to $270 weekly.

Wesley College *(☎ 9565 3333)* costs students $38 for B&B, $48 full board; everyone else $43/55.

The ***Women's College*** *(☎ 9517 5000, 15 Carillon Ave, Newtown)* has B&B singles for $36. It's $42 with dinner and $48 for full board (students and YHA members); standard rates $45/52/58. Twin rooms cost $60/72/80 (students and YHA), or $66/80/90 (standard rates).

Also worth trying are ***St Paul's College*** *(☎ 9550 7444, 9 City Rd, Newtown)* and ***Sancta Sophia College*** *(☎ 9577 2100, 8 Missenden Rd, Camperdown)*.

University of NSW Although this university is further from the city centre, it's only a short bus ride from here to the southern ocean beaches and Oxford St.

International House *(☎ 9663 0418, Gate 2, High St, Kensington)* has students' full board for $40; for several weeks around Christmas it offers B&B for $30.

New College *(☎ 9662 6066, Anzac Parade, Kensington)* has B&B accommodation for $40, with all meals $45; students get $5 discount.

Kensington Colleges *(☎ 9315 0000, The High St, Randwick)* and ***Shalom College*** *(☎ 9663 1366, Barker St, Kensington)* are also worth trying.

PLACES TO STAY – MID-RANGE

This section covers places charging about $70 to $170 for a double. It's a wide price span, and standards vary accordingly.

B&Bs

The ***B&B Sydneyside*** *(☎ 9449 4430, PO Box 555, Turramurra, NSW 2074)* finds accommodation in private homes in Sydney for about $55 to $75 a night for a single, $70 to $110 a double.

This is a good way of meeting locals and getting inside advice on things to see and do. For those who don't want B&B accommodation, but still want to meet Sydneysiders, it can sometimes arrange lunches.

Hotels & Motels

There are some mid-range hotels and guesthouses offering top-value facilities at little more than budget prices. Some hotels in

Hotels vs Pubs

First-time visitors to Australia may be confused by the distinction between hotels and ... well, hotels. There are three kinds.

Until relatively recently, any establishment serving alcohol was called a hotel and was legally required to provide accommodation. These hotels are also known as pubs (public houses). Not surprisingly, the accommodation facilities at many were minimal, designed merely to satisfy the licensing authorities. A pub room is usually pretty basic: bathrooms are almost always shared and you probably won't have a phone.

Private hotels are usually boarding-house style places with similar facilities to pubs, but without a bar. These often have 'private' in their name to distinguish them from pubs.

Hotels which provide accommodation with extra facilities, such as room service, are usually rated at three stars or higher.

Sydney has a range of all three types of hotels. Pubs are generally the cheapest and most spartan, and can be good value, especially in country areas on the fringes of the city – although if you're seeking a quiet night's rest, you might like to check the location of rowdy jukeboxes and/or bands in the downstairs bar before choosing your room.

The entrance to Taronga Zoo

MIKE COTTEE

Taronga Zoo is a short ferry ride from Circular Quay.

SIMON BRACKEN

Bondi Beach is one of the most popular beaches in Sydney and a mecca for sun-lovers. However, finding your own patch of sand in summer can sometimes prove tricky.

this section are pubs that provide slightly above-average accommodation.

City Centre (Maps 4 & 8) Excellent value for the location, ***Wynyard Hotel*** *(☎ 9299 1330)*, on the corner of Clarence and Erskine Sts, is a pleasant pub with singles/doubles with shared bathroom for $60/70 (including breakfast and use of laundry facilities). The rooms are plain, but clean and comfortable, and weekly rates are available. There's a rooftop area with views, and a good guest kitchen.

Another innercity pub is the heritage-listed ***Grand Hotel*** *(☎ 9232 3755, 30 Hunter St)* where prices are a little higher at $70/90. Triples/family rooms cost $105/115 daily. Rooms are modest, sizes vary and all have TV, fridge and tea and coffee-making facilities.

Sydney Vista Hotel *(☎ 9274 1222, 7-9 York St)* has a good, central location. Although the rack rate for a fairly ordinary room is $245, you can often get one for around $160. Apartments start at $185.

Park Regis *(☎ 9267 6511, toll-free 1800 221 138, 27 Park St)* is a fairly sparse motel-style place with plain rooms for $150 a night, and cheaper weekly rates. It has free parking, and stunning views from the 40th-floor laundry! The friendly, well-appointed ***Hyde Park Inn*** *(☎ 9264 6001, toll-free 1800 221 030, 271 Elizabeth St)* is being refurbished and charges $130/145 a for a standard single/double, $150/160 for smart 'deluxe' rooms, and $200 for an apartment. All rooms have kitchens, and prices include breakfast.

Convenient to Central station, the renovated ***Westend Hotel*** *(☎ 9211 4822, 412 Pitt St)* has 13 floors of small, fairly featureless motel-style rooms, but all are clean with bathroom, TV, fridge, air-con and phone. Singles/doubles cost $85/100 (for stays of five or more nights, take $10 off the nightly rate). There's a bar and restaurant.

Aaron's Hotel *(☎ 9281 5555, toll-free 1800 023 071, 37 Ultimo Rd, Haymarket)* is near Chinatown and Darling Harbour. It has plain, clean, light rooms with TV and attached bathroom for $130 (plus $10 for each extra person), although cheaper specials are sometimes available.

Southern Cross Hotel *(☎ 9282 0987, toll-free 1800 221 141)*, on the corner of Goulburn and Elizabeth Sts, has a rooftop pool and garden, and a piano bar; it's within walking distance of Hyde Park, Oxford St and Darling Harbour. The standard rate is $150 per night, but it often has specials.

The incongruously-named ***Country Comfort Hotel*** *(☎ 9212 2544)*, on the corner of George and Quay Sts, is in a very urban spot, near Central station and Darling Harbour and next to Her Majesty's Theatre. It's decorated in pseudo-rural style, and rates are $142 per room.

Darling Harbour (Map 4) On the western side of Darling Harbour, ***Glasgow Arms Hotel*** *(☎ 9211 2354, 527 Harris St)*, near the Powerhouse Museum, has rooms in a renovated old-style pub. B&B with bathroom, air-con and breakfast costs $90/110.

Hotel Ibis *(☎ 9563 0888, toll-free 1800 642 244, 70 Murray St)*, overlooking the harbour, is beside the Novotel (with which it shares its 1800 number). Its rooms cost $140; $160 with a harbour (and city) view.

The Rocks (Map 4) The ***Lord Nelson Brewery Hotel*** *(☎ 9251 4044, 19 Kent St, Millers Point)* is a swish boutique pub in a sandstone building on the edge of the Rocks. Rooms cost $180, $160 with shared bathroom. All rooms have fax machines.

The green-tiled ***Mercantile Hotel*** *(☎ 9247 3570, 25 George St)* is a restored pub with a strong Irish connection. Right near the bridge, it has reasonable singles/doubles from $70/100 with breakfast and shared bathroom.

Kings Cross & Around (Maps 5 & 6) The ***O'Malley's Hotel*** *(☎ 9357 2211, 228 William St)* is a friendly Irish pub with traditionally decorated, air-con rooms for $80/85 including breakfast. The rooms are well furnished. Some twins share a bathroom, but doubles have attached bathrooms. The only drawback is the noise – the traffic on William St rarely lets up.

Maksim Lodge *(☎ 9356 3399, 37 Darlinghurst Rd)* is another friendly place with singles/doubles for $70/80 nightly, $420/480 weekly; all have bathroom, fridge, phone and TV.

The ***Barclay Hotel*** *(☎ 9358 6133, 17 Bayswater Rd)* has a range of air-con rooms with TV, telephone and bathroom for $70/80, though some rooms don't get much light or fresh air. ***Metro Motor Inn*** *(☎ 9356 3511, 40 Bayswater Rd)* charges $85 for doubles with TV, kitchen and bathroom.

The hip ***L'Otel*** *(☎ 9360 6868, 114 Darlinghurst Rd)* is a stylish boutique hotel with individually designed rooms (some in retro 50s style) popular with soap stars and models. It charges $100 to $160 for a plush room with TV, telephone and attached bathroom, and $70 for plainer ones.

At the renovated ***Kingsview*** *(☎ 9358 5599, toll-free 1800 805 108, 30 Darlinghurst Rd)* in the heart of the Cross, rooms with air-con, TV, telephone and attached bathroom cost $75. The friendly ***Madison's Hotel*** *(☎ 9357 1155, 6-8 Ward Ave, Elizabeth Bay)* is in a converted 1930s building with a modern extension. Both doubles and singles cost $90 a night if you stay a week, $80 if you stay a fortnight, and $70 if you stay three weeks.

Crescent on Bayswater *(☎ 9357 7266, toll-free 1800 257 327, 33 Bayswater Rd)* is in a huge, modern brick building. A room/suite costs $160/180, which includes breakfast and car parking; there are sometimes special deals.

Top of the Town Hotel *(☎ 9361 0911, 227 Victoria St)* is near the L'Otel, and has a rooftop restaurant and swimming pool. Reasonable singles and doubles with showers cost $105, $125 with a spa; there's also a slick Internet cafe.

Potts Point (Maps 5 & 6) The ***De Vere Hotel*** *(☎ 9358 1211, 46 Macleay St)* has rooms sleeping one or two people with TV, telephone and bathroom for $100. At the lovely Art-Deco ***Manhattan Park Inn Hotel*** *(☎ 9358 1288, 8 Greenknowe Ave)* the standard rate for doubles is $145 to $165, depending on the view (the magnificent harbour on one side, a vacant lot on the other).

To the north is ***Chateau Sydney Hotel*** *(☎ 9358 2500, 14 Macleay St)*, where the rooms have small balconies, and the top floors have some great views – which are factored into the price. A dinner package (including double room, buffet dinner and breakfast) costs $205 to $225; the same deal minus dinner is $145 to $165.

Victoria Court Hotel *(☎ 9357 3200, 122 Victoria St)* is a quiet retreat in a comfortable boutique hotel occupying two restored terrace houses. There's security parking, and a pleasant courtyard. Rates range from $135 up to $180 for rooms with a balcony, and include continental breakfast. ***Holiday Inn*** *(☎ 9368 4000, 203 Victoria St)* charges $145 (includes a full buffet breakfast); the better rooms have harbour views.

Edgecliff & Rushcutters Bay (Map 5) The ***Woodmark Hotel*** *(☎ 9327 3207, 2b Mona Rd)* is near the intersection with New South Head Rd (the eastward continuation of William St), not far from Edgecliff station. The renovated rooms have a mini-kitchen with fridge and microwave, and some have good views. There's also a roof garden. Rates are $70/240 nightly/weekly.

Metro Motor Inn *(☎ 9238 7977, 230 New South Head Rd)* has slightly dreary rooms (but with great harbour views) for $90.

In Rushcutters Bay, the three-star, four storey ***Bayside*** *(☎ 9327 8511, 85 New South Head Rd)* has standard rooms for $135 – but check for specials.

Double Bay The pleasant, friendly ***Savoy Double Bay Hotel*** *(☎ 9326 1411, toll-free 1800 811 846, 41-45 Knox St)* is small but in a good location. Smaller rooms cost $135, standard doubles $145, including a light breakfast.

Watsons Bay To enjoy the harbour in a quiet locale and still be within a short ferry ride of the city, try the harbourside ***Watsons***

***Bay Hotel** (☎ 9337 4299, 1 Military Rd, Watsons Bay)*, which has B&B for $50/80 with separate bathroom (although impending renovations may raise prices).

Darlinghurst (Map 4) The 13 storey, three-star ***Oxford Koala Hotel** (☎ 9269 0645, toll-free 1800 222 144)*, on the corner of Oxford and Pelican Sts, has rooms for $130 to $150, and apartments for $180 including breakfast. During the week there are sometimes specials for $99.

Surry Hills (Map 8) The ***Crown Lodge International** (☎ 9331 2433, 289 Crown St)*, a little south of Oxford St, offers standard motel accommodation for $85 a room; there's a $5 nightly discount if you stay a week or more.

The more upmarket ***Cambridge Park Inn** (☎ 9212 1111, toll-free 1800 251 901, 212 Riley St)*, in a converted building, has a gym, sauna, heated pool and restaurant. Rates range from $190 for standard rooms, to $210 for suites with full facilities, but there are often specials.

Glebe (Map 9) With its lovely stained-glass entrance, ***Alishan International Guesthouse** (☎ 9566 4048, 100 Glebe Point Rd)* is both a guesthouse and an upmarket hostel. It boasts well-travelled, multilingual staff; good common areas, including kitchen and laundry facilities; and a small garden with a barbecue. Singles/doubles with bathroom cost $80/85, and there's a room set up for disabled travellers.

***Rooftop Motel** (☎ 9660 7777, toll-free 1800 227 436, 146-148 Glebe Point Rd)* is a simple motel charging around $80 for *en suite* rooms – some have pretty lurid green carpet, but it's a friendly place and there's a rooftop pool. Further north, on the corner of Wigram Rd, ***Haven Inn** (☎ 9660 6655, 196 Glebe Point Rd)* has decent-sized rooms (for an innercity motel) in the standard pink-and-grey colour scheme for $110 ($130 with a city view). There's a heated swimming pool, secure parking and a restaurant.

Closer to the city, ***A-Line Hotel** (☎ 9566 2111, 247-53 Broadway)* has modest, clean *en suite* rooms for $90. The foyer has interesting antique Chinese furniture.

Bondi Beach (Map 11) The peach-coloured layer-cake on the beachfront is ***Hotel Bondi** (☎ 9130 3271)*, on the corner of Campbell Parade and Curlewis St. It's an impressive old pile with small single rooms (men only) for $45, doubles for $85 (add $10 for a balcony and beach view) and renovated suites from $110 to $140.

***Bondi Beachside Inn** (☎ 9130 5311, 152 Campbell Parade)* has small, motel-style rooms. They all have air-con, phone, TV, kitchen and balcony. Rates are $98 for both singles and doubles.

The refurbished ***Beach Road Hotel** (☎ 9130 7247, 71 Beach Rd)* is a large pub two blocks back from the beach. Heavy on the beach-themed décor, it has several bars, a couple of eateries and a nightclub. The clean, bright rooms have air-con, fridge and bathroom, and go for $55/70.

***Ravesi's** (☎ 9365 4422)*, on the corner of Campbell Parade and Hall St, is an interesting, three-star hotel. There are only 16 rooms and suites, some with their own terraces. Rates start at $100, and go up to $275, depending on the view and degree of luxury. Check for special deals in winter and spring.

Coogee (Map 10) The huge ***Coogee Bay Hotel** (☎ 9665 0000)*, on the corner of Arden St and Coogee Bay Rd, is right in the centre of things. It has standard air-con singles/doubles with fridge, TV, telephone and *en suite* for $89/99; heritage suites cost from $109 to $159, quieter, renovated boutique rooms $155.

***Coogee Sands Motor Inn** (☎ 9665 8588, 165 Dolphin St)* was undergoing major renovations at the time of writing, so the new rates may reflect this.

Manly (Map 12) Because Manly's a beach resort, many places have seasonal and weekend deals; ring around to find out what's on offer.

Steyne Hotel's *(☎ 9977 4977, 75 The Corso)* rooms mostly come with shared bathroom. OK singles/doubles cost from $70/95. ***Manly Lodge*** *(☎ 9977 8655, 22 Victoria Parade)* is a guesthouse with a holiday atmosphere. Most rooms are small, but have TV, fridge, air-con and attached bathroom; some have spas. Doubles/twins start at $120 nightly, including breakfast, and there's a communal sauna, gym, and giant trampoline.

Manly Beach Resort *(☎ 9977 4188, 6 Carlton St)* is a reasonable motel with good security, offering singles/doubles from $95/105 to $105/115, which includes a continental breakfast.

Periwinkle Guest House *(☎ 9977 4668, 18-19 East Esplanade)* is an elegantly restored Victorian house facing the harbour beach at Manly Cove. Most rooms have *en suite*, and all have double beds. Room rates start from $120 nightly; rooms overlooking over the water cost $130. There's a stylish but cosy kitchen, and laundry facilities are available.

Manly Paradise Motel *(☎ 9977 5799, 54 North Steyne)* is on the beachfront. It has a rooftop pool and air-con motel rooms with TV, fridge and bathroom for $115, or $125 with a (side-on) ocean view; there's also one very small room for $90.

Serviced Apartments

Serviced apartments – which can be anything from a hotel room with a fridge and a microwave, to a full-size apartment – can be good value, especially for families.

City Centre (Map 4) The ***Sydney City Centre Apartments*** *(☎ 9233 6677/3529, 7 Elizabeth St)*, in the heart of the financial district, offers fully equipped bedsit apartments of a reasonable size, complete with washing machine and drier. Rates are $300 a week, but unfortunately there's a minimum nine week stay.

Near Hyde Park and Oxford St, ***Sydney Park Inn*** *(☎ 9360 5988, toll-free 1800 656 708, 2-6 Francis St)*, behind the NSW police headquarters, provides fully equipped studios complete with air-con, kitchenette, TV, video and personal safe. Some rooms are lighter than others. Rooms cost $115 including breakfast.

Darling Harbour (Map 4) The ***Metro Inn*** *(☎ 9290 9200, 132 Sussex St and 27-29 King St)* has good serviced apartments close to Darling Harbour. The clean, bright rooms sleep four to five people, are split level and have great views. There's a kitchenette, and a clothes washer and drier. Great value, especially for families, apartments cost $155 per night or $125 per night if you stay a week or more.

The nearby ***Savoy Apartments*** *(☎ 9267 9211, 37-43 King St)* are a little more expensive – an apartment costs $165 per night; it's $140 per night if you stay a week or more.

Downtown Serviced Apartments *(☎ 9261 4333, 336 Sussex St)* has a tennis court and swimming pool, plus a rooftop garden with good views of the harbour. The apartments have two bedrooms, kitchen and living room and cost $170 for two people (extra person $20).

Waldorf *(☎ 9261 5355, toll-free 1800 023 361, 57 Liverpool St)* has a rooftop pool, spa, barbecue area and free parking. Fully equipped singles sleeping up to three people cost $175, doubles cost $240 ($290 for six people).

Potts Point (Map 5) On the steep northern continuation of Macleay St, ***Oakford Potts Point Apartments*** *(☎ 9358 4544, toll-free 1800 657 392, 10 Wylde St)* charges $175/225 for one/two-bedroom apartments. All-in-one studio rooms cost $103, $113 with harbour views. The décor is a little chilly, but rooms are clean and modern.

Elizabeth Bay (Map 5) In Elizabeth Bay, down the road from the Cross, ***17 Elizabeth Bay Rd*** *(☎ 9358 8999)* has well-equipped, serviced one-bedroom apartments for $160, two-bedroom ones (which sleep four people) for $205 nightly. Weekly rates are $140/175 per night. The name of the place is also its address.

Medina Executive Apartments *(☎ 9356 7400, 68 Roslyn Gardens)* has bright, quiet rooms overlooking an atrium from $90 to $120 nightly.

Rushcutters Bay The four storey ***Lodge Motel*** *(☎ 9328 0666, 38-44 New South Head Rd)* has studio apartments with TV, kitchenette and bathroom for $60 a double ($320 weekly).

PLACES TO STAY – TOP END

This section covers accommodation costing from around $160 a night. There are lots of five-star and four-star establishments to choose from. Travel agents in other states or countries can book many of these, and will have access to special deals and packages.

Hotels

Airport The ***Sydney Airport Hilton*** *(☎ 9518 2000, 20 Levey St, Arncliffe)* charges around $190 to $300 a room; most rates include breakfast, free parking, and a shuttle service to and from the airport.

City Centre (Map 4) The ***Sydney Hilton*** *(☎ 9266 2000, toll-free 1800 222 255, 259 Pitt St)* is in the heart of the city. Standard singles/doubles cost $380, but there are often cheaper weekend deals for almost half this price, especially in winter. The historic Marble Bar is downstairs (see Things to See & Do chapter).

The grand ***Menzies Hotel*** *(☎ 9299 1000, 1300 363 600, 14 Carrington St)*, across from Wynyard Park, has rooms for $185 with breakfast, and package deals on weekends. ***Wentworth Hotel*** *(☎ 9230 0700, toll-free 1800 226 466, 61-101 Phillip St)* is within walking distance of Circular Quay and the Macquarie St museums. Staff are super-courteous, and there's a piano bar downstairs; rack rates range from $275 to $650, but there are often specials.

Several hotels overlook Hyde Park. The friendly ***Sheraton on the Park*** *(☎ 9286 6000, 161 Elizabeth St)* has a magnificent lobby with enormous, maroon marble columns. Good rooms with views of the city/park cost $370/450, but there are sometimes heavily discounted specials.

Sydney Marriott Hotel *(☎ 9361 8400, toll-free 1800 025 419, 36 College St)* has rooms for $235, one/two-bedroom suites for $260/350. Next door, but with the same street number, is ***Hyde Park Plaza Hotel*** *(☎ 9331 6933)* where rooms start at $235; one/two-bedroom suites cost $260/275. Both hotels are close to the nightlife and restaurants of Oxford St.

Darling Harbour (Map 4) The huge, 700 room ***Hotel Nikko*** *(☎ 9299 1231, toll-free 1800 222 700, 161 Sussex St)* charges $290 to $350 depending on the view, but often has specials.

A hotel with good views of Darling Harbour and the city is the 530-room ***Novotel Sydney Hotel*** *(☎ 9934 0000, 1300 656 565, 100 Pyrmont St)*. It's behind Harbourside, and has a swimming pool, spa, gym and tennis court; rooms cost from $235 to $430. It's somewhat cut off from the harbour and you need to walk across covered footbridges (over Darling Rd) to get there.

Furama Hotel *(☎ 9281 0400, toll-free 1800 800 555, 68 Harbour St)*, in a renovated 19th century woolstore (and a modern extension), is directly opposite Sydney Entertainment Centre. It has a walk-in rate of $170 for standard rooms, up to $210 for a deluxe room.

The Rocks & Circular Quay (Map 4) In a superb location, the charming ***Russell Hotel*** *(☎ 9241 3543, 143a George St)* is a small, friendly, boutique-style hotel with traditionally decorated rooms, pleasant lounge areas and a sunny roof garden. Single/double rooms cost $100/110 with shared bathroom, $210/220 with attached bathroom. Apartment suites cost $230.

Stafford *(☎ 9251 6711, 75 Harrington St)* has plain but comfortable self-contained studios, and single-bedroom apartments (some in a row of restored terrace houses) from $180 to $335. Weekly rates are available. ***Harbour Rocks Hotel*** *(☎ 9251 8944, toll-free 1800 251 210, 34-52 Harrington St)*, diagonally opposite, also occupies restored 19th century buildings. Rooms here start at $185.

From the rooftop pool of the ***Old Sydney Parkroyal*** *(☎ 9252 0524, toll-free 1800 221 493, 55 George St)*, there are great views of the Rocks, Sydney Harbour Bridge, the harbour and the Opera House. The rack rate for a room is $350, but the hotel offers specials with hefty discounts, such as weekend nights for $199.

Regent *(☎ 9238 0000, toll-free 1800 222 200, 199 George St)* has excellent views from the upper floors. At the time of writing, it was closed for major renovations in preparation for the Olympics. Rack rates will start from $425 for a standard double with city views.

The lovely, three storey ***Observatory Hotel*** *(☎ 9256 2222, toll-free 1800 806 245, 89-113 Kent St)*, on the Millers Point side of the Bradfield Hwy, is large for a boutique hotel, but small for a five-star one. The rack rate for its plush rooms is $580, but you can often get one for around $400 (including breakfast).

Nearby is the big ***ANA Hotel Sydney*** *(☎ 9250 6111, toll-free 1800 801 080, 176 Cumberland St)*, which has 573 stylish rooms. All suites have harbour views. Rooms cost $370 to $460, most suites $620.

The luxurious ***Park Hyatt*** *(☎ 9241 1234, 13 1234, 7 Hickson Rd)* has one of the best locations in Sydney – on the waterfront at the edge of Campbells Cove, in the shadow of the Harbour Bridge and facing the Opera House. It charges from $600 for a room and up to $1200 for most suites. Watch out for discounted weekend packages.

Ritz-Carlton *(☎ 9258 3450, 1300 361 180, 93 Macquarie St)* is in an elegant brick building. The staff are courteous and helpful; comfortable rooms cost $309 to $369, suites $459 to $519.

Hotel-Intercontinental *(☎ 9230 0200, toll-free 1800 221 828, 117 Macquarie St)*, next door, is in a beautiful sandstone building that once housed the treasury. It's one of the few hotels with an environmental 'mission statement' by which it maintains 'best-practice' use of resources. Rooms cost $385 to $505 depending on the view, suites from $775, and there are weekly rates and package deals.

Potts Point (Maps 5 & 6) Definitely worth a look if you're after a bit of luxury, ***Simpsons of Potts Point*** *(☎ 9356 2199, 8 Challis Ave)* is in a superb old house in a quiet spot a short walk from Kings Cross. It offers large, well-furnished rooms with attached bathroom for $160 to $175 for one person, $10 more for two.

Regent's Court *(☎ 9358 1533, 18 Springfield Ave)* is a boutique hotel in a converted Art Deco apartment block close to the Cross. Stylish *en suite* rooms with small kitchens stocked with Twinings teas and plunger coffee cost $170 to $185. The Italian-style rooftop garden is a great place to relax after a hard day shopping.

The 470-room ***Landmark Parkroyal Hotel*** *(☎ 9368 3000, 81 Macleay St)* is popular with flight crews as well as tourists. Rooms with views cost $300 to $360, but intermittent specials can almost halve these rates.

Elizabeth Bay (Map 5) The ***Sebel of Sydney*** *(☎ 9358 3244, 23 Elizabeth Bay Rd)* has a reputation for celebrity guests, especially from the music industry. It has some quality touches, including a gym and rooftop heated pool. Rates are $169 to $459, with seasonal specials and good weekend deals.

Double Bay With its gold and deep purple décor, ***Sir Stamford*** *(☎ 9363 0100, 22 Cross St)* perches above the Cosmopolitan shopping centre. Reception is on the 3rd floor and pleasant rooms cost $215 to $235, suites $315 to $450.

At the plush ***Ritz-Carlton*** *(☎ 9362 4455, 33 Cross St, Double Bay)*, rooms cost from $199 to $275, suites $385 to $1200. It's popular with the powerful and famous who require discretion.

Bondi Beach & Coogee (Maps 10 & 11) The top-dollar place to stay in Bondi is the huge, balustraded ***Swiss Grand*** *(☎ 9365*

5666, toll-free 1800 655 252), on the corner of Beach Rd and Campbell Parade. The entrance is on Beach Rd. Normal suites cost $190; those with beach views start at $280. Some deals include breakfast, and rates may be lower depending on availability.

In Coogee, ***Holiday Inn*** *(☎ 9315 7600, toll-free 1800 553 888, 242 Arden St)* charges $169 for views of Coogee, $189 for ocean views; another $10 gets you breakfast for two, and there's a complimentary airport bus shuttle-service.

Manly (Map 12) Manly has two four-star hotels. The ***Manly Pacific Parkroyal*** *(☎ 9977 7666, 55 North Steyne)* has a gym and swimming pool, and rooms cost from $190 to $450. ***Radisson Kestrel*** *(☎ 9977 8866, 8 South Steyne)* has double rooms with air-con, TV and bathroom from $209 to $399. At both, the more expensive rooms offer views of the ocean.

North Shore (Map 2) The ***Duxton Hotel*** *(☎ 9955 1111, toll-free 1800 807 356, 11 Alfred St)* is across from Milsons Point station. It's a stylish, modern, four star hotel, oriented to business travellers, with easy access to North Sydney and the city. Nightly rates during the week are $220 but on weekends (Friday night to Monday morning) there are specials from $159 including breakfast.

Serviced Apartments

In the Rocks, ***Quay West Sydney*** *(Map 4, ☎ 9240 6000, toll-free 1800 805 031, 98 Gloucester St)* has quality apartments with views of Sydney Harbour or the city. Rates are $305 to $1300 for up to four people.

The 11-storey ***Carrington Apartments*** *(Map 4, ☎ 9299 6556, 57-59 York St)* has rooms for $140 to $180. Reception is on the 10th floor. From the 6th-floor swimming pool at ***York Apartment Hotel*** *(Map 4, ☎ 9210 5000, 5 York St)* you can see the approaches to Sydney Harbour Bridge. Rates for its spacious rooms are $215 to $500, including free parking.

Not far from Hyde Park, ***Parkridge Corporate Apartments*** *(Map 4, ☎ 9361 8600, 6-14 Oxford St)* has decent single/double suites for $160/190. There's a minimum stay of three nights.

Grand Esplanade Crest Hotel *(Map 12, ☎ 9976 4600, toll-free 1800 334 033, 54a West Esplanade, Manly)* is directly opposite the ferry terminal; studio apartments cost $180 for two people, $195 for three.

Places to Eat

With great local produce, innovative chefs, reasonable prices and BYO licensing laws, eating out is one of the great delights of Sydney. The city has a huge variety of eateries; this chapter is just an introduction to the vast number of cafes, bistros, restaurants and takeaways on offer.

Many restaurants serve 'modern Australian' food – an amalgamation of Mediterranean, Asian and Californian cooking practices that emphasises lightness, freshness and healthy eating. It's a hybrid style, shaped by migrant influences, climatic conditions and local produce. In Sydney this style has filtered down from sophisticated restaurants to modest corner bistros, so you can savour it whatever your budget. Cafes tend to serve a near ubiquitous diet of focaccia, bagels, filled croissants and sandwiches.

Even if you can't afford to dine at the top end, there are scores of places serving decent food at reasonable prices. Eating at modest Chinese, Indian and Vietnamese restaurants can be almost as cheap as eating at home. Pub counter-meals are also good for solid, inexpensive fare, and the many brasserie-style eateries are generally cheaper than formal restaurants.

CITY CENTRE (MAPS 4 & 8)

There's no shortage of places for a snack or a meal in the city centre on weekdays, but many, especially those north of Liverpool St, close in the evenings. They're clustered around train stations, in shopping arcades and tucked away in the food courts at the base of office buildings.

Fast Food

On Pitt St Mall there's reasonably priced food in ***Mid City Centre*** food court at street level, and in the ***Centrepoint*** food hall on the ground floor. They serve Mexican, Italian, Thai etc for $4 to $7. There is a range of eateries below street level of the ***Queen Victoria Building*** (QVB), which forms an arcade through to Town Hall station. Many remain open after the shops have closed. On the ground floor of the QVB, ***Bar Cupola*** serves good coffee and Italian-style sandwiches and sweets.

Woolworths, on the corner of George and Park Sts, has a 2nd floor cafeteria open daily serving filling meals like roast lamb or pork from around $5.

YWCA *(5-11 Wentworth Ave)* has a cafeteria serving sandwiches for around $2.20 and hot meals for $7. It's open from 7 am to 7 pm weekdays, 7 am to 11 am weekends.

For innercity snacks at odd hours, ***Coles Express*** *(☎ 9221 3119)*, on the corner of

GST

The Australian government plans to introduce a controversial 10% goods and services tax (GST) as of July 2000. This tax will be automatically added to virtually everything you buy, from taxi fares and accommodation, to clothing – even a humble cup of coffee.

However, the question of food and the GST remains an almost comically complicated issue. Pressure from concerned parties led the government to agree to waive the GST on 'basic fresh foods', while prepared foods will attract the new tax. At the time of writing, the finer points of the GST were still being thrashed out in parliament, but it seems likely, for example, that a fresh supermarket lettuce will be tax-free – but the same lettuce, once dismembered, dressed and sold in the deli section, or served at a restaurant, *will* be taxed – along with 'non-basic' supermarket items like cakes and biscuits.

While the cost of home-cooked meals won't change much, eating out will become comparatively more expensive.

King and George Sts, is open from 6 am to midnight daily. There's a patisserie section, fresh fruit and vegetables, and hot meals from $3.95.

Cafes

Obelisk, on Macquarie Place, has outdoor tables in a lovely spot just near the obelisk itself. Gourmet rolls, baguettes and chunky toasted sandwiches cost $6.50, Caesar salad $7.90. ***Bar Coluzzi*** *(99 Elizabeth St)*, near the Hyde Park fountain, serves good coffee and a range of interesting snacks: most are $5 to $7.50, cakes and biscuits are $2.50.

Deli on Market, on the corner of Clarence and Market Sts, is a large cafe offering muesli with fruit and yoghurt for $5, and a range of wholesome, reasonably priced lunches.

For a quiet cup of tea or coffee away from the city bustle, follow the smell of roasted beans to ***Harris Coffee and Tea***, on the ground floor of the elegant Strand Arcade, between Pitt St Mall and George St. It has a wide choice of coffee and teas from around $2.

Further south, ***Zenergy*** *(69 Druitt St)*, near Clarence St, is part of a small chain serving wholesome vegetarian fare – cheap and tasty sandwiches, salads and vegie burgers start from around $3.50. Breakfast specials are $2.50 to $3.

There's an above-average (by shopping mall standards) collection of eateries and bars on level 3 of ***Skygarden Arcade***, a recycled building on Pitt St Mall. Take the escalators to the top, where you can eat under a glassed-in roof. On the ground floor ***Il Gianfornaio*** serves coffee and an excellent selection of breads, sweets, cakes and gelati.

Vender *(86 Liverpool St)* is a small espresso bar with funky lights and a selection of filled pide breads and salads for $7 to $9. It's near the George St cinemas, is open until 11pm, and has good hot chocolate.

For palatable fast food at the other end of town, there's ***Central Park Cafe***, on Eddy Ave, next to the coach terminal in Haymarket. The options range from fresh fruit salads to roasts; focaccia and gourmet sandwiches are $4.50.

Pubs

Hotel Sweeney *(☎ 9267 1116)*, on the corner of Clarence and Druitt Sts, has a 2nd floor bistro where you can get $12 meals, or grab a drink and surf the Internet upstairs. Upstairs at the Edinburgh Castle Hotel is the welcoming ***Pitt St Bistro*** *(☎ 9264 8616)*, on the corner of Pitt and Bathurst Sts, serving interesting and relatively inexpensive meals (around $11) in pleasant, light surrounds.

South of Pitt St Mall, ***Arizona's*** *(☎ 9261 1077, 231-47 Pitt St)*, on the 1st floor beside the City Centre monorail stop, is one of a small chain of licensed 'western' bar/restaurants. Heavy on the kitsch décor, it serves Tex-Mex food, including nachos for $10.50. ***Chamberlain Hotel*** *(☎ 9211 1929)*, on the corner of Pitt and Campbell Sts, has $6 bar meals.

Restaurants

If high-altitude rotation doesn't make you queasy, ***International Revolving Restaurant*** *(☎ 8223 3800, Level 1, Centrepoint Tower)* has main courses from $27.50 for vegetarian dishes, to $42 for lobster. It's open for dinner Tuesday to Saturday. ***Level 2 Revolving Restaurant*** *(☎ 8223 3800)* has an all-you-can-eat buffet for $40, offering a selection of meats, seafood and Asian dishes, but little for vegetarians. Children under 12 pay $15. It's open daily for lunch and dinner. Diners aren't charged for the ride to the top of the tower, so you're $10 ahead. Bookings are recommended.

Dendy Bar & Bistro *(☎ 9221 1243, MLC Centre, Martin Place)* is an agreeable, comfy downstairs space serving dishes like risotto for $12 and wok-fried noodles for $8.50. There are pool tables, occasional live music, and weekend dance parties. The bar is open until midnight (later on weekends).

Slipp-Inn *(☎ 9299 4777, 111 Sussex St)* has a range of eating options: the Thai noodle bar upstairs is open weekdays for lunch (around $7); there's a restaurant downstairs with mains for around $24 (open for lunch and dinner Tuesday to Friday); and a pizza bar ($12 to $16), open for lunch and dinner Tuesday to Friday.

Diethnes *(☎ 9267 8956, downstairs, 336 Pitt St)*, north of Liverpool St, is a large, friendly Greek restaurant, serving lunch and dinner Monday to Saturday. Lamb specials cost $10.50 to $12.50, delicious haloumi (fried cheese) is $6. Alternatively, ***Hellenic Club*** *(☎ 9261 4910, 5th floor, 251 Elizabeth St)* overlooks Hyde Park. It's open for lunch and dinner weekdays, dinner Saturday. Mains are $11 to $16 (minimum charge $10 per person).

Planet Hollywood *(☎ 9267 7827, 600 George St)* is as tacky – and popular – as ever. A near-naked, latex Sly Stallone hovers from the ceiling, and the walls are crammed with movie memorabilia. Burgers cost $11.50 to $14.25.

Spanish Town consists of a small group of Spanish restaurants and bars along Liverpool St, between George and Sussex Sts. ***Capitan Torres*** *(☎ 9264 5574, 73 Liverpool St)* has a great bar, tapas from around $3, and good seafood for $15 to $20. ***Casa Asturiana*** *(☎ 9264 1010, 77 Liverpool St)* specialises in northern Spanish cooking, and reputedly has the best tapas in Sydney, for $5 to $7. ***Grand Taverna*** *(☎ 9267 3608)*, on the corner of Liverpool and George Sts at the Sir John Young Hotel, is another popular Spanish place. Mains like lemon sole and ocean perch are $15 to $16.

Ru-Yuan Vegetarian Restaurant *(☎ 9211 2189, 768 George St)* is a clean, airy place serving tasty vegan Chinese food. Szuchen spicy beancurd on rice costs $7.80. The nearby ***Saigon*** *(☎ 9212 3822)* is a Vietnamese restaurant that gets busy at lunchtime, offering quick meals like garlic beef with fried rice for $5.

Malaya on George *(☎ 9211 0946)*, on the corner of Valentine and George Sts, is a modern, spacious Malaysian/Chinese eatery. Most mains cost between $13 and $16, and vegetarian dishes start from $12. It's licensed, and is open weekdays for lunch, nightly for dinner (closed Sunday).

Mother Chu's Vegetarian Kitchen *(☎ 9283 2828, 376 Pitt St)* is another Asian restaurant serving vegan food. It's open for dinner daily, for lunch weekdays. Noodle dishes cost around $7, main courses (like honey-glazed gluten with walnut and sesame) $9 to $12. Similar is the voluminous ***Bodhi*** *(☎ 9281 9918, 187 Hay St)*. The heavenly lunchtime yum cha upstairs is legendary, and the takeaway downstairs has $2 vegie pies.

CHINATOWN (MAP 4)

Chinatown is a dense cluster of mostly Chinese restaurants, cafes, takeaways and shops catering to the Chinese community. There are also Thai, Vietnamese, Japanese and Korean eateries. Officially, Chinatown is confined to the pedestrian mall on Dixon St, but its culinary delights have spilled over into the surrounding streets, especially around Haymarket.

You can break the bank at some outstanding Chinese restaurants, or eat well for next to nothing in a food hall. Weekend yum cha makes such a popular brunch that you may have to queue for it.

Fast Food

The best place to start is the downstairs food hall in the pagoda-style ***Harbour Plaza***, on the corner of Dixon and Goulburn Sts (open from 10 am to 10 pm daily). There's a wide range of dishes for $4.50 to $6.50. There's a food hall on the top level of the ***Sussex Centre***, diagonally across from the Harbour Plaza, fronting Dixon St and backing onto Sussex St; and another in the ***Dixon House Food Court***, on the corner of Dixon St Mall and Little Hay St.

Cafes

Open daily, ***Emperor's Garden BBQ & Noodles*** *(213 Thomas St)* is a popular cafe-style Chinese eatery specialising in meat and poultry dishes. Pork and rice costs $5.

Beneath the House of Guangzhou restaurant, on the corner of Ultimo Rd and Thomas St, is the inexpensive and spotless Japanese cafe ***Fuji San***. It has a few tables and most meals cost from $5 to $10; it also does takeaway.

A busy, budget-minded place is the pink-walled ***Ching Yip Coffee Lounge*** *(434 Sussex St)*. Obviously owned by a keen Marilyn Monroe fan, it serves cheap, plain Asian and European food. Sandwiches start at $2.50, soups from $3.80, and mains are around $6.

Restaurants

At the intimate, busy ***Chinese Noodle Restaurant*** *(☎ 9281 9051, ground floor, Prince Centre, Thomas St)*, the noodles are handmade in traditional northern Chinese style, and most meals cost around $6. Next door is the Japanese/Korean ***Green Zone***, serving beautifully presented food like beef sukiyaki for around $8 to $14.

Meals with a View

Given the city's setting, it's not surprising that it offers some seriously good combinations of food and view.

The Doyle family has been serving seafood to Sydneysiders for several generations and now owns a swag of waterfront eateries. At Watsons Bay, ***Doyle's Wharf Restaurant***, ***Doyle's on the Beach*** and the bistro at ***Doyle's Watsons Bay Hotel*** all share views of the bay. ***Doyle's at the Markets***, a bistro and takeaway at Pyrmont Fish Markets, has views of the marina and the new Glebe Island Bridge.

From ***Doyle's at the Quay***, in the Overseas Passenger Terminal on Circular Quay West, you can gaze out over the harbour, the bridge and the Opera House. ***Quay***, on the top floor, above Doyle's, offers a similar vista, somewhat elevated. Further north at the Campbell's Storehouse complex the restaurants have outdoor areas with views across the quay.

There are also good vantage points on Circular Quay East: ***Sydney Cove Oyster Bar*** is a small place right on the waterfront, and nearby is the cheaper ***Portobello Caffe***, with a scattering of outdoor tables.

The three restaurants in the Opera House complex let you ogle the harbour to your heart's content. On the western side, ***Concourse*** is on the lower concourse; ***Harbour*** is at the 'prow' of the Opera House and has an outdoor area; upstairs is the classy ***Bennelong*** restaurant.

In the Rocks at Dawes Point west of the Harbour Bridge, ***Harbour Watch*** and the voluminous ***Wharf Restaurant*** are both perched at the end of piers overlooking the water.

The highest views in Sydney are from ***International Revolving Restaurant*** and ***Level 2 Revolving Restaurant***, both of which twirl in slow motion atop the Centrepoint Tower, at the corner of Market and Pitt Sts. The top-notch ***Restaurant 41***, on the 41st floor of the Chifley Square tower, corner of Hunter and Elizabeth Sts, also affords an awe-inspiring panorama – if you're lucky enough to be dining here, the women's toilets offer what must be one of the world's best loo-bound views.

At Harbourside, Darling Harbour, several restaurants including ***Jordon's***, ***Jo Jo's*** and ***Zaaffran*** look across Cockle Bay toward the city. Restaurants at the new Cockle Bay Wharf complex (opposite) also face the water, and are well-sited for sunset-watching.

On the North Shore, in the suburb of Balmoral, the well-heeled ***Bathers Pavilion*** and ***Watermark*** on the esplanade have views across the harbour to Manly and North Head. In Manly itself, ***Armstrong's*** has outdoor tables on the wharf that overlook Manly's pretty harbour beach. On the north side of the peninsula, the cafes and restaurants at South Steyne face Manly Beach and the Pacific Ocean. Many other Sydney beachside suburbs, including Bondi Beach and Coogee, also have eateries with sea views.

The crowded Cantonese restaurant ***Hingara*** *(☎ 9212 2169, 82 Dixon St)* does good seafood mains, most in the $10 to $15 range. Others worth checking out are the large, good-value ***Old Tai Yuen*** *(☎ 9211 3782, 110 Hay St)*, which has been around a long time and has a good reputation; and the budget-minded but relatively plush ***New Tai Yuen*** *(☎ 9212 5244, 31 Dixon St)*, where seafood noodles cost $12.90, mains $8 to $15.

The popular, established ***House of Guangzhou*** *(☎ 9281 2205, 76 Ultimo Rd)*, occupying two floors, has an aquarium full of beautiful (inedible) fish, and a reputation for good seafood; bookings are essential. Most main courses cost around $11 to $19.

The huge ***Marigold*** restaurant *(☎ 9264 6744, 299-305 Sussex St)* serves Cantonese food with great style and wide-ranging prices – broccoli in oyster sauce is $9, scallops $25. Despite its size you need to book. ***Marigold 2*** *(☎ 9281 3388, 5th floor, 683-89 George St)* serves lunchtime yum cha daily.

In the same price bracket, the grand and heavily-chandeliered ***Regal*** *(☎ 9261 8988, 347-53 Sussex St)* is another large place popular for Sunday yum cha. Mains start at $16 and the emphasis is on seafood.

PLACES TO EAT

DARLING HARBOUR & PYRMONT (MAPS 4 & 9)

The biggest concentration of eateries is at ***Cockle Bay Wharf***, officially heralded as Sydney's newest dining precinct. Most are fairly slick, and few are cheap: the view from the promenade is all white tablecloths, potted palms, polished glasses, and lots of chrome.

Across the water at ***Harbourside*** are a handful of top-notch restaurants and a swag of fast-food outlets, and not a great deal in between. Many of the eateries around Darling Harbour are aimed at the tourist trade, but with an outdoor table on a sunny day, who cares? Wander around and take your pick.

Fast Food, Cafes & Pubs

Most of the fast-food outlets at Harbourside are in the food court on the ground floor. Upstairs is ***Festival Cafe***, a large tourist-style coffee lounge (without views) serving Devonshire teas, and sandwiches and burgers for around $6 to $10. For a quick, portable meal, pop downstairs to ***Shakespeare's Pies***, where pies like Thai broccoli and tandoori chicken cost between $2 and $3.80.

The Health Tree takeaway at Cockle Bay Wharf has fresh juices, a range of tasty salads for $3 to $7, and beef tortellini and vegetable lasagne for $6.50. Opposite is ***Schwob's Swiss***, a gourmet sandwich joint; the caviar and chive variety is $6.90.

Away from Darling Harbour proper you can eat with the locals at the ***Glasgow Arms Hotel*** *(☎ 9211 2354, 527 Harris St)*, near the Powerhouse Museum. It has a good bistro; burgers cost $10.90.

Restaurants

In the Harbourside complex, ***Jordon's*** *(☎ 9281 3711)* and ***Jo Jo's*** *(☎ 9281 3888)* are two of the more expensive joints. Both have in-house bars, and some of the best views. The more relaxed Jordon's is a seafood restaurant, and its 'famous fish and chips' go for $18.50. At Jo Jo's, entrées like the antipasto platter cost around $16.50, while a main dish of poached salmon is $25.

Right above Jo Jo's is ***Zaaffran*** *(☎ 9211 8900)*, a smart restaurant serving unusual Indian food; mains cost $11 to $16.50. It's open for lunch and dinner Tuesday to Sunday.

Perched on a leafy rooftop at the northern end of Cockle Bay Wharf is ***Chinta Ria*** *(☎ 9265 3211)*, a Malaysian place serving tasty, reasonably priced meals with great style. Most mains are $9 or $10; chicken laksa is $12.

Shipley's Restaurant *(☎ 9281 0400, Furama Hotel, 68 Harbour St)*, opposite the Sydney Entertainment Centre, has entrées from $10.95, and interesting main dishes (like chicken breast with orange and peach schnapps glaze) for around $20. It also does a breakfast buffet (from $15.50).

Pyrmont Fish Markets have several places to eat. ***Doyle's at the Markets*** *(☎ 9552 4339)* is a bistro, but also does takeaway. It serves fish of the day with chips for $9.80, and a seafood basket for two for $14.50. There's seating outside.

CIRCULAR QUAY (MAP 4)

Many cafes and restaurants that line the quay, especially on the western side, have good views of the harbour, although you pay for the position. Most are aimed at tourists.

Fast Food

For fuel rather than views, there are lots of cheap stalls on the wharves as you head towards the ferries, although most of what's on offer has a high grease count. A good option for hot days is ***Casa Del Gelato*** on Wharf 5, which boasts twenty flavours of gelati.

Cafes

Just beside the wharves, amid the crowds and buskers, are ***Rossini*** and the 24-hour ***City Extra***, offering fairly standard coffee, snacks and meals. City Extra has a huge menu: sticky toffee pudding for $6.50, Thai chicken fillets $17.80.

The Museum of Contemporary Art has the stylish ***MCA Cafe*** *(☎ 9241 4253)*. The outside tables have good views of the quay, the food is interesting and the service is professional; poached chicken costs $14.50, hazelnut bread with honeyed marscapone $5.

On the eastern side of Circular Quay next to Sydney Cove Oyster Bar is ***Portobello Caffe*** *(☎ 9247 8548)*, which serves pastries and cakes for $3 to $7, and expensive but decent coffee; it has some outdoor tables.

Restaurants

Doyle's at the Quay *(☎ 9252 3400, Overseas Passenger Terminal, Circular Quay West)* is a good quality seafood restaurant. Most mains, like John Dory fillets, are around $29. There's a minimum charge of $15 per adult, and patrons are implored not to feed the hovering seagulls.

More formal than Doyle's, and directly upstairs, is ***Quay*** *(☎ 9251 5600)*, one of Sydney's most highly regarded seafood restaurants. Entrées are priced from $19 to $36 and most mains (like snapper roulade) are $42 to $52. If you're still solvent, finish with passionfruit soufflé ($24).

There's a collection of restaurants, with large outdoor areas and great views overlooking the quay, further north in the renovated Campbell's Storehouse complex. They include ***Wolfie's*** *(☎ 9241 5577)*, which has seafood entrées for $13.90 to $16.90 and Tasmanian salmon for $19.50. Others are the similarly priced ***Waterfront*** *(☎ 9247 3666)* and ***Italian Village*** *(☎ 9247 6111)*.

In a sunny spot close to the Opera House, ***Sydney Cove Oyster Bar*** *(☎ 9247 2937)*, on the eastern side of Circular Quay, offers purely Australian produce, including wine. Oysters cost from $18.50 a dozen; other dishes, like a cheese and fruit platter, start from $13. It's open from mid-morning until about 8 pm daily in winter and until 11 pm or later in summer. There is a surcharge on weekends.

There are three restaurants in the Opera House complex. On the western side, ***Concourse*** *(☎ 9250 7300)* is on the lower concourse where the wall protects you from the breeze. The menu isn't huge, but the wine list is! Mains like chargrilled swordfish cost $15 to $19. It's open from 10 am daily, but not for dinner on Sunday. ***Harbour*** *(☎ 9250 7191)*, at the 'prow' of the Opera House, serves mostly seafood, with main courses for around $23.

Upstairs, maximising the building's stunning architecture, is the chic but accessible ***Bennelong Restaurant*** *(☎ 9250 7578)*. There's live jazz nightly, a seafood and crustacean bar for fishy snacks, and a cocktail lounge open till around midnight. If you eat before 7.30 pm, a three course meal costs $39; later on it's $65. Single mains cost around $29. It's open from 5.30 pm to 11.30 pm Monday to Saturday.

THE ROCKS (MAP 4)

Here too the cafes and restaurants are aimed mainly at tourists, but there are some good deals available, especially in the numerous pubs where most bar meals are around $10 or less.

Fast Food, Cafes & Pubs

There's a small food hall in the modern ***Clocktower Square Shopping Centre***, on the corner of Harrington and Argyle Sts.

Near Argyle St is ***Gum Nut Tea Garden*** *(☎ 9247 9591, 28 Harrington St)*. It's a cosy old house with several small rooms, and a courtyard where you can enjoy good coffee and cakes, and lunches from around $6.50.

Rocks Cafe *(99 Harrington St)* has snacks for $9, pastas for $15, and mains like rack of lamb for $19. It's open from 8 am to midnight most nights. ***G'Day Cafe*** *(83 Harrington St)*, just north of Argyle St, is similar but cheaper, with breakfast or focaccia for $4. It's open 5.30 am to midnight, and has a $1.50 surcharge on Sunday.

Harbour View Hotel *(☎ 9252 3769, 18 Lower Fort St)* has basic, inexpensive food; steak sandwiches cost $5. At ***The Hero of Waterloo*** *(☎ 9252 4553, 81 Lower Fort St)* you can get green chicken curry for $10.50. ***Lord Nelson Brewery Hotel*** *(☎ 9251 4044)*, on the corner of Kent and Argyle Sts, also does decent pub grub of the sausage, pie and pasta variety, for between $7 and $13.

Restaurants

Pancakes on the Rocks *(☎ 9247 6371, Metcalfe Arcade, Hickson Rd)* is a member of the Pancake Parlour chain. It has the usual huge menu (pancakes for $6 to $11, gourmet pizzas from $13) and it's open 24 hours.

Phillip's Foote *(☎ 9241 1485, 101 George St)* is an informal pub-style eatery with a salad bar, and a pleasant outdoor barbecue area where you can cook your own steak or fish for $18. It's open till midnight most nights.

The stylish ***Sailor's Thai*** *(☎ 9251 2466, 106 George St)* is a less extreme version of David Thompson's Darley St Thai (see Kings Cross & Around later), with simpler food and décor. Chicken and coconut soup costs $26. It's open for lunch weekdays, dinner Monday to Saturday. Upstairs, the noodle bar is open from noon until 8 pm daily. Stir-fries, curries, and spicy Thai salads range from $12 to $18.

Rockpool *(☎ 9252 1888, 107 George St)* is one of the best. Chef Neil Perry draws on Asian influences to create sensational dishes. The interior is space-age Art Deco, the service spot-on. Mains include grilled swordfish with artichoke for $38, and the emphasis is on freshly caught seafood – strict vegetarians should look elsewhere.

Vault *(☎ 9247 1920, 135 George St)* is in an old Gothic building that has been refurbished. Meaty mains (like suckling pig) cost between $26 and $34. The wine room has a cheaper menu; artichoke tortellini is $16.

Rocks Teppanyaki *(☎ 9250 6000)*, on the corner of Essex and Cumberland Sts, is an upmarket Japanese restaurant in a painted sandstone building with armchairs and sofas adorning the foyer. King prawns are $29.

The mellow and lovely ***Kable's*** *(☎ 9238 0000, Regent Hotel, 199 George St)* is one of Australia's best restaurants, and the prices reflect this, but there are lunchtime specials, with two courses and coffee for $42.50.

Restaurants at Pier 1 on Dawes Point, to the west of the Harbour Bridge, include ***Harbour Watch*** *(☎ 9241 2217)*, a seafood place where most mains are $25. The informal ***Harbourside Brasserie*** *(☎ 9252 3000)* nearby is cheaper, with soup for $8.90 and chicken schnitzel for $16.90. Dramatically situated in a converted warehouse near the Sydney Theatre Company, ***Wharf Restaurant*** *(☎ 9250 1761, Pier 4)* is a pleasant, open space, with a soaring ceiling and great views. Three courses will cost you about $50.

KINGS CROSS & AROUND (MAPS 6)

The Cross has fast-food joints serving quick fare that's good for soaking up beer, tiny cafes servicing locals and travellers, and some swanky top-notch eateries.

Fast Food, Cafes & Pubs

Great bargains, and popular with backpackers, are the pizzas from ***Action Pizza*** and ***House Kebab*** on Darlinghurst Rd (near the corner of Bayswater road). Action Pizza has the best deal, with three slices from $1.

PLACES TO EAT

King's Seafood, on the corner of Darlinghurst Rd, opposite the El Alamein Fountain, is a decent takeaway serving grilled fish, salad and chips for $6.50. ***Oporto*** *(☎ 9368 0257, 3c Roslyn St)* is one of a small chain that specialises in cooking chicken in a fast-food, Portuguese style. Chicken burgers start at $3.85.

There are inexpensive, no-frills cafes on William St, just off Darlinghurst Rd. You can usually find a full breakfast for under $5. ***Williams on William*** *(☎ 9358 5680, 242 Williams St)* has breakfast specials for $3.90, pasta for $5. A few doors down is ***Mamma Maria*** *(☎ 9357 2211)*, with pasta from $6.

The licensed ***Waterlily Cafe*** *(6 Bayswater Rd)* is one of the nicest cafes in the Cross, with a few outside tables and a friendly atmosphere. Thai tuna cakes cost $7, and a full cooked breakfast (with free-range eggs) $6. Another good one is the cute and reasonably priced ***Cafe 59*** *(59 Bayswater Rd)*, which serves fine coffee, hearty breakfasts and lunches and an array of nutritious drinks.

For cheap Thai food, try the nearby ***Mum's Thai*** (*☎ 9331 1577, 57 Bayswater Rd)*; the menu is extensive, with a range of seafood and vegetarian dishes for $4.50 to $12. Another cheap Thai place is ***Pad Thai*** *(15 Llankelly Place)*, a tiny takeaway with a few tables, serving soups for $5 and noodles for $7. Across the lane and further down is ***Sushi Bar***, a small, pleasant Japanese restaurant where you can eat for between $6 and $12.

Although a small section of Kellet St is devoted to the red-light trade, the quieter stretch adjoining Ward Ave contains several mid-range places for late-night eating and drinking, some of which have outside tables. Catering to avid carnivores, the increasingly slick ***Cafe Iguana*** *(☎ 9357 2609, 15 Kellet St)* has kangaroo, crocodile, and Balmain bugs on the menu; mains are around $17. The cosily bohemian ***Dean's Cafe*** *(☎ 9368 0953, 5 Kellet St)* has toasties for $6.50, a good selection of drinks, and is open late; next door is the similarly laid-back ***Venice Beach*** *(☎ 9326 9928)* serving budget mod Oz food, with nothing over $10.

Restaurants

One of the cheapest restaurants is the basic, brightly lit, busy ***New York Restaurant*** *(18 Kellett St)*. Taking no-frills dining to new heights, it serves plain, hearty meals for $5 to $7. Coffee or tea with your meal is just 70c.

There are several popular eateries near the El Alamein Fountain, where the window seats and pavement tables let you watch Kings Cross go by in all its glory. With its splendidly tacky Las Vegas décor and red-tinted lighting, the ***Bourbon & Beefsteak*** *(☎ 9358 1144, 24 Darlinghurst Rd)* is a touristy but surreal spot to quell the late-night munchies. It serves breakfast 24 hours – pancakes with maple syrup for $7.50, bacon and eggs $9.50. Next door is the ***Fountain Cafe, Restaurant & Bar*** *(☎ 9358 6009, 20 Darlinghurst Rd)*. With a large menu and breezy outside tables, it's good for postcard-writing and observing. Sandwiches cost $4.80, garlic steak $15.80.

Back on Kellet St, the mid-range ***Lime & Lemon Grass Brasserie*** *(☎ 9358 5577, 42 Kellet St)* is a Thai place with good tom yum soup for $14.50, and curry mains for $14.50 to $19.

Bayswater Rd has several upmarket eateries. ***Bayswater Brasserie*** *(☎ 9357 2177, 32 Bayswater Rd)* is a classy but casual restaurant with excellent service where if you choose carefully you needn't spend a fortune. The cheapest starter is chickpea purée with grilled flatbread ($8.50); mains ($12.50 to $27) include cuttlefish in black ink sauce.

Eating at ***Darley Street Thai*** *(☎ 9358 6530, 28-30 Bayswater Rd)* – with its gold-leaf foyer, electric blue and pink silk cushions, and undulating candy-coloured ceilings – is a sumptuous experience. The equally mind-blowing food comes courtesy of 400-year-old recipes from the royal court of Thailand, with ingredients like quail eggs and ginger flowers. Banquets are $70 per person, or you can dine à la carte for around $28.

POTTS POINT & WOOLLOMOOLOO (MAPS 5 & 6)

Victoria St, which leads north from the Kings Cross junction into Potts Point, has some good fashionable cafes and restaurants. There's also a cluster of more upmarket cafes and restaurants on Macleay St, which is the northern extension of Darlinghurst Rd.

Fast Food, Cafes & Pubs

Harry's Cafe de Wheels *(Woolloomooloo Finger Wharf)* must be one of the few pie carts in the world to be a tourist attraction. It opened in 1945, and stays open 18 hours a day, serving pies and mash galore. You might see a limousine parked up next to a skateboard, as various night-owls queue for some post-party sustenance.

The small but comfortable ***Joe's Cafe Deluxe*** *(☎ 9368 1188, 190 Victoria St)*, near Kings Cross station, has a range of pasta and bagels; a breakfast plate of scrambled eggs, bread, tomatoes and mushrooms is $9.50. Further north is ***Roy's Famous*** *(☎ 9357 3579, No 176)*, a slick Italian-style cafe with huge servings; focaccia for $9, sticky date pudding $6. It has some vegetarian dishes and is equally good for a coffee or meal.

Popular with sailors from the nearby naval base, ***Frisco Hotel*** *(☎ 9357 1800, 46 Dowling St)* in Woolloomooloo is a pub that serves meals. There's a bistro downstairs, and an upstairs restaurant with a balcony. Mondays and Tuesdays are 'spag nights', when pasta dishes are $6.

For great coffee, and fresh, tasty fare from around $6, try the diminutive and bustling ***Spring Cafe*** on Challis Ave near Macleay St. It's always busy, so you may have to improvise with seating. Next door is ***La Buvette***, with equally good coffee and delicious home-made pastries.

Restaurants

On Victoria St, near Roy's, ***Out of India*** *(☎ 9357 7055, 178 Victoria St)* is a reasonably priced Indian restaurant with spicy mains for $10 to $13.

Behind its worn and mysterious front door, ***Mére Catherine*** *(☎ 9358 3862, 146 Victoria St)* is an intimate and unpretentious French restaurant serving filling meals for around $25 to $30. Knock to be let in; it's open from 6 pm Tuesday to Sunday. ***Star Bar & Grill*** *(☎ 9356 2911, 155 Victoria St)* is a hip modern restaurant and noodle bar (part of the famous Rockpool family) offering delicious Chinese and Malaysian food. Seared scallops cost $14. It's open Tuesday to Saturday for dinner only.

On Macleay St, the long-established BYO ***Macleay St Bistro*** *(☎ 9358 4891, 73a Macleay St)* has a modern Australian menu with mains like oven-baked salmon with papaya salad, priced from $13 to $29. There's a minimum charge of $20 per head, and it's open nightly for dinner, for lunch Friday to Sunday (no bookings). Further north, and with a similar menu, is the fashionable ***Moran's Restaurant & Cafe*** *(☎ 9356 2223, 61-3 Macleay St)*. Meat and seafood feature almost exclusively; pan-fried barramundi costs $29.50. The licensed cafe section is more affordable, with mains around $15.

The Pig & the Olive *(☎ 9357 3745, 71a Macleay St)*, with its terracotta walls and pig-themed decorations, serves out-of-the-ordinary pizzas (from $12) with scrumptiously inventive toppings.

DARLINGHURST & EAST SYDNEY (MAPS 4, 5 & 6)

Ranging from the budget to the pricey, this area has the greatest concentration of cafes and restaurants in Sydney. In Darlinghurst, most are either on Oxford St or Victoria St. In East Sydney, they're mainly on Stanley St between Riley and Crown Sts and are mostly Italian-style.

Fast Food & Cafes

The northern end of Victoria St, near Kings Cross, has plenty of eateries. Most are trendy and probably transient, but not the bustling ***Bar Coluzzi*** *(322 Victoria St)*, which is a caffeine institution – often with more patrons than available seats. Another

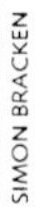
SIMON BRACKEN

After catching a ferry across the harbour ...

SIMON BRACKEN

pop into a cafe ...

SIMON BRACKEN

then do some shopping.

ROSS BARNETT

View across Camp Cove near Watsons Bay on a busy Sydney summers' day

ROSS BARNETT

Alfresco dining at Doyles, Watsons Bay

stayer is the BYO ***Una's Coffee Lounge*** *(☎ 9360 6885, 340 Victoria St)*, just south of Surrey St. An Austrian cafe that has been going strong for over 25 years, it serves solid, inexpensive fare and opens until about 11 pm. Mains cost $8 to $14.

Bills 1 *(433 Liverpool St)* has a large communal table and a great selection of glossy magazines. It's open for breakfast (until midday) and lunch only; scrambled eggs cost $7.50, sweetcorn fritters with bacon $11.50.

For a quick, good quality meal-in-a-bun, try the licensed ***Burgerman*** *(116 Surrey St)*, where delicious burgers start from $5.

At the busy ***Fez Cafe*** *(☎ 9360 9581, 247 Victoria St)* the food has a Middle-Eastern flavour; couscous is $13.50, mains are $7.50 to $16. It serves good coffee, and breakfast until 3 pm.

Bandstand Cafe on Green Park has a tranquil setting. Squeezed into a renovated bandstand, it serves coffee, cakes and basic light meals; lunch mains are around $10, and you can sit outside.

Le Petit Creme *(☎ 9361 4738, 118 Darlinghurst Rd)* is a popular French-style cafe, with some alfresco tables. Breakfasts start from $4.50. The small and appealing ***Fishface*** *(☎ 9332 4803, 132 Darlinghurst Rd)* serves delicious seafood and fills quickly in the evening. Classy beer-battered fish and chips costs $7.50.

Dov Cafe *(☎ 9360 9594, 252 Forbes St)*, a popular BYO place in an old sandstone building, has delicious Mediterranean and Israeli-inspired food. It has a long list of tasty cold dishes ($8), and good cakes ($4.50). It's also open for breakfast, and you can sit outside.

In East Sydney on Stanley St, the ultra-cheap ***No Name*** is above the Arch Coffee Lounge, near Riley St; there's no sign outside indicating it's there. Walk past the pool table and pinball machines right to the back, then climb the stairs. Filling spaghetti meals cost $5 to $6, a large salad $3. ***Bill & Toni's*** *(☎ 9360 4702, upstairs, 74 Stanley St)* is a popular dinner spot with locals. Pasta dishes start at $6.50. The cafe downstairs serves gelati and cheap focaccia.

A Guide for the Serious Foodie

Looking for the best bite for your buck? Lonely Planet's *Out to Eat – Sydney* is the best guide to Sydney's value eateries for any budget; if you're staying a while it will quickly repay your investment. The book takes its food seriously, but offers a fresh approach, with independent, wickedly unstuffy opinions on heaps of hand-picked restaurants, bars and cafes in Sydney.

For something more stylish try the licensed, mid-range ***Cafe Divino*** *(☎ 9360 9911, 70 Stanley St)* with its white tablecloths, blackboard menu and smartly dressed waiters. Chilli spaghetti costs $12.50. The BYO ***Palati Fini*** *(☎ 9360 9121, 80 Stanely St)* has similar prices and is popular at dinner time. Penne carbonara is $13.

The voluminous ***Baraza Cafe*** *(☎ 9380 5197, 91 Riley St)* is a casual place to drop in for lunch, dinner, or a game of pool; spicy cuttlefish laksa is $13.50, vegetarian frittata $13.50.

Part of a worldwide chain, the nearby ***Hard Rock Cafe*** *(☎ 9331 1116, 121-129 Crown St)* is a tourist mecca. A burger and fries with salad costs $10.75. It opens from noon to at least midnight daily.

Restaurants

The smart Hare Krishna ***Govinda's*** *(☎ 9380 5155 or 9360 7853, 112 Darlinghurst Rd)* serves healthy vegetarian food. It offers an all-you-can-gobble smorgasbord from 6 to 10.30 pm nightly, for $14.90, which also gives you admission to the cinema upstairs (see the Entertainment chapter). For great Thai food, try the bustling ***Tum Tum Thai*** *(☎ 9331 5390, 199 Darlinghurst Rd)*, where tasty curries and stir-fries start at $7.50. Seating is limited and the food's popular, so be prepared to take away.

In East Sydney the upper-crust, long-standing ***Beppi's*** *(☎ 9360 4558)*, on the corner of Stanley and Yurong Sts, serves traditional Italian fare. Expect to pay about $60 a head for a three course meal. ***Two Chefs*** *(☎ 9331 1559, 115 Riley St)* is a small, stylish restaurant with mains for $14.50 to $23.50.

The huge ***Pacifico*** *(☎ 9360 3811, upstairs, 95 Riley St)*, between Stanley and Williams Sts, is an airy Mexican cantina with enchiladas for $12.50, guacamole $8.50. ***The Edge*** *(☎ 9360 1372, 60 Riley St)*, just opposite, is popular with Sydney foodies. It serves modern Australian food in a light, pleasant space with an outside seating area and bar. Mains cost between $18 and $24.

OXFORD ST & AROUND (MAPS 4, 7 & 8)

Fast Food, Cafes & Pubs

North Indian Flavour *(129 Oxford St)*, and ***Tamana's*** nearby, offer fast, good-value North Indian and tandoori meals, including a special of rice with a choice of three curries for $3.50.

The area's prime people-watching spot is ***Cafe 191*** *(☎ 9360 4295, Taylor Square)*. You can just have a coffee, or try its eclectic menu – Thai green curry costs $12.50. If you're feeling lost, head for the welcoming ***Metronome Cafe*** *(411 Bourke St)* near Taylor Square, a peaceful haven away from the bustle and traffic. Tables are covered with maps of Sydney; there's a leafy outdoor area, a range of sweet treats, and delicious home-blended coffee.

For the best burgers in the neighbourhood, try ***Beastie Burger*** *(☎ 9361 3400)* on Bourke St opposite Taylor Square; it doesn't skimp on the ingredients – even vegetarians will be impressed. Prices start at $4.80.

The groovy, laid-back ***Roobar*** *(253 Crown St)* is another fine place to escape the hubbub. It serves open sandwiches for $7, risotto for $12.50. (It also offers international calls and Internet access.) Next door is the similarly pleasant ***Fatz*** *(251 Crown St)*, with comfortable booth seats and an interesting variety of pastas for around $12.

Cafe Belgenny *(197 Campbell St)* is a stylish little urban cafe behind Taylor Square, with a relaxed air, good coffee and cakes, groovy magazines, and tasty toasted pide (sort of a pizza) for $5 to $6.

For pasta on the cheap, visit the low-key ***Maltese Cafe*** *(310 Crown St)* where you can fill up for $4 or $5. Further down is the bohemian ***Mali*** *(348a Crown St)*, one of Sydney's cutest and smallest cafes, with low, cushioned benches and a beach-like atmosphere. Light breakfasts cost $3. Even tinier, with killer coffees and outdoor perches, is the great ***Pablo's Vice*** *(257 Crown St)*, on the corner of Goulburn St.

If you don't mind the smell of beer, the refurbished ***Burdekin Hotel*** *(☎ 9331 3066, 2 Oxford St)* near Hyde Park serves pasta mains for $11, meat ones for $15, and vegie burgers for $10.

Restaurants

The reassuringly homely ***Betty's Soup Kitchen*** *(☎ 9360 9698, 84 Oxford St)* is a better restaurant than its name might suggest. It has filling soup and damper for $5.50, pasta for $6.80 and lamb stew for $8.80. Just opposite is the modish and extremely busy ***Thai Panic***, with excellent fresh curries and stir-fries that cost from $7.50 to $9.50.

1 Burton *(☎ 9331 4745)*, off Oxford St by Oxford Square, is an upmarket Italian restaurant with outdoor tables and a name to match its address. Mains cost $18.50 to $21.

Beside Betty's on the corner of Crown St is the popular ***Tandoori Palace*** *(☎ 9331 7072, 86 Oxford St)*, where reasonably priced Indian food is served on crisp white tablecloths. Meat and vegetarian mains are around $9. Further down, cheerful ***Don Don*** *(☎ 9331 3544, 80 Oxford St)* offers delicious Japanese fare in generous portions. Udon soup with tempura is $7.50.

Along Oxford St, east of Taylor Square, is a clutch of mid-priced restaurants serving cuisine ranging from Cambodian to Californian. The long-established ***Balkan*** *(☎ 9360 4970, 209 Oxford St)* is a continental restaurant specialising in seafood, and traditional meaty raznjici and cevapcici. Ask for a filling pola-pola ($15.90) and you'll get half of each. ***Kim's*** *(☎ 9380 5429, 235 Oxford St)* is a small, popular Vietnamese restaurant, which has seafood and beef mains for $9 to $13. It's open for dinner daily, except Tuesday. Nearby at the popular ***Thai Nesia*** *(☎ 9361 4817, 243 Oxford St)*, most mains cost $10 to $15.

SURRY HILLS (MAP 8)

Surry Hills is an interesting multicultural dining area. Crown St is its main food thoroughfare, but it's a long street with cafes and restaurants in clusters. The biggest bunch is between Cleveland and Devonshire Sts, both of which also have a number of eateries.

Cafes

Bills 2 *(☎ 9360 4762, 355 Crown St)* is a stylish modern cafe open for breakfast, lunch and dinner. It's not quite as expensive as it looks; toasted coconut bread costs $4, gourmet filled rolls $10.50, and dinner mains $10 to $15.

A great pit-stop is the vibrant ***Rustic Cafe*** *(☎ 9318 1034)*, on the corner of Crown and Devonshire Sts. The menu is varied and prices are reasonable: yam chips for $6.50, pasta for $8, and rump steak for $13.90. There's a bar upstairs with sunny window seats.

BYO

You'll find many restaurants advertising that they're BYO. The initials stand for 'Bring Your Own', which means that the restaurant isn't licensed to serve alcohol, but you are permitted to bring some with you. This is a real bonus for wine-lovers on a budget because you can bring your own bottle of wine and not pay any mark-up. Many restaurants charge a nominal fee for corkage, which can cost from as little as 50c. Some licensed restaurants are also BYO, but they tend to charge a higher corkage fee.

The ***Universal Deli Cafe*** *(555 Crown St)*, opposite Thai Orchid, has quiche ($4), good sandwiches and coffee, and delicious fresh salads.

West along Devonshire St is the likeable ***Mohr Fish*** *(☎ 9218 1326, 202 Devonshire St)*, a small but popular designer fish-cafe; seafood mains cost around $17, takeaway fish and chips $7.

La Passion du Fruit, on the corner of Bourke and Devonshire Sts, is an inexpensive, popular cafe, with snacks like focaccia for around $6, main course dinners for $11. It's closed Sunday. ***Johnnies Seafood Cafe***, on Fitzroy St, has grilled fish and chips for $4.80. ***Cafe Niki*** *(☎ 9319 7517, 544 Bourke St)* is a pleasant wood-lined cafe with fruit whips for $4, open bagels for $7, and comfortable outside seats.

For a fancy sugar-fix, there's ***Maya*** *(470 Cleveland St)*, an Indian sweet shop. Try the delicious gulab jaman (a syrup-soaked dumpling), which is $1 for a generous-sized ball.

Restaurants

Prasit's Northside Thai *(☎ 9332 1792, 395 Crown St)* is a nifty box-like Thai restaurant serving consistently good, interesting meals like banana flower chicken salad for $13.50. Meals are served at a fast and furious pace to keep salivating would-be diners happy. A little south is the larger and pricier ***Prasit's Northside on Crown*** *(☎ 9319 0748, 413 Crown St)*, with a gorgeous gold and purple colour-scheme and mains at around $20. Further south again, the spacious ***Thai Orchid*** *(☎ 9698 2097, 628 Crown St)* looks upmarket, but meat mains are only $9.80. Nearby is the smaller, more intimate ***Thai Cotton*** *(☎ 9319 3206, 622 Crown St)*, with mains between $8 and $11.

Another good Thai eatery on Crown St is ***Thai Tha Poh*** *(☎ 9699 2829, 666 Crown St)*, with heavy pine furniture and a smoke-free policy. The food is fresh and colourful, and curries range from $8 to $13.

A group of Lebanese eateries line Cleveland St between Elizabeth and Wilton Sts. ***Abdul's*** *(☎ 9698 1275, 565 Elizabeth St)* and ***Nada's*** *(270 Cleveland St)* have been there longest. Abdul's is basic, but it's relaxed and friendly. Many dishes are under $6; shish kebabs are only $2. Most places charge less than $10 for mains, including ***Fatima's*** *(☎ 9698 4895, 296 Cleveland St)* and ***Emad's*** *(☎ 9698 2631)* next door.

Turkish pide is popular along Cleveland St, especially at ***Erciyes*** *(409 Cleveland St)*, diagonally opposite the junction with Crown St. Almost everything on the menu is $8. ***Golden Pide***, on the corner of Bourke and Cleveland Sts, is also popular, and serves pide for $6 or $7, doner kebabs for $3 or $4.

For inexpensive Indian fare on Cleveland St, there are several good options, including the BYO ***Tandoori Rasoi*** *(☎ 9310 2470)*, on the corner of Cleveland and Bourke Sts. It serves Indian meals such as chicken or vegetarian curry for $7.90, and you can watch your meal being prepared through a window onto the kitchen.

The Uruguayan ***Casapueblo*** *(☎ 9319 6377, 650 Bourke St)*, near the corner of Cleveland St, is one of the few South American restaurants in the city. It's open for dinner Tuesday to Saturday. Deftly spiced mains (like chicken with wine, leeks, beans and rice) cost around $14.50.

PADDINGTON (MAP 7)

Oxford St continues east from Darlinghurst through Paddington, but be aware that locating restaurants can be tricky, as the street numbers begin again at the junction with South Dowling St.

Cafes & Pubs

Sloanes *(☎ 9331 6717, 312 Oxford St)* is a modern little mini-cafe with a large vegetarian selection and a courtyard. Mains cost from $7.50 to $12.50, and it serves cooked breakfasts all day. ***Hot Gossip*** *(☎ 9332 4358, 436 Oxford St)* is a lovely place to refuel and relax. It has three rooms with cosy seats and its menu is filled with gourmet goodies.

Centennial Park Cafe, a five minute walk inside the park from the Centennial Square entrance off Oxford St, is good for those needing a touch of the rural. It's a pleasant open-sided cafe surrounded by parkland, serving modern Australian lunch mains for around $12 to $17. It's open for breakfast and lunch daily.

Fringe Bar & Cafe *(☎ 9360 3554)*, on the corner of Oxford and Hopewell Sts, is a fashionable place in a woody, renovated pub, offering filled focaccia for $6.50, and sushi for around $7.

At Five Ways (the junction of Glenmore Rd and Goodhope, Heeley and Broughton Sts), there are great views from the iron-laced balcony at ***Royal Hotel*** *(☎ 9331 2604, 237 Glenmore Rd)*. Follow the chain of painted elephants upstairs; lemon risotto with zucchini flowers costs $12.50.

Noted for its fine-dining, ***Bellevue Hotel*** *(☎ 9363 2293, 159 Hargrave St)* has mains for $17 to $18.

Restaurants

There are several good restaurants at Five Ways. The BYO ***Creperie Stivell*** *(☎ 9360 6191, 2b Heeley St)* has a pleasant courtyard area where you can eat crepes, pannequets and blintzes for $4.90 to $13.90. It's open for dinner from 6 pm daily, and for lunch Wednesday to Sunday. The simple and beautifully decorated ***Eat Thai*** *(☎ 9361 6640, 229 Glenmore Rd)*, on the corner of Heeley St, has a lovely atmosphere and a range of stir-fry dishes, including spicy duck and rice noodles, for $10.50.

Paddington has several distinguished restaurants, many of them Italian and with long-standing good reputations. They include ***Darcy's*** *(☎ 9363 3706, 92 Hargrave St)*, which serves Italian seafood dishes such as smoked salmon penne; most mains are $25.

At ***Buon Ricordo Ristorante*** *(Map 5, ☎ 9360 6729, 108 Boundary St)* you can enjoy authentic Italian food for around $60 for three courses. Northern Italian cuisine is on offer at the large ***Lucio's*** *(☎ 9380 5996, 47 Windsor St)*. Indulgent main dishes (like quails with bacon) cost $26. It's open Monday to Saturday for lunch and dinner.

GLEBE (MAP 9)

Glebe Point Rd was Sydney's original 'eat street' and though it has been left behind by the food innovations sweeping the inner east, it has a laid-back, unfaddish atmosphere and good-value, varied food.

Cafes

On the corner of Francis St is the old favourite, ***Badde Manors*** *(☎ 9660 3797, 37 Francis St)*. Popular with locals and visitors, it's a relaxed place, sometimes chaotically so. Salads cost from $6.50, pasta around $8.50, and there's a great gelati selection. Late breakfasts are popular on weekends.

Despite Glebe's 'students and bohemians' tag, many eateries have edged into higher price brackets, so it's good to see that the popular and relaxed ***The Craven***, next to the old Valhalla Cinema, remains a good, inexpensive place for a coffee or meal. Filled focaccia starts at $5 and other dishes are around $10. Most nights it's open till 10.30 pm.

The very comfortable ***Well Connected*** *(☎ 9566 2655, 35 Glebe Point Rd)* was the first Internet cafe to set up in Sydney. It offers coffee, all-day breakfasts and a good fresh menu – plus numerous couches, nooks and crannies, and two floors of terminals. A little further down is ***Lolita's***, a student hangout with some good spots to sit and read. Bruschetta costs $4.50, focaccia $6.50.

Many of the eateries along Glebe Point Rd are sugar-rush heaven, and the tiny takeaway ***Pudding Shop*** *(☎ 9660 1794, 144b Glebe Point Rd)* is a great source of the sweet and sticky. It sells hot pies too.

Bogart Pizza Cafe *(☎ 9552 4656, 211 Glebe Point Rd)*, between Bridge and St Johns Rds, is reputed to have the best pizza ($7 to $17) on the strip, and also does pasta. It's open from 5 pm.

The secret gem of Glebe is ***Blackwattle Canteen***, in the Blackwattle Studios in a converted wharf at the end of Glebe Point Rd, overlooking Rozelle Bay. It's among the studios of artists, sculptors and picture framers and has wonderful views, mega breakfasts and comfort food under $10.

Restaurants

For tapas ($6.80 to $11.80) such as king prawns cooked with chilli and ginger, try ***Different Drummer*** *(☎ 9552 3406, 185 Glebe Point Rd)*. Behind the sinister tinted windows there also lurks a well-stocked cocktail bar. It's open for dinner daily except Monday.

Several Asian places offer excellent value for money. ***Thai Intra*** *(☎ 9660 4149, 207 Glebe Point Rd)* is a large, licensed Thai restaurant in a pleasantly decorated old house. The MSG-free food is good, and the surrounds are classy. Most mains are under $10.

The friendly ***Lien*** *(☎ 9660 2079, 331 Glebe Point Rd)* serves Thai, Malaysian and Vietnamese food. It has vegetable dishes for $6.80, and seafood for $10.90. The nearby ***Lilac Restaurant*** *(☎ 9660 5172, 333 Glebe Point Rd)* serves Chinese, Malaysian and Indonesian food. Beef mains cost from $8.50, lunch specials are $5.80, and there's a good vegetarian selection.

Yak & Yeti *(☎ 9552 1220, 41 Glebe Point Rd)* is a Nepalese restaurant with vegetable dishes for around $10, meat dishes for $12 to $16; there's not much elbow room, but the food is tasty.

Flavour of India *(☎ 9692 0062, 142a Glebe Point Rd)* is next to the Pudding Shop, on the corner of Pyrmont Bridge Rd. Starters like chicken tikka (chicken marinated in yoghurt and spices and grilled in the tandoor oven) cost $6.50 to $9.50. It also has a good vegetarian selection; the pakora entrée is $6.50.

The least expensive pizzas ($6 to $19) in the area are available from ***Perry's Gourmet Pizzas*** *(☎ 9660 8440, 381 Glebe Point Rd)* another block north.

BALMAIN (MAP 3)

In Sydney's inner west, the pretty, breezy suburb of Balmain has some good places to eat. Because much of the trade is local, service is usually friendly and standards consistent. Most are on Darling St, which is a good place to visit at night.

Near the Darling St wharf in East Balmain, ***Pelicans Fine Foods*** *(81 Darling St)* opens for breakfast, fresh-roasted coffee and light meals daily – including the famous pelican burger ($4.50) – which is pelican-free, but popular nonetheless. Next door, the friendly ***Reveille*** *(☎ 9555 8874, 79 Darling St)* has a small but eclectic modern French-Australian menu and an equally select clientele. Mains cost around $23; it opens at 7 pm and is closed Sundays. It's a good idea to book.

At the pleasant ***Cafe Viva*** *(☎ 9810 9569, 189 Darling St)* you can sip your coffee at kooky formica tables, and choose from a range of toasted Turkish rolls ($7) with various tasty fillings.

Sausolito *(☎ 9810 9521, 246 Darling St)* opens for breakfast, lunch and dinner daily, and serves modern Italian and Mediterranean cuisine; focaccia starts at $6.50, pasta is $7.50. Tucked away behind the Institute Arcade is ***La Lupa Trattoria*** *(☎ 9818 1645, 332 Darling St)*, with a cool green interior and a mezzanine level. Enter through the main arcade entrance, or take the small alley to the left. Mains, mostly chicken or fish, cost $12.50 to $6.50. It's open Tuesday to Saturday.

In a house set back from the road, ***Jiyu No Omise*** *(☎ 9818 3886, 342 Darling St)* is a Japanese restaurant open for dinner. Teriyaki steak is $15.80. Nearby ***Cafe Smooth*** *(☎ 9555 7008, 348 Darling St)* is a relaxed cafe-gallery with paintings on the walls, magazines and books to read, and an unusual communal table as its centrepiece. A cooked breakfast is $10.

LEICHHARDT

Leichhardt, another interesting culinary centre in Sydney's inner west, has a reputation for Italian food. You're likely to hear a fair bit of Italian spoken on Norton St, where most of the cafes and restaurants are located. The street bustles on weekend nights; it's a short ride from George St on bus No 438 or 440.

Bar Italia *(☎ 9560 9981, 169-71 Norton St)* is an enormously popular restaurant, cafe and gelateria. It offers pasta mains for around $7.50, and bar snacks from $3.50, but one of its biggest drawcards is the delicious gelato (from $3.50). The nearby ***Cafe Barzu*** *(☎ 9550 0144, 121 Norton St)* does excellent pizzas for $10 to $15, and also has fancy cakes.

On the other side of the road, popular ***Portofino's*** *(☎ 9550 0782, 166 Norton St)* is a cafe and bar with a large, diverse Italian menu. Pastas are between $12 and $19, seafood starts at $10. The small, friendly ***Mezzapica*** *(☎ 9568 2095, 128 Norton St)* is also popular, and has outside tables.

At the Parramatta Rd end of Norton St, ***Bar Baba*** *(☎ 9564 2044)* is a pleasant Italian cafe and restaurant with good food and a tempting selection of wines. Blue cheese gnocchi costs $9.50, barbecued octopus $15; it's also a good spot for breakfast.

NEWTOWN

Newtown's long King St has a huge range of eateries, many budget-priced, with plenty of ethnic cuisines – everything from African to Vietnamese. The eateries are an interesting introduction to the suburb's rich and varied community life.

Fast Food & Cafes

The cheapest place to eat is ***Hare Krishna Centre*** near the train station (turn left as you come out, and cross the road), but it's only open from 11 am to 3 pm Monday to Saturday. Sydney's Indian fast-food phenomenon is represented by ***Tamana's Indian Diner***, which has two places on King St (Nos 196 and 236) offering three curries with rice for $4.90.

The laid-back, convivial ***Green Iguana Cafe*** *(☎ 9516 3118, 6 King St)* is at the far eastern end of King St, near the intersection with Darlington Rd. Breakfast costs $2.50 to $7, potato and coriander soup $5.90. There's a leafy courtyard, and a noticeboard with information on neighbourhood happenings.

Easily the kookiest cafe in town, the entrance to tiny ***MacDonna's*** *(☎ 9565 1102, 275 Australia St)* is decorated with a bizarre 'bead curtain' of strung-up kids' toys. It's just off King St not far from the train station,

SIMON BRACKEN

MacDonna's is one of the more unusual cafes in Sydney.

and is open until 6 pm; extravagant vegetarian burgers cost $5.50.

Restaurants

Le Kilimanjaro *(☎ 9557 4565, 280 King St)* is a bustling African restaurant with a good menu full of tempting, exotic dishes such as spiced couscous. Mains are $8.50, side dishes $5.

Peasant's Feast *(☎ 9916 5998, 121 King St)* offers hearty staples with a modern edge, served in a 'rural' restaurant setting; entrées cost $10, mains $15. ***Green Gourmet*** *(☎ 9519 5330, 115 King St)* is a roomy Asian vegetarian place. Mains start at $10, and there's a $6 lunch buffet.

Old Saigon *(☎ 9519 5931, 107 King St)* is an interesting Vietnamese restaurant with toy helicopters hanging from the ceiling, and a hands-on approach to cuisine: you can cook your own meat at the table (complete with hissing grill) and construct individualised rice-paper rolls. Mains cost about $12.

Back at the Ranch *(☎ 9519 7869, 175 King St)* is a Tex-Mex restaurant with booth seats, leather bridles and western paraphernalia dangling overhead. At lunchtime, meals are almost half what they cost in the evening. At dinner time, enchiladas and burritos are $11.90.

DOUBLE BAY

This exclusive neighbourhood has some excellent (and expensive) places to eat, many on and around Bay St.

Peron's *(☎ 9328 6004, 42 Bay St)* is part of the Cosmopolitan shopping centre and serves a range of delicious salads and snacks. The nearby ***Courtyard Cafe*** *(☎ 9326 1602, 37 Bay St)* serves good pasta; mushroom gnocchi costs $10.90. One of the city's top Italian restaurants is the spacious but intimate ***Botticelli*** *(☎ 9363 3266, 21 Bay St)*, where pasta mains cost $15 to $19. A good place for a romantic dinner, it's where former Australian prime minister Bob Hawke and his biographer Blanche d'Alpuget celebrated their nuptials.

Taste of India *(☎ 9327 5712, 370 New South Rd)*, near Knox St, is one of the best Indian restaurants in Sydney. A mushroom bhajee is $11.90, mango chicken $13.90.

BONDI BEACH & AROUND (MAP 11)

Campbell Parade is one long string of takeaways, cafes and restaurants, many with sea views. Hall St, leading away from the beach also has some interesting places.

Cafes

The good-value ***Gusto*** *(☎ 9130 4565, 16 Hall St)* is a block back from the beach near the corner of Jacques Ave. It's a popular little deli where you can eat healthy snacks at fairly low prices; generous-sized chicken and cheese melts are $7.

The nearby ***On the Rise*** *(☎ 9365 1278, 39 Hall St)* is a bakery-cum-eatery selling muffins, gourmet breads, and filled focaccia for $5. It has a good atmosphere, and you can sit outside.

Beneath the Swiss Grand hotel, the oddly-named ***Hog's Breath Cafe*** *(☎ 9130 8045, 180-186 Campbell Parade)* is part of a small chain selling reasonably priced food and drink. Chicken burgers are $9.95.

There's a strip of trendy cafe-bars at the beach's southern end. Most have outdoor seating, ocean views and Mediterranean-influenced bistro fare. At ***Lamrock Cafe*** *(☎ 9130 6313, 72 Campbell Parade)* risotto costs $12.90, vegetarian burgers $10.50. ***Hugo's Bondi Cafe*** *(☎ 9300 0900, 70 Campbell Parade)*, near Lamrock Ave, is stark, modern and a little more expensive, but it's a good place to show off your designer shades. Lunch mains are around $16.

Restaurants

In North Bondi, ***RSL Club*** *(Returned Servicemen's League, ☎ 9130 3152, 118-120 Ramsgate Ave)* has lunch specials for $4.

The popular ***Bondi Trattoria*** *(☎ 9365 4303, 34 Campbell Parade)* is known locally as 'the Tratt'. It's good for breakfast; your basic coco pops are $4, delectable marscapone and banana honey pancakes are $7.50.

The busy ***Raw*** *(☎ 9365 7200)*, on the corner of Wairoa and Warners Ave, serves bistro-style Japanese in spotlessly slick style for $3 to $29; teriyaki chicken is $12.80. ***Turenne's*** *(☎ 9365 7609, 49 Hall St)* is an unusual Caribbean restaurant with oriental-influenced food; mains start at $9.50 and go up to $16.50. Desserts (like black sticky rice with coconut and honey) are $7.50.

There are a couple of good restaurants back towards the city. ***Indochine*** *(☎ 9387 4081, 99 Bondi Rd)* is a popular Vietnamese place with braised pork for $10.30.

Laurie's Vegetarian Restaurant *(☎ 9365 0134, 286 Bondi Road)* has a great selection of cheap and tasty curries, pastas and stir-fries from $3.80.

COOGEE (MAP 10)

Fast Food & Cafes

There are numerous takeaways on Coogee Bay Rd offering cheap eats, but you're better off hitting the cafes for healthier food, sunnier demeanours and outdoor tables. ***Cafe Congo*** *(☎ 9665 3101, 208 Arden St)*, north of Coogee Bay Rd, is popular, inexpensive and colourful, and has aerosol murals on the walls. There's nothing African about the menu, which is mostly Italian with a mix of Mexican. Nachos cost $7, lasagne $8. The nearby ***La Casa*** is similarly priced, with spaghetti or fish and chips for $9.

There are several bright, pleasant places on Coogee Bay Rd serving standard cafe fare for between $5 and $11, including the beach-themed ***Coogee Cafe*** *(221 Coogee Bay Rd)* where most lunches are $8, and the colourful ***Globe*** *(203 Coogee Bay Rd)*, with breakfasts (until 3 pm) from $4, sandwiches from around $5.

Restaurants

Renato's *(☎ 9665 8975, 237 Coogee Bay Rd)* is a good-value, busy Italian restaurant, which has pasta from $7 to $9. Nearby is ***Erciyes 2*** *(240 Coogee Bay Rd)*, which is an offshoot of the popular Erciyes Turkish restaurant in Surry Hills. The food is tasty and inexpensive, with nothing over $8.50; doner kebabs cost $7, and there are good dips and salads.

At the northern end of the beach, on Dolphin St, is the Beach Palace Hotel; on the 1st floor is the large ***Regal Pearl*** *(☎ 9665 3308)*, an upmarket Chinese restaurant specialising in seafood. Lobster tail goes for $35.

Just around the corner is ***Human*** *(☎ 9664 5573, 104 Beach Rd)*, serving interesting food in warm surrounds. Entrées cost up to $12, mains from $14 to $19, and it has a BYO license. You can also drop in for dessert or a coffee.

WATSONS BAY

The long-established ***Doyle's on the Beach*** *(☎ 9337 2007, 11 Marine Parade, Watsons Bay)* specialises in seafood, and main courses average around $25. Bookings are advisable. Next door, at ***Doyle's on the Quay***, which shares the fabulous view, most mains are similarly priced, although indulgent dishes like lobster and smoked salmon salad cost around $43.

Right on the water, ***Doyle's Wharf Restaurant*** *(☎ 9337 1572, Watsons Bay Wharf)* is open daily for lunch, Wednesday to Saturday for dinner. Lobster straight from the tank is $60.

On the other side of Robertson Park in the beautiful old Dunbar House, ***Fisherman's Lodge*** *(☎ 9337 1226)* is a slightly less expensive option (the Atlantic salmon costs $23.50).

Getting There & Away

On weekdays at lunchtime, you can catch Doyle's own water taxi from the Harbour Master's Steps on the western side of Circular Quay. The taxi costs $6/10 one way/return, and services start at 11.30 am. An ordinary water taxi would cost about $50 between four people. Ferries run from Circular Quay to Watsons Bay every two hours on weekends, but only until 5.15 pm. For the non-nautical, bus Nos 324 and 325 run from Circular Quay.

NORTH SHORE

Crows Nest

Crows Nest, north-west of North Sydney, has many popular eating places. Most are clustered on or near the three-way intersection of the Pacific Highway (Hwy), Falcon St and Willoughby Rd.

At ***Wood Fire Pizza Company*** *(☎ 9439 3113, 308 Pacific Hwy)* the dish comes as close as it can to being a health food. The pizzas aren't cheap ($12.90 to $16.90) but the quality is good, with such exotic toppings as artichokes, brie, snow peas, and scallops. West of the junction is the Thai restaurant ***Hot Basil*** *(☎ 9437 4075, 318 Pacific Hwy)*. The large and varied menu offers vegetarian mains for around $10 and seafood dishes for $13.50. It's open for lunch weekdays, and daily for dinner.

Along Willoughby Rd, the main shopping precinct, places to try include ***Blue Elephant*** *(☎ 9439 3468, upstairs, 36-38 Willoughby Rd)*; it has Sri Lankan food for around $15, and is closed Sunday. ***Talay Thai*** *(☎ 9906 3535, 88 Willoughby Rd)* has stir-fried dishes for $9 to $12.50 (takeaways are a little cheaper); there are outside tables and it's open daily for dinner, weekdays for lunch.

Borderland *(☎ 9436 3918, 97 Willoughby Rd)* is a Mexican restaurant offering lunches like dips for $5.50 and nachos for $5.80; dinner mains cost $10.90 to $17.50. The crowded but low-key ***Ten-Sun*** *(☎ 9906 2956, 103 Willoughby Rd)*, in the arcade north of Albany St, is a Japanese noodle bar with meals under $10.

Nearby Alexander St also has some good restaurants including the large ***Rangoon Racquet Club Restaurant*** *(☎ 9906 4091, 70 Alexander St)*. Its walls are lined with shelves of antique books. It doesn't serve Burmese food, but rather, the 'aromatic cuisine of British colonial India'. Elephant boy curry (beef marinated in a spicy sauce) costs $15.50, dhal $8.95. It's open daily for dinner, weekdays for lunch.

Across the road and further down is ***Montezuma's*** *(☎ 9901 3533, 51 Alexander St)*, another Mexican restaurant. Part of a chain, it's open daily; nachos cost $5.95 to $7.50, chicken enchiladas $10.95. It also does takeaway.

North Sydney (Map 2)

North Sydney Noodle Market *(☎ 9417 3256)* is a praiseworthy attempt to capture the atmosphere of Asian street-food markets. It's held in the park near the corner of Miller and McLaren Sts in North Sydney on Friday night from 5.30 pm during the warmer months, and Sunday lunchtime from 11.30 am during winter. Numerous stalls serve Chinese, Indian, Malaysian, Nepalese and Vietnamese food.

Prasit's Northside Thai *(☎ 9957 2271, 77 Mount St)*, on the corner of Elizabeth Plaza, is a licensed Thai restaurant with good spiced fish cakes for $9.90, and most mains priced at around $15.50. It's open for lunch on weekdays and for dinner Tuesday to Saturday.

Balmoral

In the quiet suburb of Balmoral, you'll find a number of good restaurants, most with good views across the harbour.

Between Raglan St and Botanic Rd are some inexpensive cafes, including ***Sam's Espresso Bar***, which has filling sandwiches and rolls for $3 to $4, and a good array of pies, muffins and cakes. Nearby is ***Bottom of the Harbour*** *(21 East Esplanade)*, with fresh sushi, good salads, and some of the best fish and chips ($5.65) in Sydney.

Two restaurants have prime locations on the foreshore itself – and prices to match. ***Bathers Pavilion*** *(☎ 9968 1133, 59 East Esplanade)* is in a beautiful old building and has views across the harbour to North Head. Major renovations were underway at the time of writing, but there are plans for a stylish cafe and restaurant. The similarly swanky ***Watermark*** *(☎ 9968 3433, 2a East Esplanade)*, at the junction with Botanic Rd, has well-heeled patrons, and views of the marina and across to Manly. Scallop ravioli is $22. It's open for breakfast, lunch and dinner.

PLACES TO EAT

MANLY (MAP 12)

Fast Food & Cafes

In Manly, you don't have to go any further than the wharf to eat for $4 to $7; the Corso is jammed with places, and there are others along North and South Steyne.

Next to the Le Kiosk Restaurant on Shelly Beach east of the main beach is ***Shelly Beach Kiosk*** where you can get sandwiches for $4.50 and ice creams.

Cafe Steyne *(☎ 9977 0116, 14 South Steyne)* serves everything from daiquiris to melts, though an average dish on the large menu is pasta from $6.80 to $12.30. The chic but laid-back Tunisian eatery, ***Cafe Tunis*** *(☎ 9976 2805, 30-31 South Steyne)*, has good coffee and interesting food. Pita bread rolls with a choice of fillings cost from $10.50.

BarKing Frog *(☎ 9977 6307, 48 North Steyne)* is a fashionable bar and cafe with good coffee, entrées like baked bruschetta for $9.80 and interesting mains from $18.

For quick and tasty budget fare, try ***Fresh*** *(1/49 North Steyne)*. There's homemade muesli and fresh juices, and giant cheese melts for a paltry $3.50.

Restaurants

For a reasonably priced, MSG-free Thai meal, try ***Wi Marn*** *(☎ 9976 2995, 47 North Steyne)*, which has entrées for $6 and seafood dishes from $13. Next door is a low-frills seafood specialist, ***Fishmongers*** *(☎ 9977 7513)*, with mains for $11 to $15. (The old-school shrimp cocktail is alive and well here.)

Follow the foreshore path east from the main ocean beach to reach the small ***Bower Restaurant*** *(☎ 9977 5451, 7 Marine Parade)*, within spray's-breadth of tiny Fairy Bower beach. It has snacks and coffees, and main courses of modern Australian food for around $23. It's BYO and is open for breakfast and lunch daily. Further around at Shelly Beach is the upmarket ***Le Kiosk Restaurant*** *(☎ 9977 4122, 1 Marine Parade)*, serving mostly Asian-influenced seafood with a view. Expect to pay about $55.

For tasty Malay and Thai dishes, ***Malacca Straits Satay Restaurant*** *(☎ 9977 6627, 49 Sydney Rd)* has a good reputation, if a slightly dubious colour scheme. Main courses cost $7 to $13.

There's a seafood buffet at ***Manly Pacific Parkroyal*** *(☎ 9977 7666, 55 North Steyne)* – on weekdays it's downstairs and costs $31.50, weekends it's upstairs for $34.50. It has a champagne and jazz lunch on Sunday for $26.50.

On Manly Wharf, ***Armstrong's*** *(☎ 9976 3835)*, at the western end, has a good reputation for modern Australian food, with the emphasis on seafood. Crisp-skinned salmon with asparagus is $15.

Entertainment

With a thriving arts and cultural scene and plenty of nightlife, Sydney has something for everyone. Attractions range from gay dance clubs, stand-up comedy, live bands in crowded pubs and films at one of the many cinemas, to opera and ballet at the Opera House and shows at the city's many theatres. Call the City Events Infoline (☎ 9265 9007) for information on current events.

One of the best sources of 'what's on' information is the *Sydney Morning Herald*'s 'Metro' section. It's published on Friday and lists happenings for the week ahead. The free weekly *Sydney City Hub* is a street-smart rag bursting with news on music and arty events. For more-specialised music listings pick up one of the free and widely available weekly papers such as *Drum Media*, *Revolver* or *3D World*.

Ticketek (Map 4, ☎ 9266 4800), 195 Elizabeth St, is the city's main booking agency for theatre, concerts, sports and other events. Phone bookings can be made from 7.30 am to 10 pm weekdays, 9 am to 4 pm Saturday, and 9 am to 8 pm Sunday. It also has agencies around town and publishes a bi-monthly *Entertainment Guide*.

Halftix (Map 4, ☎ 9966 1622), 201 Sussex St, near Cockle Bay Wharf, sells half-price seats to shows. Tickets are only available for shows that night. Halftix is open daily except Sunday. You can also book through the Web site at www.halftix.com.au.

Try to catch something at the Sydney Opera House (see Performing Arts later) – in addition to opera and ballet, it hosts a wide range of musical events, live theatre, films, children's entertainment and even rock concerts.

FREE ENTERTAINMENT

On summer weekends there's free music in many parks, especially in the Domain during the Sydney Festival and Carnivale (January). There's often free lunchtime music in the amphitheatre at Martin Place (12.15 to 1.15 pm); at Darling Harbour's Tumbalong Park amphitheatre; and at St Andrews Cathedral next to the Town Hall (Tuesday at 1.10 pm during the school term), courtesy of students from the Conservatorium of Music. Over the Labour Day long weekend (early October), there are free outdoor jazz concerts at the Manly Jazz Festival. You can be entertained by buskers around the Opera House and Circular Quay, in the Rocks and Kings Cross, and along the Corso in Manly. Alternatively, you can listen to the mad and the erudite venting their obsessions at Speakers' Corner in the Domain on Sunday afternoon.

There's a free Aboriginal dance performance at the Art Gallery of NSW, Tuesday to Saturday at noon. There's also free entertainment at many of Sydney's weekend flea markets (see Markets in the Shopping chapter).

Tropfest (☎ 9368 0434) is a one-day short film festival in late February, which screens simultaneously at the Domain, and in Victoria St (which is blocked off for the occasion), Darlinghurst. Entries must fit a loosely interpreted theme; the theme for 2000 is 'bugs'.

PUBS WITH MUSIC

Sydney doesn't have an especially dynamic pub music scene, but there are enough pubs offering live music for you to be able to find something most nights of the week. Five-star hotels often have famous cabaret artists, and sometimes more adventurous acts, at prices that aren't outrageous as long as you watch your alcohol intake. A few of the many venues are listed here; for other places with music on the menu, see Pubs & Bars in this chapter.

The Basement *(Map 4, ☎ 9251 2797, 29 Reiby Place, Circular Quay)* has good food, good jazz, sometimes big international names – it's a smoke-free venue.

The Bridge *(☎ 9810 1260, 135 Victoria Rd, Rozelle)* has rock, DJs, and comedy.

Sometimes big Aussie names and overseas acts perform here.

The ***Cat & Fiddle Hotel*** *(☎ 9810 7931, 456 Darling St, Balmain)* has bands nightly except Monday: jazz, blues, pop. rock, metal etc.

Golden Sheaf Hotel *(☎ 9327 5877, 429 New South Head Rd, Double Bay)* has a free band on Sunday night, and DJs Wednesday to Saturday (lounge, funk and groove). It has good food and is popular with travellers.

Grand Hotel *(☎ 9389 300, 489 Ebley St, Bondi Junction)* has several bars, cover bands Friday and Saturday, and DJs (retro and commercial dance) Thursday to Sunday.

Harbourside Brasserie *(☎ 9252 3000, Pier 1, Hickson Rd, Walsh Bay)* has good live music and entertainment seven nights. The kitchen is open from 7 pm to 11 pm.

The ***Hopetoun Hotel*** *(Map 8, ☎ 9361 5257, 416 Bourke St, Surry Hills)* has live music every night: indie, rock, jazz, groove, and electronic.

Kinselas *(Map 8, ☎ 9331 3299, 383 Bourke St, Darlinghurst)* is a large Art Deco building with a basement bar downstairs and a pool table (DJs playing cruisey sounds) and a cocktail bar upstairs. The nightclub upstairs may also be reopening.

Lansdowne Hotel *(Map 9, ☎ 9211 2325, 2 City Rd, Chippendale)* has bands Sunday to Thursday, DJs Friday (underground house) and Saturday (Sounds of Seduction – kooky cocktail-lounge tunes and go-go dancers, $5).

Rose, Shamrock & Thistle Hotel – 'The Three Weeds' *(☎ 9810 2244, 193 Evans St)*, on the corner of Belmore St, Rozelle, has bands Thursday to Sunday: rock, pop, blues and folk (sometimes big names).

Sandringham Hotel *(☎ 9557 1254, 387 King St, Newtown)* has live acoustic music on weekends.

Selina's *(Map 10, ☎ 9665 0000, Coogee Bay Hotel, Coogee Bay Rd, Coogee)* has rock (often top Australian and international bands) for which you can pay a fair bit; the main nights are Friday and Saturday, but there are cheaper bands most other nights.

Strawberry Hills Hotel *(Map 8, ☎ 9698 2997, 453 Elizabeth St, Surry Hills)* has interesting jazz most nights.

NIGHTCLUBS

Dance music has taken off in recent years, and you'll find beats of almost every description if you're prepared to seek them out. Sydney has some good local DJs, as well as touring internationals from mega-clubs overseas. However, nightclubs can be fickle things and exclusive clubs or specific nights can pop up and vanish in the blink of an eye. Check the street press mentioned at the start of this chapter, and flyers in record stores, for up-to-the-minute information.

Cauldron *(Map 6, ☎ 9331 1523, 207 Darlinghurst Rd)*, on the corner of Farrel Ave, Darlinghurst, is a long-running, slick basement club with a strict door policy. Music ranges from retro to house.

Cave *(Map 3, ☎ 9566 4755, Star City Casino, Pyrmont)* is a flashy joint. The music is predominantly house and techno and there are good one-off nights. Open seven nights till 4 am.

DCM *(Map 4, ☎ 9267 7380, 33 Oxford St, Darlinghurst)* is a large, mixed gay-straight disco with weekend drag shows.

EP1 *(Map 6, ☎ 9358 3990, 1 Earl Place, Kings Cross)* is a mainstream club with varied music. Backpackers' night is Wednesday (retro) and entry is cheap.

Home *(Map 4, ☎ 9266 0600, Cockle Bay Wharf, Darling Harbour)* is a huge, hip and happening club playing mostly house music. It has international DJs on Saturday ($20).

Midnight Shift *(Map 4, ☎ 9360 4319, 85-91 Oxford St, Darlinghurst)* is a popular two level gay club with a big dance floor and great lighting; open from 9 pm.

Mister GoodBar *(Map 7, ☎ 9360 6759, 11 Oxford St, Paddington)* is a small, terribly cool club with strict door and dress policies. The music includes house, big beat, hip hop, funk, disco and rare groove.

Power Cuts Reggae Club *(Map 8)*, on the corner of Cleveland and Chalmers Sts, Redfern, has reggae and dub Friday and Saturday night.

Q Bar *(Map 4, ☎ 9360 1375, Level 2, 44 Oxford St)* is a groovy, hard-to-find pool hall-bar-club tucked away above a record shop. It has lounge, funk, house, trip-hop and drum and bass, and is open extra late.

Slipp-Inn *(Map 4, ☎ 9299 4777, 111 Sussex St)* is a hip joint playing a mish-mash of breakbeat, house, garage, drum and bass and hip-hop; 'Chinese Laundry' on Friday and Saturday nights.

Soho Bar *(Map 6, ☎ 9358 4221, 171 Victoria St, Potts Point)* is four different bars in one; watch the attitude on the door. It has funk, groove and commercial house.

Underground Cafe *(Map 6, ☎ 9368 1067, 22 Bayswater Rd, Kings Cross)* is a decent, established house-music club, with local and international DJs. There's a $2 entry fee on Thursday.

PUBS & BARS

Pubs and bars are an important part of Sydney's social scene. Try going to a few during the week because they often have a totally different atmosphere on the weekends, when the roving hordes are out on the town. Pubs vary from the traditional with tiled walls, to the modern stylish Art Deco bar. Pubs are often multipurpose, and many now have the ubiquitous poker machines and betting (see the Gambling section later); most serve food and some have a variety of live entertainment.

The Rocks & Circular Quay (Map 4)

There are some nice old pubs in the Rocks, but determining just *how* old they are seems to be a less than exact science. ***Fortune of War*** *(137 George St)*, opposite the back of the Museum of Contemporary Art, claims to hold Sydney's oldest hotel licence – but a couple of other old pubs nearby disagree.

Both in Millers Point, ***Hero of Waterloo*** *(81 Lower Fort St)*, on the corner of Windmill St, and ***Lord Nelson Brewery Hotel*** *(19 Kent St)*, are probably Sydney's best-known pubs, and two of its busiest. Both vie for the title of 'Sydney's oldest pub' – while other equally ambitious establishments lay claim to the title of 'oldest continually operating pub'. Hero of Waterloo has music on weekends, including traditional Irish music, and the Lord Nelson brews its own beer.

One of Sydney's best places for Guinness and regular live Irish music is the beautifully green-tiled ***Mercantile Hotel*** *(25 George St)*, near the bridge.

The more upmarket ***Harts Pub***, on the corner of Gloucester and Essex Sts, the Rocks, has live music on Thursday and Friday. The ***George St Bar (GSB)*** *(199 George St)* is another upmarket (but more modern) boozer.

If you're feeling sophisticated, the bar at the smart ***Bennelong*** restaurant in the Opera House is a good spot to drop in for a cocktail, hear some live jazz, and check out the awesome architecture – dress respectably and you'll be welcome. ***Legends*** is an upmarket bar on Bligh St under the Wentworth Hotel. A neon sign promises 'free beer tomorrow'.

City Centre (Map 4)

A must for most visitors is the richly ornate ***Marble Bar*** *(☎ 9266 0610, 259 Pitt St)* beneath the Royal Arcade and Hilton Hotel; most nights it has live music of the funk, blues and jazz persuasion.

At the intersection of York and King Sts, two contrasting pubs face each other diagonally. The charming, multistorey ***Forbes Hotel***, with leadlights, wood-panelled walls and a tiny wrought-iron balcony, is the more traditional and cosy, while ***CBD Hotel*** has a trendy Art Deco layout. Both are popular with city workers.

Scruffy Murphy's *(43 Goulburn St)*, near the corner of George St, is popular with twenty-somethings, serves good Guinness and has live music every night.

As yet untouched by the renovating squad, ***Century Tavern***, on the corner of George and Liverpool Sts, has a downbeat rock and roll charm, and curved glass windows looking down onto the street.

Super stylish and popular with sharply-dressed types, the nevertheless cosy ***Wine Banc***, on the corner of Martin Place and

Castlereagh St, is a modern cigar-cum-wine bar tucked away in an old bank vault.

Darling Harbour & Pyrmont (Maps 4 & 9)

For real ale fans a good option is ***Pumphouse Tavern Brewery*** *(17 Little Pier St)* near the Sydney Entertainment Centre, which offers a variety of beers brewed on the premises.

Pyrmont Bridge Hotel *(96 Union St)* on the corner of Murray St near Pyrmont Bridge, is a typical Sydney pub that's pleasantly unpretentious beside the Darling Harbour and casino glitz. The less casual upstairs bar has a good view of the city.

There are several other old-style pubs along Pyrmont Bridge Rd, including ***Quarrymans Hotel***, on the corner of Harris St.

Near Darling Harbour, in an old sandstone building squeezed between Hotel Nikko and the Takashimaya duty free store on Sussex St, is ***Dundee Arms Tavern***. This upmarket pub is in a heritage-listed sandstone building.

Kings Cross & Around (Maps 5 & 6)

Kings Cross and the surrounding areas have plenty of watering holes. The huge, rowdy ***Kings Cross Hotel***, at the junction of Victoria St, Darlinghurst Rd and William St, is a boozy hang-out for backpackers and predominantly young out-of-towners. Pricier places in the Cross include the slick ***Cafe Iguana*** and the cool ***Dean's Cafe*** *(5 Kellett St)*, both with front courtyards.

Mansions Hotel *(18 Bayswater Rd)* on the corner of Kellett St is a cavernous, modern place with a pool table and a decent bistro.

The tiny ***Piccolo's*** bar *(6 Roslyn St)* is crammed with movie memorabilia and local insomniacs, sells beer and vegemite toast, and is open around the clock. The extremely laid-back The ***Amsterdam Cafe*** *(☎ 8356 9018, 9a Roslyn St)* across the road has a similar ambience, and serves munchies (but not alcohol).

Several hostels are close to ***Soho Bar*** *(Piccadilly Hotel, 171 Victoria St)*, where you can get good cocktails.

Old Fitzroy Hotel, on the corner of Cathedral and Dowling Sts, Woolloomooloo, is popular with British backpackers, and has good live theatre nights. ***Woolloomooloo Bay Hotel*** *(2 Bourke St)* gets busy at weekend lunchtimes and evenings.

A good place for a drink is the funky ***Darlo Bar***, on the corner of Darlinghurst and Liverpool Sts. Occupying its own tiny block, this is surely the narrowest pub in Sydney. It's pretty much a neighbourhood pub, but it's a very interesting neighbourhood. Good food, drinks and cocktails are available, and the service is friendly.

South of the Cross, ***Green Park Hotel*** *(360 Victoria St, Darlinghurst)*, with its blue-tiled walls and bar, is a popular local watering hole and a cool hang-out for pool-shooters.

Oxford St & Around (Maps 4, 7 & 8)

There are a number of good pubs along Oxford St, including ***Burdekin Hotel*** *(2 Oxford St)*, which has a stylish cocktail bar downstairs and a fashionable restaurant upstairs. ***Lizard Lounge*** *(Exchange Hotel, 34 Oxford St)* is a casual bar popular with lesbians. Further east is the discreet but groovy ***Q Bar*** *(44 Oxford St)*, a cavernous bar/nightclub-cum-pool hall above Central Station Records.

On the other side of Taylor Square, ***Albury Hotel*** *(6 Oxford St)* in Paddington is a gay pub that often has good entertainment, including drag shows. Other gay pubs in the area include ***Beauchamp Hotel***, on the corner of Oxford and South Dowling Sts; ***Flinders Hotel*** *(63 Flinders St)*; and ***Beresford Hotel*** *(354 Bourke St)*.

Lively pubs for twenty-somethings include ***Fringe Bar*** *(106 Oxford St)*, near the Victoria Barracks, and ***Palace Hotel*** *(122 Flinders St)* at the junction with South Dowling St.

Glebe (Map 9)

The eccentric ***Friend in Hand Hotel*** *(58 Cowper St)*, full of old photos and crazy bric-a-brac, has a reputation as a party pub. It stages events such as crab racing

(Wednesday) and poetry slams (Tuesday); there's music Friday and Sunday, and generous discounts on drinks and food. Don't offer your beer to the resident cockatoo.

Another popular Glebe pub is ***Harold Park Hotel*** *(115 Wigram Rd)*, which has a sunny courtyard-cum-beer garden.

Surry Hills (Map 8)

Cricketers Arms *(106 Fitzroy St)* is popular with locals and British backpackers, and sometimes has DJs.

The renovated ***Dolphin Hotel*** *(412 Crown St)*, on the corner of Fitzroy St is good for a quiet drink or a meal in the large restaurant. ***Bentley Bar*** *(320 Crown St)* on the corner of Campbell St is another reasonable local.

Woollahra (Map 7)

Lord Dudley Hotel *(236 Jersey Rd)* in Woollahra is as close as Sydney gets to an English pub atmosphere.

Newtown (Map 9)

The trendy ***Bank Hotel*** *(324 King St)* has a beer garden and is a popular lesbian hang-out, especially on Wednesday. Another pub with a beer garden is ***Iron Duke Hotel***, on the corner of Botany and McEvoy Rds; it sometimes has live music on weekends. The busy ***Botany View Hotel*** *(597 King St)* serves decent Guinness on tap. ***Marlborough Hotel*** *(145 King St)* has live music on weekends and a Wednesday night trivia quiz.

GAMBLING

Australians love to gamble, and Sydney provides plenty of opportunities for punters to be separated from their cash.

Star City Casino

This huge casino, theatre, retail, restaurant and hotel complex is located on the waterfront in Pyrmont, on the north-eastern headland of Darling Harbour (Map 4). It's open 24 hours; for information call ☎ 1300 300 711. A free shuttle bus connects the Rocks and city centre with the casino, or you can catch the ferry to the Pyrmont Bay Wharf, just across the road from the casino.

Horse & Greyhound Racing

Sydney has four horse racing venues. These are ***Canterbury Park*** *(☎ 9930 4000, King St, Canterbury)*, south-west of the city centre; ***Rosehill Gardens*** *(☎ 9930 4070, Grand Ave, Rosehill)*, near Parramatta; ***Royal Randwick*** *(☎ 9663 8400, Alison Rd, Randwick)*, closest to the city, near Centennial Park; and ***Warwick Farm*** *(☎ 9602 6199, Hume Hwy, Rosehill)*, near Liverpool.

Horse racing alternates between these tracks throughout the year. However, it's more colourful and exciting during the spring and autumn carnivals, when major events like the Golden Slipper at Rosehill or the Sydney Cup at Randwick take place.

A little down the social scale are trotting/pacing (harness racing) meetings at ***Harold Park Paceway*** *(Map 9, ☎ 9660 3688, Ross St, Glebe)*, and greyhound racing at ***Wentworth Park*** *(Map 9, ☎ 9552 1799, Wentworth Park Rd)*, also in Glebe.

Pokies

Coin-fed gambling machines known as 'pokies' (short for poker machines) are the most common form of gambling. They're everywhere. You'll find them in many pubs and in leagues, RSL (Returned Servicemen's League) and other clubs, which they help to keep profitable.

COMEDY

Sydney has several comedy venues. The ***Comedy Store*** *(☎ 9564 3900, 450 Parramatta Rd)*, on the corner of Crystal St in Petersham, is open Tuesday to Saturday. Tuesday, when new comics test their gags, is the cheapest night.

The prize for best supporting act goes to ***The Comedy Cellar*** *(Map 9, ☎ 9692 0564)*, on the corner of Bay St and Broadway, Glebe. It has a range of live music and comedy Thursday to Saturday.

CINEMAS

There's a cluster of mainstream multiscreen cinemas on George St south of Town Hall between Bathurst and Liverpool Sts (Map 4). These include ***Greater Union*** *(☎ 9267*

SARA-JANE CLELAND

The night lights at Darling Harbour

SARA-JANE CLELAND

The Sydney Opera House ready for a night of entertainment

SARA-JANE CLELAND

Sunset on Sydney Harbour

Sydney's internationally renowned Gay & Lesbian Mardi Gras draws huge crowds. The parade is the culmination of a month of events including theatre, arts, sporting events and parties, parties, parties.

8666), ***Hoyts*** *(☎ 9273 7431)* and ***Village*** *(☎ 9264 6701)*. New releases at these major cinemas cost $12.50 for adults, but they're cheaper on Tuesday.

Two cinemas on the North Shore are the ***Greater Union*** *(☎ 9969 1988, 9 Spit Rd, Mosman)* and the ***Manly Twin Cinemas*** *(Map 12, ☎ 9977 0644, 43 East Esplanade, Manly)*.

One cinema that shows inexpensive mainstream films is the ***Ritz Theatre*** *(☎ 9611 4811, 43 St Paul's St, Randwick)*. It's not far from Coogee, and charges just $7 ($4 children) for all sessions.

The new ***Fox Studios*** film and entertainment complex *(Map 7, ☎ 9383 4000, Moore Park, Paddington)* has a whopping 16 Hoyts cinemas. There are 12 for mainstream films and four for specialist and art-house screenings.

For further unusual fare, try the independent ***Dendy*** *(Map 4, ☎ 9264 1577, 624 George St)*, opposite the major cinema complexes, which shows alternative as well as commercial films. It has other cinemas around town. One of these is on the corner of Castlereagh St *(Map 4, ☎ 9233 8166, 19 Martin Place)* – there's a bar and bistro here too, with regular music nights. The other is in Newtown *(☎ 9550 5699, 261 King St)* opposite Le Kilimanjaro restaurant – turn right out of the train station. Tickets are $12 ($7.50 on Monday).

There are other cinemas showing foreign and alternative films. ***Academy Twin*** *(Map 7, ☎ 9361 4453, 3a Oxford St)* is on the corner of South Dowling St in Paddington. ***Hayden Orpheum Picture Palace*** *(☎ 9908 4344)*, at the junction of Military and Cremorne Rds, Cremorne, is a fabulous Art Deco gem. ***Verona Cinema*** *(Map 7, ☎ 9360 6099, upstairs, 17 Oxford St, Paddington)* is also an excellent Art Deco cafe and bar, with views over Oxford St. You could also try ***Encore Cinema*** *(Map 8, ☎ 9281 6493, 64 Devonshire St, Surry Hills)* and ***Walker Cinema*** *(Map 2, ☎ 9959 4222, 121 Walker St, North Sydney)*.

In Darlinghurst south of Kings Cross, the cushioned ***Movie Room*** *(Map 5, ☎ 9360 7853 or 9380 5155, 112 Darlinghurst Rd)* above Govinda's restaurant shows mainstream blockbusters, art-house fare and old favourites. Admission is $14.90, but includes an all-you-can-eat smorgasbord at Govinda's. There are screenings nightly at 7.30 and 9.30 pm. Govinda's opens from 6 pm.

The future of the much-loved ***Valhalla Cinema*** *(Map 9, ☎ 9660 8050, 166 Glebe Point Rd)* in Glebe is currently in suspended animation, but there are hopes that it will resume screening sometime.

The Australian Film Institute (AFI, ☎ 9332 2111) screens interesting new work and classics at the ***Sydney Film Centre/Chauvel Cinemas*** *(Map 7, ☎ 9361 5398, Paddington Town Hall)*.

The ***State Theatre*** *(Map 4, ☎ 9373 6655, 49 Market St)*, tucked between Pitt and George Sts, is the main venue for the Sydney Film Festival in June.

Centennial Park is the outdoor venue for the excellent twilight ***Moonlight Cinema*** *(☎ 1900 933 899 or 13 6100 for bookings)*, which has screenings during summer. ***Flickerfest*** *(☎ 9365 6877)* is a touring international short-film festival and competition held at the Bondi Pavilion in the first week of January. See Free Entertainment earlier in this chapter for information on the Tropfest short-film festival.

PERFORMING ARTS

The ***Sydney Opera House*** *(Map 4, ☎ 9250 7777)* is the performing arts centre of Sydney. The Australian Opera, Australian Ballet, Sydney Symphony Orchestra, Sydney Philharmonia Choirs, Musica Viva Australia and the Sydney Theatre Company stage regular performances here. See also Arts in the Facts About Sydney chapter.

For more information on companies' programs contact:

Australian Ballet
(☎ 9223 9522) Level 15, 115 Pitt St
Australian Opera
(☎ 9319 1088) 480 Elizabeth St, Surry Hills
Musica Viva Australia
(☎ 9698 1711) 120 Chalmers St, Surry Hills

Sydney Dance Company
(☎ 9221 4811) Pier 4, Hickson Rd, Walsh Bay
Sydney Philharmonia Choirs
(☎ 9251 2024) Pier 4, Hickson Rd, Walsh Bay
Sydney Symphony Orchestra
(☎ 9334 4644) 52 William St, East Sydney

THEATRE

Sydney may not have a distinct theatre district, but it has numerous theatres and a vigorous calendar of productions. These range from Broadway and West End shows at mainstream theatres to experimental theatre at smaller inner-suburban venues. Most tickets cost from $20 to $50.

Sydney Opera House *(Map 4, ☎ 9250 7777)* has three main theatres: the ***Drama Theatre*** regularly puts on plays by the Sydney Theatre Company, and the offerings at the ***Playhouse*** range from Aboriginal performances to Shakespeare; the new ***Studio*** venue hosts interesting contemporary arts and musical events. The Sydney Theatre Company, the city's top theatre company, has its own venue at the ***Wharf Theatre*** *(Map 4, ☎ 9250 1777, Pier 4, Hickson Rd, Walsh Bay)*.

The major commercial theatres are the restored ***Capitol Theatre*** *(Map 4, ☎ 9320 5000, 17 Campbell St, Haymarket)*; ***Her Majesty's Theatre*** *(Map 4, ☎ 9212 3411, 107 Quay St)* near Railway Square; and the ***Theatre Royal*** *(Map 4, ☎ 9320 9191, MLC Centre, King St)* in the city. A sight in itself

Aboriginal Performance

Dance and song have always played an important part in the culture of Australia's indigenous peoples (both Torres Strait Islanders and Aborigines), and the stories expressed through these activities draw upon ancient myths and spiritual links with the land.

You can see traditional Aboriginal dance performed by the community-oriented ***Aboriginal Dance Theatre*** *(☎ 9699 2171, 88 Renwick St, Redfern)*, which has been operating for 20 years, and also runs courses and workshops. The acclaimed ***Bangarra Dance Theatre*** *(☎ 9251 5333, Pier 4, Hickson Rd, Walsh Bay)* regularly performs indigenous song and dance, fusing ancient and modern styles.

The ***National Aboriginal and Islander Skills Development Association (NAISDA)*** *(Map 6, ☎ 9252 0199, 3 Cumberland St, the Rocks)* is an indigenous performing arts college that presents one-off performances including dance, song and spoken word.

JIM MCFARLANE

Miranda Coney, The Australian Ballet, and Albert David, Bangarra Dance Theatre: *Rites* (1997)

At Harbourside in Darling Harbour, ***Gavala*** *(Map 6, ☎ 9212 7232)* presents Aboriginal dancers who perform traditional dances, play didgeridoos and recount stories, at 4 pm on Wednesday and Sunday. Entry costs $15. There's also a free Aboriginal dance performance at the Art Gallery of NSW, Tuesday to Saturday at noon.

is the lush and opulent ***State Theatre*** *(Map 4, ☎ 9373 6655, 49 Market St)*, between Pitt and George Sts – they don't make them like this any more! These theatres are often the venues chosen for imported big-budget productions.

On the North Shore, the small ***Ensemble Theatre*** *(Map 2, ☎ 9929 0644, 78 McDougall St, Milsons Point)* presents mainstream theatre in a great setting on the waterfront at Careening Cove, a few blocks from Milsons Point station.

The ***National Institute of Dramatic Art*** *(NIDA, Map 2, ☎ 9697 7600, 215 Anzac Parade, Kensington)* at the University of NSW regularly stages excellent productions by its students. At the University of Sydney, the ***Footbridge Theatre*** *(Map 9, ☎ 9692 9955, Parramatta Rd, Glebe)* is also worth keeping an eye on.

The ***Seymour Theatre Centre*** *(Map 9, ☎ 9364 9444)*, on the corner of Cleveland St and City Rd, Chippendale, houses three theatres offering a variety of performances.

The ***Belvoir Street Theatre*** *(Map 8, ☎ 9699 3444, 25 Belvoir St, Surry Hills)* and ***Stables Theatre*** *(Map 6, ☎ 9361 3817, 10 Nimrod St, Kings Cross)* feature original, experimental Australian works.

Although it has been around a long time, the ***New Theatre*** *(☎ 9519 3403, 542 King St, Newtown)* produces some cutting-edge drama in addition to more-traditional pieces.

SPECTATOR SPORTS

You'll find vocal crowds and world-class athletes in action on just about every weekend of the year.

Football

The football season runs through autumn and winter (March to September).

Sydney is one of the world capitals of rugby league. The main competition, run by the Australian Rugby League, is the Optus Cup, which includes interstate sides. Games are played at various grounds, but the sell-out finals are played in September at the architecturally stunning ***Sydney Football Stadium*** *(Map 7, ☎ 9360 6601, Moore Park)* in Paddington. Tickets to most games cost from $15 to $25.

The other big rugby league series is the State of Origin, played in Sydney, Brisbane and Melbourne. The NSW versus Queensland game generates a lot of passion.

A breakaway competition, the Super League, run by media giant Rupert Murdoch's News Limited Corporation, began its first official season in 1997.

Rugby union is a less brutal game and has a less fanatical following, but the Wallabies (the Australian rugby union team) are world-beaters. You can occasionally see them in action against international teams.

Aussie Rules football is a unique, exciting sport – only Gaelic football is anything like it. The Sydney Swans are Sydney's – and NSW's – only contribution to the Australian Football League (AFL) and their home ground is the 40,000 seat ***Sydney Cricket Ground*** *(SCG, Map 7, ☎ 9360 6601, Moore Park)* in Paddington. Tickets cost from $14.60 to $27.

Soccer is slowly gaining popularity, thanks in part to the success of the national team and to the high profile of some Aussies playing overseas. The national league is only semiprofessional and games attract a relatively small following. In the past, most clubs were ethnically based, but they now appeal to the broader community. As well as Sydney Football Stadium, games are played at the grounds of ***Sydney United*** *(☎ 9823 6418, Edensor Rd, Edensor Park)* and ***Marconi*** *(☎ 9823 2222, Marconi Rd, Bossley Park)*, among others. For information, contact Soccer Australia (☎ 9380 6099), Sydney Football Stadium.

Cricket

The SCG *(Map 7, ☎ 9360 6601, Moore Park)* in Paddington is the venue for sparsely attended Sheffield Shield (interstate) matches, well-attended test (international) matches and sell-out World Series Cup (one-day, international) matches. Local district games are also played here. The cricket season in Australia is from October to March.

AARON J ORANSKY

Surf life-saving carnivals have long been tradition in Sydney. This carnival occurred on Queenscliff beach in the late 1940s.

Tennis

Major tournaments are held at ***White City*** *(Map 7, ☎ 9360 4113, 30 Alma St)* in Paddington; this is also the home of the NSW Tennis Association. The year's biggest event is the NSW Open, held the second week in January as a prelude to the Australian Open in Melbourne. Indoor games are played at the ***Sydney Entertainment Centre*** *(Map 4, ☎ 9320 4200, 1900 957 333 for recorded information, Harbour St)*, near Darling Harbour.

Basketball

Australia's basketball league has all the razzmatazz of US pro basketball (and quite a few US players as well), thanks largely to the TV coverage it receives. The basketball season runs from April to November and games are played on weekends at the Sydney Entertainment Centre (see the Tennis section earlier for details). The teams in Sydney are the Kings (men) and the Flames (women).

Netball

Netball doesn't have as high a profile as basketball in Australia due to the fact that it's not an Olympic sport and because, generally, womens' sports don't receive as much coverage in the media. However, the game can be just as exciting to watch; finals matches in particular. Sydney's National Netball League teams (women) are the Sydney Swifts and the Sydney Sandpipers. The netball season runs from April to August and games are played on weekends at the ***Anne Clark Centre*** in Lidcombe. They are covered by ABC and Optus, which televise games and highlights.

Surf Life-Saving Carnivals

The volunteer surf life-saver is one of Australia's icons. Australia was one of the first places in the world to have surf life-saving clubs. Despite the macho image often associated with life-saving, many surf life-savers are female. You can see life-savers in action each summer at surf carnivals held all along the coast. Check at a local surf life-saving club for dates or contact Surf Life Saving NSW (☎ 9984 7188), PO Box 430, Narrabeen NSW.

Yachting

On weekends, hundreds of yachts weave around ferries and ships on Sydney Harbour. Many are racing, and the most spectacular are the speedy 18-footers. The 18-footer races carry big prize money and the boats are covered in sponsors' logos, like racing cars. The 18-footer racing season runs from mid-September to late March. The oldest and largest 18-footer club is the Sydney Flying Squadron (☎ 9955 8350), 76 McDougall St, near Milsons Park on Careening Cove on the northern side of Kirribilli Point.

The greatest yachting event on Sydney Harbour is the Boxing Day (26 December) start of the Sydney to Hobart Yacht Race. The harbour is crammed with competitors, media boats and a huge spectator fleet. Special ferries are scheduled by Sydney Ferries to follow the boats; call ☎ 131500 in November to find out when tickets go on sale.

Shopping

Avoid tacky souvenirs like plastic boomerangs, 'Aboriginal' ashtrays or cuddly koalas. They're probably made overseas anyway. If you want to buy a souvenir of Australia, check that it was made here.

WHAT TO BUY

Aboriginal Art

The main traditional forms of Aboriginal art were body painting, cave painting and rock engraving. Only in the last few decades have Aboriginal artists begun using western materials like canvas and acrylic paints. These works have quickly gained wide appreciation. The paintings depict traditional stories and ceremonial designs, and some have particular spiritual significance.

Much of the Aboriginal art available in Sydney, especially traditional styles, comes from other areas of Australia, and because it captures the essence of the Australian outback, it makes a wonderful reminder of a trip to Australia.

The best works range in price from $500 to $1500, but among the cheaper artworks on sale are prints, baskets, small carvings and beautiful screen-printed T-shirts produced by Aboriginal craft cooperatives. Although there are numerous commercial rip-offs, Sydney has some reputable outlets selling Aboriginal art and crafts, who pay the artists properly. It's worth shopping around and paying a few dollars more for the real thing.

A large range of traditional and contemporary Aboriginal art is available from the following outlets (Maps 4 & 7):

Aboriginal Art Gallery
(☎ 9264 9018) Shop 47, Level 2, Queen Victoria Building (QVB), 455 George St, city

Aboriginal Art Shop
(☎ 9247 4344) Upper Concourse, Sydney Opera House

Aboriginal & Tribal Art Centre
(☎ 9241 5998) 117 George St, the Rocks

Australia's Northern Territory & Outback Centre
(☎ 9283 7477) Shop 28, 1/25 Harbour St, Darling Walk, Darling Harbour

Boomalli Aboriginal Artists Co-operative
(☎ 9698 2047) 191 Parramatta Rd, Annandale

Coo-ee Aboriginal Emporium & Art Gallery
(☎ 9332 1544) 98 Oxford St, Paddington

Gavala Art Shop & Cultural Centre
(☎ 9212 7232) Harbourside, Darling Harbour

Hogarth Galleries Aboriginal Art Centre
(☎ 9360 6839) 7 Walker Lane, Paddington

Balarinji, an Aboriginal clothing company that combines Aboriginal art with modern graphic design, has a store at the airport, and a design studio in the new Customs House complex. Aboriginal athlete Cathy Freeman promotes its clothing, and its distinctive, brightly coloured work has adorned the bodies of two Qantas 747s.

Australiana

The term 'Australiana' describes the things you buy as gifts for the folks back home or to remember your visit by, and which are supposedly representative of Australia. Arts, crafts, T-shirts, designer clothing and bush gear are sold practically everywhere. Apart from the usual kitsch there's much that's of high quality, with prices to match, though you can pick up the odd bargain. Check out the huge range in the Rocks and Darling Harbour to see what's available, then compare prices in other areas. The places mentioned here are on Map 4.

The shops at galleries and museums frequently have a good range of interesting and novel gifts and some excellent books, posters and postcards with Australian themes. The shops at the Museum of Contemporary Art, National Gallery of NSW and the Powerhouse Museum are particularly good.

For Australian-made, environmentally friendly souvenirs visit the Wilderness Society Shop (☎ 9233 4674), on the 1st floor of Centrepoint, or the Australian Conservation

Foundation (ACF) shop (☎ 9247 4754), 33 George St, the Rocks (open from 10 am to 5.30 pm weekdays). Both have T-shirts, posters and other good-quality souvenirs.

The *Australian Geographic* magazine has stores in Harbourside (☎ 9212 6539), Darling Harbour, and in Centrepoint (☎ 9231 5055), on Pitt St. The shops are full of Australian memorabilia.

At the Gardens Shop (☎ 9231 8125) in the Royal Botanic Gardens Visitors Centre, there are souvenirs, posters, and books on Australian flora.

Poster prints and silkscreen prints by Sydney artist Ken Done are available from the Ken Done Gallery (☎ 9247 2740), 1 Hickson Rd, the Rocks. There are also several Done & Design shops around town, including one nearby at 123 George St (☎ 9251 6099), selling greeting cards, T-shirts etc.

Australia boasts some of the best wines in the world. The Australian Wine Centre (☎ 9247 2755), downstairs in Gold Fields House, behind Circular Quay at 1 Alfred St, opens daily and has wines from every Australian wine-growing region. It will package and send wine overseas. Tastings for the general public take place after 4 pm Friday.

Aussie Clothing The places mentioned here are on Map 4. The must-buy Aussie item is an Akubra, one brand of the classic stockman's hat. These are sold everywhere tourists converge, but if you want good advice and the right size, try the Strand Hatters (☎ 9231 6884), 8 Strand Arcade on Pitt St Mall. This excellent shop sells a variety of hats, none very cheap, but the staff are friendly and knowledgeable.

RM Williams (☎ 9262 2228), 389 George St, is an established manufacturer and distributor of Aussie outdoor gear such as Driza-bones (oilskin riding coats), elastic-sided boots and moleskin trousers. Thomas Cook Boot & Clothing Company (☎ 9212 6616), 790 George St near Railway Square, is similar.

Many companies that produce surfing equipment also make a range of beach clothing (see Outdoor Gear later).

Opals The opal is Australia's national gemstone, and opals and opal jewellery are popular souvenirs, but buy wisely and shop around – quality and prices vary widely (see the boxed text). Many Sydney jewellers and duty-free shops sell opals, especially in the Rocks (see Map 4).

Some shops to try include Opal Fields (☎ 9247 6800), 155 George St; Opal Minded (☎ 9247 9885), 36-64 George St; and Opal Beauty (☎ 9241 4050), 22 Argyle St in the Rocks Centre.

Fashion

Oxford St (Maps 4 & 7) is the perfect place to rack up some serious credit-card bills: from the Centennial Park end, there are a string of Australian designer stores including

Buying Opals

Precious opal exhibits a play of colour. It comes in several varieties, including jelly (transparent opal with little colour), crystal (jelly with more colour), white, milky (somewhere between crystal and white) and black (transparent to opaque opal with a dark background colour). Potch is opal without a play of colour and hence has no value.

Prices can be astronomical; up to $2000 a carat or $3000 for a black opal, but you can pay as little as $50 for a stone of lower quality. The price depends on flaws and brilliance of colour. The variation in shades of colour is enormous and, if you're lucky, the one you like won't be one of the most expensive.

Much less expensive are non-solid opals. Doublets are precious opals stuck (by a jeweller) to a potch of non-precious opal. Domed doublets are worth more than flat doublets because the section of precious opal is thicker. Triplets are flat doublets with a dome of glass or quartz crystal stuck on top, protecting and magnifying the opal.

Lisa Ho, Zimmerman, Bettina Liano, Scanlan and Theodore, Ellin Ambin, Saba for Men, and Collette Dinnegan (on William St, off Oxford St).

For funky streetwear and slightly less daunting price-tags, try the Oxford St end of Crown St – check out Wheels and Doll Baby (259 Crown St) for rock-chic gear.

If you want to get *really* dressed up, Drag Bag, upstairs at 185 Oxford St on the corner of Taylor Square, sells sparkly glamwear for the gay crowd, including wigs, shoes, jewellery and make-up. They also do full make-overs (guys and girls).

For quirky threads from Asian designers, there are scores of excellent little boutiques in the numerous shopping arcades in and around Chinatown.

Newtown's King St is full of second-hand clothing stores: try Chiconomy at No 399 or Rip Off at No 129.

Cheap factory outlets and seconds stores abound both in Redfern, on the corner of Regent and Redfern Sts, and in western Surry Hills (from Albion St, head south towards Redfern). Here you'll find everything from bikinis to ball gowns – although the emphasis is on utilitarian clothing, underwear and footwear, rather than on cutting-edge fashion.

Antiques

Look for early Australian colonial furniture made from cedar or Huon pine; Australian silver jewellery; ceramics, either early factory pieces or studio pieces (especially anything by the Boyd family); glassware, such as Carnival glass; and Australiana collectables and bric-a-brac, such as old signs, tins, bottles, etc – anything featuring the Opera House, Harbour Bridge or kookaburras.

Updated annually, *Carter's Price Guide to Antiques in Australia* is an excellent price reference. Also available is the free, large-format quarterly magazine *Antiques in New South Wales*.

Queen St in Woollahra is the main centre for antiques in Sydney. Woollahra Antiques Centre (☎ 9327 8840), 160 Oxford St (opposite the eastern end of Centennial Park), is an agglomeration of 50 shops. Sydney Antique Centre (Map 8, ☎ 9361 3244), 531 South Dowling St, Surry Hills, has 60 shops and opens from 10 am to 6 pm daily.

Craft & Design

You'll find many shops and galleries displaying crafts by local artists. The local craft scene is especially strong in the fields of ceramics, jewellery and stained glass. To see some of the best, call into the Arts & Crafts Society of NSW (Map 4, ☎ 9241 1673), in the Metcalfe Arcade, 80-84 George St. It houses a gallery and a sales outlet. You could also try Australian Craftworks (Map 4, ☎ 9247 7156), 127 George St, in the old police station.

Cohav at 371 King St, Newtown crafts and sells lovely handmade silver jewellery set with semiprecious stones. From the ceiling of the wonderful Puppet Shop (Map 4), 77 George St in the Rocks, there dangles all manner of stringed things and bizarre jointed toys, priced from $5.

Dinosaur Designs is noted for its excellent range of inexpensive jewellery and homewares made from jewel-coloured resins, gold, silver and bone. It has two stores: Strand Arcade (Map 4, ☎ 9223 2953) and 339 Oxford St, Paddington (Map 7, ☎ 9361 3776).

There are several other good stores selling modern knick-knacks. Combo Design (Map 8, ☎ 9360 2222), at 500 Crown St in Surry Hills, is a huge warehouse filled with desirable objects, including a good selection of glassware. At Cockle Bay Wharf you'll find the stylish MCA shop (☎ 9266 0226), full of tastefully mod goodies. The Object store (☎ 9247 7318) at Customs House sells funky creations by contemporary designers.

Outdoor Gear

Australians are among the world's keenest travellers, so it's no surprise that Sydney's outdoor and adventure shops carry an excellent range of both Australian-made and imported gear. In many cases, local products are cheaper than imports, and of equal quality. The shops listed are on Map 4.

There's a good selection of shops on Kent St, near Bathurst St and the YHA Membership & Travel Centre. Among the Australian firms here are Kathmandu (☎ 9261 8901), Paddy Pallin (☎ 9264 2685) and Mountain Designs (☎ 9267 3822).

It's also worth checking out 'disposal' stores (listed in the *Yellow Pages*), which handle ex-army gear. They can be good for rugged clothing and less hi-tech camping gear, and are often a lot cheaper than the specialists. One of Sydney's many disposal stores is Mitchell King Camping & Disposals, which has several shops on Pitt St – the one at No 327 (☎ 9264 5440) specialises in backpacks, and is open daily.

Australia produces some of the world's best surfing equipment; there are shops selling it at major surf beaches. See Surfing under Activities in the Things to See & Do chapter. One company, Mambo, is noted for producing off-the-wall designs. To see its complete range (which also includes watches and backpacks) visit the Mambo shop in the Verona cinema complex (Map 7), 17 Oxford St, Paddington. Hot Tuna has an emporium stacked with gear at 180 Oxford St, Paddington (Map 7). Other manufacturers include Billabong and Rip Curl, whose products are available from surf shops and department stores. See also 'Surfing Equipment & Supplies – Retail' in the *Yellow Pages*.

Duty-Free

Prices for duty-free shopping in Sydney compare favourably with the rest of the world. Remember that a duty-free item may not have had much duty on it originally and might be cheaper in an ordinary store. Look around before buying. Duty-free shops abound in the city, especially on Pitt St (Map 4) and include:

Allders Duty Free
(☎ 9241 5844) 22 Pitt St
Angus & Coote Duty Free
(☎ 9247 7611) 19 Pitt St
City International Duty Free
(☎ 9232 1555) 88 Pitt St
Downtown Duty Free
(☎ 9221 4444) 105 Pitt St
Harbourside Duty Free
(☎ 9283 8900) 249 Pitt St

Music

Big stores selling recorded music include the heavyweights HMV Megastore (☎ 9221 2311) and Sanity (☎ 9223 8488), which face each other across Pitt St Mall (Map 4). Both also have suburban outlets.

There are many specialist shops. The ABC Shop (Map 4, ☎ 9333 1635) in the QVB is the national broadcaster's retail outlet. It sells CDs and cassettes linked associated with its programming.

For dance and electronic music, Oxford St (Maps 4 & 7) is the place to go: try Central Station at No 46 or Reachin' Records on the corner of Oxford and Crown Sts. Good Groove is a very funky little record shop at 350 Crown St.

Red Eye Records (☎ 9233 8177), 66 King St in the city, is a huge store stocking music of almost every genre, from blues and jazz to world music, funk, country and pop. The staff have good import connections, and are adept at hunting down hard-to-find releases.

For others see the *Yellow Pages* under 'Compact Discs, Records & Tapes'.

For guitar repairs and stringed instruments, try Venue Music (☎ 9267 7288) on Druitt St, opposite the Town Hall.

Books

Dymocks and Angus & Robertson are two large Sydney chains. Dymocks' main branch (Map 4, ☎ 9235 0155), 424-30 George St, is an enormous shop with a huge range of stock and a cafe. It has several other city stores. You'll find an Angus & Robertson (Map 4, ☎ 9235 1188) in the Imperial Arcade, 168 Pitt St.

There are plenty of bookshops catering to more specialised tastes.

The Travel Bookshop (Map 4, ☎ 9261 8200) at 175 Liverpool St, specialising in travel books and maps, opens from 9 am to 6 pm weekdays, 10 am to 5 pm Saturday.

The friendly Abbey's Bookshop (Map 4, ☎ 9264 3111), 131 York St opposite the QVB, has a wide range of literature, including many foreign-language titles.

Oxford St (Maps 4 & 7) has a handful of excellent bookshops. The Bookshop Darlinghurst (☎ 9331 1103), 207 Oxford St near Taylor Square, specialises in gay and lesbian literature. Ariel (☎ 9332 4581), at No 42-44, Paddington, focuses on art and design and provides a couple of couches for comfortable browsing. Berkelouw's Books (☎ 9360 3200), at No 19 opposite Ariel, specialises in second-hand and antique books and has a good travel section; it has the added pull of a small cafe. All three stock general fiction and are open late daily.

Further east, the Humanities Bookshop (☎ 9331 5514), in Paddington Town Hall on Oxford St, sells interesting second-hand titles, including first editions. New Edition bookshop (☎ 9360 6913), at No 328, has general fiction.

In Glebe (Map 9), Gleebooks (☎ 9660 2333), 49 Glebe Point Rd, is worth checking out for new books, as is its other outlet (☎ 9552 2526), at No 189, for second-hand and children's books. Half a Cow (☎ 9565 2886), 74 Glebe Point Rd, sells second-hand comics and books (plus CDs and records).

Newtown has lots of second-hand bookshops. Easily the largest is Gould's Book Arcade (☎ 9519 8947), 32 King St opposite the Hard Nox Cafe; it's jam-packed, from wall to wall and floor to ceiling.

In Double Bay, the best-known second-hand bookseller is Nicholas Pounder (☎ 9328 7410) on the 1st floor, 346 New South Head Rd.

WHERE TO SHOP

The most fashionable shops tend to be around Oxford St, which, in Paddington east of the Royal Women's Hospital, is packed with boutique clothing stores. There are several groovy clothes shops wedged between the cafes and restaurants at the Oxford St end of Crown St.

Newtown's King St is popular for grunge shopping, alternative lifestyle fashions, creative furnishings and second-hand books and clothes.

If you're looking for bargains, there are several factory clothing outlets and seconds shops in Redfern and Surry Hill's south-west.

Military Rd, between Neutral Bay and Mosman, is one long stretch of shops, catering to the surrounding affluent suburbs.

Shopping Centres

The following are on Map 4. The magnificent QVB on George St, with dozens of shops on four levels, is the city's most beautiful shopping centre. You'll find Jag, Guess, Benetton, Jigsaw, Crabtree & Evelyn, Portmans, Country Road, Esprit and Osh Kosh here, among others. On the lower ground floor is Earth's Natural Wonders (shop 55), a gem and opal shop, and the luxurious Aveda store (shop 16), stocking aromatherapy skincare. The lower level, which connects to Town Hall station, also has food bars, shoe repair shops, drycleaners and newsagents to service the rushing commuters.

Several leading Australian fashion designers and craftspeople have shops at the impressive, carefully restored and more intimate Strand Arcade (1892), between Pitt St Mall and George St. Designer boutiques include Dinosaur Designs, Third Millenium, Indigo, Wayne Cooper, Lili, Von Trotska, Black Vanity, Rox and Love & Hatred. Other city arcades are the Royal, beneath the Hilton Hotel, and the Imperial, connecting Pitt St Mall and Castlereagh St.

Beside the Imperial Arcade and beneath the Sydney Tower, the four-storey Centrepoint shopping centre has a range of fashion and jewellery shops. Nearby is the seven-storey Skygarden, which has a number of art galleries in addition to shops. Two newer shopping centres are Piccadilly, south of Pitt St Mall opposite the Hilton Hotel, and the upmarket Chifley Plaza, 2 Chifley Square on the corner of Elizabeth and Hunter Sts where you'll find Tiffanys. At the renovated MLC Centre, on the corner of King and Castlereagh Sts, you'll find some of the world's top names in fashions and accessories.

GLENN BEANLAND

The QVB is a shopper's paradise – loads of shops in beautiful surrounds.

The Argyle Centre, 18 Argyle St, the Rocks, is a huge shopping area, as is the Rocks Centre, on the corner of Playfair and Argyle Sts. Harbourside at Darling Harbour has over 150 stores on its two floors.

The biggest shopping centre in North Sydney (Map 2) is Greenwood Plaza, above North Sydney station.

Department Stores

The following stores are on Map 4. Of the department stores, Gowings (☎ 9264 6321), on the corner of Market and George Sts, is the oldest; it has been operating since 1868 and sells moderately priced modern clothing for men and boys as well as traditional bush clothing. The seven-level Grace Brothers (☎ 9238 9111), 436 George St, is one of Sydney's largest stores and sells just about everything.

David Jones (☎ 9266 5544) is considered the city's premier department store and is a good place to look for top-quality goods. It has two stores on Market St. The one on the corner of Castlereagh St has menswear, electrical goods and a food hall with luxury food items. The one on the corner of Elizabeth St sells women's and children's goods.

Grace Brothers and David Jones also have suburban stores around Sydney.

Markets

Sydney has lots of weekend markets. The most interesting, Paddington Bazaar (☎ 9331 2646), St John's Church, 395 Oxford St, is held from 10 am to 4.30 pm Saturday. It offers everything from vintage clothing and funky, up-to-the-minute designer fashions, to jewellery, massage, health foods and holistic treatments. More unusual wares include temporary henna-tattoos, butterflies under glass, and hammocks.

There are two Paddy's markets (☎ 1300 361 589). The one on the corner of Hay and Thomas Sts in Haymarket in the heart of Chinatown, is a Sydney institution where you'll find the usual market fare at rock-bottom prices, alongside less predictable wares such as wigs, board games, cheap cosmetics, mobile phones and live budgies. There's also a good selection of fresh fruit, vegetables, and seafood. It's open from 9 am to 4.30 pm Saturday and Sunday. Paddy's Market in Flemington, on Parramatta Rd near Sydney Olympic Park, operates (along with the huge Sydney fruit and vegetable market) from 10.30 am to 3.30 pm Friday, 9 am to 4.30 pm Sunday.

In the Rocks, the top end of George St, under the bridge, is closed to traffic for a craft market (☎ 9255 1717) from 10 am to 5 pm weekends. A little on the touristy side, it's still good for a browse – wares include jewellery, antiques, souvenirs, fossils, gems, crystals, retro postcards, musical instruments and a good selection of juggling paraphernalia.

Balmain Markets (☎ 9818 2674), at St Andrew's Church, on Darling St, is also good and is held from 8.30 am to 4 pm Saturday. Besides offering stuff like handmade

SIMON BRACKEN

The Rocks market has an eclectic mix of goodies on offer.

candles, kids' clothing and essential oils, it's a good spot to hunt out the perfect hat, bag, or pair of shades. Glebe's weekend market (☎ 4237 7499) is held at Glebe Public School at the corner of Glebe Point Rd and Derby Place from 10 am to 4 pm Saturday; it has an assortment of books, clothing, ceramics, glassware, leather goods, herbal teas, oddities and curios. Bondi Beach Market (☎ 9398 5486) is good for funky clothing, swimwear, jewellery and assorted knick-knacks. It's held at Bondi Beach Public School at the northern end of Campbell Parade from 9 am to 4 pm Sunday.

Excursions

Sydney sprawls over a coastal plain, hemmed in by rugged country on three sides and by the Pacific Ocean on the fourth.

The city is at the centre of the largest concentration of population in Australia, with at least 100 people per sq km from Wollongong to Newcastle. More than two-thirds of NSW's population is crammed into this area; and about a quarter of all Australians live within 150km of Sydney.

This might sound like a recipe for overcrowding, but the region has historic small towns, stunning waterways, uncrowded beaches, superb national parks and vast tracts of forest. The proximity of Sydney also means that public transport is pretty good, so day trips are feasible even without a car.

You will find the following places on Map 17.

Highlights

- Walking the coastal trail in Royal National Park, the world's oldest gazetted national park
- Enjoying spectacular water views while bushwalking in Ku-ring-gai Chase National Park
- Travelling the Hawkesbury River on the *Riverboat Postman* mail boat
- Bushwalking or cycling in the deep gorges of the Blue Mountains
- Touring the Jenolan Caves, some of which are still unexplored
- Driving along Bells Line of Road or Kangaroo Valley
- Tasting fabulous reds at a Hunter Valley winery
- Catching waves at a Central Coast surf beach

WILDLIFE PARKS

In addition to the large national parks on Sydney's fringes, there are several outer suburban places where you can see native animals. The larger parks are listed here, but you can also meet indigenous critters at the Hawkesbury Heritage Farm near Wilberforce (see Macquarie Towns Area later in this chapter) and at the Australian Reptile Park near Gosford (see Central Coast later in this chapter).

Waratah Park

Popular Waratah Park (☎ 9450 2377) on Namba Rd, Terrey Hills, on the edge of Ku-ring-gai Chase National Park, is a good place to see native fauna. The TV series 'Skippy' was filmed here in the 60s. It's open from 10 am to 5 pm daily; admission is $12.90 (children $6.50). You can get here on Forest Coach Lines' (☎ 9450 2277) bus No 284, which meets trains at Chatswood station on the North Shore line, but there are only three buses on weekdays, fewer on weekends. Call ☎ 9450 1236 for bus times.

Koala Park

If a tactile koala encounter is all you're after, head for Koala Park (☎ 9484 3141) on Castle Hill Rd, in West Pennant Hills, north-west Sydney. It's open from 9 am to 5 pm daily; admission is $10 (children $5). The koalas are fed at 10.20 and 11.45 am, and at 2 and 3 pm. Take a train to Pennant Hills station, and from there catch any bus Nos 661 to 665.

Featherdale Wildlife Park

Featherdale Wildlife Park (☎ 9671 4984) on Kildare Rd, Doonside, has a wide variety of native fauna, including koalas. It's between Parramatta and Penrith, and opens from 9 am to 5 pm daily. Admission is $12 for adults and $6 for children. From the city, take a train to Blacktown, then catch bus No 725.

Australia's Wonderland

This amusement park, off the Western Motorway (M4) west of the city, includes the large Australian Wildlife Park, which houses all sorts of native Australian animals. Admission to the wildlife park is $13 (children $9), and it's open from 9 am to 5 pm daily.

There are also pools and water slides at the amusement park next door, so bring your cossie (swimsuit) in summer. Admission to both is $37 ($26 for children aged four to 13). Call ☎ 9830 9187 for information.

BOTANY BAY

Many first-time visitors to Sydney mistakenly believe that the city is built on the shores of Botany Bay. Sydney is actually built around the harbour of Port Jackson, some 10 to 15km north of Botany Bay, although the city's sprawling southern suburbs now encompass the bay too.

Botany Bay was the place where Captain Cook first stepped ashore in Australia. The bay was named by Joseph Banks, the expedition's naturalist, because of the many botanical specimens he found here. Cook's landing place is marked by monuments at Kurnell, on the southern side of the bay, in **Botany Bay National Park**.

The **Discovery Centre** (☎ 9668 9111) in the park has material relating to Cook's life and expeditions, and information on the surrounding wetlands. It's open from 11 am to 3 pm weekdays, 10 am to 4 pm on weekends. There are bushland walking tracks and picnic areas in the park, which is open from 7.30 am to 7 or 8 pm. From Cronulla station (10km away), take bus No 987; admission is $5 per car.

La Perouse is on the northern side of the bay entrance, at the spot where the French explorer of that name arrived in 1788, just six days after the arrival of the First Fleet. He gave the Poms a good scare – they weren't expecting the French to materialise in this part of the world quite so soon! La Perouse and his men camped at Botany Bay for a few weeks, then sailed off into the Pacific and vanished. Many years later the wrecks of their ships were discovered on a reef near Vanuatu.

There's a monument at La Perouse commemorating the explorer, built in 1828 by French sailors searching for him. There's also the **La Perouse Museum** (☎ 9311 3379), with expedition relics and antique maps, as well as an Aboriginal gallery. It's open from 10 am to 4 pm daily during school holidays, Tuesday to Sunday the rest of the year; admission is $5, and you can book guided tours.

Bus Nos 394 and 398 run here from Circular Quay.

ROYAL NATIONAL PARK

This coastal park of dramatic cliffs, secluded beaches, scrub and lush rainforest is the oldest gazetted national park in the world. It begins at Port Hacking, 30km south of Sydney, and stretches 20km southward. A road runs through the park, with detours to the small township of Bundeena on Port Hacking, to the beautiful Wattamolla beach, and on to windswept Garie beach. There's a large network of walking tracks, including a spectacular and highly recommended 26km coastal trail that runs the length of the park.

The bushfires of 1994 devastated 95% of the park, but some sections escaped unharmed and the area has been regenerating well since then.

The sandstone plateau at the park's northern end is a sea of low scrub. Tall forest can only be found in the river valleys, and on the park's southern boundary on the edge of the Illawarra escarpment. In late winter and early spring, the park is carpeted with wildflowers.

There's a visitors centre (☎ 9542 0648) on the hilltop at the park's main entrance, off the Princes Highway (Hwy). It's open daily from 8.30 am to 4.30 pm (closed 1 to 2 pm). You can hire rowboats and canoes at the Audley Boat Shed (☎ 9545 4967) for $12 an hour or $24 a day. Bikes cost $10/24 an hour/day.

Garie, **Era**, **South Era** and **Burning Palms** are popular surf beaches; swimming and surfing at Marley beach is dangerous (Little

Marley is safe). Garie beach has a surf-life-saving club and **Wattamolla beach** has a calm lagoon for swimming.

A walking and cycling trail follows the Port Hacking River south from Audley, and other walking tracks pass tranquil, freshwater swimming holes. You can swim in **Kangaroo Creek** but not in the Port Hacking River.

Admission to the park is $9 per car, but pedestrians and cyclists can enter for free. The road through the park and the offshoot to Bundeena are always open, but the detours to the beaches close at sunset.

The park surrounds the sizeable town of **Bundeena**, on the southern shore of Port Hacking. Bundeena has its own beaches and you can walk for 30 minutes to **Jibbon Head**, which has a good beach and Aboriginal rock art. Bundeena is the starting point of the 26km coastal walk.

Places to Stay

The only ***camp site*** accessible by car is at Bonnie Vale, near Bundeena, where sites start at $10 for two people. Free bush camping is allowed in several areas – one of the best places is Burning Palms beach – but you must obtain a permit beforehand from the visitors centre. The small, basic (no electricity or phone) and secluded ***Garie Beach YHA Hostel*** is close to one of the best surf beaches and has beds for YHA members only for $7. You need to book; collect a key and get detailed directions from the YHA Travel Centre (☎ 9261 1111), 422 Kent St, Sydney.

Getting There & Away

Train The Sydney-Wollongong railway line forms the western boundary of the park. The closest station is Loftus, 4km from the park entrance and another 2km from the visitors centre. Bringing a bike on the train is a good idea because there's a 10km ride along a vehicle-free forest track about half an hour's ride from Sutherland station. The stations of Engadine, Heathcote, Waterfall and Otford are on the park boundary and have walking trails leading into the park.

Car & Motorcycle From Sydney, take the Princes Hwy and turn off south of Loftus to reach the northern end of the park. From the south, enter via Otford on the coast road north of Wollongong. It's a beautiful drive through thick bush and there are great views from Bald Hill Lookout, just north of Stanwell Park on the park's southern boundary. There's a third entrance at Waterfall, just off the Princes Hwy.

Ferry A scenic way to reach the park is to take a train from Sydney to the suburb of Cronulla (changing at Sutherland on the way; $3.40), then the Cronulla National Park Ferries (☎ 9523 2990) boat to Bundeena in the north-eastern corner of the park ($2.60, children $1.30). Ferries depart from the Cronulla wharf, just below the train station. Cronulla Ferries also offers Hacking River cruises on Sunday, Monday and Wednesday for $10.

KU-RING-GAI CHASE NATIONAL PARK

This 15,000 hectare national park (☎ 9457 9322), 24km north of the city centre, borders the southern edge of Broken Bay and the western shore of Pittwater. It has that classic Sydney mixture of sandstone, bushland and water vistas, plus walking tracks, horse-riding trails, picnic areas, Aboriginal rock engravings and spectacular views of Broken Bay. The park has over 100km of shoreline. There are several through-roads and four entrances; admission is $9 per car.

Large areas of Ku-ring-gai Chase, especially around West Head, were burned in the 1994 bushfires but the area is quickly regenerating.

Kalkari visitors centre (☎ 9457 9853), on Ku-ring-gai Chase Rd about 4km into the park from the Mt Colah entrance, is open from 9 am to 5 pm daily. The road descends from the visitors centre to the picnic area at Bobbin Head on Cowan Creek, then heads south to the Turramurra entrance. At Bobbin Head, Halvorsen (☎ 9457 9011) rents rowing boats for $12 for the first hour and $4 for subsequent hours. Eight-seater motorboats cost $50 for two hours.

The best places to see **Aboriginal engravings** are on the Basin Track and Garigal Aboriginal Heritage Walk at West Head.

It's unwise to swim in Broken Bay because of sharks, but there are safe netted **swimming** areas at Illawong Bay and the Basin.

Elevated parts of the park offer superb views across inlets such as Cowan Creek and Pittwater. From West Head, there's a fantastic view across Pittwater to Barrenjoey Head. You may also see lyrebirds at West Head during their May to July mating season.

Places to Stay

Camping is permitted at the Basin on the western side of Pittwater. It's a walk of about 2.5km from the West Head road, or a ferry ride from Palm Beach. A camp site costs around $10 for two people and you have to book in advance. Call ☎ 9451 8124 for information; call ☎ 9972 7378 for bookings.

Idyllic ***Pittwater YHA Hostel*** *(☎ 9999 2196)*, a couple of kilometres south of the Basin, is noted for its friendly wildlife. Dorm beds cost $16, twin rooms $20 per person (Saturday night costs extra). Non-members pay $3 more. Book ahead and bring food.

If you're lucky you might get to see or hear a lyrebird in the Ku-ring-gai Chase National Park.

Getting There & Away

There are four road entrances to the park: Mt Colah, on the Pacific Hwy; Turramurra, in the south-west; and Terrey Hills and Church Point, in the south-east.

Bus From Wynyard station in the city, take bus No 190 to Mona Vale, then pick up bus No 155, 157 or 159 to Church Point. Bus No 190 continues north to Palm Beach (the trip from Wynyard takes about an hour). Bus Nos 155 and 157 run from Manly.

Shorelink Buses (☎ 9457 8888) has a fairly frequent service from Turramurra train station to the nearby park entrance ($2.20).

STA buses service the Terrey Hills and Church Point entrances, but it's quite a walk to the Pittwater YHA Hostel or the camp sites from these entrances.

Ferry The Palm Beach Ferry Service (☎ 9918 2747) runs to the Basin hourly (except noon) from 9 am to 5 pm, for $7 return ($3.50 children). A ferry departs Palm Beach for Bobbin Head (via Patonga) at 11 am daily, returning at 3.30 pm. The return fare is $25 ($12 children).

To get to the Pittwater YHA Hostel take a ferry (☎ 9999 3492) from Church Point to Halls Wharf ($6 return); the hostel is just a short walk from here.

MACQUARIE TOWNS AREA

Windsor, Richmond, Wilberforce, Castlereagh and Pitt Town are the five 'Macquarie Towns' established by Governor Lachlan Macquarie in 1810 on fertile agricultural land on the upper Hawkesbury River.

The upper Hawkesbury is popular for water-skiing, but before you're tempted to get wet, check that there isn't a blue-green algae problem. Call the Environment Protection Authority (EPA) Pollution Line (☎ 9325 5555) for information.

The Hawkesbury visitors centre (☎ 4588 5895), across from the Richmond RAAF (Royal Australian Air Force) base on the

ROSS BARNETT

The Three Sisters, Katoomba, Blue Mountains National Park

ROSS BARNETT
Early morning mist in the Megalong Valley, Blue Mountains National Park

ROSS BARNETT
The Empress Falls, Blue Mountains National Park

SIMON BRACKEN
Kookaburras are easily spotted in the bush.

road between Richmond and Windsor, is the main information centre for the upper Hawkesbury area. It's open daily 9 am to 5 pm weekdays, until 3 pm Sunday, and 10 am to 3 pm Saturday. Windsor has its own information centre (☎ 4577 2310) in the 1843 Daniel O'Connell Inn on Thompson Square, off Bridge St. In Richmond the National Parks & Wildlife Service (NPWS, ☎ 4588 5247) is at 370 Windsor St.

Windsor

Set on the banks of the Hawkesbury River, Windsor has many fine old colonial buildings. The **Hawkesbury Museum** is in the same building as the information centre. It's open daily; admission is $2.50 (children 50c).

Windsor's other old buildings include the convict-built **St Matthew's Church** (1820), designed, like the old **courthouse** (1822), by convict architect Francis Greenway. George St has other historic buildings, and the **Macquarie Arms Hotel**, built in 1815 under orders from the governor, is reckoned to be the oldest pub in Australia (but several other pubs disagree).

On the edge of town is the tiny **Tebbut Observatory**, which used to feature on the $100 note.

Wilberforce & Around

Tiny Wilberforce, 6km north of Windsor, is on the edge of the riverflat farmland. **Hawkesbury Heritage Farm** (☎ 4575 1457) is a collection of old buildings gathered to form a small historical park. It includes **Rose Cottage** (1811), probably the oldest surviving timber building in the country. There are also native animals and regular entertainment. The village opens from 10 am to 5 pm daily; admission is $10 (children $6). Next door is **Butterfly Farm**, an insect museum. You can get here by public transport – take a CityRail train to Windsor and then an (infrequent) bus – phone to check times.

The originally Presbyterian (now Uniting) **Ebenezer Church** (1809) on Coromandel Rd, 5km north of Wilberforce, is said to be the oldest church in Australia still used as a place of worship. The old **Tizzana Winery** (☎ 4579 1150), 518 Tizzana Rd, near Ebenezer, is open from noon to 6 pm weekdays, weekends by appointment.

Pitt Town & Around

Pitt Town, a few kilometres north-east of Windsor, is another Macquarie Town. Its old buildings include the restored **Bird in Hand Hotel** (1825). North of Pitt Town on the road to Wisemans Ferry is the small **Cattai National Park** (☎ 4572 3100). It comprises two parts: Cattai Farm, containing the remains of a homestead (c. 1799); and Mitchell Park (2km east), with pristine forest and walking trails.

Richmond

Richmond is 6km west of Windsor, at the end of the CityRail line and at the start of the Bells Line of Rd across the Blue Mountains (see the Blue Mountains section later in this chapter). The town dates from 1810 and has some fine Georgian and Victorian buildings. These include the **courthouse** and **police station** on Windsor St, and, around the corner on Market St, **St Andrew's Church** (1845). A number of notable pioneers are buried in the cemetery at **St Peter's Church** (1841).

Putty Rd

On the Putty Rd about 20km north of Windsor there's a long descent to the lovely **Colo River**, a picturesque spot popular for swimming, canoeing and picnicking. It's a little village with a service station, shop and tourist information. There's camping at ***Riverside Tourist Park*** *(☎ 4575 5253)*, where you can hire canoes for $12 an hour ($20 for two hours).

Getting There & Away

Train CityRail trains run from Sydney to Windsor and Richmond, but getting to the other Macquarie Towns involves connecting with an infrequent local bus service.

Car & Motorcycle From Sydney the easiest routes to Windsor are on Windsor Rd

(Route 40), the north-western continuation of Parramatta's Church St; and via Penrith, heading north from either the Western Motorway (M4) or the Great Western Hwy on Route 69 (Parker St and the Northern Rd).

The Putty Rd runs north from Windsor to Singleton, 160km north in the upper Hunter Valley. From Windsor take Bridge St across the river then turn right onto the Wilberforce Road (Route 69).

From Richmond, Bells Line of Rd runs west up into the Blue Mountains (see the Blue Mountains section later in this chapter). This is a more interesting (but considerably longer) route to Katoomba than the crowded Great Western Hwy.

THE BLUE MOUNTAINS

The Blue Mountains, part of the Great Dividing Range, have some truly fantastic scenery, excellent bushwalks and gorges, gum trees and cliffs galore. The foothills begin 65km inland from Sydney and rise up to 1100m, but the mountains are really a sandstone plateau riddled with spectacular gullies formed by erosion over millennia. The blue haze, which gave the mountains their name, is a result of the fine mist of oil given off by eucalyptus trees.

For more than a century, the area has been a popular getaway for Sydneysiders seeking to escape the summer heat. Despite intensive tourist development, much of the area is so precipitous that it's still only open to bushwalkers.

In the 1994 fires, large areas of the Grose Valley were burned, but the Blue Gum Forest escaped almost intact.

Be prepared for the climatic difference between the Blue Mountains and the coast – you can swelter in Sydney but shiver in Katoomba. Autumn's mists and drizzle can make bushwalking a less attractive option. In winter the days are often clear, and in the valleys it can be almost warm. There is usually some snowfall some time between June and August, and the region has a Yulefest in July, when many restaurants and guesthouses have good deals on mid-year 'Christmas' dinners.

History

The first Europeans to explore the area found evidence of extensive Aboriginal occupation, but few Aborigines. It seems quite likely that catastrophic European-introduced diseases had spread from Sydney long before.

The colonists at Port Jackson attempted to cross the mountains within a year or so of arrival, driven not just by the usual lust for exploration but also by an urgent need to find agriculturally useful land for the new colony. However, the sheer cliffs and tough terrain defeated their attempts for nearly 25 years. Many convicts came to believe that China, and freedom, was just on the other side of the mountains.

The first crossing was made in 1813, by Blaxland, Wentworth and Lawson. They followed the ridge-tops and their route was pretty much the same as today's Great Western Hwy. The first road across the mountains was built in just six months, and the great expansion into the western plains began.

After the railway across the mountains was completed in the 1860s, wealthy Sydneysiders began to build mansions here, as summer retreats from the heat and stench of Sydney Town. By the beginning of the 20th century, grand hotels and guesthouses had opened to cater for the increasing demand. This early tourist boom had tapered off by the 1940s, but today there's a resurgence, with some of the old guesthouses making a comeback and new resorts being built.

Orientation

The Great Western Hwy from Sydney follows a ridge from east to west through the Blue Mountains. Along this less-than-beautiful road, the Blue Mountains towns often merge into each other – Glenbrook, Springwood, Woodford, Lawson, Wentworth Falls, Leura, Katoomba (the main accommodation centre), Medlow Bath, Blackheath, Mt Victoria and Hartley. Just west of Mt Victoria township, the road falls down the steep and winding Victoria Pass. On the western fringe of the mountains is the large town of Lithgow.

To the south and north of the highway's ridge the country drops away into precipitous valleys, including the Grose Valley to the north, and the Jamison Valley south of Katoomba. There is a succession of turn-offs to waterfalls, lookout points and scenic alternative routes along the highway.

The Bells Line of Rd, much more scenic (and less congested) than the Great Western Hwy, is a more northerly approach from Sydney. From Richmond it runs north of the Grose Valley to emerge in Lithgow, although you can cut across from Bell to join the Great Western Hwy at Mt Victoria.

Information

There's a visitors centre (☎ 4739 6266) on the highway at Glenbrook and another one (☎ 4782 0756) at Echo Point in Katoomba. The excellent NPWS Blue Mountains Heritage Centre (☎ 4787 8877) is on Govett's Leap Rd near Blackheath, about 3km north of the highway.

Katoomba has its own tourist radio station (88 FM).

The Heritage Centre at Govett's Leap is the best place to ask about walks; it also sells maps and some books. Maps suitable for walkers are also sold at information centres. Megalong Books (☎ 4784 1302), 82 Railway Parade in Leura, stocks books about the Blue Mountains, and is open daily.

How to See the Blue Mountains by Jim Smith is useful and has details of day walks, as does Neil Paton's *Walks in the Blue Mountains*. Lonely Planet's *Bushwalking in Australia* goes into the details of the Blue Gum Forest Walk.

Accommodation ranges from camp sites and hostels to expensive guesthouses and resorts. Katoomba is the main accommodation centre. Most places charge more on weekends, and are often booked out on long weekends. Camping is banned in some parts of the national parks and in others you need a permit, so check with the NPWS first.

Information centres (including many in Sydney) stock brochures listing accommodation options in the Blue Mountains. Check prices before heading off – there are numerous packages available, and rates fluctuate seasonally.

National Parks

The **Blue Mountains National Park** protects large areas to the north and south of the Great Western Hwy. It's the most popular and accessible of the three national parks in the area, and offers great bushwalking, scenic lookouts, breathtaking waterfalls and Aboriginal stencils.

Wollemi National Park, north of Bells Line of Rd, is the state's largest forested wilderness area (nearly 500,000 hectares). It stretches as far as Denman in the Hunter Valley, and has good rugged bushwalking and lots of wildlife. Access is limited and the park's centre is so isolated that a new species of tree, named the Wollemi pine, was only discovered in 1994.

Kanangra Boyd National Park is south-west of the southern section of the Blue Mountains National Park. It has bushwalking, limestone caves and grand scenery, including the spectacular Kanangra Walls Plateau, which is surrounded by sheer cliffs. The park can be reached on unsealed roads from Oberon or Jenolan Caves.

Lookouts

Clichés have been used to describe the Blue Mountains' views for so long that it's a little surprising to find that the vistas *are* breathtaking. Don't miss the famous Three Sisters at **Echo Point** at Katoomba. **Cliff Drive**, running along the edge of the Jamison Valley between Leura and Katoomba, also offers some great views. **Govett's Leap** (near Blackheath, and the NPWS Heritage Centre) and **Evans Lookout** (north of the highway – turn off before Blackheath) afford spectacular vistas. Less famous but just as breath-taking are the viewpoints off Bells Line of Rd, such as **Walls Lookout**. **Hawkesbury Heights**, between Springwood and Bells Line of Rd, has views across the Nepean River to Sydney, sometimes muddied by a cloud of tan-coloured smog.

Further from the main centres, there are more views from **McMahon's Lookout** on

Kings Tableland, 22km from the Queen Victoria Memorial Hospital (south of Wentworth) – for the last 10km you'll need a 4WD (or a mountain bike).

Glenbrook to Katoomba

From **Marge's Lookout** and **Elizabeth's Lookout**, just north of Glenbrook, there are good views back to Sydney. The section of the Blue Mountains National Park south of Glenbrook contains **Red Hand Cave**, which is an old Aboriginal shelter with hand stencils on the walls. It's an easy 7km return walk south-west of the NPWS information centre.

Springwood The famous artist and author Norman Lindsay lived in Springwood from 1912 until he died in 1969. His home at 14 Norman Lindsay Crescent is now the **Norman Lindsay Gallery & Museum** (☎ 4751 1067), with exhibits of his paintings, cartoons, illustrations and sculptures. It's open from 10 am to 4 pm daily; admission is $6 (children $2).

Wentworth Falls South of town there are views of the Jamison Valley and of the lovely 300m Wentworth Falls from **Falls Reserve**, the starting point for a network of walking tracks.

Getting Active in the Blue Mountains

Rugged terrain and superb scenery make the Blue Mountains ideal for bushwalking and other outdoor activities.

There are walks lasting from a few minutes to several days. The two most popular areas, spectacular from the tops of the cliffs and the bottoms of the valleys, are the **Jamison Valley** immediately south of Katoomba and the **Grose Valley** area north-east of Katoomba, and Blackheath. South of Glenbrook is another good area.

Visit a NPWS visitors centre for information or, for shorter walks, ask at a tourist information centre. It's very rugged country and walkers sometimes get lost, so it's crucial that you get reliable information, go with other walkers and tell someone where you're going and when you expect to return. Most Blue Mountains watercourses are polluted, so you have to sterilise water or take your own. Be prepared for rapid weather changes.

Blue Mountains Backpackers in Katoomba takes guests to trailheads. There's free parking for bushwalkers' cars near the trailhead for the Grand Canyon Walk on Evans Lookout Rd.

There's a fairly easy three day walk from Katoomba to Jenolan Caves along the **Six Foot Track** (see Jenolan Caves in the Katoomba section). On weekends and public holidays the NPWS runs a series of excellent guided walks, many of which have an historical or ecological theme; it also runs Aboriginal discovery tours (walks with an indigenous focus). All these tours have to be booked. Call ☎ 4787 8877 for information.

The cliffs, gorges and valleys of the Blue Mountains offer outstanding abseiling, rock climbing and 'canyoning' (exploring gorges by climbing, abseiling, swimming, walking etc). **Narrow Neck**, **Mt Victoria** and **Mt Peddington** are among the popular sites. Most outfits offering guided adventure activities and courses are based in Katoomba (see Activities in the Katoomba section).

Cycling is permitted on most national park trails and, except for the hassle of carrying your bike down to the valley floor and back up again, there's good riding. See Activities under Katoomba for bike rentals and guided rides.

Several horse-riding outfits in the Megalong Valley have trail rides (see Megalong Valley in the Blue Mountains section).

Leura This quaint, tree-lined town is full of country stores and cafes. **Leuralla** (☎ 4784 1169), 36 Olympian Parade, is an Art Deco mansion which has a fine collection of 19th century Australian art, as well as a toy and model-railway museum. The historic house, set in 5 hectares of gardens, is a memorial to HV 'Doc' Evatt, a former Labor Party leader and first president of the United Nations; it's open from 10 am to 5 pm daily except Christmas; admission is $6 (children $2).

South of Leura, **Sublime Point** is a great clifftop lookout. **Gordon Falls Reserve** is a popular picnic spot; from there you can follow the road back past Leuralla, then take the Cliff Drive or the more scenic Prince Henry Cliff Walk to Katoomba's Echo Point.

Places to Stay There are NPWS ***camping areas*** accessible by road at Euroka Clearing near Glenbrook, Murphys Glen near Woodford and Ingar near Wentworth Falls. To camp at Euroka Clearing, you need a permit from the Richmond NPWS (☎ 4588 5247). The tracks to Ingar and Murphys Glen may be closed after heavy rain.

Leura Village Caravan Park *(☎ 4784 1552)*, on the corner of the Great Western Hwy and Leura Mall, has tent sites (starting at $18), on-site vans (starting at $40) and cabins (starting at $50).

Leura House *(☎ 4784 2035, 7 Britain St)* is a grand Victorian home (c. 1880) with the feel of a country retreat. Comfortable singles cost $99, doubles are $138 to $158 with breakfast. Weekend prices may be a little higher, depending on demand, but there are sometimes specials in summer.

The new ***Hawkesbury Heights YHA***, built to replace the Springwood YHA hostel razed by the 1994 bushfires, is surrounded by bush. It's a 'green' hostel with solar power, an 'eco-friendly' toilet and a wood stove. For rates and bookings, phone YHA NSW (☎ 9261 1111).

Leura's plush, 210 room ***Fairmont Resort*** *(☎ 4782 5222, Sublime Point Rd)* is right on the edge of the escarpment. Its prices start at $157 per person midweek, $195 on the weekend.

Katoomba (Map 13)

Katoomba and the adjacent centres of Wentworth Falls and Leura form the tourism centre of the Blue Mountains. Katoomba, with a population of 17,700, has long been a popular summer getaway spot for Sydney 'plains-dwellers', but despite the number of tourists and its proximity to Sydney, it remains a relaxed place, full of character and thankfully devoid of touristy glitz. The town has the uncanny ambience of another time and place, an atmosphere accentuated by its Art Deco and Art Nouveau guesthouses and cafes, its thick mists and occasional snowfalls.

Information The visitors centre (☎ 1300 653 408), at Echo Point, about 2km down Katoomba St from the train station, is open from 9 am to 5 pm daily. The post office is tucked in behind the shopping centre, one street back from Katoomba St as you head downhill towards Waratah St.

Things to See The major scenic attraction is **Echo Point**, near the southern end of Katoomba St about 1km from the shopping centre. Here you'll find some of the best views of the Jamison Valley and the magnificent **Three Sisters** rock formation – floodlit at night, it's an awesome spectacle. A walking track follows the road. The story goes that the three sisters were turned to stone to protect them from the unwanted advances of three young men, but the sorcerer who helped them died before he could turn them back into women.

West of Echo Point, at the junction of Cliff Drive and Violet St, are the **Scenic Railway** and **Scenic Skyway** (☎ 4782 2699). The railway drops 200m to the bottom of the Jamison Valley ($3/5 one way/return) where there's good bushwalking (see the Activities section). The railway was built in the 1880s to transport coal miners and its 45° incline is one of the steepest in the world. The Scenic Skyway cable car glides some 200m above the valley floor, traversing **Katoomba Falls gorge** ($5 return).

The **Explorers Tree**, just west of Katoomba near the Great Western Hwy, was marked by Blaxland, Wentworth and Lawson, who, in 1813, were the first Europeans to find a way over the mountains.

Activities The 12km-return **bushwalk** to the **Ruined Castle** rock formation on Narrow Neck Plateau, which divides the Jamison and Megalong valleys another couple of kilometres west, is one of the best – watch out for leeches after rain. The **Golden Stairs** lead down from this plateau to more bushwalking tracks.

Several companies offer **abseiling, rock climbing, canyoning** and **caving** adventure activities. The competition keeps the deals fairly similar – expect to pay about $90 for a day's abseiling.

At the Paddy Pallin shop at 166b Katoomba St, the Australian School of Mountaineering offers a two day basic rock-climbing course for $195. We have received good feedback about this. The two-day bush survival courses ($250) also sound interesting. Upstairs in the Mountain Designs shop at No 190, Australian Outdoor Consultants (☎ 4782 3877) offers abseiling, rock climbing and canyoning, while the shop (☎ 4782 5999) stocks a good range of camping and outdoor paraphernalia (including maps). With the Blue Mountains Adventure Company (☎ 4782 1271), 84a Main St, abseiling and canyoning cost $89 a day, and rock climbing starts at $110.

At High 'n' Wild (☎ 4782 6224), 3/5 Katoomba St across from the station, a half-day's abseiling, rock climbing, or canyoning will cost you $49/55/65; it can also help with mountain-biking, wilderness walking and bushcraft.

Extreme Mountain Bike Tours (☎ 4787 7281, ☎ 0412 706 541) is a small outfit offering experienced mountain-bikers some great riding.

Places to Stay – Budget The ***Katoomba Falls Caravan Park*** *(☎ 4782 1835)*, on Katoomba Falls Rd about 2km south of the highway, has tent sites for $10 per person and on-site vans for $36.

Katoomba YHA Hostel *(☎ 4782 1416)*, on the corner of Lurline and Waratah Sts, is in a nice old guesthouse near the centre of town. It's clean and has excellent communal areas, and Internet access. Dorm beds cost from $14 and twins/doubles with *en suites* are $20 to $25 per person; nonmembers pay $3 more. Nearby, ***Katoomba Mountain Lodge*** *(☎ 4782 3933, 31 Lurline St)* is an old brick guesthouse and hostel charging $16 for beds in tiny dorms, and around $23 per person for acceptable singles/doubles with shared bathroom. There are also more expensive rooms in the guesthouse section.

Blue Mountains Backpackers *(☎ 4782 4226, 190 Bathurst Rd)* is on the westward continuation of Main St, in a worn but cosy old house close to the train station. Tent sites start at $10, beds in large dorms cost $16, and reasonable twins/doubles are $43 (VIP/YHA members pay $3/4 less); there are also weekly rates. This popular place receives good reviews from travellers. You need to book; this usually requires a money order or a credit card number.

The Art Deco ***Hotel Gearin*** *(☎ 4782 4395, 273 Great Western Hwy)* is a good local pub with singles and doubles for $25 per person. Some of the rooms are much better than average pub rooms. There are also dorm beds for $15. The century-old ***Katoomba Hotel*** *(☎ 4782 1106)*, on the corner of Parke and Main Sts, is a smoky Aussie local with unglamorous (but heated) singles/doubles for $25/45 ($30/50 on weekends). Dorm beds are $12, and rates are reduced if you stay a week or more.

Places to Stay – Mid-Range & Top End There are numerous motels and guesthouses in the Katoomba area. Rates tend to rise on weekends, and on long weekends accommodation can be scarce.

The ***Clarendon Guesthouse Motor Inn*** *(☎ 4782 1322)*, on the corner of Lurline and Waratah Sts, has both old-fashioned and motel-style singles/doubles from $48/68 midweek, with weekend dinner-and-show packages for around $100 per person.

Rates at most of the more expensive places vary widely, depending on the time of the week and the time of the year. ***3 Sisters Motel*** *(☎ 4782 2911)*, ten minutes walk from town at the bottom end of Katoomba St, is an average cheaper motel, charging $60/75 to $80/95.

In the style of the grand guesthouses but with a lower tariff than many, the lovely ***Cecil Guesthouse*** *(☎ 4782 1411, 108 Katoomba St)* charges $45 to $55 per person, with a full breakfast. (There's a larger frontage on Lurline St.)

At the top of the hotel scale is the lovingly restored ***Hydro Majestic Hotel*** *(☎ 4788 1002, Great Western Hwy)*. A massive relic of an earlier era, it's a few kilometres west of Katoomba at Medlow Bath. Double rooms with views of the valley (and light breakfast) start at $650 midweek, when rooms with a less awe-inspiring view start at $205. You'll pay even more on weekends. The grand ***Carrington Hotel*** *(☎ 4782 1111, 10-16 Katoomba St)* is another gorgeous old place that has been refurbished; rooms start at $195 midweek, $225 weekends, including breakfast. The swish, well-appointed ***Lilianfels Blue Mountains*** *(☎ 4780 1200, toll-free 1800 024 452, Lilianfels Ave)*, near Echo Point, charges from $362 for a single or double; add $50 for a valley view.

Places to Eat Katoomba St, between Gang Gang and Waratah Sts, has plenty of good places to eat. The pleasantly quirky, Art Deco ***Savoy*** *(No 12)* has an interesting menu including focaccia, pasta and Asian-inspired food. Salads cost $7, pastas from $9; the servings are large.

The cosy ***Blues Cafe*** *(No 57)* has mostly vegetarian (and vegan) food – a jumbo vegie burger is $7.90, sticky date pudding $5.90. It's also Art Deco in style, but nearby is Katoomba's undisputed Art Deco masterpiece, the ***Paragon Cafe*** *(No 65)*. While the menu is fairly standard, the ambience alone makes it worth a visit – if only for a cup of coffee, or some handmade chocolates. Check out the cocktail bar and the motif figures on the wood-panelled walls. Pasta is $10, steak $15; it's only open during the day.

Back on the other side of the street, the licensed ***Cafe Restaurant*** *(No 40)* opens for breakfast and serves burgers and chips for $7.90, gourmet sandwiches for $4.90. Further down Katoomba St is ***Go West Cafe*** *(No 181)*, a small place with outside seats; focaccia costs $4.50, good spinach-and-cheese filo parcels are $2.50.

Towards the corner of Waratah St, ***Tom's Eats*** *(No 200)* has meals for well under $10; chicken burgers are $6. It's closed Monday. For good fast food and bad puns, try the nearby ***Grillers in the Mist*** *(No 208)*, a tiny seafood takeaway with cheap and inventive fishy snacks. The sociable ***Parakeet Cafe*** *(No 195)* has tables outside and vegie burgers for $7.50, steak sandwiches for $8.50. Across Waratah St, the Thai ***Chork Dee*** *(☎ 4782 1913)* has gingered chicken for $10.60, vegetarian dishes from around $7.50; it's open for dinner only.

Near the station, upstairs and along a mysterious corridor, is the relaxed and pleasantly eccentric ***Avalon Cafe Restaurant*** *(98 Main St)*. It's open for dinner seven nights and lunch Thursday, Friday and Sunday. Pasta dishes start at $9.50; other mains are around $14.

Entertainment ***Carrington Bar*** on Katoomba St, with its green-tiled façade, often has live music on weekends. Other pubs with local bands on weekends are ***Katoomba Hotel*** and ***Hotel Gearin*** – there's a blues jam at Gearin on Wednesday night.

There's a theatre restaurant/cabaret at ***Clarendon Guesthouse Motor Inn***, with shows on Friday and Saturday nights – some of the acts are big names.

The giant-screen ***Edge Cinema*** *(☎ 4782 8928, 235 Great Western Hwy)* shows feature films and a stunning Blue Mountains documentary. See Mt Victoria later for information about the Mt Vic Flicks.

Getting Around Katoomba-Woodford Bus Company (☎ 4782 4213) runs from opposite the Carrington Hotel to the Scenic

Railway, approximately hourly until about 4.30 pm on weekdays and a few times on Saturday ($1.60). Mountainlink (☎ 4782 3333) runs a service between Echo Point and Gordon Falls via Katoomba St and Leura Mall. There's roughly one service an hour midweek, fewer on weekends.

If you're driving, beware of the parking restrictions, because they're strictly enforced. Cullen Utility Rental (☎ 4782 5535), 60 Wilson St, rents cars from $58 a day including insurance and 250 free kilometres.

You can hire mountain bikes at the Katoomba YHA Hostel for $25 a day ($15 for guests). If all its bikes are out, try the Cecil Guesthouse, further up Lurline St. Cycletech (☎ 4782 2800), on Gang Gang St, hires mountain bikes for $6 an hour or $15/25 for a half/full day. Katoomba Mountain Bike Hire (☎ 4782 6000), 38 Waratah St, has similar rates.

See also Getting Around at the end of the Blue Mountains section for information on the Blue Mountains Explorer bus.

Blackheath & Around

This town, 10km west of Katoomba on the Great Western Hwy, is a good base for visiting the Grose and Megalong valleys. It has the closest train station to the NPWS Blue Mountains Heritage Centre (☎ 4787 8877), about 3km north-east along Govett's Leap Rd. The centre is open from 8.30 am to 4.30 pm daily.

There are superb lookouts east of town, among them **Govett's Leap**, the adjacent **Bridal Veil Falls** (the highest in the Blue Mountains), and **Evans Lookout** (turn off the highway south of Blackheath). To the north-east, via Hat Hill Rd, are **Pulpit Rock**, **Perry's Lookdown** and **Anvil Rock**.

A long cliff-edge track leads from Govett's Leap to Pulpit Rock and there are walks down into the Grose Valley itself. Get details on walks from the NPWS Heritage Centre. Perry's Lookdown is at the beginning of the shortest route to the beautiful **Blue Gum Forest** in the bottom of the valley – about four hours return, but you'll want to linger longer.

To the west and south-west of Blackheath lie the Kanimbla and Megalong valleys, with yet more spectacular views from places like **Hargreaves Lookout**.

Places to Stay The nearest NPWS ***camp site*** is Acacia Flat in the Grose Valley, near the Blue Gum Forest. It's a steep walk down from Govett's Leap or Perry's Lookdown. You can camp at Perry's Lookdown, which has a car park and is a convenient base for Grose Valley walks.

Blackheath Caravan Park *(☎ 4787 8101, Prince Edward St)* is off Govett's Leap Rd, about 600m from the highway. Tent sites are $7 a single, vans $38 a double. ***Lakeview Holiday Park*** *(☎ 4787 8534, Prince Edward St)* has *en suite* cabins from $50 a double. The cosy ***Gardners Inn*** *(☎ 4787 8347, Great Western Hwy, Blackheath)* is the oldest hotel (1831) in the Blue Mountains. Reasonable rooms cost $30 per person midweek and $35 on weekends, including breakfast.

On the road to Evans Lookout, ***Federation Garden Lodge*** *(☎ 4787 7767)* has two-bedroom apartments for $90 a double midweek (an extra person costs $25). The grounds are large and the facilities are good. On weekends it's $290 minimum for Friday and Saturday night. Set in secluded bushland, ***Jemby-Rimbah Lodge*** *(☎ 4787 7622, 336 Evans Lookout Rd)* has good self-contained cabins sleeping six people for $98 midweek, $135 weekends. It can organise activities through the NPWS.

Megalong Valley

The Megalong Valley feels like rural Australia, a refreshing change from the quasi-suburbs strung out along the ridges. It's largely cleared farmland, but it's still beautiful. The road down from Blackheath passes through pockets of rainforest; you can wander along the beautiful 600m **Coachwood Glen Nature Trail**, a couple of kilometres before the small settlement of Werribee.

Megalong Valley Farm (☎ 4787 8188) has shearing, milking and other activities as well as Clydesdale horses and native animals. It's open from 10 am to 5 pm daily; admission is $3 (children $2). There's also bunkhouse accommodation, with dorm beds for $15.

There are several **horse-riding** companies, such as Werriberri Trail Rides (☎ 4787 9171), Megalong Rd near Megalong Valley Farm, and Pack Saddlers (☎ 4787 9150), at the end of the valley in Green Gully. Both offer riding by the hour ($20) and longer treks, as well as accommodation.

Mt Victoria

Mt Victoria, the highest point in the mountains, is a small village with a semi-rural atmosphere 16km north-west of Katoomba on the Great Western Hwy.

Everything is an easy walk from the train station, where there's the **Mt Victoria Museum of Australiana**, open from 2 to 5 pm on weekends. Interesting buildings include the **Victoria & Albert Guesthouse**, the 1849 **Tollkeeper's Cottage** and the 1870s **church**.

The charming **Mt Vic Flicks** (☎ 4787 1577) is a cinema of the old school, with 'usherettes' and the occasional piano player. Movies ($5 to $10) are shown from Thursday to Sunday.

Off the highway at **Mt York** there's a memorial to the explorers who first crossed the Blue Mountains.

Places to Stay & Eat The fine, old ***Imperial Hotel*** *(☎ 4787 1233, Great Western Hwy)* has arguably the best backpackers' rooms in the region, at $20 for a dorm bed. It also has singles/doubles for $60/78 midweek (starting at $70/109 on weekends), and various packages. The hotel faces the highway and quieter Station St.

Nearby, the lovely ***Victoria & Albert*** *(☎ 4787 1588, 19 Station St)* is a comfortable guesthouse in the grand old style. B&B costs from $45 midweek ($60 weekends), $10 more with bathroom. There's a cafe and a good restaurant. Another old-style guesthouse is the distinguished ***Manor House*** *(☎ 4787 1369, Montgomery St)*, which has rooms from $90 to $125 per person, including dinner and breakfast.

Hartley Historic Site

The government established Hartley in the 1830s as a police post to protect travellers crossing the mountains from bushrangers. The village became a popular place to break the journey, due to its safe atmosphere – and welcome pubs. Some fine sandstone buildings were constructed, notably the Greek Revival **courthouse** (1837). Many remain today, although the village is now deserted.

The NPWS information centre (☎ 6355 2117) in the Farmer's Inn is open from 10 am to 1 pm and 2 to 4.30 pm daily. You can wander around the village for free, but entry to the Courthouse comes with a guided tour that costs $4 ($3 children).

The village is 10km west of Mt Victoria, off the Great Western Hwy.

Jenolan Caves

South-west of Katoomba on the western fringe of Kanangra Boyd National Park, are the Jenolan Caves (☎ 6359 3311), the best-known limestone caves in Australia. One cave has been open to the public since 1867, although parts of the system are still unexplored. There are nine caves you can visit by guided tour. There are about 10 tours between 10 am and 4 pm daily, and weekly evening tours at 8 pm; tours last one to two hours and prices start at $12. It's advisable to arrive early during holiday periods, as the best caves can be 'sold out' by 10 am.

Walks There's a network of walking trails through the bush surrounding the Jenolan Caves.

The **Six Foot Track** from Katoomba to the Jenolan Caves is a fairly easy three day walk. The Department of Conservation & Land Management (DCLM) has a detailed brochure. Great Australian Walks (☎ 9555 7580) conducts guided walks along the track, with accommodation, for $370. The guides carry everything for you.

Organised Tours See the Organised Tours at the end of the Blue Mountains section for information on the popular Wonderbus tour. Fantastic Aussie Tours (☎ 4782 1866,

9938 5714 in Sydney) has day tours to the caves from Katoomba from $48 (including cave entry). Walkers can be dropped off at and collected from the Six Foot Track at Jenolan from $25, but you have to book.

Places to Stay There are ***camp sites*** near Jenolan Caves House for $10 per site. The self-contained ***Binda Bush Cabins*** *(☎ 6359 3311)*, on the road from Hartley about 8km north of the caves, can accommodate six people in bunks for $75 midweek. The revamped 1889 ***Jenolan Caves House*** *(☎ 6359 3322)* is a big old-style guesthouse. Rooms cost from $100 midweek, but there are a range of other options including a cottage (with doubles from $65), a motel section, and backpacker bunks for $15.

There are other cheap options, including a ***caravan park***, in Oberon, about 30km north-west of the caves.

Bells Line of Road

The scenic Bells Line of Rd was constructed in 1841 as an alternative route (to what is now the Great Western Hwy) across the mountains. It runs from near Richmond across the mountains to Lithgow, although you can cut across to join the Great Western Hwy near Mt Victoria. Bells Line of Rd is much quieter than the highway, and is lined with bush, small farms and apple orchards.

Mt Tomah Botanic Garden Midway between Bilpin and Bell, the delightful Mt Tomah Botanic Garden (☎ 4567 2154) is a cool-climate annexe of Sydney's Royal Botanic Gardens. As well as native plants there are displays of exotic species, including some magnificent rhododendrons. The gardens are open daily; admission is $5 per car or motorcycle and $2 for pedestrians and cyclists.

Mt Wilson Settled by people with a penchant for re-creating England, Mt Wilson is a tiny, beautiful village of hedgerows, large gardens and lines of European trees. It's 8km north of the Bells Line of Rd; the turn-off is 7km east of Bell. Near the Post House there's an information board with details of public gardens and some short walks in the area.

A kilometre or so from the village centre is a lovely remnant of rainforest thick with tree ferns, the **Cathedral of Ferns**.

The ***Post House*** *(☎ 4756 2000)* serves tea and can help with B&B accommodation, or you could try ***Blueberry Lodge*** *(☎ 4756 2022)*, which has self-contained log chalets sleeping up to six for $280 a double midweek.

Zig Zag Railway The Zig Zag Railway (☎ 6353 1795) is at Clarence about 10km east of Lithgow. It was built in 1869 and was quite an engineering wonder in its day. Trains descended from the Blue Mountains by this route until 1910. A section has been restored, and steam trains run daily. The fare for the 12km trip is $13 (children $6.50).

Organised Tours

The major Sydney tour companies have day trips to the Blue Mountains for about $60.

Backpacker-friendly Wonderbus (☎ 9555 9800) runs day tours of the Blue Mountains ($55) and overnight trips ($180 for YHA members) that include the Jenolan Caves, dorm accommodation at the Blue Mountains YHA Hostel (you don't have to be a YHA member) and a choice of either abseiling or horse riding. Book in person at the Sydney YHA Travel Centre or the YHA hostels in Sydney.

Another inexpensive tour operator that gets good feedback is Oz-Trek (☎ 9360 3444), 448 Bourke St in Sydney's Surry Hills. From Sydney, Wayward Bus Company (☎ 08-8232 6646, toll-free 1800 882 823), based in Adelaide, has two-day tours of the Blue Mountains and the Jenolan Caves for $110 (not including accommodation). See Getting Around under Katoomba later for information about the Blue Mountains Explorer bus.

Getting There & Away

Katoomba, 109km from Sydney's city centre, is almost a satellite suburb. CityRail trains run roughly hourly from Central station

($9.40 one way, two hours). Countrylink buses meet trains at Mt Victoria on Tuesday, Friday and Sunday for the run to Oberon.

To get there by car from Sydney, exit via Parramatta Rd and detour onto the Western Motorway ($1.50) at Strathfield. West of Penrith the motorway becomes the Great Western Hwy. To reach the Bells Line of Rd, exit the city on Parramatta Rd and from Parramatta head north-west on Windsor Rd to Windsor. Richmond Rd from Windsor becomes the Bells Line of Rd west of Richmond.

See also Organised Tours earlier in this section.

Getting Around

Bus Mountainlink (☎ 4782 3333) runs between Leura, Katoomba, Medlow Bath, Blackheath and Mt Victoria, with some services along Hat Hill Rd and Govett's Leap Rd, which lead respectively to Perry's Lookdown and Govett's Leap. It'll take you to within about 1km of Govett's Leap, but for Perry's Lookdown you'll have to walk about 6km from the last stop. Services are less frequent on weekends. In Katoomba the bus leaves from the top of Katoomba St, outside the Carrington Hotel.

On weekends and public holidays the Blue Mountains Explorer bus offers all-day travel for $18 (children $9). It departs regularly from the train station and visits the Scenic Railway, Skyway, Echo Point, Leura village and other places. The full circuit takes an hour, but you can get on or off where you like, and loiter at your leisure. Contact Fantastic Aussie Tours (☎ 4782 1866), 283 Main St, Katoomba.

Blue Mountains Bus Company (☎ 4782 4213) runs between Katoomba, Leura, Wentworth Falls, and east as far as Woodford. There's roughly one service every 45 minutes from Katoomba train station.

Train There are train stations in most Blue Mountains towns along the Great Western Hwy. Trains run roughly hourly between stations east of Katoomba and roughly two-hourly between stations to the west.

MACARTHUR COUNTRY

The Hume Freeway heads south-west from Sydney, flanked by the rugged Blue Mountains National Park to the west and the coastal escarpment to the east. This cleared and rolling sheep country has some of the state's oldest towns, although many have been swallowed by Sydney's steamrolling suburbs. For a more rural vista than the freeway allows, take the **Northern Rd** between Penrith and Narellan (just north of Camden).

Liverpool and, 20km further south, **Campbelltown**, are unattractive outer suburbs of Sydney, though both do have some interesting old buildings.

Camden & Around

This large country town is almost a dormitory suburb of Sydney. Camden itself retains its integrity, but the surrounding countryside is fast filling up with weekend attractions for Sydneysiders. John Oxley Cottage on the northern outskirts houses the Camden information centre (☎ 4658 1370), open from 10 am to 3 pm daily. The **Camden Museum**, at 40 John St, behind the library, is open from 1.30 to 4.30 pm on weekends; admission is $1 (children 50c).

The Macarthurs' home, **Camden Park House** (1835), is only open to the public the on last weekend in September.

Gledswood (☎ 9606 5111), Camden Valley Way, in Catherine Field near Narellan, is an old homestead (1827) now housing a winery and a restaurant. There are also sheep shearing, boomerang throwing and other activities. It's open from 10 am to 4 pm daily; entry is $12 ($6 children). **Strugletown** (☎ 4648 2424), on Sharman Close, is a collection of galleries in historic cottages; it's open from 10 am to 5 pm Wednesday to Sunday. Not far from Narellan, **Australiana Park** (also called El Caballo Blanco), Camden Valley Way, has a grab-bag of things to see and do, including sheep shearing, water-sliding, horse riding and koala cuddling. The star attractions are the Andalusian Dancing Stallions; phone (☎ 9606 6266) for performance times. Admission is $18 (children $9.50).

Midway between Camden and Campbelltown is the **Mt Annan Botanic Garden** (☎ 4648 2477), which is an offshoot of Sydney's Royal Botanic Gardens and displays native flora on over 400 hectares. It is open from 10 am to 6 pm daily from October to March and to 4 pm from April to September; admission is $5 per car or motorcycle, $2 for pedestrians. You can get here on bus No 896, which runs approximately hourly from Campbelltown train station to Camden.

Picton & Around

South of Camden and more rural, pretty Picton is an old village originally called Stonequarry. A number of historic buildings still stand, including the train station and the 1839 **George IV Inn** (☎ 4677 1415), which brews Bavarian-style beer and provides modest accommodation. Upper Menangle St is listed by the National Trust.

Elizabeth Macarthur Agricultural Institute, 710 Morton Park Rd, is a research station in Menangle, north-east of Picton. It takes in **Belgenny Farm** (☎ 4655 9651), the Macarthurs' first farm in the area and the oldest in Australia. It can be visited on organised tours; call for details.

South of Picton in **Thirlmere**, the **Rail Transport Museum** (☎ 4681 8001) on Barbour Rd has a huge collection of engines and rolling stock. The museum is open from 10 am to 3 pm weekdays, 9 am to 5 pm weekends; admission is $8 (children $2). There are steam-train excursions (☎ 9744 9999) every Sunday, and Monday and Wednesday during school holidays.

Getting There & Away

From Sydney take Parramatta Rd and turn south onto the Hume Hwy. The Narellan Rd exit on the Hume Hwy runs west to Camden and east to Campbelltown. Alternatively take the Camden Valley Way (Route 89) as it forks off the Hume Hwy south of Liverpool.

To reach Picton, stay on the Hume Hwy past Campbelltown and turn off at the Picton exit. From Camden or Narellan, head south on Remembrance Drive.

The Mac's Magnificent Merinos

The Macarthur Country area was originally called Cow Pastures because a herd of escapee cattle from Sydney Cove thrived here, but it was John and Elizabeth Macarthur's sheep, arriving in 1805, which made the area famous. The couple's experiments with sheep-breeding led to the development of merino sheep suited to Australian conditions. These became the foundation of the Australian wool industry.

CityRail trains stop at Liverpool, Campbelltown and Picton.

SOUTHERN HIGHLANDS

The southern highlands, 100km south of Sydney, was one of the earliest inland areas to be settled by whites – so early, in fact, that many settlers still saw themselves as English landed gentry rather than Australian farmers, and promptly cleared the surrounding land of unruly native foliage in favour of English-style villages.

There was a second bout of nostalgia for the 'homeland' in the 1920s, which resulted in the building of lavish guesthouses catering to wealthy Sydneysiders.

The main source of information on the area is the Southern Highlands visitors centre (☎ 4871 2888) on Main St in Mittagong; it's open from 8 am to 5.30 pm daily. It also provides a free accommodation-booking service (☎ 1300 657 559). Craigie's *Visitors Map of the Southern Highlands* ($4.95) covers the area in detail.

Some of the towns in the highlands area include: **Mittagong**, the gateway to the highlands; **Bowral**, with an excellent museum devoted to its most famous son, Sir Donald Bradman, and other cricketing greats; **Berrima**, a village with some fine old buildings and a good museum; and **Bundanoon**, near the spectacular northern escarpments of **Morton National Park** (☎ 4887 7270).

Getting There & Away

Bus Buses running along the Hume Hwy between Sydney and Melbourne call in at Mittagong, but most don't go on to Bowral or Moss Vale.

Berrima Coaches (☎ 4871 3211) runs fairly frequent weekday services between Mittagong, Moss Vale and Bowral, with a few continuing on to Berrima, Sutton Forest, Exeter and Bundanoon. There are Saturday services between Mittagong, Moss Vale and Bowral. Buses also link Wollongong and Moss Vale, some via Bundanoon.

Train CityRail trains run to Mittagong, Bowral and Moss Vale. Some Countrylink trains on the Sydney-Canberra run stop at these stations and at Bundanoon. The XPT to/from Melbourne stops at one or more of them. Check with CityRail and Countrylink for schedules.

HAWKESBURY RIVER

The Hawkesbury River enters the sea 30km north of Sydney at Broken Bay. Dotted with coves, beaches, picnic spots and some fine riverside restaurants, it's one of Australia's most beautiful rivers and is a popular centre for boating. The Hawkesbury's final 20-odd kilometres before it enters the ocean are fringed by inlets like Berowra Creek, Cowan Water and Pittwater to the south, and Brisbane Water to the north.

The river flows between Marramarra and Ku-ring-gai Chase national parks in the south; and Dharug, Brisbane Water and Bouddi national parks to the north. Windsor and Richmond are about 120km further upstream from there.

Riverboat Postman

The *Riverboat Postman* (☎ 9985 7566) mail boat is an excellent way to get a feel for the river. It does a 40km round trip weekdays, running upstream as far as Marlow, near Spencer. It leaves Brooklyn at 9.30 am and returns at 1.15 pm. A shorter afternoon run on Wednesday leaves at 1.30 pm and returns at 4 pm. It costs $28 or $22 for a concession. See Getting There & Away later in this section for details on connecting with the *Riverboat Postman*.

Houseboats

You can hire houseboats in Brooklyn, Berowra Waters, Bobbin Head and Wisemans Ferry. These aren't cheap but renting midweek during the low season can be affordable for a group. As a rough guide, ***Able Houseboats*** *(☎ 4566 4308)* on River Rd, Wisemans Ferry, offers two nights on a four berth boat starting at $325. Other companies include ***Holidays-A-Float*** *(☎ 9985 7368)* in Brooklyn, and ***Ripples on the Hawkesbury*** *(☎ 9985 7333, 87 Brooklyn Rd, Brooklyn)*.

Brooklyn & Berowra Waters

The settlements along the river have their own distinct character. Life in Brooklyn revolves totally around boats and the river. The town is on the Sydney-Newcastle railway line, just east of the Pacific Hwy.

The small town of Berowra Waters, further upstream on a narrow, forested waterway, is clustered around a free 24-hour winch-ferry that crosses Berowra Creek. It's a pretty location, with boat hire and walking tracks through the bush. The main weekend drawcard for Sydneysiders is ***Berowra Waters Inn*** *(☎ 9456 1027)*, one of Australia's best-known restaurants. It's open for lunch and dinner on Friday and Saturday, for lunch only Thursday and Sunday. The excellent modern Australian set menu costs $60 per person. Bookings are essential. There are also several cafes overlooking the water.

Berowra Waters is 5km west of the Pacific Hwy. There is a train station at Berowra, but from there it's a 6km hike down to the ferry.

Wisemans Ferry & St Albans

The tranquil settlement of Wisemans Ferry is a popular spot on the Hawkesbury River, about halfway between Windsor and the mouth of the river. A free 24-hour winch-ferry is the only means of crossing the river here. The NPWS shop (☎ 4566 4382) has information on the area. The historic ***Wisemans Ferry Inn*** *(☎ 4566 4301)* has cramped but clean rooms for $55 a double. There are several caravan parks, including ***Del Rio Riverside Resort*** *(☎ 4566 4330)*, 3km south-west of the village centre, where powered sites cost $19 a double.

Unsealed roads on both sides of the river run north from Wisemans Ferry to the tiny hamlet of St Albans. It's a pretty drive, with bush on one side, river flats on other side, and the occasional old sandstone house. The friendly ***Settlers Arms Inn*** *(☎ 4568 2111)* dates from 1848, and the public bar is worth having a beer in. It has a few pleasant rooms from $100 a double, and there's a basic ***camp site*** opposite the pub. There's also B&B in the wonderful old ***Court House*** *(☎ 4568 2042)* for $120 midweek.

It may be unwise to swim in the Hawkesbury River between Windsor and Wisemans Ferry in summer due to blue-green algae. Call the EPA Pollution Line (☎ 9325 5555) for information.

National Parks Across the river, **Dharug National Park** (14,834 hectares) is a wilderness noted for its Aboriginal rock carvings, which date back nearly 10,000 years. There's camping at Mill Creek and Ten Mile Hollow.

Yengo National Park (139,861 hectares), a rugged sandstone area covering the foothills of the Blue Mountains, stretches from Wisemans Ferry to the Hunter Valley. It's a wilderness area with no facilities and limited road access.

South of the Hawkesbury, **Murramarra National Park** (11,760 hectares) has vehicle access from the Old Northern Rd south of Wisemans Ferry. ***Camping*** is allowed here. Contact the NPWS (☎ 4324 4911), at 207 Albany St in Gosford.

Getting There & Away

Train Trains run from Central station to Brooklyn's Hawkesbury River train station. The 8.16 am train from Central station ($4.60 one way) gets you to Brooklyn's Hawkesbury River station in time to meet the morning *Riverboat Postman.*

Car & Motorcycle To reach Berowra Waters, turn off Pacific Hwy at Berowra, or take the longer scenic road through the Galston Gorge, north of Hornsby in Sydney's north-east.

A road leads to Wisemans Ferry from Pitt Town, near Windsor. You can also get there from Sydney on Old Northern Rd, which branches off Windsor Rd north of Parramatta.

Both of these routes culminate in a choice of two car ferries: the ferry in the west of town (at the bottom of the steep hill) takes you to St Albans Rd, which runs to St Albans; the ferry on the north-eastern side (just out of town, near the park) takes you to Settlers Rd, which also leads to St Albans; in the other direction it leads to Central Mangrove and, eventually, the central coast or the Sydney-Newcastle Freeway.

An unsealed road runs north-east from St Albans to Bucketty, from where you can travel on to Wollombi and Cessnock in the Hunter Valley.

To reach Brooklyn by car, take the Sydney-Newcastle Freeway or follow the old Pacific Hwy.

Ferry The *Riverboat Postman* (☎ 9985 7566) runs a ferry service from Brooklyn to Patonga beach five times a week for $12 return ($6 children). Bookings are necessary.

There's also a daily ferry between Palm Beach, Patonga and Bobbin Head in Ku-ring-gai Chase National Park. From Patonga, Peninsula Bus Lines (☎ 4341 4133) has infrequent buses to Gosford, where you can catch a northbound bus or train.

THE CENTRAL COAST

The central coast has superb surf beaches, lakes and national parks, but rampant suburban housing.

Its beautiful waterways include **Broken Bay** and **Brisbane Water** in the south and three contiguous lakes in the north. The northern lakes are **Tuggerah Lake**; **Lake Budgewoi**, near Toukley; and **Lake Munmorah**. A few kilometres north of Lake Munmorah is **Lake Macquarie**, which stretches north to Newcastle.

West of the lakes, in the modest Watagan Mountains, are 13 **state forests** that run north to the Hunter Valley. The forests have walking trails; camping is permitted, except in picnic areas. The old village of **Cooranbong** is the main access point to the mountains. Further west again, you come to the vast national parks of the Blue Mountains.

Gosford is the main town in the area. Larger beachside centres include **Terrigal** and **The Entrance**.

Gosford visitors centre (☎ 4385 4430, toll-free 1800 806 258), 206 Mann St, is near the train station and is open from 9 am to 5 pm weekdays, to 3 pm on weekends. There are also visitors centres at Terrigal and The Entrance (for information call same telephone numbers as for Gosford). Information is also available from Umina (☎ 4343 2200) and Toukley (☎ 4392 4666). There is an NPWS office (☎ 4324 4911) in Gosford.

Accommodation is scarce during school holidays.

Gosford & Around

Gosford, the largest town in the area, is 12km inland on the shores of Brisbane Water, about 85km north of Sydney. Gosford has good transport links with Sydney, and is a good base from which to explore the region, including Brisbane Water National Park.

Brisbane Water National Park On the northern side of the Hawkesbury River, across from Ku-ring-gai Chase National Park, Brisbane Water National Park is 9km south-west of Gosford. It extends from the Pacific Hwy in the west to Brisbane Water in the east but, despite its name, this national park has only a short frontage onto that body of water.

In rugged sandstone country, the park is known for its **wildflowers** in early spring, and there are many walking trails. South of the township of Kariong is the turn-off for the **Bulgandry Aboriginal Engraving Site**, where there are interesting rock carvings.

The main road access is at Girrakool; travel west from Gosford or exit the Sydney-Newcastle Freeway at the Calga interchange. Wondabyne train station, on the Sydney-Newcastle line, is inside the park near several walking trails (including part of the Great North Walk). You must tell the guard that you want to get off at Wondabyne, and travel in the rear carriage. Ferries from Palm Beach run to Patonga; ferries from Brooklyn run to Wobby beach, on a peninsula south of the park near some walking trails.

For more information contact the Gosford NPWS (☎ 4324 4911).

Old Sydney Town Off the freeway 9km south-west of Gosford, Old Sydney Town (☎ 4340 1104) is a major reconstruction of early Sydney with street theatre retelling events from the colony's early history. It's open from 10 am to 4 pm Wednesday to Sunday, daily during school holidays; admission is $18 (children $10.50). Peninsula Bus Lines runs here from Gosford and several tours run from Sydney.

Other Things to See & Do West of Gosford on the Pacific Hwy in Somersby, the **Australian Reptile Park** (☎ 4340 1022) has native animals and birds as well as reptiles. It's open from 9 am to 5 pm daily; admission is $11.95 (children $5.95). Off Brisbane Water Drive in West Gosford is **Henry Kendall Cottage** (☎ 4325 2270), a small museum in the home of an early poet. It's open 10 am to 4 pm Wednesday and weekends, and daily during school holidays; admission is $3 (concession $1.50). Another attraction is the **Forest of Tranquillity** (☎ 4362 1855), a private forest reserve and bird sanctuary west off the freeway at Ourimbah. It's open from 10 am to 5 pm Wednesday to Sunday, daily in school holidays; admission is $7 (children $4).

South of the national park is **Patonga**, a small fishing village on Broken Bay, with camping available at ***Patonga Beach Caravanning & Camping Area*** *(☎ 4379 1287)*. Off the road to Patonga is the worthwhile **Warrah Lookout**.

Not far away, but screened from the housing estates of Umina and Woy Woy by a steep road over Mt Ettalong, **Pearl beach** is a lovely National Trust hamlet on the eastern edge of the national park. The only way to stay here is to rent a holiday house or apartment, and they're scarce.

Terrigal & Around

Terrigal, on the ocean about 12km east of Gosford, is probably the most upmarket of the central coast's beachside towns. The big ***Holiday Inn Crowne Plaza*** *(☎ toll-free 1800 024 966)* dominates the foreshore; rooms start from around $165, weekend packages from around $420. There's also a good, quiet hostel, ***Terrigal Beach Lodge YHA*** *(☎ 4385 3330, 10 Campbell Crescent)*, a block from the beach. Dorm beds cost $20, doubles $45 (members pay about $3 less).

South of Terrigal is the tiny beachside town of **Copacabana**. North of Terrigal, **Bateau Bay** meets the southern section of the small **Wyrrabalong National Park**. It's popular for surfing and the beach is patrolled by life-savers.

Bouddi National Park, 19km south-east of Gosford, extends south from MacMasters beach to the north head of Broken Bay. It also extends out to sea as a marine reserve. There's camping in the park, but you have to book through the Gosford NPWS (☎ 4324 4911).

The Entrance & Tuggerah Lake

The Entrance on the sea inlet of Tuggerah Lake, 15km north of Terrigal, is a suburban sprawl of relentlessly cheerful cream brick, palm trees and plastic chairs, set beside a beautiful lake and superb surf beach. You can reach The Entrance either by driving north from Terrigal or by taking the Tuggerah exit off the Sydney-Newcastle Freeway.

The **pelicans** are fed daily at 3.30 pm on the beachfront near the visitors centre.

On the peninsula north of The Entrance is the northern section of the small **Wyrrabalong National Park**, which has walking trails and diverse flora habitats. North of the park are the towns of **Toukley** and **Budgewoi**, popular bases for boating and fishing.

Running up the coast for 12km is **Munmorah State Recreation Area**. State recreation areas (SRAs) are similar to national parks but have less-strict conservation rules. There are three ***camping areas*** – at Freemans, Frazer and Geebung beaches – but they're usually full at peak times; book at the office (☎ 4358 1649), off the road south of Elizabeth Bay.

Getting There & Away CityRail trains running between Sydney and the Hunter Valley stop at central coast destinations including Gosford and Wyong.

The central coast is easily accessible from Sydney via the Sydney-Newcastle Freeway.

A ferry (☎ 9918 2747) runs from Palm Beach, a northern beachside suburb of Sydney, to Patonga in Broken Bay four or five times daily during winter (more frequently during summer, weekends and school holidays). The fare is $12 (YHA $8), plus about $2 for big packs and bikes. From Patonga, Peninsula Bus Lines (☎ 4324 1255) has infrequent buses to Gosford. The 11 am ferry continues on to Bobbin Head in Ku-ring-gai Chase National Park.

From Brooklyn you can get to Patonga on a cruise boat (☎ 9985 7566) for about $10 return, or to Wobby beach for $6 return with the Dangar Island Ferry Service (☎ 9985 7605), near the trailhead for a walking track through Brisbane Water National Park. Hawkesbury River train station in Brooklyn is near the ferry wharf.

Getting Around The two local bus services covering the main centres in the area are The Entrance Red Bus Services (☎ 4332 8655), and Peninsula Bus Lines (☎ 4341 1433).

HUNTER VALLEY WINERIES (MAP 14)

Only a two hour drive north of Sydney, the Hunter Valley is a superb scenic area sprinkled with vineyards. The lower Hunter is the largest wine-growing area, but there are also wineries in the less-visited upper Hunter, especially around the village of **Denman**.

The lower Hunter has more than 50 vineyards concentrated in a small, pretty area around tiny **Pokolbin Village**, north-west of Cessnock. It's a popular weekend destination, so visit midweek if possible.

The main towns in the wilder upper Hunter Valley are **Scone** and **Muswellbrook**.

The lower Hunter's efficient information centre (☎ 4990 4477), on Aberdare Rd in Cessnock, is open daily (but closes at 3.30 pm on Sunday). Drop in for brochures and maps (Broadbent's is a handy one) before setting out for the wineries.

For information on the upper Hunter Valley, contact the Denman (☎ 6547 2731) or Scone (☎ 6545 1526) information centres.

Things to See & Do

Most wineries encourage casual visits, but several also have tours. They include McWilliams (☎ 4998 7505; 11 am daily); Hunter Estate (☎ 4998 7777; 9 and 11 am, 2 pm daily); McGuigan Brothers (call ☎ 4998 7400 for times); Tyrrells (☎ 4993 7000; 1.30 pm Monday to Saturday) and Rothbury Estate (☎ 4998 7555 for times).

Balloon Aloft (☎ toll-free 1800 028 568) has **flights** over the valley for around $200.

You can hire bicycles from Grapemobile (☎ 4998 7639), on the corner of McDonalds and Gillards Rds near Pokolbin, for $15/25 a half/full day.

The Hunter Vintage Festival, held during harvest period (January to March), attracts hordes of wine buffs for tasting, and grape-picking and treading contests. Accommodation can be scarce, but with some planning you can find good package deals. In September there's the Wine & Food Affair.

Organised Tours

Hunter Vineyard Tours (☎ 4991 1659) has daily departures from Newcastle and other Hunter Valley centres and charges $50 (children $25), or $34 without lunch.

Grapemobile (☎ 4991 2339) offers one-day bike rides through the wineries, with a support bus, overnight accommodation and all meals for $189 per person. It also has day tours ($98).

Places to Stay

Accommodation prices rise on weekends, and beds can be scarce – it's wise to book ahead. The Cessnock (☎ 4990 4477) information centre books accommodation and knows about special deals.

In Cessnock, ***Valley View*** *(☎ 4990 2573, Mt View Rd)* has tent sites for $12, on-site vans for $35 and *en suite* cabins from $55. ***Cessnock Park*** *(☎ 4990 5819)*, off Allandale Rd north of Cessnock, has sites for $7, on-site vans start at $30 and cabins start at $50.

Black Opal Hotel *(☎ 4990 1070, 220 Vincent St)*, at the southern end of the main street, has OK rooms for $20 per person from Monday to Thursday, $25 Friday to Sunday. ***Cessnock Hotel*** *(☎ 4990 1002, 234 Wollombi Rd)* has renovated rooms from $35 per person midweek (including cooked breakfast) and noisier (but more character-filled) unrenovated rooms from $25 midweek. Friendly ***Wentworth Hotel*** *(☎ 4990 1364, 36 Vincent St)* has decent rooms for $25 per person, including breakfast.

Midweek, you can get a double for $59 at ***Cessnock Motel*** *(☎ 4990 2699, 13 Annandale Rd)* or ***Hunter Valley Motel*** *(☎ 4990 1722, 30 Allandale Rd)*. Prices at all local motels rise steeply on weekends.

Many vineyards offer accommodation. Most charge well over $100 a night on weekends, but midweek a few charge between $60 and $70 a double. These include the well-equipped, private ***Belford Country Cabins*** *(☎ 4991 2777, Hermitage Rd)* north of the Hunter Estate and the more motel-style ***Potters Inn*** *(☎ 4998 7648, De Beyers Rd)* south of Pokolbin Village. ***Pokolbin Cabins*** *(☎ 4998 7611, Palmers Lane)* is a large complex with four to six-person cabins costing from $30 per person midweek ($60 weekends). The ***Hunter Country Lodge*** *(☎ 4938 1744, Branxton Rd)* is about 12km north of Cessnock. It charges $95 a double midweek.

Probably the top place to stay is the ***Peppers Hunter Valley Guesthouse*** *(☎ 4998 7739, Ekerts Rd)*, which charges from $240 midweek for relatively unspectacular double rooms in lovely surrounds.

Getting There & Away

Air Yanda (book with Qantas) flies between Sydney and Singleton for $132 one way.

Bus Rover Motors (☎ 4990 1699) runs between Newcastle and Cessnock ($8.50) six times a day on weekdays and four times on Saturday, but not at all on Sunday. The last bus from Newcastle to Cessnock departs from Watt St at 6.30 pm weekdays, at 4.45 pm on Saturday. There are also services between Cessnock and Maitland. Rover's office is on Vincent St in Cessnock, opposite the Black Opal Hotel. Kean's (☎ toll-free 1800 625 587) stops at Cessnock ($24) daily on the run from Sydney to Scone. In Sydney, book at the Sydney Coach Terminal (☎ 9281 9366) on Eddy Ave.

Train CityRail runs from Sydney to Newcastle about 25 times daily, taking nearly three hours. The one-way fare is $14.60; an off-peak return is $17.60. Some trains connect with Rover Motors buses to Cessnock.

Car & Motorcycle There are several routes into the Hunter Valley from Sydney. The quickest is the Sydney-Newcastle Freeway.

The Putty Rd between Windsor and Singleton is longer, but more interesting (see the Macquarie Towns section earlier in this chapter). There's also an interesting but bumpy route from Wisemans Ferry, passing through Wollombi.

From Newcastle, follow the New England Hwy and turn off to Kurri Kurri and Cessnock about 4km west of Hexham Bridge.

Phrasebooks

Lonely Planet phrasebooks are packed with essential words and phrases to help travellers communicate with the locals. With colour tabs for quick reference, an extensive vocabulary and use of script, these handy pocket-sized language guides cover day-to-day travel situations.

- handy pocket-sized books
- easy to understand Pronunciation chapter
- clear & comprehensive Grammar chapter
- romanisation alongside script to allow ease of pronunciation
- script throughout so users can point to phrases for every situation
- full of cultural information and tips for the traveller

'...vital for a real DIY spirit and attitude in language learning'

– Backpacker

'the phrasebooks have good cultural backgrounders and offer solid advice for challenging situations in remote locations'

– San Francisco Examiner

Arabic (Egyptian) • Arabic (Moroccan) • Australian *(Australian English, Aboriginal and Torres Strait languages)* • Baltic States *(Estonian, Latvian, Lithuanian)* • Bengali • Brazilian • British • Burmese • Cantonese • Central Asia • Central Europe *(Czech, French, German, Hungarian, Italian, Slovak)* • Eastern Europe *(Bulgarian, Czech, Hungarian, Polish, Romanian, Slovak)* • Ethiopian (Amharic) • Fijian • French • German • Greek • Hebrew phrasebook • Hill Tribes • Hindi/Urdu • Indonesian • Italian • Japanese • Korean • Lao • Latin American Spanish • Malay • Mandarin • Mediterranean Europe *(Albanian, Croatian, Greek, Italian, Macedonian, Maltese, Serbian, Slovene)* • Mongolian • Nepali • Papua New Guinea • Pilipino (Tagalog) • Quechua • Russian • Scandinavian Europe *(Danish, Finnish, Icelandic, Norwegian, Swedish)* • South-East Asia *(Burmese, Indonesian, Khmer, Lao, Malay, Tagalog Pilipino, Thai, Vietnamese)* • South Pacific Languages • Spanish (Castilian) *(also includes Catalan, Galician and Basque)* • Sri Lanka • Swahili • Thai • Tibetan • Turkish • Ukrainian • USA *(US English, Vernacular, Native American languages, Hawaiian)* • Vietnamese • Western Europe *(Basque, Catalan, Dutch, French, German, Greek, Irish)*

Guides by Region

Lonely Planet is known worldwide for publishing practical, reliable and no-nonsense travel information in our guides and on our Web site. The Lonely Planet list covers just about every accessible part of the world. Currently there are nine series: travel guides, shoestring guides, walking guides, city guides, phrasebooks, audio packs, travel atlases, diving and snorkeling guides and travel literature.

AFRICA Africa – the South • Africa on a shoestring • Arabic (Egyptian) phrasebook • Arabic (Moroccan) phrasebook • Cairo • Cape Town • Central Africa • East Africa • Egypt • Egypt travel atlas • Ethiopian (Amharic) phrasebook • The Gambia & Senegal • Healthy Travel Africa • Kenya • Kenya travel atlas • Malawi, Mozambique & Zambia • Morocco • North Africa • South Africa, Lesotho & Swaziland • South Africa, Lesotho & Swaziland travel atlas • Swahili phrasebook • Tanzania, Zanzibar & Pemba • Trekking in East Africa • Tunisia • West Africa • Zimbabwe, Botswana & Namibia • Zimbabwe, Botswana & Namibia travel atlas
Travel Literature: The Rainbird: A Central African Journey • Songs to an African Sunset: A Zimbabwean Story • Mali Blues: Traveling to an African Beat

AUSTRALIA & THE PACIFIC Auckland • Australia • Australian phrasebook • Bushwalking in Australia • Bushwalking in Papua New Guinea • Fiji • Fijian phrasebook • Islands of Australia's Great Barrier Reef • Melbourne • Micronesia • New Caledonia • New South Wales & the ACT • New Zealand • Northern Territory • Outback Australia • Out To Eat – Melbourne • Papua New Guinea • Papua New Guinea (Pidgin) phrasebook • Queensland • Rarotonga & the Cook Islands • Samoa • Solomon Islands • South Australia • South Pacific Languages phrasebook • Sydney • Tahiti & French Polynesia • Tasmania • Tonga • Tramping in New Zealand • Vanuatu • Victoria • Western Australia
Travel Literature: Islands in the Clouds • Kiwi Tracks • Sean & David's Long Drive

CENTRAL AMERICA & THE CARIBBEAN Bahamas and Turks & Caicos • Bermuda • Central America on a shoestring • Costa Rica • Cuba • Dominican Republic & Haiti • Eastern Caribbean • Guatemala, Belize & Yucatán: La Ruta Maya • Jamaica • Mexico • Mexico City • Panama • Puerto Rico
Travel Literature: Green Dreams: Travels in Central America

EUROPE Amsterdam • Andalucía • Austria • Baltic States phrasebook • Barcelona • Berlin • Britain • British phrasebook • Brussels, Bruges & Antwerp • Canary Islands • Central Europe • Central Europe phrasebook • Corsica • Croatia • Czech & Slovak Republics • Denmark • Dublin • Eastern Europe • Eastern Europe phrasebook • Edinburgh • Estonia, Latvia & Lithuania • Europe • Finland • France • French phrasebook • Germany • German phrasebook • Greece • Greek phrasebook • Hungary • Iceland, Greenland & the Faroe Islands • Ireland • Italian phrasebook • Italy • Lisbon • London • Mediterranean Europe • Mediterranean Europe phrasebook • Norway • Paris • Poland • Portugal • Portugal travel atlas • Prague • Provence & the Côte d'Azur • Romania & Moldova • Rome • Russia, Ukraine & Belarus • Russian phrasebook • Scandinavian & Baltic Europe • Scandinavian Europe phrasebook • Scotland • Slovenia • Spain • Spanish phrasebook • St Petersburg • Switzerland • Trekking in Spain • Ukrainian phrasebook • Vienna • Walking in Britain • Walking in Italy • Walking in Ireland • Walking in Switzerland • Western Europe • Western Europe phrasebook
Travel Literature: The Olive Grove: Travels in Greece

INDIAN SUBCONTINENT Bangladesh • Bengali phrasebook • Bhutan • Delhi • Goa • Hindi/Urdu phrasebook • India • India & Bangladesh travel atlas • Indian Himalaya • Karakoram Highway • Kerala • Mumbai • Nepal • Nepali phrasebook • Pakistan • Rajasthan • Read This First: Asia & India • South India • Sri Lanka • Sri Lanka phrasebook • Trekking in the Indian Himalaya • Trekking in the Karakoram & Hindukush • Trekking in the Nepal Himalaya
Travel Literature: In Rajasthan • Shopping for Buddhas

LONELY PLANET

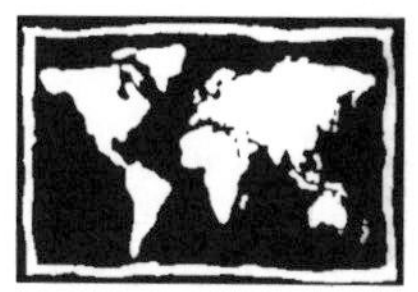

Mail Order

Lonely Planet products are distributed worldwide. They are also available by mail order from Lonely Planet, so if you have difficulty finding a title please write to us. North and South American residents should write to 150 Linden St, Oakland, CA 94607, USA; European and African residents should write to 10a Spring Place, London NW5 3BH, UK; and residents of other countries to PO Box 617, Hawthorn, Victoria 3122, Australia.

ISLANDS OF THE INDIAN OCEAN Madagascar & Comoros • Maldives • Mauritius, Réunion & Seychelles

MIDDLE EAST & CENTRAL ASIA Arab Gulf States • Central Asia • Central Asia phrasebook • Hebrew phrasebook • Iran • Israel & the Palestinian Territories • Israel & the Palestinian Territories travel atlas • Istanbul • Istanbul to Cairo • Jerusalem • Jordan & Syria • Jordan, Syria & Lebanon travel atlas • Lebanon • Middle East on a shoestring • Syria • Turkey • Turkish phrasebook • Turkey travel atlas • Yemen
Travel Literature: The Gates of Damascus • Kingdom of the Film Stars: Journey into Jordan

NORTH AMERICA Alaska • Backpacking in Alaska • Baja California • California & Nevada • Canada • Chicago • Florida • Hawaii • Honolulu • Las Vegas • Los Angeles • Louisiana • Miami • New England USA • New Orleans • New York City • New York, New Jersey & Pennsylvania • Pacific Northwest USA • Puerto Rico • Rocky Mountain States • San Francisco • Seattle • Southwest USA • Texas • USA • USA phrasebook • Vancouver • Washington, DC & the Capital Region
Travel Literature: Drive Thru America

NORTH-EAST ASIA Beijing • Cantonese phrasebook • China • Hong Kong • Hong Kong, Macau & Guangzhou • Japan • Japanese phrasebook • Japanese audio pack • Korea • Korean phrasebook • Kyoto • Mandarin phrasebook • Mongolia • Mongolian phrasebook • North-East Asia on a shoestring • Seoul • South-West China • Taiwan • Tibet • Tibetan phrasebook • Tokyo
Travel Literature: Lost Japan

SOUTH AMERICA Argentina, Uruguay & Paraguay • Bolivia • Brazil • Brazilian phrasebook • Buenos Aires • Chile & Easter Island • Chile & Easter Island travel atlas • Colombia • Ecuador & the Galapagos Islands • Latin American Spanish phrasebook • Peru • Quechua phrasebook • Rio de Janeiro • South America on a shoestring • Trekking in the Patagonian Andes • Venezuela
Travel Literature: Full Circle: A South American Journey

SOUTH-EAST ASIA Bali & Lombok • Bangkok • Burmese phrasebook • Cambodia • Hanoi • Healthy Travel Asia & India • Hill Tribes phrasebook • Ho Chi Minh City • Indonesia • Indonesia's Eastern Islands • Indonesian phrasebook • Indonesian audio pack • Jakarta • Java • Laos • Lao phrasebook • Laos travel atlas • Malay phrasebook • Malaysia, Singapore & Brunei • Myanmar (Burma) • Philippines • Pilipino (Tagalog) phrasebook • Singapore • South-East Asia on a shoestring • South-East Asia phrasebook • Thailand • Thailand's Islands & Beaches • Thailand travel atlas • Thai phrasebook • Thai audio pack • Vietnam • Vietnamese phrasebook • Vietnam travel atlas

ALSO AVAILABLE: Antarctica • The Arctic • Brief Encounters: Stories of Love, Sex & Travel • Chasing Rickshaws • Lonely Planet Unpacked • Not the Only Planet: Travel Stories from Science Fiction • Sacred India • Travel with Children • Traveller's Tales

LONELY PLANET

Lonely Planet Journeys

JOURNEYS is a unique collection of travel writing – published by the company that understands travel better than anyone else. It is a series for anyone who has ever experienced – or dreamed of – the magical moment when they encountered a strange culture or saw a place for the first time. They are tales to read while you're planning a trip, while you're on the road or while you're in an armchair in front of a fire.

These outstanding titles explore our planet through the eyes of a diverse group of international writers. JOURNEYS books catch the spirit of a place, illuminate a culture, recount a crazy adventure or introduce a fascinating way of life. They always entertain, and always enrich the experience of travel.

ISLANDS IN THE CLOUDS
Travels in the Highlands of New Guinea
Isabella Tree

This is the fascinating account of a journey to the remote and beautiful Highlands of Papua New Guinea and Irian Jaya: one of the most extraordinary and dangerous regions on the planet. Tree travels with a PNG Highlander who introduces her to his intriguing and complex world, changing rapidly as it collides with twentieth-century technology. *Islands in the Clouds* is a thoughtful, moving book.

SEAN & DAVID'S LONG DRIVE
Sean Condon

Sean and David are young townies who have rarely strayed beyond city limits. One day, for no good reason, they set out to discover their homeland, and what follows is a wildly entertaining adventure that covers half of Australia.

'a hilariously detailed log of two burned out friends' – *Rolling Stone*

DRIVE THRU AMERICA
Sean Condon

If you've ever wanted to drive across the USA but couldn't find the time (or afford the gas), *Drive Thru America* is perfect for you. In his search for American myths and realities – along with comfort, cable TV and good, reasonably priced coffee – Sean Condon paints a hilarious road-portrait of the USA.

'entertaining and laugh-out-loud funny' – *Alex Wilber, Travel editor, Amazon.com*

BRIEF ENCOUNTERS
Stories of Love, Sex & Travel
edited by Michelle de Kretser

Love affairs on the road, passionate holiday flings, disastrous pick-ups, erotic encounters... In this seductive collection of stories, 22 authors from around the world write about travel romances. Combining fiction and reportage, *Brief Encounters* is must-have reading – for everyone who has dreamt of escape with that perfect stranger.

Includes stories by Pico Iyer, Mary Morris, Emily Perkins, Mona Simpson, Lisa St Aubin de Terán, Paul Theroux and Sara Wheeler.

Lonely Planet Travel Atlases

Lonely Planet has long been famous for the number and quality of its guidebook maps. Now we've gone one step further and produced a handy companion series: Lonely Planet travel atlases – maps of a country produced in book form.

Unlike other maps, which look good but lead travellers astray, our travel atlases have been researched on the road by Lonely Planet's experienced team of writers. All details are carefully checked to ensure the atlas corresponds with the equivalent Lonely Planet guidebook.

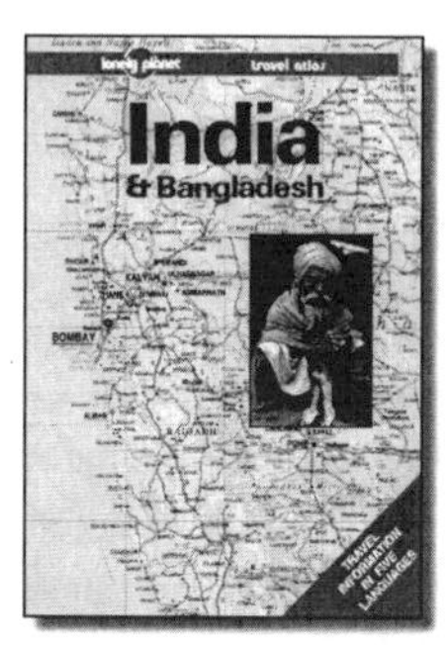

- full-colour throughout
- maps researched and checked by Lonely Planet authors
- place names correspond with Lonely Planet guidebooks
- no confusing spelling differences
- legend and travelling information in English, French, German, Japanese and Spanish
- size: 230 x 160 mm

Available now: Chile & Easter Island • Egypt • India & Bangladesh • Israel & the Palestinian Territories • Jordan, Syria & Lebanon • Kenya • Laos • Portugal • South Africa, Lesotho & Swaziland • Thailand • Turkey • Vietnam • Zimbabwe, Botswana & Namibia

---

Lonely Planet TV Series & Videos

Lonely Planet travel guides have been brought to life on television screens around the world. Like our guides, the programs are based on the joy of independent travel, and look honestly at some of the most exciting, picturesque and frustrating places in the world. Each show is presented by one of three travellers from Australia, England or the USA and combines an innovative mixture of video, Super-8 film, atmospheric soundscapes and original music.

Videos of each episode – containing additional footage not shown on television – are available from good book and video shops, but the availability of individual videos varies with regional screening schedules.

Video destinations include: Alaska • American Rockies • Australia – The South-East • Baja California & the Copper Canyon • Brazil • Central Asia • Chile & Easter Island • Corsica, Sicily & Sardinia – The Mediterranean Islands • East Africa (Tanzania & Zanzibar) • Ecuador & the Galapagos Islands • Greenland & Iceland • Indonesia • Israel & the Sinai Desert • Jamaica • Japan • La Ruta Maya • Morocco • New York • North India • Pacific Islands (Fiji, Solomon Islands & Vanuatu) • South India • South West China • Turkey • Vietnam • West Africa • Zimbabwe, Botswana & Namibia

The Lonely Planet TV series is produced by: Pilot Productions
The Old Studio
18 Middle Row
London W10 5AT, UK

Lonely Planet On-line

Whether you've just begun planning your next trip, or you're chasing down specific info on currency regulations or visa requirements, check out Lonely Planet On-line for up-to-the minute travel information.

As well as mini guides to more than 250 destinations, you'll find maps, photos, travel news, health and visa updates, travel advisories, and discussion of the ecological and political issues you need to be aware of as you travel. You'll also find timely upgrades to popular guidebooks which you can print out and stick in the back of your book.

There's also an on-line travellers' forum where you can share your experience of life on the road, meet travel companions and ask other travellers for their recommendations and advice.

And of course we have a complete and up-to-date list of all Lonely Planet travel products including travel guides, diving and snorkeling guides, phrasebooks, atlases, travel literature and videos, and a simple on-line ordering facility if you can't find the book you want elsewhere.

Lonely Planet Diving & Snorkeling Guides

Beautifully illustrated with full-colour photos throughout, Lonely Planet s Pisces Books explore the world s best diving and snorkeling areas and prepare divers for what to expect when they get there, both topside and underwater.

Dive sites are described in detail with specifics on depths, visibility, level of difficulty, special conditions, underwater photography tips and common and unusual marine life present. You ll also find practical logistical information and coverage on topside activities and attractions, sections on diving health and safety, plus listings for diving services, live-aboards, dive resorts and tourist offices.

FREE Lonely Planet Newsletters

We love hearing from you and think you'd like to hear from us.

Planet Talk

Our FREE quarterly printed newsletter is full of tips from travellers and anecdotes from Lonely Planet guidebook authors. Every issue is packed with up-to-date travel news and advice, and includes:

- a postcard from Lonely Planet co-founder Tony Wheeler
- a swag of mail from travellers
- a look at life on the road through the eyes of a Lonely Planet author
- topical health advice
- prizes for the best travel yarn
- news about forthcoming Lonely Planet events
- a complete list of Lonely Planet books and other titles

To join our mailing list, residents of the UK, Europe and Africa can email us at go@lonelyplanet.co.uk; residents of North and South America can email us at info@lonelyplanet.com; the rest of the world can email us at talk2us@lonelyplanet.com.au, or contact any Lonely Planet office.

Comet

Our FREE monthly email newsletter brings you all the latest travel news, features, interviews, competitions, destination ideas, travellers' tips & tales, Q&As, raging debates and related links. Find out what's new on the Lonely Planet Web site and which books are about to hit the shelves.

Subscribe from your desktop: www.lonelyplanet.com/comet

Index

Text

Bold indicates maps.

Boxed Text

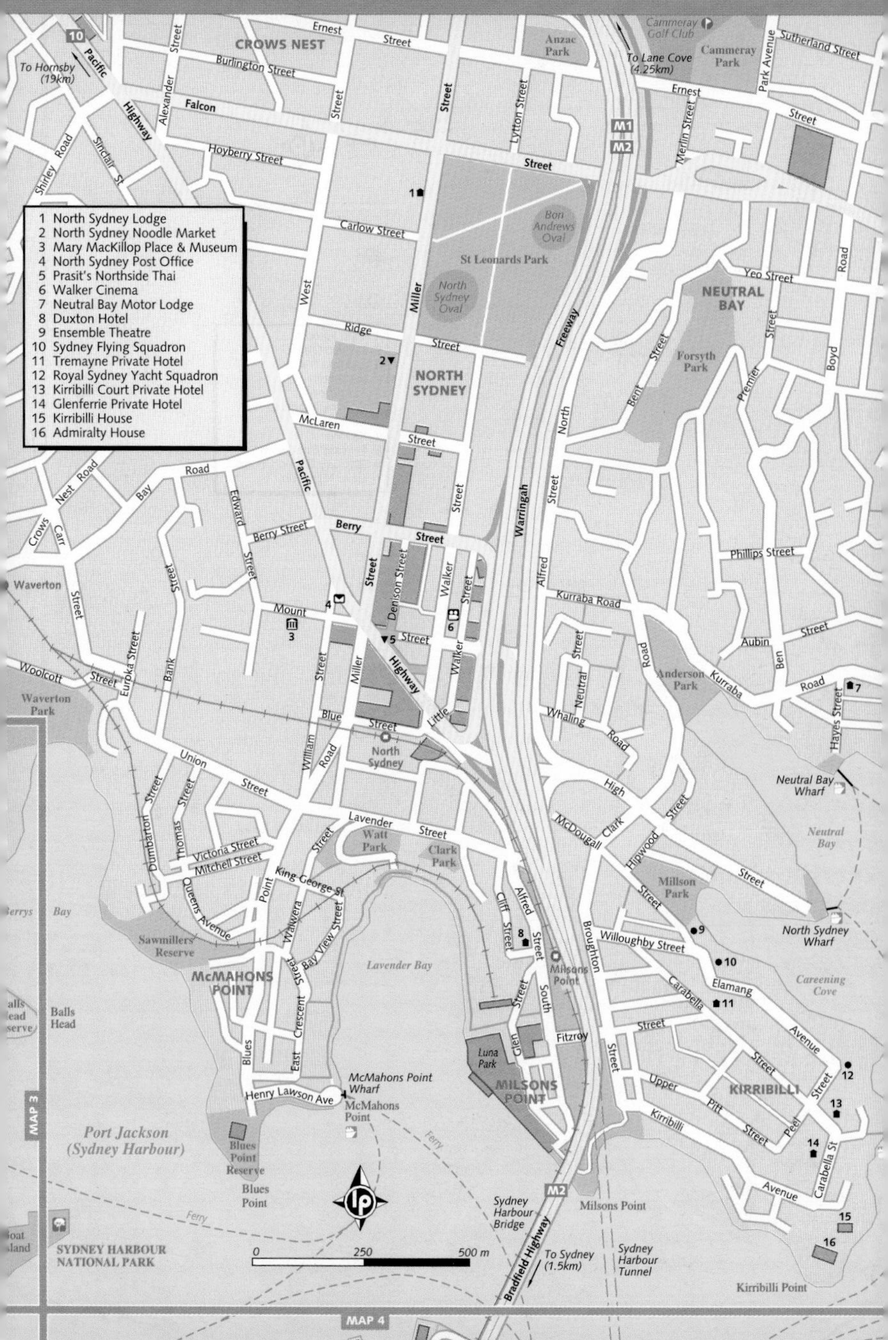
1 North Sydney Lodge
2 North Sydney Noodle Market
3 Mary MacKillop Place & Museum
4 North Sydney Post Office
5 Prasit's Northside Thai
6 Walker Cinema
7 Neutral Bay Motor Lodge
8 Duxton Hotel
9 Ensemble Theatre
10 Sydney Flying Squadron
11 Tremayne Private Hotel
12 Royal Sydney Yacht Squadron
13 Kirribilli Court Private Hotel
14 Glenferrie Private Hotel
15 Kirribilli House
16 Admiralty House
CROWS NEST
NORTH SYDNEY
NEUTRAL BAY
McMAHONS POINT
MILSONS POINT
KIRRIBILLI
To Hornsby (19km)
To Lane Cove (4.25km)
To Sydney (1.5km)
Cammeray Golf Club
Cammeray Park
Anzac Park
St Leonards Park
Bon Andrews Oval
North Sydney Oval
Forsyth Park
Anderson Park
Millson Park
Watt Park
Clark Park
Sawmillers Reserve
Waverton Park
Blues Point Reserve
Luna Park
Port Jackson (Sydney Harbour)
Lavender Bay
Neutral Bay
Careening Cove
Neutral Bay Wharf
North Sydney Wharf
McMahons Point Wharf
Sydney Harbour Bridge
Sydney Harbour Tunnel
Bradfield Highway
Warringah Freeway
Pacific Highway
SYDNEY HARBOUR NATIONAL PARK
Kirribilli Point
Balls Head
Blues Point
Milsons Point
Waverton
North Sydney
MAP 3
MAP 4
0 250 500 m

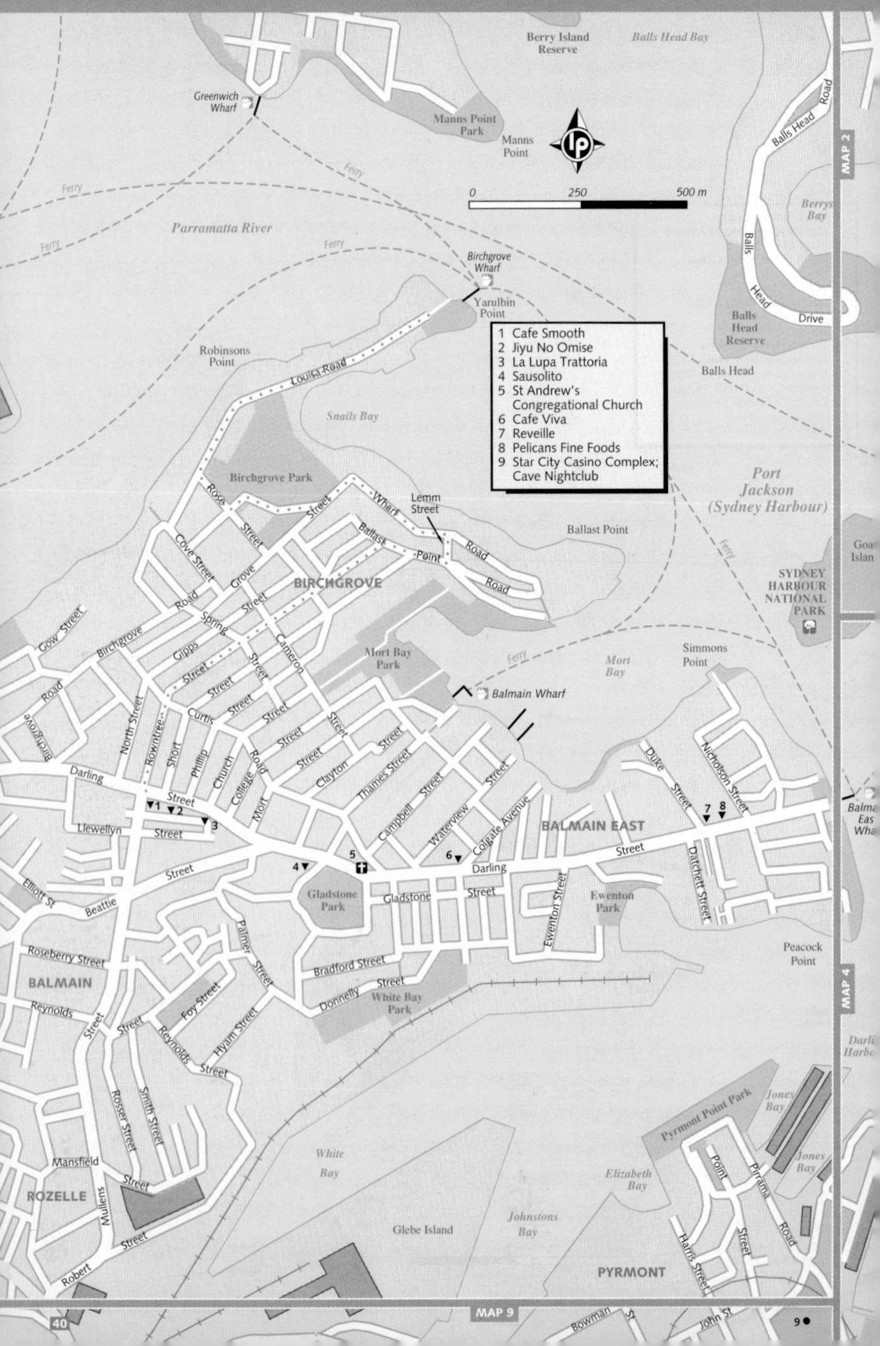
1 Cafe Smooth
2 Jiyu No Omise
3 La Lupa Trattoria
4 Sausolito
5 St Andrew's Congregational Church
6 Cafe Viva
7 Reveille
8 Pelicans Fine Foods
9 Star City Casino Complex; Cave Nightclub
0 250 500 m
Berry Island Reserve
Balls Head Bay
Greenwich Wharf
Manns Point Park
Manns Point
Parramatta River
Ferry
Birchgrove Wharf
Yarulbin Point
Robinsons Point
Louisa Road
Snails Bay
Birchgrove Park
Balls Head Reserve
Balls Head
Balls Head Road
Balls Head Drive
Berrys Bay
Port Jackson (Sydney Harbour)
Lemm Street
Ballast Point
Ballast Point Road
Wharf Road
BIRCHGROVE
SYDNEY HARBOUR NATIONAL PARK
Mort Bay Park
Mort Bay
Simmons Point
Balmain Wharf
BALMAIN EAST
Darling Street
Gladstone Park
Gladstone Street
Ewenton Park
Ewenton Street
Peacock Point
White Bay Park
BALMAIN
ROZELLE
White Bay
Glebe Island
Johnstons Bay
Elizabeth Bay
Pyrmont Point Park
Jones Bay
PYRMONT
MAP 2
MAP 4
MAP 9
40

RICHARD I'ANSON

View of North Sydney and beyond

RICHARD I'ANSON

Picturesque East Balmain

COLIN K BARNES

The *QEII* and ferries, Sydney Harbour

MAP 4 – CENTRAL SYDNEY

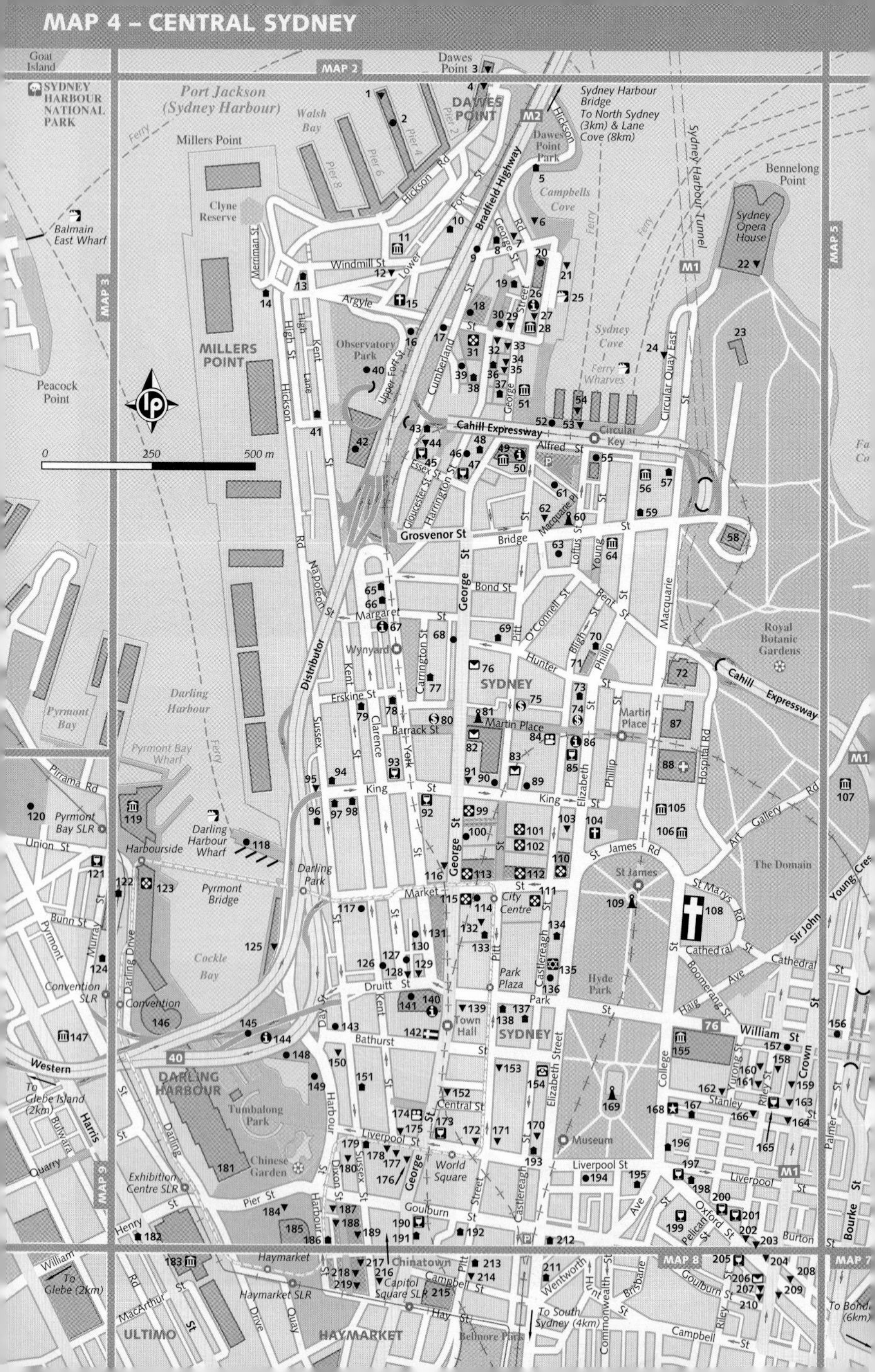

PLACES TO STAY

5 Park Hyatt
8 Mercantile Hotel
10 Harbour View Hotel
13 Lord Nelson Brewery Hotel
14 Palisade Hotel
19 Old Sydney Parkroyal Hotel
36 Harbour Rocks Hotel
37 Russell Hotel
38 Stafford Hotel
41 Observatory Hotel
43 ANA Hotel
48 Regent Hotel; Kables
57 Ritz-Carlton Hotel
59 Hotel Intercontinental
65 York Apartment Hotel
66 Sydney Vista Hotel
69 Grand Hotel
70 Wentworth Hotel
73 Sydney City Centre Apartments
77 Menzies Hotel
78 Carrington Apartments
79 Wynyard Hotel
94 Metro Inn
96 Hotel Nikko
97 Metro Inn Apartments
98 Savoy Apartments
122 Hotel Ibis
124 Novotel Sydney Hotel
133 Sydney Hilton; Marble Bar
134 Sheraton on the Park
137 Park Regis
138 Criterion Hotel
151 Downtown Serviced Apartments
167 Sydney Park Inn
179 Waldorf
182 Glasgow Arms Hotel
186 Furama Hotel; Shipley's Restaurant
191 George Hotel
192 CB Private Hotel
193 Hyde Park Inn
195 YWCA; YWCA Cafe
196 Hyde Park Plaza Hotel; Sydney Marriot Hotel
198 Parkridge Corporate Apartments
211 Sydney Central Private Hotel
212 Southern Cross Hotel
213 Westend Hotel

PLACES TO EAT

1 Wharf Restaurant
3 Harbour Watch
4 Harbourside Brasserie
6 Campbell's Storehouse (Wolfie's; Waterfront; Italian Village)
7 Metcalfe Arcade; Pancakes on the Rocks
12 Hero of Waterloo
21 Quay (restaurant); Doyle's at the Quay
22 Bennelong Restaurant; Harbour; Concourse
24 Sydney Cove Oyster Bar; Portobello Caffe
27 Sailor's Thai
29 G'day Cafe
32 Gum Nut Tea Garden
33 Phillip's Foote; Rocks Cafe
34 Rockpool
35 Vault; Fortune of War
44 Rocks Teppanyaki
53 City Extra; Rossini
54 Casa Del Gelato
62 Obelisk
91 Coles Express; NRMA
95 Slipp-Inn; Dundee Arms Tavern
103 Bar Coluzzi
116 Deli on Market
125 Cockle Bay Wharf (The Health Tree; Schwob's Swiss; Chinta Ria; Home Nightclub)
128 Hotel Sweeney
129 Zenergy
132 Arizona's
139 Woolworths
150 Marigold
152 Planet Hollywood
153 Edinburgh Castle Hotel & Pitt St Bistro
158 The Edge
159 Hard Rock Cafe
160 Baraza Cafe
161 Pacifico
162 Beppi's
163 Bill & Toni; Cafe Divino; Palati Fini
164 No Names Restaurant; Arch Coffee Lounge
166 Two Chefs
170 Hellenic Club
171 Diethnes
172 Mother Chu's Vegetarian Kitchen
175 Vender
176 Sir John Young Hotel; Grand Taverna
177 Casa Asturiana
178 Capitan Torres
180 Regal
184 Pumphouse Tavern Brewery
187 Harbour Plaza
188 New Tai Yuen
189 Sussex Centre
202 1 Burton
203 Don Don
204 Thai Panic
207 Roobar; Fatz
208 Betty's Soup Kitchen; Tandoori Palace
209 Tamana's; North Indian Flavour
210 Pablo's Vice
214 Chamberlain Hotel
216 Ching Yip Coffee Lounge
217 Dixon House Food Court
218 Hingara
219 Old Tai Yuen

PUBS & CLUBS

45 Harts Pub; Quay West Sydney
47 George St Bar
85 Wine Banc
92 Forbes Hotel
93 CBD Hotel; Eden Travel
121 Pyrmont Bridge Hotel
165 Lord Roberts Hotel
173 Century Tavern
190 Scuffy Murphy's
197 Burdekin Hotel
199 DCM
200 Exchange Hotel; Oxford Koala Hotel
201 Q Bar
205 Midnight Shift

OTHER

2 Pier Four (Sydney Dance Company; Sydney Theatre Company; Wharf Theatre; Bangarra Dance Theatre)
9 NAISDA Studios (Indigenous Dance); Bridgeclimb
11 Colonial House Museum
15 Garrison Church
16 Pedestrian Access to Harbour Bridge
17 Argyle Cut
18 Argyle Centre
20 Ken Done Gallery
23 Government House
25 Overseas Passenger Terminal
26 Sydney Visitors Centre
28 Cadman's Cottage
30 Rocks Centre
31 Clocktower Square Shopping Centre
39 Susannah Place
40 Sydney Observatory
42 National Trust Centre
46 Site of Public Gallows; Sydney's First Jail
49 Gold Fields House
50 City Host Visitor Information Booth
51 Museum of Contemporary Art; MCA Cafe
52 Australian Travel Specialists (CQ)
55 Customs House Arts and Cultural Centre
56 Justice & Police Museum
58 Conservatorium of Music
60 Obelisk
61 The Basement
63 Lands Department Building
64 Museum of Sydney
67 Countrylink Travel Centre
68 Paxton's
71 Qantas Centre
72 State Library
74 Commonwealth Bank
75 American Express
76 Post Restante
80 Westpac Bank; National Australia Bank
81 Cenotaph
82 GPO (Martin Place)
83 GPO (counter service)
84 Dendy Cinema; Dendy Bar & Bistro
86 City Host Visitor Information Booth
87 Parliament House
88 Sydney Hospital
89 Theatre Royal
90 Thomas Cook
99 Strand Arcade; Harris Coffee and Tea
100 Dymocks Bookshop; Travellers Contact Point
101 Skygarden Arcade; Il Gianfornaio
102 Imperial Arcade
104 St James' Church
105 Sydney Mint Museum
106 Hyde Park Barracks Museum
107 Art Gallery of NSW
108 St Mary's Cathedral
109 Archibald Memorial Fountain
110 David Jones
111 David Jones
112 Sydney Tower; Centrepoint; Revolving Restaurants
113 Grace Brothers
114 State Theatre
115 Gowings
117 Halftix
118 Sydney Aquarium
119 Australian National Maritime Museum
120 Star City Casino Complex
123 Harbourside (Gavala; Festival Cafe; Zaaffran; Shakespeare's Pies; Jordon's; Jo Jo's)
126 YHA Membership & Travel Centre
127 Innes Bicycles
130 Abbey's Bookshop
131 Queen Victoria Building; Bar Cupola
135 Great Synagogue
136 Ticketek
140 City Host Information Kiosk
141 Town Hall
142 St Andrew's Cathedral
143 Paddy Pallin; Mountain Design
144 Darling Harbour Visitors' Centre
145 IMAX Theatre
146 Motor Vehicle Museum
147 Sydney Convention Centre
148 Darling Walk; Sega World
149 Australia's Northern Territory & Outback Centre
154 Telstra Payphone Centre
155 Australian Museum
156 Eastern Distributor Tunnel Exit
157 Thrifty Car Rental
168 NSW Police Headquarters
169 Anzac Memorial
174 Cinema Complex
181 Sydney Exhibition Centre
183 Powerhouse Museum
185 Sydney Entertainment Centre
194 Travel Bookshop
206 Post Office
215 Capitol Theatre

MAP 5 – POTTS POINT

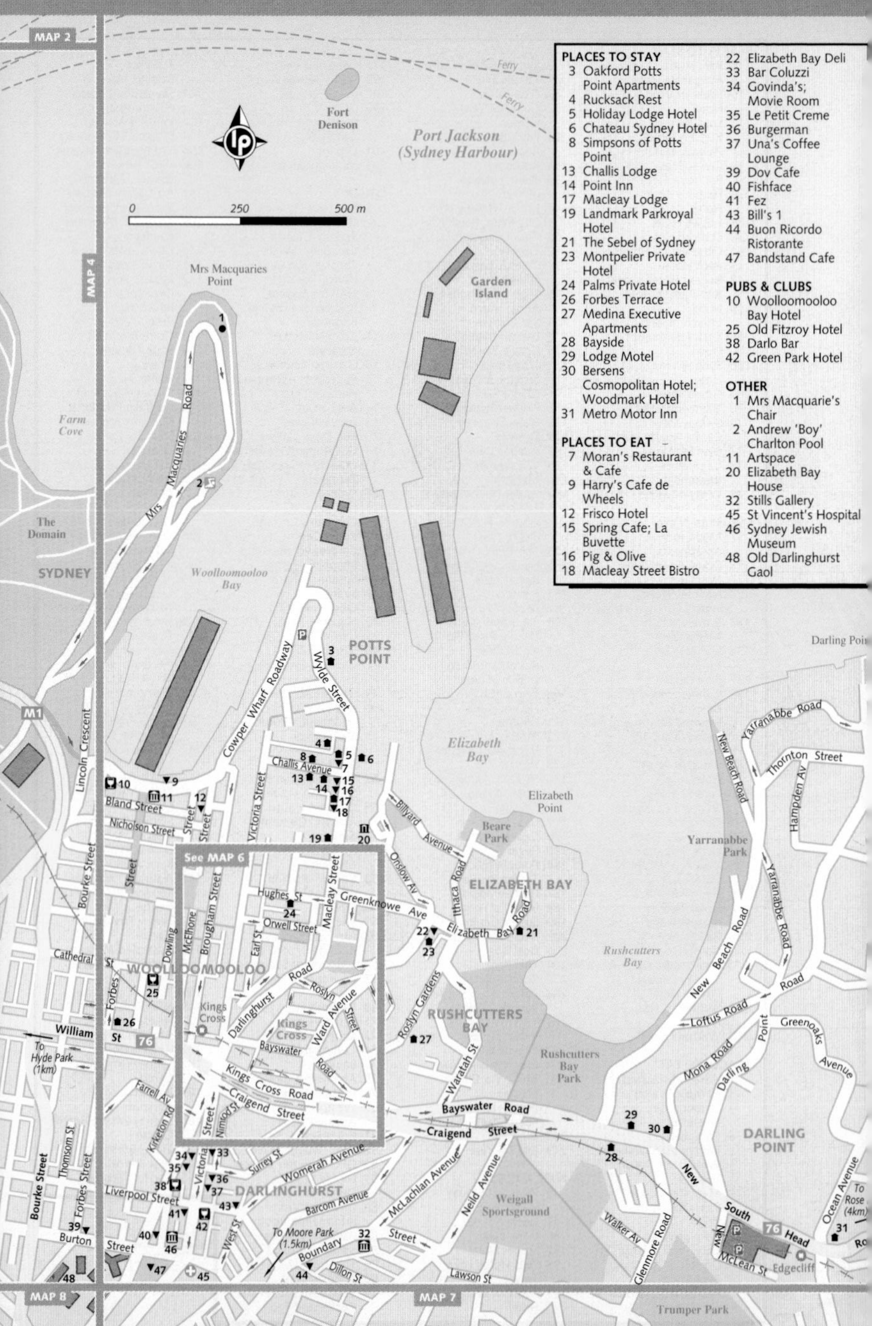
PLACES TO STAY
3 Oakford Potts Point Apartments
4 Rucksack Rest
5 Holiday Lodge Hotel
6 Chateau Sydney Hotel
8 Simpsons of Potts Point
13 Challis Lodge
14 Point Inn
17 Macleay Lodge
19 Landmark Parkroyal Hotel
21 The Sebel of Sydney
23 Montpelier Private Hotel
24 Palms Private Hotel
26 Forbes Terrace
27 Medina Executive Apartments
28 Bayside
29 Lodge Motel
30 Bersens Cosmopolitan Hotel; Woodmark Hotel
31 Metro Motor Inn
PLACES TO EAT
7 Moran's Restaurant & Cafe
9 Harry's Cafe de Wheels
12 Frisco Hotel
15 Spring Cafe; La Buvette
16 Pig & Olive
18 Macleay Street Bistro
22 Elizabeth Bay Deli
33 Bar Coluzzi
34 Govinda's; Movie Room
35 Le Petit Creme
36 Burgerman
37 Una's Coffee Lounge
39 Dov Cafe
40 Fishface
41 Fez
43 Bill's 1
44 Buon Ricordo Ristorante
47 Bandstand Cafe
PUBS & CLUBS
10 Woolloomooloo Bay Hotel
25 Old Fitzroy Hotel
38 Darlo Bar
42 Green Park Hotel
OTHER
1 Mrs Macquarie's Chair
2 Andrew 'Boy' Charlton Pool
11 Artspace
20 Elizabeth Bay House
32 Stills Gallery
45 St Vincent's Hospital
46 Sydney Jewish Museum
48 Old Darlinghurst Gaol
MAP 2
MAP 4
MAP 6
MAP 7
MAP 8
See MAP 6
Ferry
Fort Denison
Port Jackson (Sydney Harbour)
0
250
500 m
Mrs Macquaries Point
Mrs Macquaries Road
Farm Cove
The Domain
SYDNEY
Woolloomooloo Bay
Garden Island
POTTS POINT
Elizabeth Bay
Elizabeth Point
Beare Park
ELIZABETH BAY
Rushcutters Bay
RUSHCUTTERS BAY
Rushcutters Bay Park
Yarranabbe Park
Darling Point
DARLING POINT
WOOLLOOMOOLOO
Kings Cross
DARLINGHURST
Weigall Sportsground
Trumper Park
Edgecliff
Cowper Wharf Roadway
Wylde Street
Challis Avenue
Victoria Street
Bland Street
Nicholson Street
Lincoln Crescent
Bourke Street
Billyard Avenue
Onslow Av
Ithaca Road
Elizabeth Bay Road
Greenknowe Ave
Hughes St
Orwell Street
Macleay Street
Brougham Street
McElhone
Dowling
Earl St
Cathedral St
Forbes
William St
To Hyde Park (1km)
Darlinghurst Road
Roslyn
Ward Avenue
Bayswater
Kings Cross Road
Craigend Street
Bayswater Road
Roslyn Gardens
Waratah St
Farrell Av
Kirketon Rd
Nimrod St
Surrey St
Womerah Avenue
Liverpool Street
Barcom Avenue
McLachlan Avenue
Neild Avenue
Thomson St
Forbes Street
Burton Street
West St
To Moore Park (1.5km)
Boundary Street
Dillon St
Lawson St
Walker Av
Glenmore Road
New South Head Road
New McLean St
Ocean Avenue
To Rose Bay (4km)
Yarranabbe Road
New Beach Road
Thornton Street
Hampden Av
Loftus Road
Mona Road
Darling Point Road
Greenoaks Avenue
M1
76

The bustling Harbour in front of the Rocks

RICHARD I'ANSON

The famous Lord Nelson pub at the Rocks

SIMON BRACKEN

Detail of the Powerhouse Museum

TOM SMALLMAN

Elizabeth Bay House was the finest in the colony.

SIMON BRACKEN

MAP 6 – KINGS CROSS

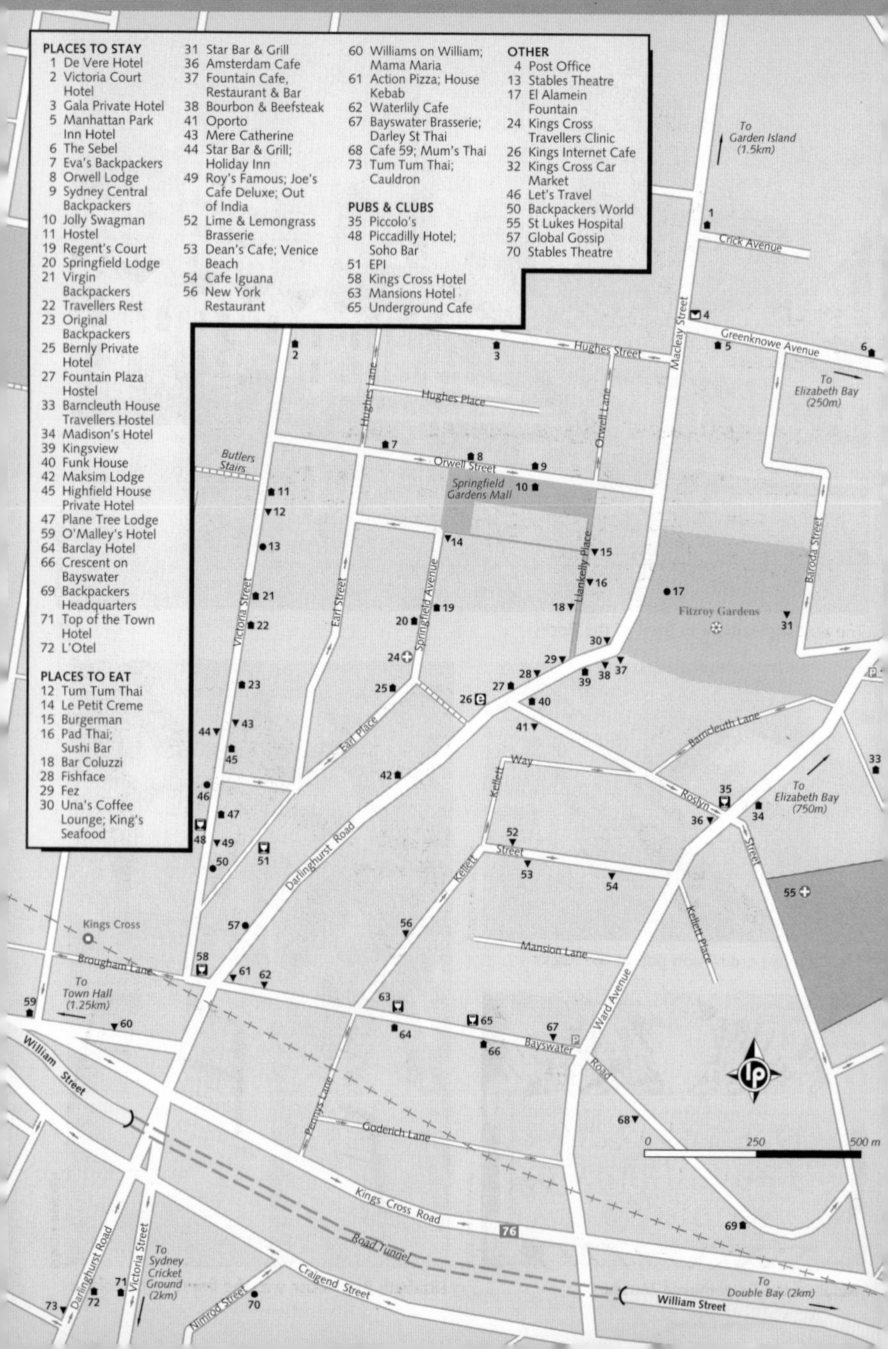

RICHARD I'ANSON

Inside the beautiful Queen Victoria Building

MAP 7 – PADDINGTON

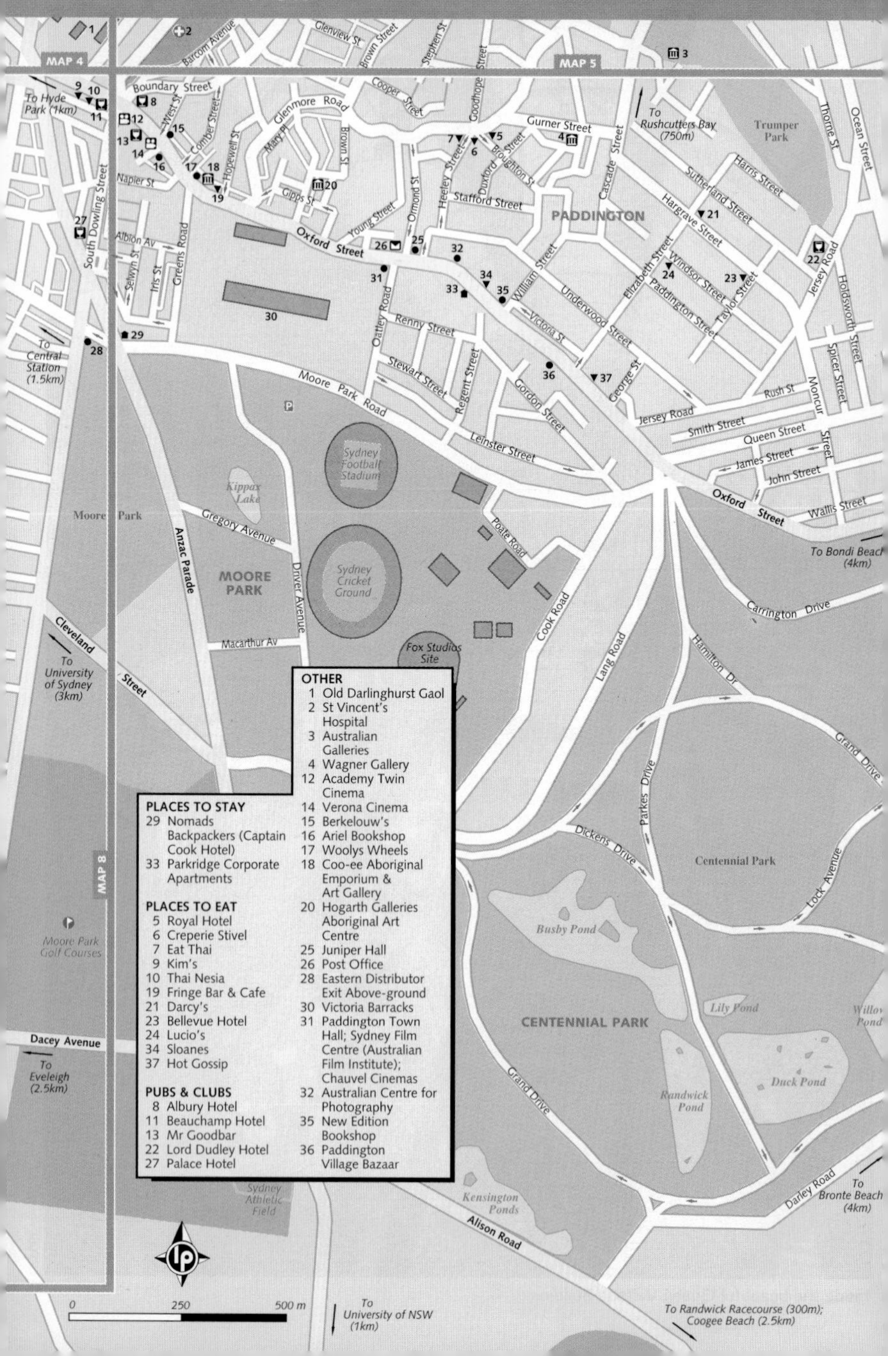

MIKE COTTEEE

Spaghetti-eating contest at Norton Community Festival, Leichhardt

SIMON BRACKEN

Vaucluse House in the exclusive suburb of Vaucluse

MAP 8 – SURRY HILLS

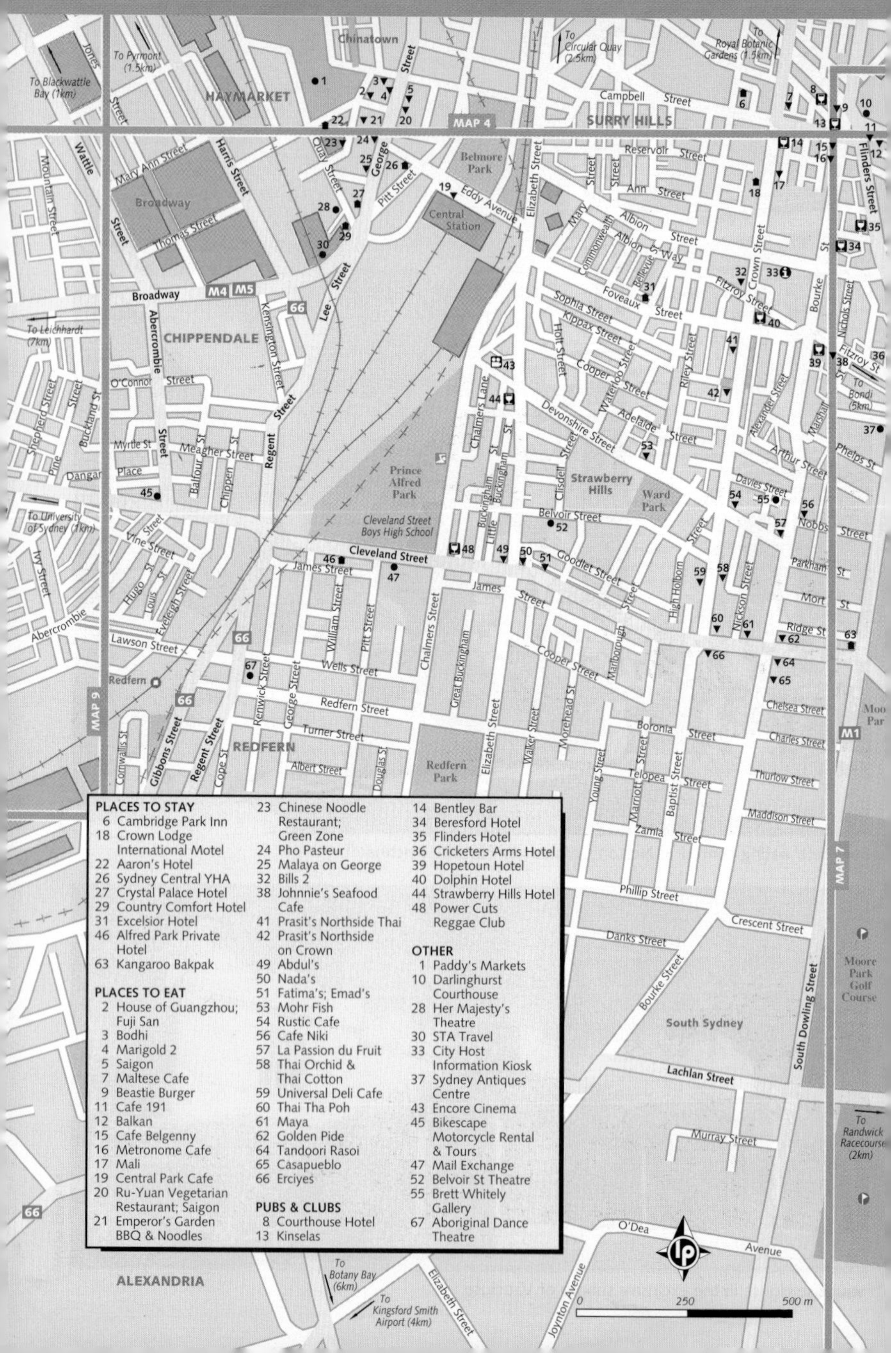

SIMON BRACKEN

The small fortified island of Fort Denison was originally used to isolate troublesome convicts.

SIMON BRACKEN

Archibald Memorial Fountain, Hyde Park ...

ROSS BARNETT

... more statues in the fountain

ROSS BARNETT

Anzac War Memorial, Hyde Park

MAP 9 – GLEBE

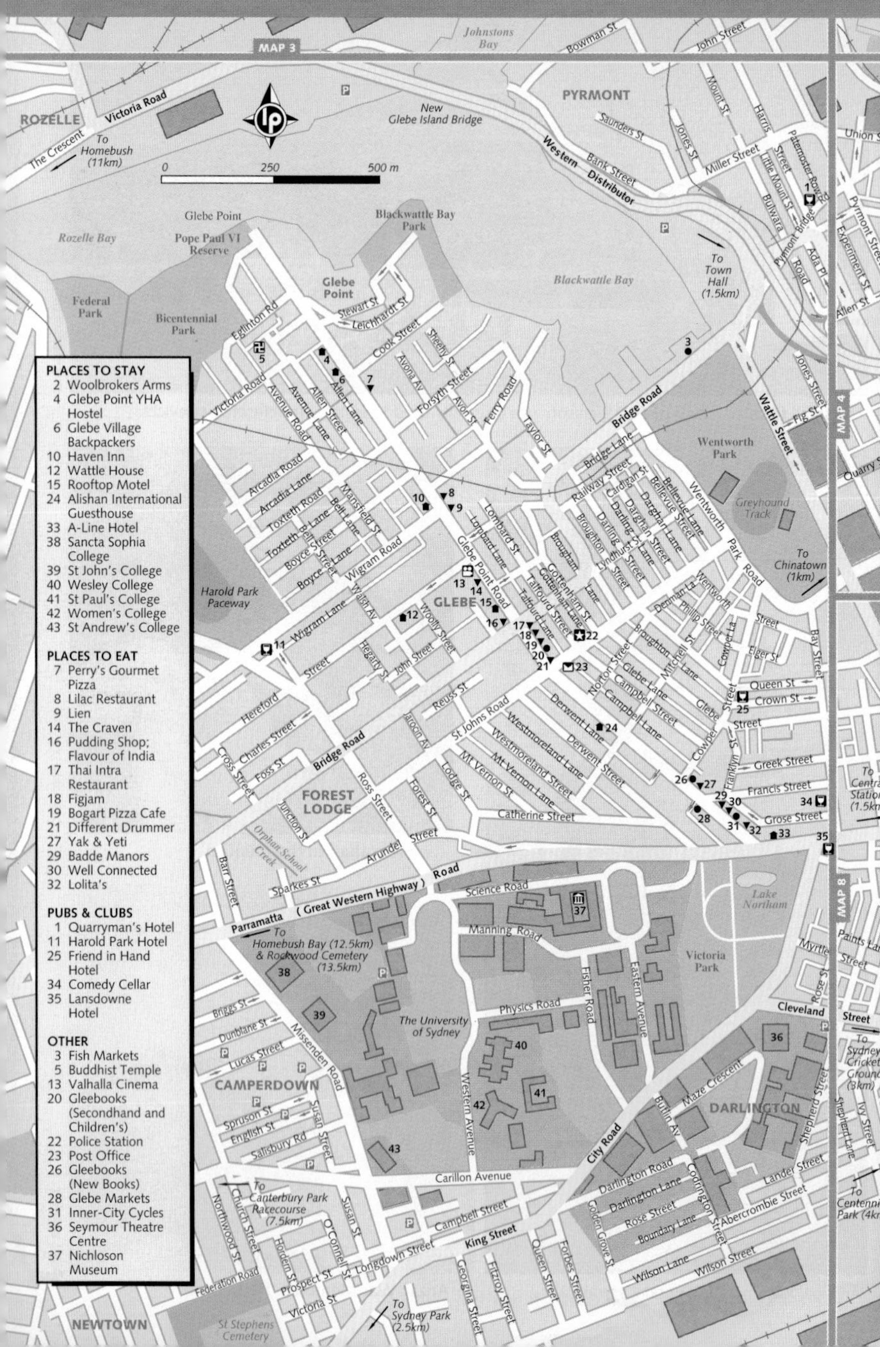

PLACES TO STAY
2 Woolbrokers Arms
4 Glebe Point YHA Hostel
6 Glebe Village Backpackers
10 Haven Inn
12 Wattle House
15 Rooftop Motel
24 Alishan International Guesthouse
33 A-Line Hotel
38 Sancta Sophia College
39 St John's College
40 Wesley College
41 St Paul's College
42 Women's College
43 St Andrew's College
PLACES TO EAT
7 Perry's Gourmet Pizza
8 Lilac Restaurant
9 Lien
14 The Craven
16 Pudding Shop; Flavour of India
17 Thai Intra Restaurant
18 Figjam
19 Bogart Pizza Cafe
21 Different Drummer
27 Yak & Yeti
29 Badde Manors
30 Well Connected
32 Lolita's
PUBS & CLUBS
1 Quarryman's Hotel
11 Harold Park Hotel
25 Friend in Hand Hotel
34 Comedy Cellar
35 Lansdowne Hotel
OTHER
3 Fish Markets
5 Buddhist Temple
13 Valhalla Cinema
20 Gleebooks (Secondhand and Children's)
22 Police Station
23 Post Office
26 Gleebooks (New Books)
28 Glebe Markets
31 Inner-City Cycles
36 Seymour Theatre Centre
37 Nichloson Museum
MAP 3
MAP 4
MAP 8
0
250
500 m
ROZELLE
PYRMONT
GLEBE
FOREST LODGE
CAMPERDOWN
DARLINGTON
NEWTOWN
Johnstons Bay
Rozelle Bay
Blackwattle Bay
Glebe Point
Pope Paul VI Reserve
Blackwattle Bay Park
Federal Park
Bicentennial Park
Harold Park Paceway
Wentworth Park
Greyhound Track
Victoria Park
Lake Northam
The University of Sydney
St Stephens Cemetery
New Glebe Island Bridge
Western Distributor
Victoria Road
The Crescent
Bridge Road
Glebe Point Road
Wattle Street
Parramatta (Great Western Highway) Road
City Road
Cleveland Street
King Street
Carillon Avenue
To Homebush (11km)
To Town Hall (1.5km)
To Chinatown (1km)
To Central Station (1.5km)
To Homebush Bay (12.5km) & Rockwood Cemetery (13.5km)
To Sydney Cricket Ground (3km)
To Canterbury Park Racecourse (7.5km)
To Sydney Park (2.5km)
To Centennial Park (4km)

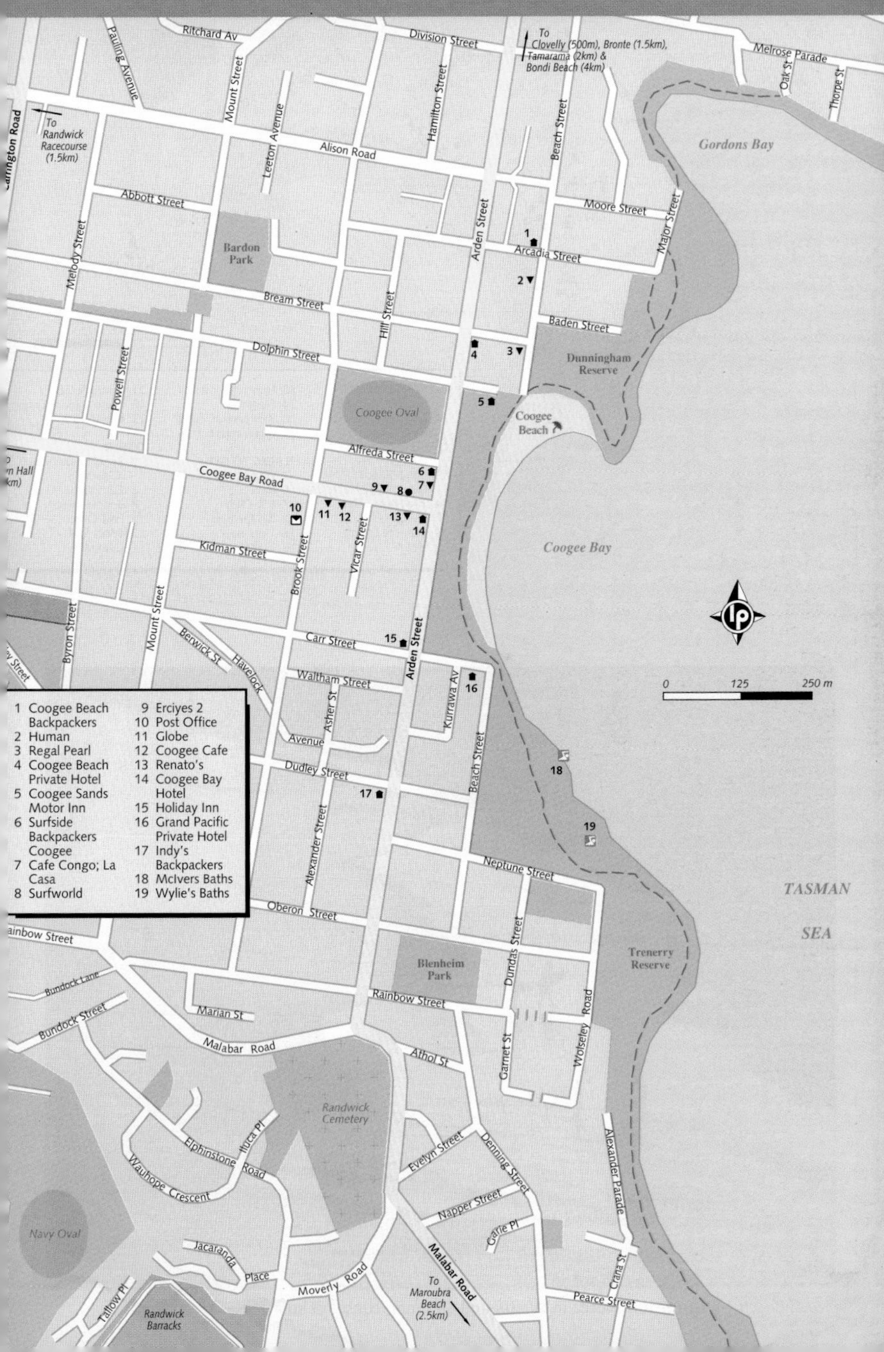

Ritchard Av
Division Street
To Clovelly (500m), Bronte (1.5km), Tamarama (2km) & Bondi Beach (4km)
Melrose Parade
Oak St
Thorpe St
Pauling Avenue
Mount Street
Leeton Avenue
Hamilton Street
Beach Street
To Randwick Racecourse (1.5km)
Alison Road
Gordons Bay
Abbott Street
Moore Street
Major Street
Melody Street
Bardon Park
Arden Street
Arcadia Street
Bream Street
Hill Street
Baden Street
Dolphin Street
Dunningham Reserve
Powell Street
Coogee Oval
Coogee Beach
Alfreda Street
Coogee Bay Road
Kidman Street
Brook Street
Vicar Street
Coogee Bay
Byron Street
Carr Street
Berwick St
Havelock
Waltham Street
Kurrawa Av
Asher St
Avenue
Dudley Street
0 125 250 m
Alexander Street
Neptune Street
TASMAN SEA
Oberon Street
Dundas Street
Trenerry Reserve
Rainbow Street
Blenheim Park
Bundock Lane
Marian St
Wolseley Road
Bundock Street
Malabar Road
Athol St
Garnet St
Randwick Cemetery
Elphinstone Road
Ilfuca Pl
Evelyn Street
Denning Street
Alexander Parade
Wauhope Crescent
Napper Street
Navy Oval
Carrie Pl
Jacaranda Place
Crana St
Moverly Road
To Maroubra Beach (2.5km)
Pearce Street
Tallow Pl
Randwick Barracks
1 Coogee Beach Backpackers
2 Human
3 Regal Pearl
4 Coogee Beach Private Hotel
5 Coogee Sands Motor Inn
6 Surfside Backpackers Coogee
7 Cafe Congo; La Casa
8 Surfworld
9 Erciyes 2
10 Post Office
11 Globe
12 Coogee Cafe
13 Renato's
14 Coogee Bay Hotel
15 Holiday Inn
16 Grand Pacific Private Hotel
17 Indy's Backpackers
18 McIvers Baths
19 Wylie's Baths

MAP 11 – BONDI BEACH

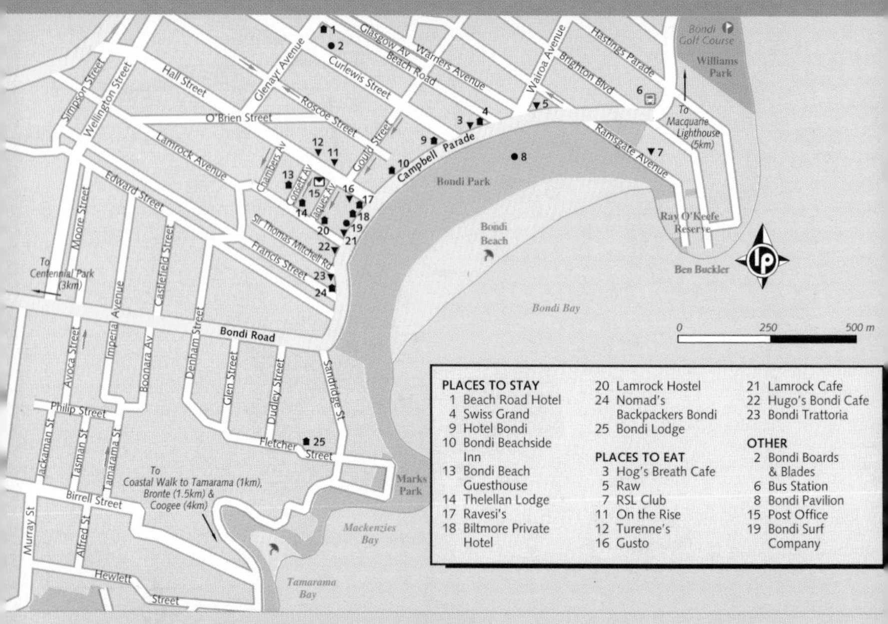

Bondi Beach – a sun & surf mecca in Winter and Summer, sunset or sunrise

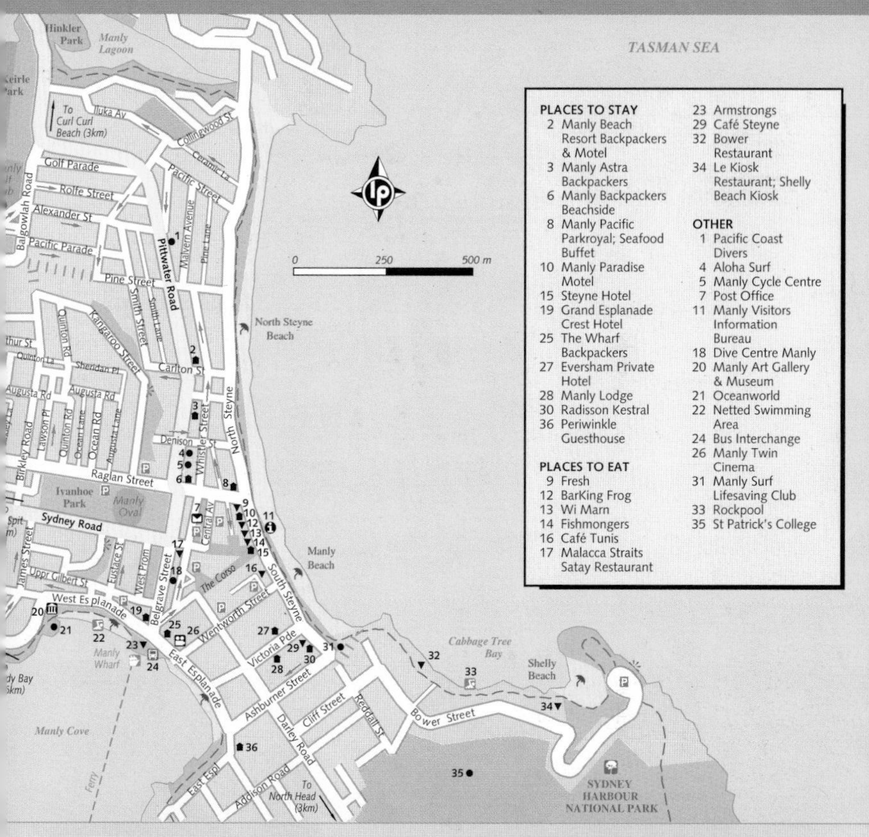

RICHARD I'ANSON

Manly Oceanworld – the best place for fresh seafood!

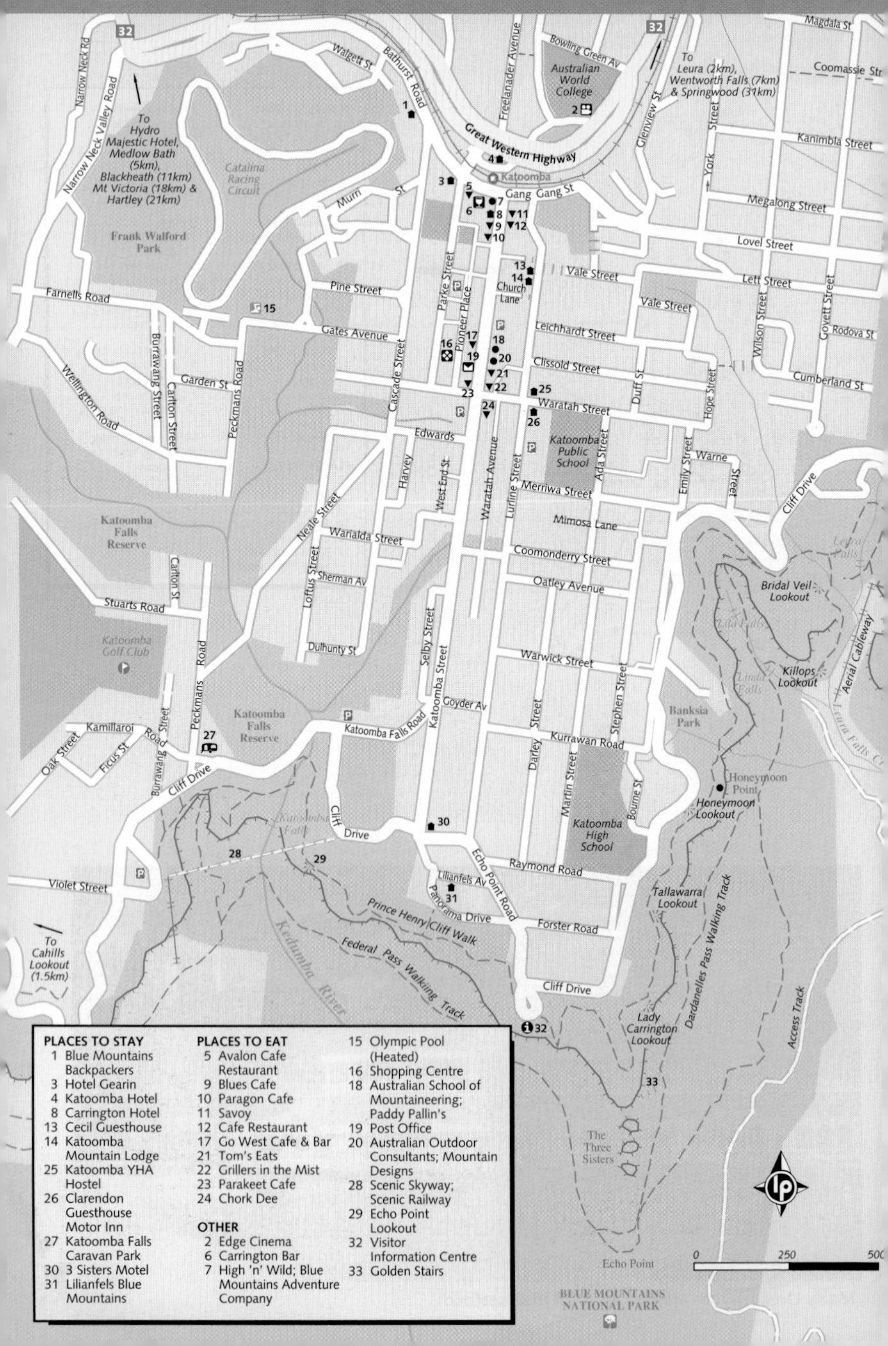

PLACES TO STAY
1 Blue Mountains Backpackers
3 Hotel Gearin
4 Katoomba Hotel
8 Carrington Hotel
13 Cecil Guesthouse
14 Katoomba Mountain Lodge
25 Katoomba YHA Hostel
26 Clarendon Guesthouse Motor Inn
27 Katoomba Falls Caravan Park
30 3 Sisters Motel
31 Lilianfels Blue Mountains
PLACES TO EAT
5 Avalon Cafe Restaurant
9 Blues Cafe
10 Paragon Cafe
11 Savoy
12 Cafe Restaurant
17 Go West Cafe & Bar
21 Tom's Eats
22 Grillers in the Mist
23 Parakeet Cafe
24 Chork Dee
OTHER
2 Edge Cinema
6 Carrington Bar
7 High 'n' Wild; Blue Mountains Adventure Company
15 Olympic Pool (Heated)
16 Shopping Centre
18 Australian School of Mountaineering; Paddy Pallin's
19 Post Office
20 Australian Outdoor Consultants; Mountain Designs
28 Scenic Skyway; Scenic Railway
29 Echo Point Lookout
32 Visitor Information Centre
33 Golden Stairs
To Hydro Majestic Hotel, Medlow Bath (5km), Blackheath (11km) Mt Victoria (18km) & Hartley (21km)
To Leura (2km), Wentworth Falls (7km) & Springwood (31km)
To Cahills Lookout (1.5km)
Great Western Highway
Katoomba
Australian World College
Catalina Racing Circuit
Frank Walford Park
Katoomba Falls Reserve
Katoomba Golf Club
Katoomba Public School
Katoomba High School
Banksia Park
Bridal Veil Lookout
Leura Falls
Lila Falls
Linda Falls
Killops Lookout
Aerial Cableway
Honeymoon Point
Honeymoon Lookout
Tallawarra Lookout
Lady Carrington Lookout
Dardanelles Pass Walking Track
Access Track
The Three Sisters
Echo Point
Katoomba Falls
Prince Henry Cliff Walk
Federal Pass Walking Track
Kedumba River
BLUE MOUNTAINS NATIONAL PARK
Narrow Neck Valley Road
Narrow Neck Rd
Walgett St
Bathurst Road
Freelanader Avenue
Bowling Green Av
Glenview St
York Street
Magdala St
Coomassie St
Kanimbla Street
Megalong Street
Lovel Street
Lett Street
Vale Street
Gang Gang St
Murri St
Parke Street
Pioneer Place
Church Lane
Pine Street
Farnells Road
Gates Avenue
Leichhardt Street
Clissold Street
Cumberland St
Rodova St
Wilson Street
Govett Street
Hope Street
Duff St
Garden St
Burrawang Street
Carlton Street
Peckmans Road
Wellington Road
Cascade Street
Waratah Street
Edwards
Harvey
West End St
Waratah Avenue
Lurline Street
Ada Street
Emily Street
Warne Street
Merriwa Street
Mimosa Lane
Neale Street
Warialda Street
Loftus Street
Sherman Av
Coomonderry Street
Oatley Avenue
Cliff Drive
Stuarts Road
Carlton St
Dulhunty St
Selby Street
Katoomba Street
Warwick Street
Stephen Street
Goyder Av
Katoomba Falls Road
Darley Street
Kurrawan Road
Martin Street
Bourne St
Kamillaroi Road
Oak Street
Ficus St
Raymond Road
Echo Point Road
Lilianfels Av
Panorama Drive
Forster Road
Violet Street
0
250
500

LOWER HUNTER VALLEY WINERIES – MAP 14

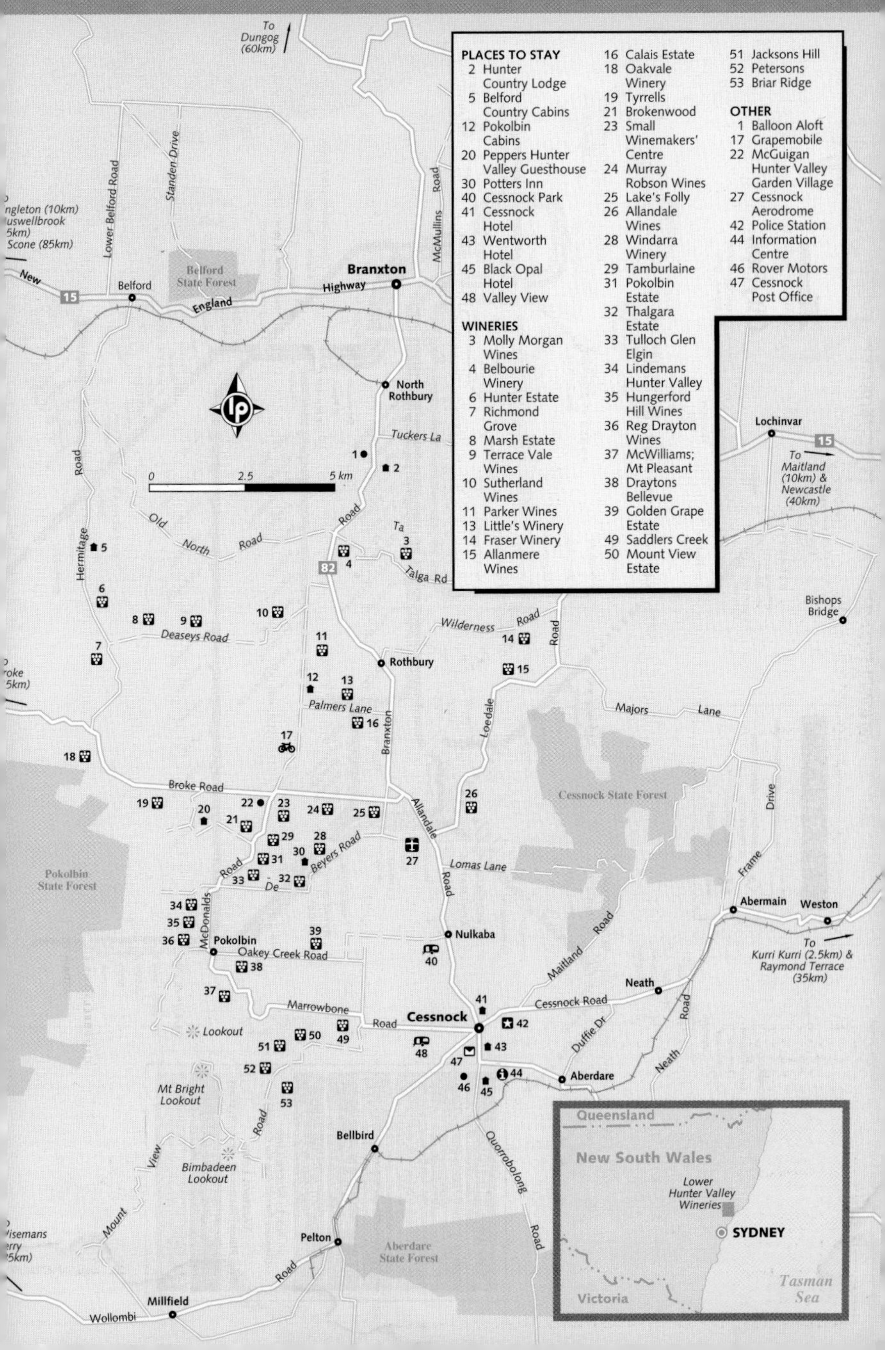

SYDNEY RAIL NETWORK

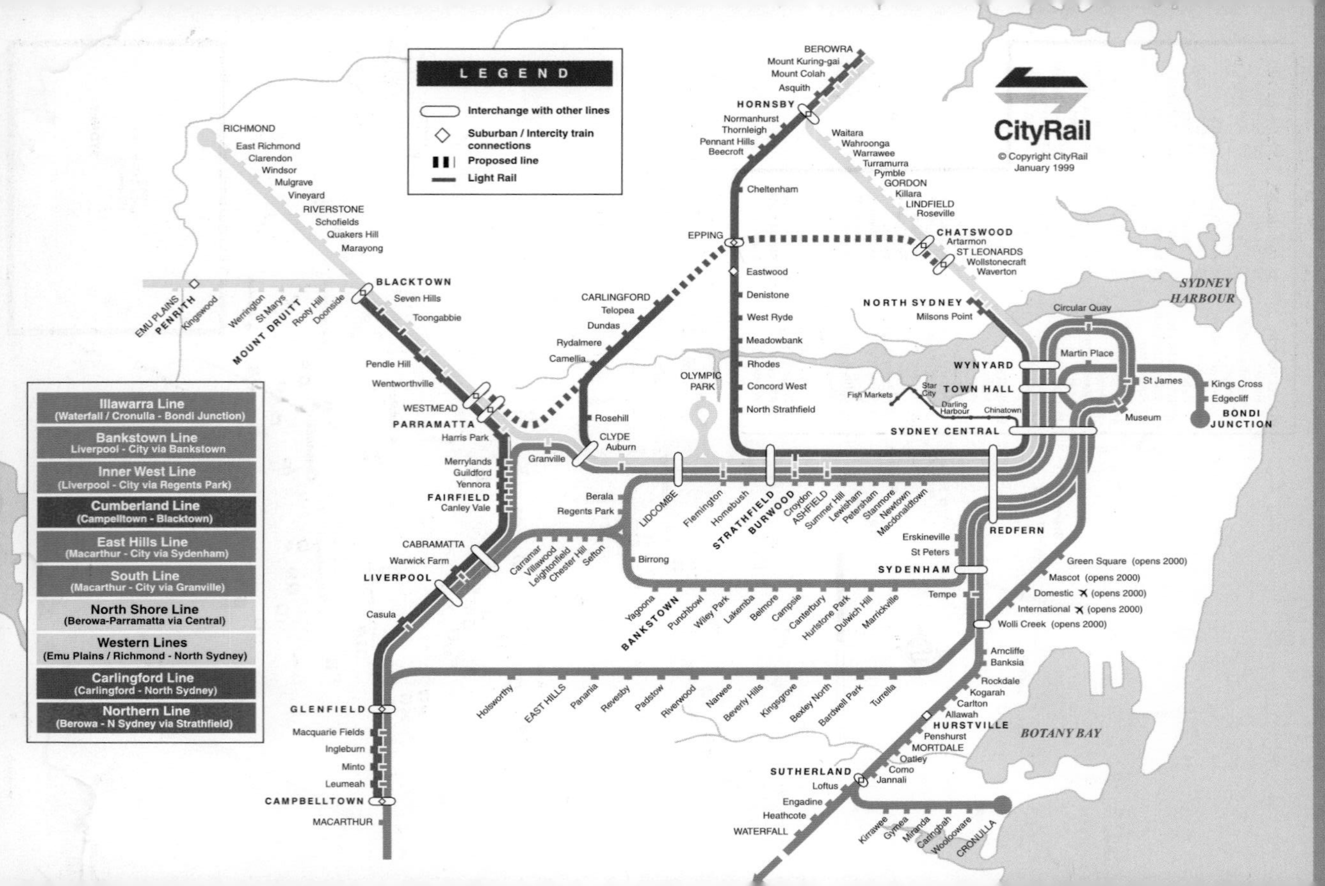

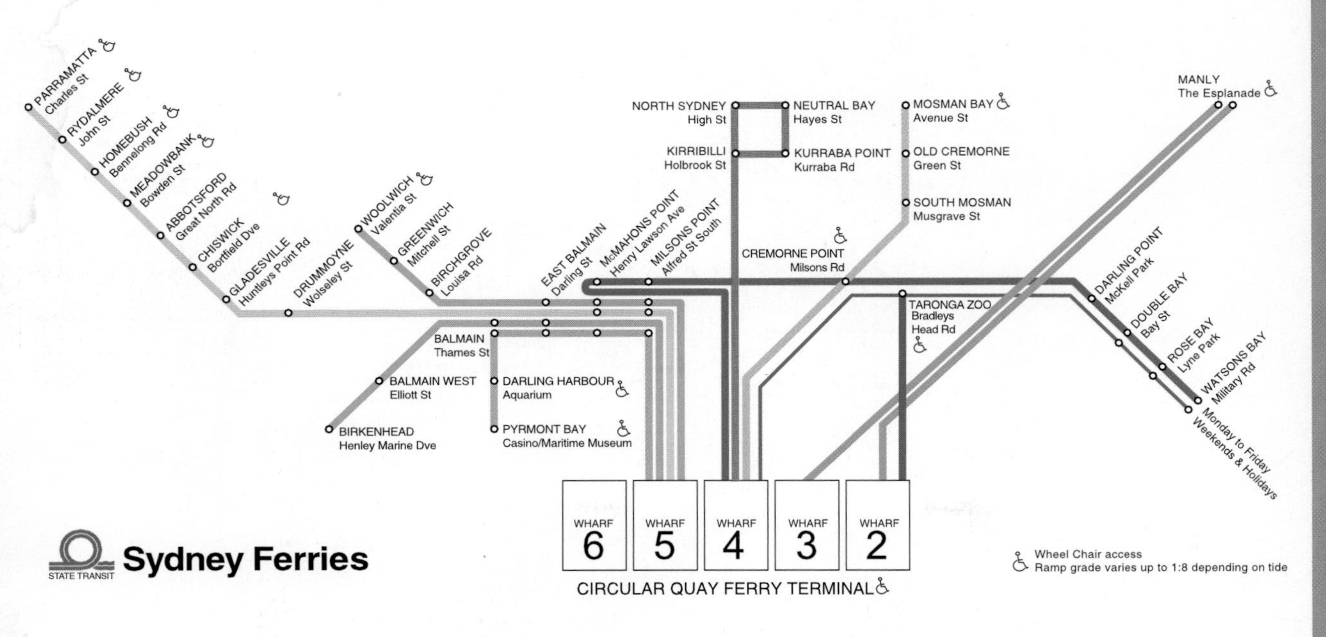

PARRAMATTA
Charles St
RYDALMERE
John St
HOMEBUSH
Bennelong Rd
MEADOWBANK
Bowden St
ABBOTSFORD
Great North Rd
CHISWICK
Bortfield Dve
GLADESVILLE
Huntleys Point Rd
DRUMMOYNE
Wolseley St
WOOLWICH
Valentia St
GREENWICH
Mitchell St
BIRCHGROVE
Louisa Rd
EAST BALMAIN
Darling St
McMAHONS POINT
Henry Lawson Ave
MILSONS POINT
Alfred St South
NORTH SYDNEY
High St
KIRRIBILLI
Holbrook St
NEUTRAL BAY
Hayes St
KURRABA POINT
Kurraba Rd
MOSMAN BAY
Avenue St
OLD CREMORNE
Green St
SOUTH MOSMAN
Musgrave St
CREMORNE POINT
Milsons Rd
TARONGA ZOO
Bradleys
Head Rd
MANLY
The Esplanade
DARLING POINT
McKell Park
DOUBLE BAY
Bay St
ROSE BAY
Lyne Park
WATSONS BAY
Military Rd
Monday to Friday
Weekends & Holidays
BALMAIN
Thames St
BALMAIN WEST
Elliott St
BIRKENHEAD
Henley Marine Dve
DARLING HARBOUR
Aquarium
PYRMONT BAY
Casino/Maritime Museum
WHARF 6
WHARF 5
WHARF 4
WHARF 3
WHARF 2
CIRCULAR QUAY FERRY TERMINAL
STATE TRANSIT
Sydney Ferries
Wheel Chair access
Ramp grade varies up to 1:8 depending on tide

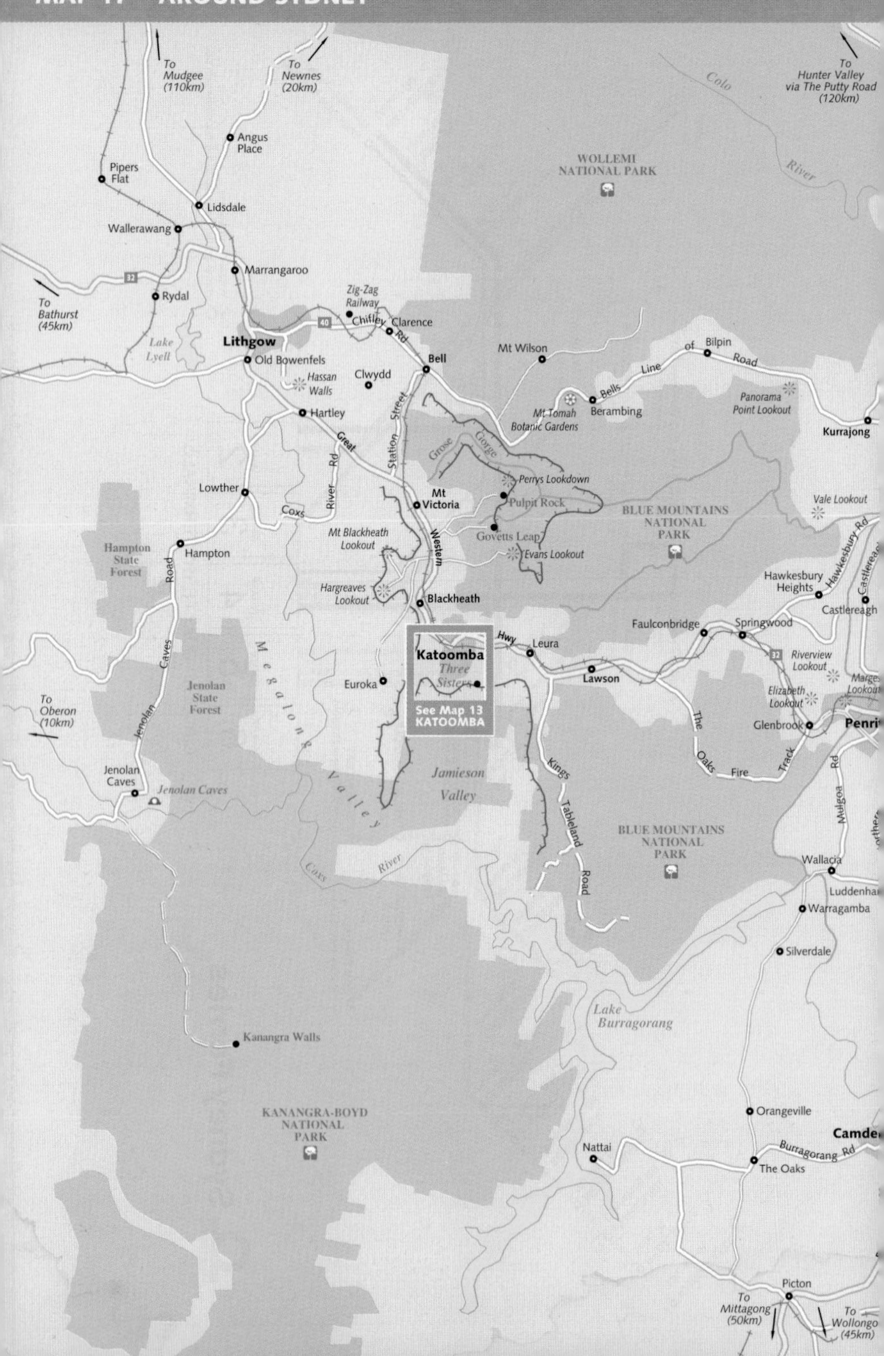
To Mudgee (110km)
To Newnes (20km)
To Hunter Valley via The Putty Road (120km)
Colo River
Angus Place
Pipers Flat
Lidsdale
Wallerawang
Marrangaroo
WOLLEMI NATIONAL PARK
To Bathurst (45km)
Rydal
Zig-Zag Railway
Chifley Rd
Clarence
Lake Lyell
Lithgow
Old Bowenfels
Bell
Mt Wilson
Bilpin
Bells Line of Road
Hassan Walls
Clwydd
Mt Tomah Botanic Gardens
Berambing
Panorama Point Lookout
Kurrajong
Hartley
Great Western Hwy
Station Street
Grose Gorge
River Rd
Perrys Lookdown
Pulpit Rock
Lowther
Coxs River Rd
Mt Victoria
Govetts Leap
BLUE MOUNTAINS NATIONAL PARK
Vale Lookout
Mt Blackheath Lookout
Hampton
Hampton State Forest
Evans Lookout
Hawkesbury Rd
Hawkesbury Heights
Castlereagh
Hargreaves Lookout
Blackheath
Jenolan Caves Road
Faulconbridge
Springwood
Katoomba
Three Sisters
Leura
Riverview Lookout
Lawson
To Oberon (10km)
Jenolan State Forest
Euroka
See Map 13 KATOOMBA
Megalong Valley
Elizabeth Lookout
The Oaks Fire Track
Glenbrook
Jenolan Caves
Jamieson Valley
Kings Tableland Road
Mulgoa Rd
Coxs River
BLUE MOUNTAINS NATIONAL PARK
Wallacia
Warragamba
Silverdale
Lake Burragorang
Kanangra Walls
KANANGRA-BOYD NATIONAL PARK
Orangeville
Nattai
Burragorang Rd
The Oaks
Picton
To Mittagong (50km)
To Wollongo (45km)

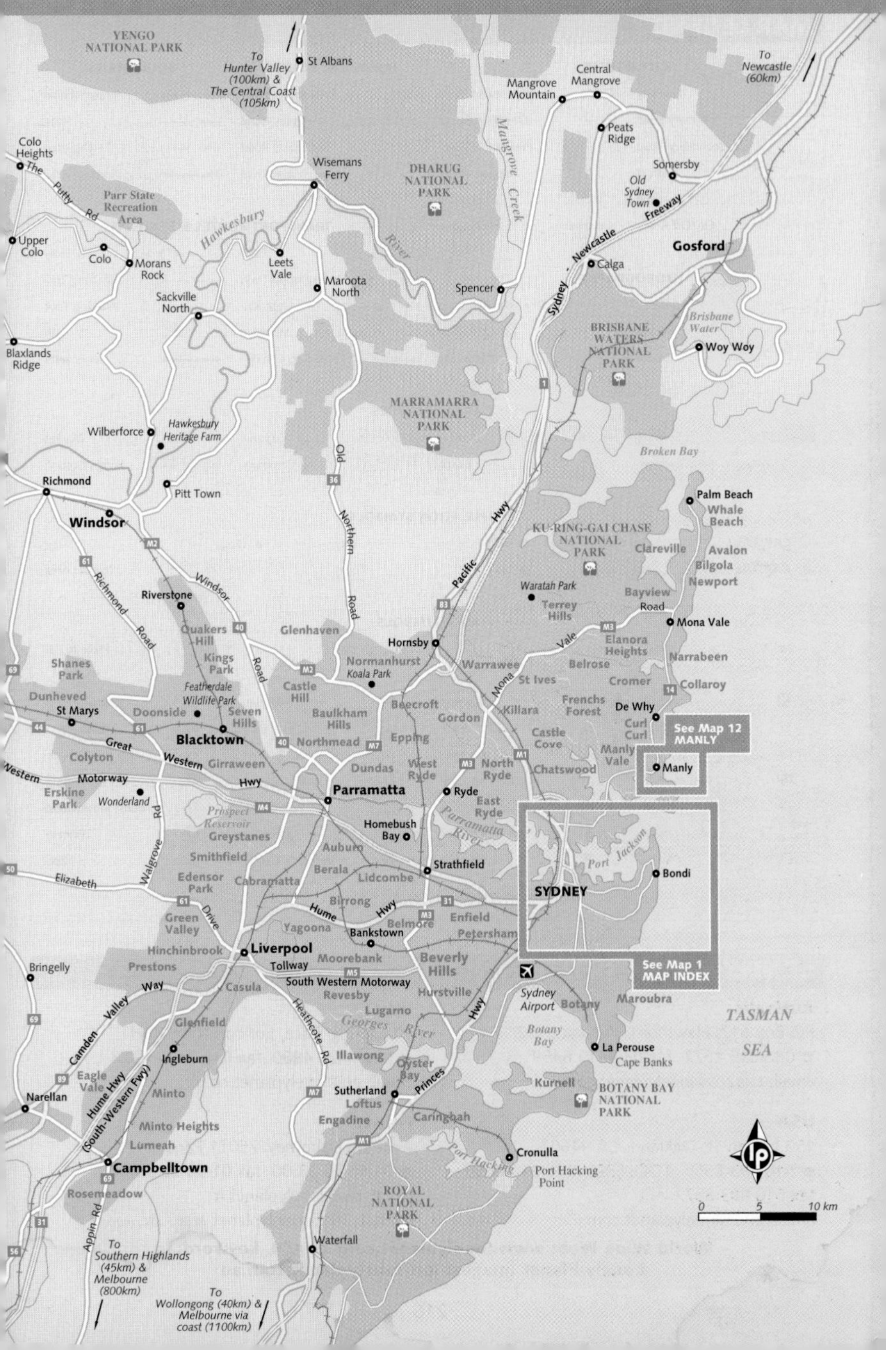

Yengo National Park
To Hunter Valley (100km) & The Central Coast (105km)
St Albans
Colo Heights
The Putty Rd
Parr State Recreation Area
Upper Colo
Colo
Morans Rock
Hawkesbury
Wisemans Ferry
Leets Vale
Maroota North
Sackville North
Blaxlands Ridge
Dharug National Park
River
Mangrove Creek
Mangrove Mountain
Central Mangrove
Peats Ridge
Somersby
Old Sydney Town
To Newcastle (60km)
Sydney - Newcastle Freeway
Gosford
Calga
Spencer
Brisbane Water
Woy Woy
Brisbane Waters National Park
Marramarra National Park
Wilberforce
Hawkesbury Heritage Farm
Broken Bay
Richmond
Pitt Town
Windsor
Old Northern Road
Palm Beach
Whale Beach
Ku-ring-gai Chase National Park
Clareville
Avalon
Bilgola
Newport
Pacific Hwy
Waratah Park
Bayview Road
Richmond Road
Windsor Road
Riverstone
Terrey Hills
Mona Vale
Quakers Hill
Glenhaven
Hornsby
Elanora Heights
Kings Park
Shanes Park
Normanhurst
Koala Park
Warrawee
Narrabeen
Belrose
Mona Vale Rd
St Ives
Cromer
Collaroy
Castle Hill
Featherdale Wildlife Park
Dunheved
St Marys
Doonside
Seven Hills
Baulkham Hills
Beecroft
Gordon
Killara
Frenchs Forest
De Why
Curl Curl
See Map 12 MANLY
Blacktown
Great Western Hwy
Colyton
Northmead
Epping
Castle Cove
Manly Vale
Manly
Girraween
Dundas
West Ryde
North Ryde
Chatswood
Western Motorway
Erskine Park
Wonderland
Walgrove Rd
Parramatta
Ryde
East Ryde
Prospect Reservoir
Homebush Bay
Parramatta River
Greystanes
Auburn
Port Jackson
Smithfield
Strathfield
Bondi
Elizabeth Dr
Edensor Park
Cabramatta
Berala
Lidcombe
SYDNEY
Birrong
Green Valley
Hume Hwy
Yagoona
Belmore
Enfield
Petersham
Bankstown
Hinchinbrook
Liverpool
Moorebank
Beverly Hills
See Map 1 MAP INDEX
Bringelly
Prestons
Tollway
South Western Motorway
Casula
Camden Valley Way
Revesby
Hurstville
Sydney Airport
Botany
Maroubra
Glenfield
Lugarno
Georges River
Botany Bay
Tasman Sea
Heathcote Rd
Ingleburn
Illawong
La Perouse
Cape Banks
Oyster Bay
Princes Hwy
Eagle Vale
Hume Hwy (South-Western Fwy)
Minto
Sutherland
Loftus
Kurnell
Botany Bay National Park
Narellan
Engadine
Caringbah
Minto Heights
Lumeah
Cronulla
Port Hacking
Port Hacking Point
Campbelltown
Rosemeadow
Royal National Park
Appin Rd
0 5 10 km
Waterfall
To Southern Highlands (45km) & Melbourne (800km)
To Wollongong (40km) & Melbourne via coast (1100km)

MAP LEGEND

CITY ROUTES

Freeway
Primary Road
Secondary Road
Street
Lane
On/Off Ramp
Unsealed Road
One Way Street
Pedestrian Street
Stepped Street
Tunnel
Footbridge

REGIONAL ROUTES

Tollway, Freeway
Primary Road
Secondary Road
Minor Road

BOUNDARIES

International
State
Disputed
Fortified Wall

TRANSPORT ROUTES & STATIONS

Train
Underground Train
Light Rail
Monorail
Cable Car, Chairlift
Ferry
Walking Trail
Walking Tour
Path
Pier or Jetty

HYDROGRAPHY

River, Creek
Canal
Lake
Dry Lake, Salt Lake
Spring, Rapids
Waterfalls

AREA FEATURES

Building
Park, Gardens
Airport
Beach
Campus
Cemetery
Market
Sports Ground

POPULATION SYMBOLS

CAPITAL National Capital
CAPITAL State Capital
CITY City
Town Town
Village Village
Urban Area

MAP SYMBOLS

Point of Interest
Place to Stay
Place to Eat

Airport
Bank
Bus Terminal
Caravan Park
Cave
Church
Cinema
Cycling
Golf Course
Hospital
Internet Cafe
Lookout
Monument
Mosque
Museum
National Park
Parking
Police Station
Post Office
Pub or Bar
Shopping Centre
Swimming Pool
Synagogue
Telephone
Temple
Tourist Information
Winery
Zoo

Note: not all symbols displayed above appear in this book

LONELY PLANET OFFICES

Australia
PO Box 617, Hawthorn, Victoria 3122
☎ 03 9819 1877 fax 03 9819 6459
email: talk2us@lonelyplanet.com.au

UK
10a Spring Place, London NW5 3BH
☎ 020 7428 4800 fax 020 7428 4828
email: go@lonelyplanet.co.uk

USA
150 Linden St, Oakland, CA 94607
☎ 510 893 8555 TOLL FREE: 800 275 8555
fax 510 893 8572
email: info@lonelyplanet.com

France
1 rue du Dahomey, 75011 Paris
☎ 01 55 25 33 00 fax 01 55 25 33 01
email: bip@lonelyplanet.fr
minitel: 3615 lonelyplanet *(1,29 F TTC/min)*

World Wide Web: www.lonelyplanet.com *or* AOL keyword: lp
Lonely Planet Images: lpi@lonelyplanet.com.au